KU-206-030

# INQUISITION
# AND
# MEDIEVAL SOCIETY

Also by James B. Given

*Society and Homicide in Thirteenth-Century England*

*State and Society in Medieval Europe: Gwynedd and Languedoc
under Outside Rule*

# INQUISITION AND MEDIEVAL SOCIETY

Power, Discipline, and
Resistance in Languedoc

James B. Given

CORNELL UNIVERSITY PRESS

ITHACA AND LONDON

Copyright © 1997 by Cornell University

All rights reserved. Except for brief quotations in a review, this book, or parts thereof, must not be reproduced in any form without permission in writing from the publisher. For information, address Cornell University Press, Sage House, 512 East State Street, Ithaca, New York 14850.

First published 1997 by Cornell University Press.

Printed in the United States of America.
Design and composition by Rohani Design, Edmonds, Washington.

Cornell University Press strives to utilize environmentally responsible suppliers and materials to the fullest extent possible in the publishing of its books. Such materials include vegetable-based, low-VOC inks and acid-free papers that are either recycled, totally chlorine-free, or partly composed of nonwood fibers.

Library of Congress Cataloging-in-Publication Data

Given, James Buchanan.
    Inquisition and medieval society: power, discipline, and resistance in Languedoc / James B. Given.
        p.   cm.
    Includes bibliographical references and index.
    ISBN 0-8014-3358-4 (cloth : alk. paper)
    1. Inquisition. 2. Church history—Middle Ages, 600–1500. 3. Languedoc (France)—History. 4. Languedoc (France)—Politics and government.
I. Title.
    BX1712.G58    1997
    272'.2'09448—dc21                                            97-11596

Cloth printing            10  9  8  7  6  5  4  3  2  1

Undergraduate Lending Library

*To Ruth*

# CONTENTS

# ACKNOWLEDGMENTS

T he first words I wrote about the inquisitors of Languedoc were typed in the fall of 1983. Since then I have been occupied in one way or another with the inquisitors and their enemies for over a decade. In that time I have amassed many debts. I owe special gratitude to the staffs of the various libraries and record repositories, named in the bibliography, which today house the remains of the inquisitors' archives.

A National Endowment for the Humanities Fellowship made it possible for me to take time off from teaching responsibilities to complete the first draft of this book. A generous grant from the Committee on Research of the University of California, Irvine, permitted the acquisition of microfilm of almost all the unpublished records of the Languedocian inquisition.

Over the years I have also acquired many personal debts. Edward Peters, Richard Kieckhefer, Gavin I. Langmuir, and Steven Epstein read manuscript versions of this book and offered many helpful suggestions. I am also indebted to Scott Waugh, Steven Topik, Timothy Tackett, Alan Bernstein, Walter L. Wakefield, Marjorie Beale, and Henry Ansgar Kelly for their advice and support. A special word of thanks should go to Edward Peters. Had it not been for his support in the very early days of my research, this book would undoubtedly never have been written.

Most of the work on this project was done during a period of unusual domestic upheaval. Without the unfailing support and friendship of Margaret Shepard, Robert Shepard, Margaret McManigal, and Kevin McManigal, I would have found the completion of this book a much more trying experience. Aliz and Gizmo, who, observed, often from my lap, the actual business of putting words on paper, always reminded me that there is far more to life than the study of medieval history. Finally, I would like to express my gratitude to my wife, Ruth. Despite embarking on a demanding Ph.D. program while I was writing this book, she still found time not only to read and critique numerous versions of it but also to listen to what must have seemed never-ending chatter about a variety of matters undoubtedly tedious to anyone other than myself.

Parts of this work, reprinted with permission, have appeared as "A Medieval Inquisitor at Work: Bernard Gui, 3 March 1308 to 19 June 1325," in *Portraits of Medieval and Renaissance Living: Essays in Memory of David Herlihy*, edited by

Steven A. Epstein and Samuel K. Cohn, Jr. (University of Michigan Press, 1996); "Social Stress, Social Strain, and the Inquisitors of Medieval Languedoc," in *Christendom and Its Discontents: Exclusion, Persecution, and Rebellion, 1000–1500*, edited by Scott L. Waugh and Peter D. Diehl (Cambridge University Press, 1996); "The Inquisitors of Languedoc and the Medieval Technology of Power," *American Historical Review* 94 (1989): 336–59; "Factional Politics in a Medieval Society: A Case Study from Fourteenth-Century Foix," *Journal of Medieval History* 14 (1988): 233–50, © 1988, reprinted with kind permission from Elsevier Science–NL, Sara Burgerhartstraat 25, 1055 KV Amsterdam, The Netherlands; and "Pursuing Heretics in Medieval Languedoc: An Essay on the Social Context of a Campaign of Repression," in *Die Enstehung des öffentlichen Strafrechts*, edited by Dietmar Willoweit (Böhlau, forthcoming).

J. G.

# ABBREVIATIONS


Add. MS 4697   London, British Library, Add. MS 4697

AM   Archives Municipales

*Bullaire*   Jean-Marie Vidal, ed., *Bullaire de l'inquisition française au XIV<sup>e</sup> siècle et jusqu'à la fin du Grand Schisme* (Paris, 1913)

Collectorie 404   Vatican City, Archivio Segreto Vaticano, Collectorie 404

Doat   Paris, Bibliothèque Nationale, Collection Doat

*Documents*   Célestin Douais, ed., *Documents pour servir à l'histoire de l'inquisition dans le Languedoc*, 2 vols. (Paris, 1900)

*HL*   Claude Devic and Joseph Vaissète, *Histoire générale de Languedoc*, ed. Auguste Molinier, 16 vols. (Toulouse, 1872–1904)

*LS*   Bernard Gui's *Liber sententiarum*, published in Philipp van Limborch, *Historia inquisitionis, cui subjungitur Liber sententiarum inquisitionis Tholosanae ab anno Christi MCCCVII ad annum MCCCXXIII* (Amsterdam, 1692)

Mansi   J. D. Mansi, ed., *Sacrorum conciliorum nova et amplissima collectio*, 39 vols. (Paris, 1901–27)

MS 609   Toulouse, Bibliothèque de la Ville, MS 609

MS 4030   Vatican City, Bibliotheca Apostolica Vaticana, MS Vat. Latin 4030

MS 4270   Paris, Bibliothèque Nationale, MS Lat. 4270

MS 12856   Paris, Bibliothèque Nationale, MS Lat. 12856

*Registre*   Jean Duvernoy, ed., *Le Registre d'inquisition de Jacques Fournier (1318–1325)*, 3 vols. (Toulouse, 1965)

# A NOTE ON CITATIONS
# FROM UNPUBLISHED MANUSCRIPTS

In Bernard Gui's *Liber sententiarum* (London, British Library, Add. MS 4697) two systems are used in numbering the folios. One, apparently of the seventeenth or eighteenth centuries, uses Arabic numerals. The other, evidently the original, uses Roman numerals, each of which has been canceled with a line drawn through it. (This is the numbering system that Limborch used in his edition of the *Liber sententiarum*.) When references are given to this MS, they are given in Arabic numbers *but refer to the folios as numbered with Roman numerals*. The first folios of the MS do not have Roman numerals. Roman numerals begin with the *Tabula omnium personarum sequentis libri* and run from 1r through 8v (corresponding to folios 10r–17v in the numbering system that uses Arabic numerals). With the first page of the first *sermo generalis*, the Roman numerals begin again with 1r (corresponding to 18r in Arabic numerals). Where there is any ambiguity as to the folio I am citing, I give references in both Roman and Arabic numerals.

The folios in Toulouse, Bibliothèque de la Ville, MS 609 are numbered in both Roman and Arabic numerals. These two systems of numbering do not always agree. Where the two systems differ, I use the Arabic numerals in my citations.

All citations of Jean Duvernoy, ed., *Le Registre d'inquisition de Jacques Fournier (1318–1325)*, 3 vols. (Toulouse, 1965), an edition that is full of errors, have been checked against a microfilm of Fournier's original register, Vatican City, Bibliotheca Apostolica Vaticana, MS Vat. Latin 4030. Where my reading of the manuscript differs from that of Duvernoy, this is indicated in the notes.

In quotations of unpublished manuscript material, I have modernized punctuation and changed "u" to "v" where appropriate.

# INQUISITION
# AND
# MEDIEVAL SOCIETY

# INTRODUCTION

EW SUBJECTS OF medieval history arouse as much passion as the inquisition of heretical depravity. Polemicists, propagandists, novelists, and historians—amateur and professional—have all tried their hands at this topic. For several centuries monographs, treatises, diatribes, and apologies have spilled from the presses. The 1983 edition of Vekené's *Bibliotheca bibliographica historiae Sanctae Inquisitionis*, the fundamental guide to the literature of all the inquisitions, both medieval and early modern, lists 4,808 titles. The fascination of the subject for writers of all stripes has itself become the subject of scholarly study. Edward Peters's *Inquisition* (1988) brilliantly outlines the ways in which the history of the inquisition has been created, reshaped, reinvented, falsified, and mythologized by generations of writers pursuing agendas that have ranged from the scientific to the romantic and from the scholarly to the perverse.

Given this abundance, the reader might well wonder what could justify yet another work on the inquisition of the Middle Ages, especially one that restricts itself to the region of southern France known as Languedoc. My justification for returning to such an oft-studied subject is that it gives us an unusual opportunity to construct a case study of the sociology of medieval politics.

## A CASE STUDY OF THE EXERCISE OF MEDIEVAL POLITICAL POWER

Among the most important aspects of European history in the late Middle Ages and the early modern period was the progressive elaboration of ever more powerful political organizations and the development of more coherent, intrusive, and coercive forms of governance. These phenomena have often been discussed. Library shelves contain an imposing array of books devoted to the histories of the proto-states of medieval Europe, to their administrative and financial histories, and to the legal-juridical apparatuses they devised to justify and rationalize their authority.

Yet much of this scholarship has a strangely bloodless feel to it. We know a great deal about the ways in which medieval rulers and administrators organized themselves, kept their records, and justified their authority to one another and to their subjects. However, our picture of the actual process of governance in this critical period when the first lineaments of European states were being hammered

1

out is very one-sided. It is essentially a top-down, administrator's view. We know much less about how the efforts of rulers and administrators were received by those over whom they claimed authority. In part this is due to the nature of the surviving documents. Medieval administrators, when they preserved office correspondence, tended to keep only their "out-mail," that is, a record of the orders they dispatched. They did not display the same interest in keeping copies of the correspondence they received from agents in the field.

But the primary reason we know so little about how governance worked itself out on a concrete, day-to-day basis is the illiteracy of the masses whom medieval administrators sought to rule. The governed were, of course, not completely inarticulate. Under certain conditions, peasants and workers were not shy about informing their masters of what they felt about their activities. Nevertheless, simple prudence, coupled with the fact that petitions and complaints had to be drawn up by clerks whose very literacy made them almost inevitably part of the ruling elite, meant that these remonstrances were couched in terms of the ideologies that the rulers used to legitimate their dominant position in society. Direct action in the form of riots and rebellions has also left dramatic evidence, but the chronicle accounts that describe these uprisings and the judicial archives that record their repression once again reflect the perspectives of the rulers rather than the ruled.[1]

The records produced by the inquisitors of Languedoc, however, allow us to peek, even if only momentarily, behind the veil that so often hides the realities of medieval governance. The inquisitors were careful record keepers. They produced and preserved registers in which they recorded the sentences they imposed, as well as copies of the depositions they received from witnesses and suspects. Thousands of individuals found themselves recorded, willy-nilly, in these documents. For example, the register kept by Bernard de Caux and Jean de Saint-Pierre in the mid-1240s, which records only a portion of their activity, indicates that some 5,518 people appeared before them.[2] Unfortunately, most of these records have perished. Much of that which has survived is often very terse, a dry catalogue of stereotypical heretical actions and opinions. Yet, tucked away amid the seemingly endless recital of routine heretical acts and beliefs, one can find depositions that contain details that are both enlightening and arresting.[3] Some inquisitors also composed manuals designed to describe the functioning of the inquisition and the beliefs and practices of different types of heresy. Finally, opponents of the inquisitors not infrequently produced petitions and complaints directed to popes and kings.

---

[1] For an interesting discussion that tries to elucidate the ideological conceptions of rebellious English peasants, see Justice, *Writing and Rebellion.*

[2] Number derived from MS 609.

[3] The most prolix register was that kept by Bishop Jacques Fournier, who ran an inquisitorial tribunal at Pamiers in the early fourteenth century. The printed edition runs to over 1,500 pages in length.

Taken as a whole, this material gives us an almost unrivaled opportunity to examine closely how a medieval governing institution interacted with the people it sought to control. We can observe in detail how the inquisitors went about the business of repressing heresy. At times we can also perceive how their activities were "received" by the people of Languedoc. The ways in which some people sought to evade the inquisitors, how some assisted them, and how yet others tried to manipulate them to serve their own ends can all be discerned in the surviving records. Thus, this book can be read as a case study in medieval governance and administration. It can also be read as an investigation of the nature of political power in a medieval society. Power is a fundamental aspect of human social relations, yet it is a phenomenon that is very hard to define in a satisfactory fashion.[4] Many definitions of power are couched in terms of the intentions and will of specific individuals. Power is thus defined as the production of intended effects or as the capacity to produce those effects. For Max Weber, power was "the probability that one actor within a social relationship will be in a position to carry out his will despite resistance."[5] Very frequently these intended effects are understood as the control of the behavior of one set of individuals by another individual or set of individuals.[6]

Many social theorists, especially those of a structuralist bent, have criticized definitions of power that stress the will, intentions, or interests of individuals for giving only a partial account of such a complex, multifaceted phenomenon. For these thinkers, power is not a thing that belongs to a particular individual, set of individuals, or institution; instead, it is a dynamic relationship, a process that is the product of the total ensemble of all social relations found within a particular social formation. This concept can be expressed in either weak or strong terms. It can take the form of the simple realization, such as we find with Weber, that he who exercises power must be able to overcome resistance to his will.[7] Or it can, as with Foucault, take a strong form, in which power becomes diffused throughout a social formation. For Foucault there can be no power without an "economy of discourses of truth," which not only shapes the way people view the world but makes it impossible for them to view it in any other way: "We are forced to produce the truth of power that our society demands, of which it has need, in order to function: we *must* speak the truth; we are constrained or condemned to confess or to discover the truth. Power never ceases its interrogation, its inquisition, its registration of truth: it institutionalizes, professionalizes and rewards its pursuit."[8] Power is thus both everywhere and nowhere. It is not something that belongs to one individual, one group, or one class and is exercised

---

4 For an introduction to this problem, see Lukes's stimulating remarks in Lukes, ed., *Power*, pp. 1–18, to which the following discussion is heavily indebted.

5 Weber, *Economy and Society*, 1: 53.

6 See, for example, Dahl, "The Concept of Power," cited in Lukes, ed., *Power*, p. 2.

7 Weber, *Economy and Society*, 2: 926.

8 Foucault, *Power/Knowledge*, p. 93.

by that individual or class over others. Power is an entity that constantly circulates through society, forming a net in which all individuals participate, simultaneously undergoing and exercising it.[9]

It is not my intention to enter the discussion of what ultimately is the best way to define power. Instead, as a historian I have merely tried to ask a few questions (and certainly not all possible questions) about the exercise of power in one particular society, Languedoc in the late thirteenth and early fourteenth centuries. What the inquisitors sought to control above all else was *behavior*. So it is with this aspect of power that I have primarily concerned myself. I have asked, and tried to answer, some very concrete questions about what the inquisitors tried to do and how and to whom they did it. The answers to these questions are presented in section I. The chapters in this section are thus very much concerned with the intention and will of specific individuals and with their capacity to enforce that will and realize those intentions. The questions posed in this section may seem old-fashioned to some, but they are legitimate and the answers to them are not without interest.

Nevertheless, I have also tried to take account of the fact that power cannot simply be reduced to a matter of the will and intention of would-be rulers. The will and intentions of the ruled must also be examined. Given the nature of medieval records, this is a much more difficult question, but in the chapters of section II I try to provide some answers. Chapters 4 and 5 examine the ways in which some Languedocians tried to resist the inquisitors. Chapter 6 addresses the different, but allied, question of how certain Languedocians endeavored to capture the resources of the inquisition and exploit them for their own purposes.

Finally, in section III I have tried to take account of the fact that power is more than the simple result of the interaction of the contesting wills of the dominators and the dominated; it is also the product of the structures of society as a whole. If nothing else, a society's economic, social, and cultural structures set the parameters within which power must be exercised as well as resisted. Neither resources nor possibilities are infinite; and I have tried to understand how the underlying structures of Languedocian society and politics both facilitated and restrained the work of the inquisitors.

In examining the work of the Languedocian inquisitors, I have focused on the years between 1275 and 1325. My reasons for doing so are twofold. First, this is the period of inquisitorial activity that is most thoroughly documented. From this period we have registers recording the depositions given by witnesses who appeared before inquisitorial tribunals in Carcassonne, Albi, and Pamiers.[10] From Toulouse we have the large register of sentences imposed by Bernard Gui, which gives us very full information on the inquisitors' penal system.[11] Gui also

---

[9] Ibid., p. 98.

[10] See respectively Pales-Gobilliard, ed., *Geoffroy d'Ablis*; MS 12856; Davis, ed., *The Inquisition at Albi*; and *Registre*.

[11] This is published as an appendix to Limborch, *Historia inquisitionis*.

wrote a manual of inquisitorial procedure, which provides considerable insight into his mode of operation.[12] Other documents also throw light on the activities of the inquisitors in this period. These include royal letters and the findings of various papal commissions that investigated the treatment of inquisitorial prisoners and the activities of Bernard de Castanet, bishop of Albi.[13] Finally, much valuable information on the important movement of opposition to the inquisitors that took shape immediately after 1300 can be gleaned from the lengthy record of the 1319 trial of the Franciscan friar Bernard Délicieux on charges that he had poisoned Pope Benedict XI, engaged in necromancy, and aided and abetted heresy by opposing the inquisitors.[14]

My second reason for concentrating on the period after 1275 is that by this date the inquisitors had fully developed their techniques for identifying, prosecuting, and condemning heretics and their supporters. The early, formative years of the Languedocian inquisition have been described by many historians. Since my goal has been not to explore the process by which the inquisitors hammered out their techniques but to examine how those techniques, once fully matured, were applied, my choice seemed logical. I have, of course, not completely ignored the period before 1275. Where the records of this early phase of inquisitorial activity throw light on the problems with which I have concerned myself, I have not hesitated to use them.

## MEDIEVAL HERESY AND LANGUEDOC

Since my purpose is to examine certain aspects of the sociology of medieval political behavior and social control, I shall not here attempt to give a full account of either the medieval inquisition or the heresies that it combated. Interested readers can find many excellent works that deal with these subjects. However, the following background information on both heresy and Languedoc will help readers unfamiliar with these subjects to follow the discussion.

The twelfth century saw the appearance of widespread, popular heretical movements in much of western Europe. The causes of this phenomenon are complex and remain the subject of considerable debate.[15] In part, popular heresy was the result of profound changes in the religious culture of medieval Europe. These included the spread of literacy and a growing religious sophistication among the laity. The quest by many lay men and lay women for ways in which they could realize their desires for a more authentic engagement in the spiritual

---

[12] Gui, *Practica inquisitionis*; a portion of this work has been reedited and translated into French as *Manuel de l'inquisiteur*.

[13] The depositions collected during the investigation of the bishop of Albi are in Collectorie 404.

[14] MS 4270.

[15] See, for example, Asad, "Medieval Heresy"; Nelson, "Society, Theodicy, and the Origins of Heresy"; Russell, "Origins of Medieval Heresy"; Lambert, *Medieval Heresy*, pp. 3–61; and Moore, *Origins of European Dissent*, pp. 263–83, and "Heresy, Repression, and Social Change."

life led some into conflict with a church whose hierarchical structures had been worked out at a time when the great mass of believers had been illiterate peasants largely concerned with matters of ritual. In the new spiritual climate of the twelfth and thirteenth centuries, many people felt strongly attracted by the model of the *vita apostolica* lived by Christ and his immediate disciples, a way of life that seemed to center on poverty and preaching.[16] But the *vita apostolica* could also provoke unfavorable comparisons with the contemporary church, which was fabulously wealthy and not overly concerned with preaching.

Moreover, the spread of heresy was linked to developments within the church hierarchy itself. Great churchmen, bishops and abbots, were also wielders of significant political authority and hence sensitive to any religious critique that called into question the structures of lay society. The church at this time was in the midst of defining both its organization and its belief ever more precisely. The intellectual revival that we associate with the twelfth-century renaissance and the thirteenth-century rise of the universities had powerful consequences for the church. Legal scholars studied, rationalized, and refined its law. Theologians, trained in the logical disciplines of the schools, subjected the church's received body of belief and practice to a similar rationalizing and refining process. The successful efforts of the bishops of Rome to make themselves the recognized leaders of the Latin-speaking church endowed that church with a source of final and authoritative decisions on matters of belief, practice, and discipline. The church of the twelfth and thirteenth centuries was thus much more highly defined and self-conscious than it had been in previous centuries. It was therefore much better equipped to identify behavior and belief that did not accord with its newly articulated norms and to stigmatize such behavior and belief as heterodox and hence culpable.

One region where heresy became well established was the area of southern France known as Languedoc. This area, roughly centered on the cities of Toulouse, Carcassonne, and Narbonne, was in the Middle Ages a rich and prosperous region. Languedoc, with its diversified agriculture, was densely populated and relatively highly urbanized.[17] The social structure of late-twelfth- and early-thirteenth-century Languedoc was highly complex; but to simplify greatly, we can say that in general it was less highly feudalized and manorialized than northern France.[18] At the beginning of the thirteenth century, there were in Languedoc a number of great princely houses, such as those of the counts of Toulouse, the counts of Foix, and the viscounts of Carcassonne. The region also contained a large number of petty nobles. In matters of inheritance, the greater local dynasties practiced primogeniture. The lesser gentry, however, did not. Although it was

---

[16] See Chenu, *Nature, Man, and Society in the Twelfth Century*, pp. 202–69, and Grundmann, *Religiöse Bewegungen im Mittelalter*, pp. 13–50.

[17] The usual estimate of the size of the Languedocian population in the early fourteenth century is 1.5 million. See Wolff, ed., *Histoire du Languedoc*, p. 217.

[18] For a highly compressed sketch of Languedoc on the eve of the Albigensian crusades, see Given, *State and Society*, pp. 19–25.

possible for a father to privilege his eldest son, inheritance customs tended to favor equal partition among male heirs.[19] To counteract the tendency toward progressive impoverishment that resulted from these inheritance customs, many lesser lords pooled their holdings in joint lordships, which were a common feature of the Languedocian political landscape.[20] Relations of domination and subordination among the local nobility were not as organized or rationalized as in certain other areas of medieval Europe. Some nobles were vassals and held fiefs in return for various services; but vassalage and fief-holding were not as important in aristocratic life as they were in northern France. The obligations that vassals owed their lords were few and the authority exercised over them by their lords correspondingly light.[21]

Peasants enjoyed a relatively large amount of personal freedom and control over their land. Manorial organization, in the sense of a tight linking of tenants' estates with the working of a seignorial demesne through compulsory labor services, does not seem to have been particularly developed.[22] Although peasants owed many dues to their lords and were subject to *tailles* and various *banalités*, they had a large degree of control over their land.[23] On the payment of the proper dues, they were able to alienate or subinfeudate their holdings.[24] During the twelfth and thirteenth centuries many settlements gained an important degree of self-government. In the eleventh and twelfth centuries large, compact, walled settlements known as *castra* (sing., *castrum*) appeared in much of Languedoc. In these communities local notables played an active role in guiding religious and charitable activities. They assumed responsibility for maintaining the physical fabric of the local church and in many places undertook the administration of hospitals, leper houses, and other charitable institutions. In some *castra* these notables fused with the men who served the local lord to form the nucleus of the self-governing consulates that many *castra* and villages acquired after 1200.[25]

One of the most distinctive features of medieval Languedocian society was its relatively dense network of towns and cities. With the revival of commerce from the eleventh century on, the region's towns, many of which could trace their history back to the days of the Roman Empire, experienced marked demographic and economic growth. Languedocian merchants constructed a far-flung trade network that extended into both the Mediterranean and the Atlantic. Many

[19] A. Molinier, "Etude sur l'administration féodale dans le Languedoc," p. 151; Bourin-Derruau, *Villages médiévaux en Bas-Languedoc*, 1: 149–52.

[20] Griffe, *Le Languedoc cathare de 1190 à 1210*, p. 144.

[21] See Giordanengo, "La Féodalité," p. 191; Higounet, "Le Groupe aristocratique en Aquitaine et en Gascogne," pp. 569–71; and Ourliac, "Le Pays de la Selve," p. 582. For a contrasting view, however, see Bourin-Derruau, *Villages médiévaux en Bas-Languedoc*, 1: 266.

[22] Magnou-Nortier, *La Société laïque et l'église*, pp. 141–42.

[23] On the dues that peasants in the hinterland of the city of Béziers had to pay their lords, see Bourin-Derruau, *Villages médiévaux en Bas-Languedoc*, 1: 128–33, 228–37.

[24] Partak, "Structures foncières et prélèvement seigneurial," pp. 10–11.

[25] Bourin-Derruau, *Villages médiévaux en Bas-Languedoc*, 1: 273–326.

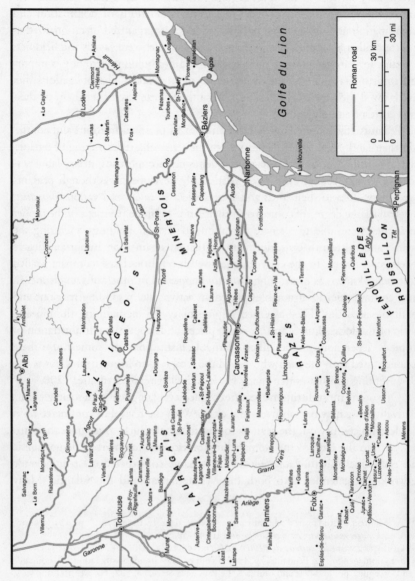

Source: Adapted from Belperron, *La Croisade contre les albigeois*, endpapers.

towns, enriched by the growth of trade and manufacturing, managed to win for themselves important degrees of political autonomy. Of these the most powerful and successful was the city of Toulouse. Located at the intersection of several trade routes, its population grew dramatically in the twelfth century; by 1200 it was the largest city in Languedoc. Over time the townspeople acquired from their count the right to manage their own affairs through an elected consulate and to exercise jurisdiction over most important legal matters concerning themselves. In the early thirteenth century the people of Toulouse expanded their power and influence beyond the city walls, compelling local nobles to abolish or curtail tolls on the city's trade. No other town in Languedoc acquired as much independence from its traditional lord or as much power over its surrounding countryside, but many others also managed to win an important degree of political autonomy.[26]

This rich, dynamic region proved receptive to many of the heretical currents that circulated in twelfth- and thirteenth-century Europe. Historians have advanced many explanations for this receptivity. Some have claimed that the region's culture was, by the standards of the rest of medieval Europe, unusually cosmopolitan and that this made Languedocians tolerant of religious diversity. The presence of a rural nobility whose anticlericalism was excited by its recent loss of control over tithes and church property has also been advanced as an explanatory factor. Some have argued that the chronic political disunity and military conflict that devastated much of Languedoc in the late twelfth century made it difficult for ecclesiastical and secular authorities to cooperate in repressing heterodox ideas. Finally, it has been claimed that the local clerics, while perhaps no more corrupt than anywhere else in Europe, were not very deeply touched by the new intellectual and spiritual currents that were transforming the church; hence, they lacked both the will and the ability to combat heresy effectively.[27] Whatever the causes that made Languedoc fertile ground for heterodoxy, by the early thirteenth century heresy had become well established there.

The most popular heresy was the strange, dualist sect known as Catharism.[28] The Cathars believed that this world and everything in it was the creation of Satan (variously interpreted as either a fallen angel or an evil god co-eternal with the good god who had created heaven). The world was also a prison in which Satan kept confined those angels whom he had managed to lure out of the good god's heaven. To make these spirits forget their heavenly origins, Satan had shut them up in human bodies. When an individual died, his soul—his angelic self— left the body, to be harried through the air by demons until it took refuge in the womb of the first pregnant creature it happened upon, whether human or

---

26 Wolff, ed., *Histoire du Languedoc*, pp. 161–63.

27 For brief summaries of why Languedoc was fruitful ground for the propagation of heresy, see Wakefield, *Heresy, Crusade, and Inquisition*, pp. 77–80, and Lambert, *Medieval Heresy*, pp. 81–85.

28 A brief introduction to the sect, with bibliographical references, is in Lambert, *Medieval Heresy*, pp. 105–46. See also *Historiographie du Catharisme* and Borst, *Die Katharer*. The question of the origins of the Cathar sect is a vexed and obscure matter and need not detain us here.

animal. To redeem these captive souls, the good god sent one of his angels, whom the Cathars identified with the Jesus of the New Testament, into the world to reveal to them their true nature. Unlike the Christ of the Catholic Church, this savior figure was not god himself, nor did he assume a human body or actually die on the cross. The Cathar savior bequeathed his followers the power to perform the central ritual of the Cathar faith, the *consolamentum*. This was a baptism of the holy spirit, conferred by the laying on of hands. Those who received it were freed of the taint of sin; when they died, their souls were not reincarnated but instead returned to heaven.

The sect was divided into two groups, which the inquisitors referred to as the "perfect" (*perfecti*; fem. pl., *perfectae*) and the "believers" (*credentes*; sing., *credens*). The *perfecti*, whom the Cathars themselves called Good Christians or Good Men and Good Women, were individuals who, after a period of probation, had received the *consolamentum*. They devoted their lives to preaching and performing the *consolamentum* on those who were about to die, thus liberating them from the prison of this world. Part of the appeal of the Good Men was the life of strict asceticism they led. Since sexual intercourse was the means by which the fleshly tunics that kept souls imprisoned in this world were produced, the *perfecti* lived lives of total sexual abstinence. Moreover, they abstained from the eating of all animal flesh and products, including meat, cheese, milk, eggs, and so forth. They also scrupulously avoided all other sins, such as lying, since any sin—fornication, murder, or the eating of an egg— canceled out the effects of the *consolamentum*.[29]

The *credentes* were, strictly speaking, not members of the Cathar church at all. Not having received the *consolamentum*, they remained mired in this world of sin and condemned to reincarnation. What made them believers was their having agreed that when their final hour came, they would receive from the hands of the Good Men the salvation-conferring *consolamentum*. This adhesion to the sect was figured in the ritual known as the *melioramentum* (which the inquisitors understood as an act of "adoration"), in which the believer prostrated himself before a Good Man, exchanged kisses with him, and called on him to intercede on his behalf with God.

In the early thirteenth century Catharism became very widespread in Languedoc. It seems to have found favor with all segments of society, ranging from members of the great princely houses to lowly peasants. Cathar Good Men and Good Women lived openly in convents that were to be found in many towns and villages. They were also organized into territorial dioceses, presided over by bishops who were assisted by figures known as "elder" and "younger" sons.

---

[29] When the inquisitors used the term "heretic," they almost invariably meant the Cathar Good Men. Most of the people prosecuted and condemned by the inquisitors were not "heretics" in this narrow sense. To describe this group the inquisitors employed a large vocabulary distinguishing different forms of aiding and abetting of the heretics proper. To avoid excessive circumlocution, I shall refer to all those who supported heresy of all types, whether Cathar Good Men or not, as "heretics."

The other heresy that enjoyed significant support in Languedoc in the early thirteenth century was Waldensianism. This group's beliefs did not differ from those of the Catholic Church as radically as did those of the Cathars. Indeed, the first Waldensians were inspired by the same fascination with the *vita apostolica* of Christ and his immediate followers that later moved St. Francis of Assisi to take up his mission. The movement's founder, a merchant of Lyon named Valdès, decided sometime in the mid-1170s to give up his wealth and devote himself to a life of poverty and preaching. He arranged to have parts of the Bible, as well as some works of the church fathers, translated into the vernacular.

Initially Valdès was completely orthodox. But as his mission enjoyed success and he gathered followers, he came into collision with the local church authorities. The chief bone of contention was his desire and that of his followers to preach. According to canon law, preaching required the permission of the local bishop. The situation reached such an impasse that Valdès and his followers appealed to Pope Alexander III. Valdès and the pope met in 1179 during the Third Lateran Council in Rome. Alexander was favorably impressed by Valdès; indeed, he approved Valdès's vow of poverty. Yet on the key issue of preaching, Alexander required him and his followers to secure the permission of local church authorities.

The Waldensians, however, failed to reach an accommodation with the archbishop of Lyon. Denied permission to preach, they nevertheless did so. Sometime around 1182 they were excommunicated and expelled from the city. Some of them made their way to Languedoc, where they seem to have undertaken propaganda against the Cathars. In 1184 Pope Lucius III excommunicated them as heretics. Only after their excommunication did the Poor of Lyon, as they came to be known, develop heterodox ideas. Persecution by church authorities, combined with their enthusiasm for Holy Scripture, gradually led many to decide that whatever aspects of current church organization and practice did not have scriptural warrant were illegitimate. They thus rejected the swearing of oaths and the shedding of blood; this, of course, struck at the foundations of all secular authority. They also denied that the church had the right to prohibit them from preaching; moreover, in their early days they even allowed women to preach. They developed the practice of confession to laymen. Their scriptural fundamentalism led them to deny the existence of purgatory and thus the value of prayers for the dead. In addition, they argued that the veneration of images and the performance of pilgrimages were of no spiritual benefit. One splinter group in Languedoc, repudiated by Valdès himself, claimed that its members alone could confer true baptism. Finally, many Waldensians adopted a Donatist position, holding that the efficacy of a sacrament depended on the moral status of the priest who performed it.[30]

---

[30] Brief introductions to the history of the Waldensians are in Lambert, *Medieval Heresy*, pp. 62–77, 147–71, and Wakefield, *Heresy, Crusade, and Inquisition*, pp. 43–47. See also Selge, *Die ersten Waldenser*; Gonnet and Molnár, *Les Vaudois*; and Audisio, *Les "Vaudois."*

By the late twelfth century the extent of heresy in Languedoc had alarmed the papacy. Innocent III (1198–1216) launched a multifold attack on the problem. He set out to reform the upper ranks of the Languedocian clergy, to persuade the local rulers to assist in the repression of heresy, and to foster the efforts of St. Dominic to combat the Cathars through a campaign of preaching by friars whose austerity of life was intended to rival that of the Cathar *perfecti*. The results on all fronts, however, were meager. When Innocent III's legate, Pierre de Castelnau, was assassinated on 14 January 1208, the pope concluded that the count of Toulouse had been responsible. He decided that the time had come to use force to expel the Languedocian princes from their lordships and to replace them with men who would persecute the heretics. He therefore called for a crusade. His summons was answered by a large number of nobles, most of them from northern France. Their invasion of Languedoc in June 1209 touched off a series of wars, known as the Albigensian crusades, that dragged on for twenty years. The crusaders elected Simon de Montfort, a northern French baron, as their leader. Although Simon and his followers enjoyed considerable initial success, they never managed to reduce all of Languedoc to obedience. Indeed, following Simon's death in 1218 during a siege of the city of Toulouse, the count of Toulouse, Raimond VII, managed to reassert control over much of the region.

The French monarchy, preoccupied by its problems with the English, had avoided entanglement in the early stages of the conflict. Not until the 1220s did the Capetian monarchs become seriously engaged in the struggle. In 1226 King Louis VIII, having bought out the claims of Simon de Montfort's heir, led an army into Languedoc. Although Louis died on his way home from this campaign, his lieutenants carried on the war. In 1229 Count Raimond VII of Toulouse was persuaded to come to terms. By the provisions of the Treaty of Paris, eastern Languedoc was incorporated directly into the royal domain. Raimond VII kept his county of Toulouse, but his daughter and heiress was married to the brother of King Louis IX, Alfonse de Poitiers. When Raimond died in 1249, Alfonse inherited the county. Since he and his wife produced no heirs, the county fell into the hands of the monarchy following their deaths in 1271.

The Albigensian crusades thus produced a major territorial windfall for the French kings, but they did not eliminate heresy from Languedoc. Armed resistance by Cathar followers remained a problem for many years. Not until the reduction of the castles of Montségur in 1244 and Quéribus in 1255 was this problem finally solved. Ultimately, the crusades and the assertion of French royal control made it impossible for Cathars and Waldensians to live and preach openly. Yet, although driven underground, the heretics remained entrenched in the countryside. To root them out required the creation of a new institution: the inquisition of heretical depravity.

## THE ORIGINS OF THE INQUISITION OF HERETICAL DEPRAVITY

When popular heresy became a significant problem in the twelfth century, the church experienced some embarrassment in dealing with it. Canon law was unclear on the proper procedure for handling heretics, and effective institutional means for identifying, prosecuting, and punishing them were lacking. Church authorities were long confused about what heretics believed and practiced, and the temptation to identify contemporary dissidents with those found in the pages of the church fathers was strong.

The burden of dealing with heretics lay on local bishops, many of whom showed little zeal for the task. Even if those suspected of heresy were apprehended, the methods available for proving their guilt, which relied on ordeals and the swearing of oaths, were primitive and unreliable.[31] Canon law was also unclear about what should be done with convicted heretics. Bishops could turn such people over to lay authorities for appropriate treatment, but until 1157 they were not required to do so. If lay rulers did not arrogate to themselves the right of punishment, bishops in this early period usually excommunicated heretics and expelled them from the diocese, although at times they also imprisoned them.[32] Some heretics were lynched by enraged mobs.

In the course of the late twelfth and early thirteenth centuries, the church remedied these deficiencies in its treatment of heretics. Decrees of councils and popes defined canon law concerning heretics. In 1184 Pope Lucius III issued the decretal *Ad abolendam*. This declared all heretics and their believers, defenders, and favorers to be excommunicate. Those found guilty of heresy were to be turned over to the lay powers for appropriate punishment (the nature of which was left unspecified). Bishops were required twice a year to visit those parishes where heresy was reported and search out suspected heretics.[33] In 1199 Innocent III in the decretal *Vergentis in senium* took the important step of assimilating heresy to treason as defined in Roman law. The property of heretics was to be confiscated by secular lords and their heirs disinherited.[34] As the church clarified its laws concerning heretics, so did lay rulers. The emperor Frederick II incorporated the canon law strictures into imperial law and decreed that the punishment for unrepentant heretics was to be death at the stake.[35] This became the penalty universally applied throughout western Europe, including the kingdom of France. Canon lawyers, church councils, and popes continued to discuss and legislate on the appropriate treatment of heretics and their supporters. By the

---

[31] Lambert, *Medieval Heresy*, pp. 66–67.

[32] Moore, *Origins of European Dissent*, p. 252.

[33] There is an English translation of this decretal in Peters, ed., *Heresy and Authority*, pp. 170–73.

[34] Peters, *Inquisition*, p. 48.

[35] Powell, ed. and trans., *The Liber Augustalis*, pp. 7–10.

end of the thirteenth century, the church possessed an elaborate and well-developed body of law dealing with the problem of heresy.[36]

During the course of the thirteenth century, the church also gained a better grasp of the nature of the heresies it was trying to combat. Catholic apologists and polemicists, in order effectively to refute heretical doctrines, felt it necessary first to describe them. Once papal inquisitors were established, their investigations yielded information on the nature of heretical belief and practice, information that a number of inquisitors set forth in treatises designed to instruct other inquisitors.[37] By the mid-thirteenth century, heresy hunters thus possessed solid information on the nature of the deviants they pursued.

Central to the medieval church's campaign against heresy was the creation of a specialized institution, the papal inquisition, charged specifically with the task of identifying, prosecuting, and punishing heretics and their sympathizers. When the exertions of local bishops did not succeed in stamping out heresy, the papacy embarked on a policy of appointing special judges delegate to pursue heretics. In selecting men to carry out this task, the pope turned to the new mendicant orders that had come into existence in the early thirteenth century, the Dominicans and Franciscans. The Dominicans in particular had a special vocation for combating heresy. Indeed, it had been the desire to wean the people of Languedoc away from Catharism that had inspired St. Dominic to found his order of Preachers in the early 1200s. In 1231 Pope Gregory IX commissioned the prior of the Dominican convent of Regensburg in Germany as a judge delegate and charged him with seeking out suspected heretics.

Not long after, the first papal inquisitors were appointed in Languedoc. In April 1233 Gregory IX called on the provincial priors of the Dominicans in Languedoc to select men suitable to serve as inquisitors. Ultimately inquisitorial tribunals, staffed by Dominicans, were established in the cities of Toulouse and Carcassonne. The setting-up of papal inquisitors did not debar bishops from conducting their own inquisitions. Indeed, from 1317 on, inquisitors and bishops were required to cooperate with one another in dealing with heretics.[38] Most bishops were content to let the main burden of repressing heresy fall on the shoulders of the papal inquisitors. At times, however, some Languedocian prelates, in cooperation with the Dominican inquisitors, established their own inquisitorial tribunals. As we shall see, the bishops of Albi and Pamiers were especially zealous in prosecuting heretics.

Once inquisitors went to work in Languedoc, they dealt primarily with Cathars and their supporters and secondarily with Waldensians. Over time the inquisitors also acquired jurisdiction over other types of offenders. These

---

[36] The best introduction is Maisonneuve, *Etudes sur les origines de l'inquisition*, pp. 151–98, 243–368.

[37] The fundamental guide to this literature is Dondaine, "Le Manuel de l'inquisiteur."

[38] Lea, *Inquisition of the Middle Ages*, 2: 96–97.

included those who dabbled in magic as well as Jewish converts to Christianity who returned to their original faith. A scattering of individuals prosecuted under these heads can be found in the surviving records. More serious was a new heresy that emerged in the early years of the fourteenth century, which I shall call Beguinism. The Béguins, usually members of the Franciscan Third Order, were followers of the Spiritual Franciscans.[39] They adhered to a rigid interpretation of the meaning and role of poverty in St. Francis's rule, regarded as martyrs the Franciscans who were burned at Marseilles in 1318 for refusing to accept the precepts concerning poverty contained in Pope John XXII's bull *Quorundam exigit*, revered the Languedocian friar Pierre-Jean Olivi as a great teacher and saint, and looked on Pope John XXII (1316–34) as the mystical antichrist.

Although it is common practice to speak of the medieval inquisition—and in the following pages I shall refer to the various inquisitorial tribunals that functioned in thirteenth- and fourteenth-century Languedoc as the "inquisition"—this is something of a misnomer. In the Middle Ages there was no single Inquisition, with a Grand Inquisitor supervising the holy office from Rome. Instead, there were simply a number of inquisitorial tribunals, staffed by papal judges delegate, some Dominicans, some Franciscans, scattered across Europe. These were never integrated into one unified organization; indeed, virtually no provision was made to assure mutual cooperation between them.[40]

Nevertheless, inquisitorial tribunals, although not part of a single, pan-European institution, shared common attributes. As papal judges delegate, the inquisitors were directly subject to the pope and hence normally exempt from ordinary episcopal control and oversight. The inquisitors proceeded against suspected heretics *ex officio*, by virtue of their office, without having to wait for a formal accusation to be brought against a suspect. Those who appeared before the inquisitors were required to take an oath and testify against themselves under pain of prosecution for either contumacy or perjury. All proceedings were secret. Moreover, the accused were normally denied the assistance of attorneys or notaries. They were also usually not told the names of those who had testified against them. In addition, inquisitorial tribunals accepted depositions from individuals ordinarily barred by canon law from giving testimony: children, convicted criminals, accomplices, and heretics.[41]

---

[39] The fundamental work on the Béguins is Manselli, *Spirituali e Beghini in Provenza* (translated into French as *Spirituels et Béguins du Midi*). These heretics are not to be confused with the beguines of northern Europe, who were women who led a religious life, often in groups, but without taking religious vows or adhering to a formal rule. On these women and their difficulties with church authorities, see McDonnell, *Beguines and Beghards*.

[40] See Kieckhefer, *Repression of Heresy in Medieval Germany*, pp. 3–6, and "The Office of Inquisition and Medieval Heresy."

[41] This is the customary interpretation of the inquisition's operation. Kelly, however, has argued that "there was not a single provision of the original *ordo juris* or rules of procedure for inquisition that privileged heresy cases over all other kinds of cases or limited due process for persons

## THE INQUISITORS IN THE LANGUEDOCIAN POLITICAL ARENA

The political arena in which the Languedocian inquisitors had to operate was very complex. Although in the early thirteenth century the French kings successfully asserted their overlordship in the region, political power remained widely dispersed. Moreover, although the thirteenth and early fourteenth centuries saw local rulers of all stripes elaborating and perfecting their organs of governance, government in many ways remained amateurish and personalistic.

After the Albigensian crusades the most important political team in Languedoc was constituted by the servants of the French crown. The French monarchy had acquired extensive lands and rights in the south of France, and it deployed a fairly impressive number of servants to manage these assets. In Languedoc the most important unit of royal administration was the *sénéchaussée*. In the aftermath of the Albigensian crusades several of these were set up. For our purposes, those worth taking note of are the *sénéchaussées* of Toulouse-Albigeois, Carcassonne, and Beaucaire. The seneschals who presided over these districts combined in their hands all royal authority: military, administrative, legal, and fiscal. *Sénéchaussées* were further subdivided into *vigueries* (except for Toulouse-Albigeois, which was divided into *jugeries*). These were presided over by *viguiers*, who were responsible to the seneschal. In addition, each *sénéchaussée* had a number of subaltern officials, among them *sous-viguiers* and *bayles*. *Bayles* functioned at the village level and were primarily concerned with collecting royal revenues.[42] Each *sénéchaussée* also had a number of specialized financial officers. For example, each *jugerie* in the *sénéchaussée* of Toulouse-Albigeois was equipped with an officer called a procurator. In the *vigueries* of Carcassonne, the official who played this role was termed a *clavier*. Finally, the Languedocian *sénéchaussées* acquired a flock of petty officials—sergeants, messengers, beadles, jailers, foresters, *banniers* (a species of rural police), and notaries.[43]

The establishment of this administrative framework was an impressive achievement. Nevertheless, it had some flaws. For one thing, the boundaries of various jurisdictions were often fairly unstable, because the extent of royal authority in the region was itself at times uncertain. For a time the kings of Aragon maintained claims to lordship over several areas in Languedoc.[44] The

---

charged with heresy in ways that were not permitted for persons charged with other crimes" ("Inquisition and the Prosecution of Heresy," p. 443). But Kelly's views should be compared with the careful survey of papal decrees relating to the powers of inquisitors in Shannon, *The Popes and Heresy*, pp. 48–89.

[42] A. Molinier, "Etude sur l'administration de Louis IX," pp. 490–93, 496–99; and Strayer, "Viscounts and Viguiers," pp. 216–19. See also Bourin, "Fortunes foncières," pp. 90–92.

[43] Lot and Fawtier, *Histoire des institutions*, 1: 94; Strayer, *Reign of Philip the Fair*, p. 136; A. Molinier, "Etude sur l'administration de Louis IX," pp. 504, 508; Michel, *L'Administration*, pp. 90–93; Friedlander, "Les Sergents royaux du Languedoc"; and *HL*, 6: 793–94.

[44] Sivéry, *Saint Louis et son siècle*, pp. 602–3; *HL*, 9: 12–21.

kings of England, who were also dukes of Gascony, claimed overlordship of lands that lay on the border of their duchy and Languedoc. Indeed, the Agenais, although ruled for much of the thirteenth century by the French, was ultimately ceded to the English king-dukes.[45] Finally, even in areas whose suzerainty was not contested, the process by which royal authority expanded was often slow, a matter of the piecemeal acquisition of estates and jurisdictional rights. These factors combined to create an administrative geography that was often anything but clearly defined.[46]

Although the French kings were recognized as suzerains throughout Languedoc, large areas remained outside the immediate grasp of the royal administration. Many of the political organizations that had existed before the wars of the early thirteenth century lived on after the assertion of royal hegemony. Among these were the numerous urban corporations. In the early days of French rule, towns not infrequently lost some of their political and legal privileges. Beaucaire, for example, was deprived of its consulate.[47] Yet, despite the trimming of the powers and autonomy of some towns, the French did not launch an all-out attack on them. Indeed, from the middle of the thirteenth century King Louis IX began restoring privileges to those towns that had lost them in the early days of royal rule.[48]

French rule was thus not inherently inimical to the preservation of traditional centers of political authority. Indeed, some members of the local ruling elites found that French hegemony was not incompatible with progress for themselves. Under the umbrella of royal overlordship, a number of lords were able to consolidate and expand their own authority. Prominent among these were the prelates of the Languedocian church. Before the crusades, for example, the authority of the bishops of Toulouse had been limited. Bishop Fulk, however, successfully exploited the turmoil of the war, enhancing—among other things—his judicial authority. He also significantly improved the material situation of his see, prying tithes and church property out of the hands of the local aristocracy.[49] Other bishops had similar success in enhancing their secular authority.[50]

Ecclesiastical lords were not the only rulers who enhanced their authority. Many lay lords found that the imposition of royal control was no bar to the consolidation of their own power. Although the count of Toulouse, Raimond VII,

[45] Lodge, *Gascony under English Rule*; Gavrilovitch, *Le Traité de Paris de 1259*, pp. 68–75, 82–83; and Trabut-Cussac, *L'Administration anglaise en Gascogne*, pp. xxiv–xxv, 59–65, 72–77.

[46] For examples of the slow process by which administrative boundaries were laid down, the confusion over their exact whereabouts, and the frequent changes that often took place in them, see Friedlander, "The Seneschalsy of Carcassonne," pp. 25, 51, 58–62, 135–36, 205–7; Dossat, ed., *Saisimentum comitatus tholosani*, pp. 36–39, 40–41; and Ménard, *Histoire de Nîmes*, 1: 346.

[47] Michel, *L'Administration royale*, p. 40.

[48] A. Molinier, "Etude sur l'administration de Louis IX," pp. 561–66.

[49] Mundy, *Liberty and Political Power in Toulouse*, pp. 164–65, 390 n. 14.

[50] For examples from Lodève and Albi, see E. Martin, *Histoire de la ville de Lodève*, 1: 46, 64; A. Molinier, "Etude sur les démêlés entre l'évêque"; and Biget, "Un Procès d'inquisition."

made significant concessions to the French in the Treaty of Paris of 1229, he used the next twenty years to cement his control of that which he still retained. In the city of Toulouse, he curtailed the townspeople's exemption from tolls, revived his judicial authority, and even succeeded in arrogating to himself the right to select the town's consuls.[51] Elsewhere in the county Raimond also enjoyed considerable success in expanding his authority. He increased the size of his domain and founded approximately forty new settlements of the type known as *bastides*.[52] Ultimately, all of Raimond's efforts served to enrich the French monarchy, which ultimately fell heir to his lordship in 1271; but this fact should not blind us to the very real success that he enjoyed in laying the groundwork for a strong territorial principality. Another lord who improved the mechanisms for governing his territories while under French dominion was the count of Foix in the eastern Pyrenees, an area that will figure prominently in the following pages. In the thirteenth and fourteenth centuries the counts of Foix gradually built up an elaborate administrative structure, complete with seneschals, *bayles*, procurators, and castellans. By 1320 their administration had become both ambitious enough and competent enough to carry out an enumeration of all the hearths in the county as well as all the services and dues owed the count.[53] The counts also experimented with the calling of general assemblies of the inhabitants of their lordship.[54]

Finally, even the peasantry was able to consolidate its political position under the umbrella of royal overlordship. It was during the period of the Albigensian crusades and their aftermath that the institution of the consulate spread widely through the villages of the region. For example, in the area of the county of Toulouse known as the Lauragais, an area heavily infected with the Cathar heresy, no village consulates seem to have existed before 1200. When Count Raimond VII acquired the Lauragais in 1237, consulates began to appear, although their number remained limited. Under the count's French heir, Alfonse de Poitiers, who arrived in 1249, consulates became more numerous, spreading to even the tiniest villages. When King Philip III inherited the county of Toulouse in 1271, his agents recorded consulates in ninety-six communities.[55]

Languedoc was thus a very complex political arena, in which lords of all types and various communities were engaged in a process of political consolidation and elaboration. In this arena one of the most important players, or group of players, consisted of the clergy of the Catholic Church. Not only were certain prelates great secular lords—masters of cities, castles, vassals, and dependent peasants—but all ecclesiastics belonged to a highly self-conscious, supranational organization

---

[51] Mundy, *Liberty and Political Power in Toulouse*, p. 136; Wolff, ed., *Histoire de Toulouse*, pp. 125, 138.

[52] Ramière de Fortanier, *Chartes de franchises*, pp. 17–18; Saint-Blanquat, "Comment se sont crées les bastides," p. 280.

[53] Dufau de Maluquer, "Le Pays de Foix," pp. 3–5.

[54] For example, in 1333 a body called the *Tres Status Comitatus* met at Pamiers; *HL*, 9: 464 n. 1.

[55] Ramière de Fortanier, *Chartes de franchises*, pp. 40–46.

whose final head was the pope in Rome. Moreover, this transnational institution possessed its own legal system, with its own law. Although the exact extent of ecclesiastical jurisdiction was often unclear, it was acknowledged that the church's courts had the right to settle matters involving many aspects of social and economic life. It was recognized that matters involving the clergy and its discipline belonged to church courts. These courts also exercised an extensive jurisdiction over what were regarded as "spiritual" affairs, which included such things as heresy, the sacraments, religious vows, canonical censures, the policing of holy sites, and the regulation of religious confraternities. Church courts also claimed the right to deal with matters relating to church property, tithes, offerings made to churches, church benefices, and questions involving marriage. So broad were the claims of the church and so frequently did they impinge on what secular rulers regarded as "temporal" matters that disputes over the boundaries between secular and ecclesiastical jurisdictions were a chronic feature of medieval European life.[56]

It was in this decentered political arena, characterized by a plethora of power holders and chronic disputes over jurisdiction, that the inquisitors of heretical depravity had to carry out their tasks. And they had to do so with the limited tools of governance available to medieval rulers. Although medieval governing institutions were experiencing major development in this period and were becoming increasingly professionalized and systematic in their operations, they were still anything but modern, bureaucratic organizations. Most governing institutions possessed virtually no formal criteria for the selection, training, evaluation, and advancement of administrators. Salaries were low. Some royal servants, such as many Languedocian *bayles*, received no salaries; instead, they "farmed" their offices, being allowed to keep whatever profits they made from the exercise of their duties in return for a lump sum payment to the royal treasury.[57]

Most of the governing agencies of Languedoc, in common with their counterparts throughout Europe, did not have much "relative autonomy" with regard to their social formations.[58] That is, rulers and administrators did not function in the political sphere as a separate social category, with a specific set of group interests and coherent policies designed to serve those interests. This was true even of the royal government, which, since it was relatively new to the region and was often staffed in its upper reaches by individuals not native to Languedoc, might have been expected to enjoy the largest degree of such autonomy. However, the continued authority of local power holders enabled them to impose themselves on the royal government, securing appointments for them-

---

[56] A brief but useful introduction to ecclesiastical jurisdiction can be found in Lot and Fawtier, *Histoire des institutions*, 3: 257–79. See also Bellomo, *Common Legal Past of Europe*, pp. 75–77.
[57] Strayer, *Reign of Philip the Fair*, p. 102.
[58] On the "relative autonomy" of the state, one can consult Skocpol, "Bringing the State Back In" and *States and Social Revolutions*; Krasner, "Approaches to the State"; Carnoy, *The State and Political Theory*, pp. 54–55, 108–9, 200–202; and Poulantzas, *Political Power and Social Classes*, pp. 255–321.

selves or their clients in the royal administration. The retention of significant authority by native Languedocians meant that the loyalty of the servants of the French crown was often divided. Royal agents were not infrequently also servants or clients of one of the local potentates. The fact that many royal administrators were recruited locally meant that these officials often had intimate ties with the people whose conduct they were required to supervise.[59] Finally, given the tiny staffs that medieval rulers could afford to field, all administrators, if they were to accomplish much of anything, were dependent on the active cooperation or at least acquiescence of those they ruled. The combination of these factors made it difficult for the rulers of Languedoc to conduct themselves as though they were a specific social group with interests and loyalties that set them apart from the other social networks in Languedoc.

All of this meant that for the most part government was a relatively passive affair. Administrators, whether they worked for a king or a less exalted lord, were primarily concerned with collecting tribute and preserving their masters' rights. Active intervention by rulers in the affairs of their subjects, designed to shape the behavior of the governed in accordance with consciously articulated policy goals, was uncommon. In large part the relative rarity of such intervention was due to the fact that medieval rulers lacked effective tools for the job. However, from the twelfth century on rulers developed judicial institutions whose operations began to open up possibilities for more active intervention in and regulation of the affairs of their subjects.

Indeed, judicial systems became one of the primary mechanisms by which political authority could be both asserted and legitimated in the developing polities of the High Middle Ages. There were many reasons why judicial institutions came to play such an important role in the medieval art of governance. The intensive study of law that was such a prominent feature of European culture in the twelfth and thirteenth centuries allowed rulers to recruit an ever more skillful and accomplished set of jurists. Royal and seignorial intervention into local affairs could, if undertaken under a judicial guise, be clothed in an ideologically acceptable, indeed attractive, garb. Finally, such intervention often addressed the felt needs of at least a segment of the governed.

Whether or not one wishes to accept this argument, it is clear that in the twelfth and thirteenth centuries a major movement was under way: older judicial mechanisms were being replaced by courts whose procedures were not merely new but more authoritarian. Before the twelfth-century courts had expressed the will of local communities assembled to do justice more than they had expressed the controlling aspirations of rulers. Directed by judges who functioned more as their courts' presidents than as authoritative interpreters of the law, judicial tribunals had been theaters for the negotiation of settlements based on compromise

---

[59] On the relations between the agents of the royal government and local power holders, see Given, *State and Society*, pp. 166–79.

rather than the sites of judgments authoritatively imposed upon litigants. Actions had normally been initiated by private suitors, not by public authority, and the modes of proof employed—ordeals, compurgation, battle—were largely beyond the control of judges. But in the twelfth and thirteenth centuries, courts increasingly became the agents of rulers. A better-trained and more professionalized judiciary came into existence, modes of proof more susceptible to their control were devised,[60] and a more activist and interventionist role was adopted by the courts.[61] If courts in the earlier Middle Ages had primarily been places where small, face-to-face communities sought to repair injuries to ongoing relationships and fashion a workable peace that would allow the community to continue to function,[62] by the period with which we are concerned they were well on their way to becoming places where judges endeavored to impose definitive verdicts that accorded less with community sentiments and more with abstract conceptions of justice and legality that were the products of a learned, elite culture.

It is against this background that the development of inquisitorial techniques should be understood. In the earlier Middle Ages criminal cases had proceeded by means of the *accusatio*, derived from Roman law. Such an action could be brought only by the victim, his kinsmen, or his lord. In this procedure the court and its judge played a largely passive role. The burden of proof was borne by the accuser who, if he failed in his suit, was subject to the same penalties the accused would have had inflicted on him had he been condemned. The accused could clear himself by means of the ordeal, by producing compurgators, or offering to fight a duel with his accuser or his compurgators. In the twelfth century the church courts began to develop procedures that allowed them a more active role in the prosecution of crime. Ecclesiastical judges claimed the right to proceed *ex officio* against perpetrators of notorious crimes. A procedure of *denunciatio* in which a person could accuse another of crime without taking on the awful burdens and risks entailed by *accusatio* was developed; in this case the judge proceeded *ex officio* and as if there were no accuser to require the

---

[60] For example, in French royal courts by the end of the thirteenth century civil cases were being settled not by appeal to such modes of proof as trial by battle, but by the examination and weighing by judges of written evidence. (For a brief description of the procedures of the French royal court at the end of the thirteenth century, see Lot and Fawtier, *Histoire des institutions*, 2: 386–89.) It should be noted that Robert Bartlett has argued that the unilateral ordeal, frequently interpreted as a "therapeutic" and "popular" form of proof, utilized by small, face-to-face communities that valued consensus and saw in the judicial process primarily a means to restore peace in the community, was in actuality a device for the assertion of royal or princely authority over the judicial process; see *Trial by Fire and Water*, especially pp. 34–42.

[61] A classic example of this is the development in England of the presenting jury, a device that allowed public authorities to prosecute crime without relying on the cumbrous and, for the accuser, perilous appeal by a private party. For a recent discussion, see Green, *Verdict According to Conscience*, pp. 3–27. On the greater activism of courts and judges in thirteenth-century Siena, see Pazzaglini, *The Sienese Commune*, pp. 102–3.

[62] This is basically the argument of Brown, "Society and the Supernatural," pp. 310–16, and Hyams, "Trial by Ordeal," pp. 95–99.

suspect to purge himself by oath or ordeal. By the end of the twelfth century, the procedure of *inquisitio* had been introduced into church courts. This allowed a judge to initiate action against someone suspected of crime solely on the basis of public rumor. In prosecuting such suspects, the judge could take an active role, seeking witnesses or other proof of guilt. Procedure by *inquisitio* was quickly adopted by lay jurisdictions, including the cities of northern Italy and the French monarchy.[63]

The papacy, when it decided to entrust the task of forcible repression of heresy to a special judicial tribunal utilizing inquisitorial procedures, was thus drawing on a body of techniques that was being used increasingly widely in thirteenth-century Europe. The men who staffed the inquisitorial tribunals in Languedoc made the most of their opportunity. By the beginning of the fourteenth century they had come close to eradicating Catharism and containing the other heretical movements. In evaluating their achievement, it should be remembered that they did not have available many of the resources at the command of their contemporary power-wielders. The Dominican inquisitors had no independent revenue sources of their own and were largely dependent on royal largesse to finance their activities. Their staffs were tiny. Finally, as special papal judges delegate, who had to operate in a fractured and fragmented political world, they did not enjoy the luxury of representing a unified system of authority. All medieval rulers had constantly to negotiate and renegotiate the spheres of their activity with other power holders; but the inquisitors confronted an unusually difficult situation. In section I we shall observe how they went about executing their task in the complex, decentered, and highly fragmented political world of medieval Languedoc.

---

[63] On the development of inquisitorial procedures, see Esmein, *History of Continental Criminal Procedure*, pp. 88–93; Cheyette, "Inquest, Canonical and French"; Trusen, "Der Inquisitionsprozeß" and "Von den Anfängen des Inquisitionsprozeßes"; and Fowler-Magerl, *"Ordines iudiciarii,"* pp. 85–90. For a thirteenth-century jurist's discussion of the *inquisitio* procedure in criminal trials, see Albertus Gandinus, "Tractatus de maleficiis," in Kantorowicz, *Albertus Gandinus*, 2: 37–48. One should also consult the essays of Fraher: "Conviction According to Conscience," "Preventing Crime in the High Middle Ages," and "Theoretical Justification for the New Criminal Law."

# SECTION I

# THE INQUISITORS
# AND THEIR TECHNIQUES

O NE CAN CONCEIVE of the power exercised by a governing institution as the product of three factors. The first factor consists of the
activity of the members of the institution itself: their strategies, their
techniques, and the resources they can mobilize. The second, almost a mirror
image of the first, is composed of the strategies, techniques, resources, and organization of the people whose behavior the governing institution seeks to control.
The third factor consists of the social formation's structures. These constitute the
economic, political, technological, and cultural resources on which both governors and governed can draw. The way in which these resources are structured can
both facilitate and constrain the actions of the governors and the governed.
Governance is therefore a dialectical process in which rulers and ruled, acting
within the parameters of a specific, historically given situation, mutually condition and shape each other's behavior. The outcome of this process is not
necessarily willed by either party; to a large extent it is the unintended and unexpected product of their interaction.

The chapters in section I deal with aspects of the first factor mentioned
above. They examine the ways in which the inquisitors sought to pursue their
task of detecting, prosecuting, and punishing heretics and their sympathizers. I
have not sought here to produce a general treatment of inquisitorial organization
and procedure. Instead, I have tried to understand the Languedocian inquisition
not so much as a judicial or administrative organization but as a political organization, that is, as a group of men endeavoring to win for themselves enough
power to accomplish their goal of extirpating heresy. Accordingly, I deal only
in a secondary fashion with the details of inquisitorial organization and the
niceties of judicial reasoning about inquisitorial procedure. I focus primarily
on an examination of the actual techniques that the inquisitors employed in
their efforts to combat heresy.

To understand how the inquisitors sought to acquire enough power to
accomplish their goals, it is useful to think of their activity as a form of production. Like all other forms of production, political activity is a labor process in
which raw materials are transformed into a new commodity. Power wielders
must take men as they find them, already organized in various competing and
cooperating social groups, and transform them, through the application of the

economic and cultural resources that their social formation offers, into organized groups that can produce the desired commodity, the realization of a policy goal.[1] In effect, political activity can be understood as a form of technology, as a body of specific techniques for manipulating social relations.

In case this conceptualization of the problem sounds to the reader too Marxist, we can instead use a game-playing analogy. Politics can be understood as an arena in which various games are played. These are governed by rules: some normative and explicit, others implicit and pragmatic. The normative rules define the prizes, the nature of the teams, and what behavior is acceptable or unacceptable. What I have referred to as the technology of power can be understood as the pragmatic rules: a set of unspoken and occasionally secret prescriptions, not about how to play the game in a normatively acceptable way but about how to play it to win.[2]

The chapters in section I examine the way in which the inquisitors used three different technologies in their pursuit of heresy and heretics: record keeping, coercive forms of interrogation (primarily imprisonment), and punishment. In fashioning their techniques for manipulating the objects of their inquiries, the inquisitors took few steps that can be regarded as completely innovative; but the way in which they incorporated existing techniques of rule into a peculiarly coherent and effective engine of repression is possibly without parallel in medieval Europe.

[1] My discussion here leans on that of Hindess and Hirst in *Pre-Capitalist Modes of Production*, pp. 36–37.
[2] I have taken this analogy from Bailey, *Stratagems and Spoils*, pp. 3–7.

# CHAPTER 1

# THE TECHNOLOGY
# OF DOCUMENTATION

A MAJOR DEVELOPMENT IN the art of governance during the Middle Ages was the dramatic increase in the use of the technologies of writing and document preservation. The rulers of Europe moved away from traditional ways of doing business, which had relied on human memory, toward systems that made extensive use of writing as a way of creating a perpetual, undying memory of their activity.[1] This age of document production and archive creation began in the late twelfth and early thirteenth centuries. Rulers produced documents in ever-increasing numbers. At the beginning of the thirteenth century, for example, Pope Innocent III (1198–1216), whose output of letters was higher than that of his predecessors, issued an average of 303 surviving letters per year. By the end of the century, Boniface VIII (1294–1303) in an average year sent out around 50,000.[2]

From the historian's point of view, even more significant than the increased volume of document production was the systematic effort that governments began to make to archive at least a part of this ever-growing stream of documents. The English kings were among the first to show a serious concern for the preservation and protection of their records. By the middle of the twelfth century, copies of the Exchequer's Pipe Rolls were being preserved. In the 1190s the Crown began to keep copies of many of its other documents, such as letters issued by the royal chancery and the proceedings of its courts.[3] Other rulers lagged behind the English, but in the course of the thirteenth century most European governments began systematically to preserve some of their records. By the fourteenth century no ruler could govern effectively without the assistance of such an institutionalized, archival memory.

Outside the world of the bureaucrat, the twelfth and thirteenth centuries also saw important developments in the technologies of book making. Monastic culture, in which reading had been a spiritual exercise bound up with prayer and meditation, gave way to the culture of the schools, in which reading "involved

---

[1] The fundamental study of this phenomenon is Clanchy, *From Memory to Written Record*, to which I am heavily indebted.
[2] Ibid., pp. 60–61.
[3] Ibid., pp. 68–72, 162–66.

a more ratiocinative scrutiny of the text and consultation for reference pur-poses."[4] New ways of reading required new ways of presenting texts. Scholars analyzed the structure of texts more closely and emphasized the articulation of the different parts of a work through division into chapters, *causae*, *quaestiones*, and *distinctiones*. Stages of an argument were indicated by *litterae notabiliores* and paraph marks. The need for material that could be readily used in teaching, research, and preaching led schoolmen and members of the new mendicant orders to develop tools to enhance the searchability of texts so as to enable users to find rapidly and efficiently the particular piece of information for which they were looking. These tools included analytical lists of chapter headings, concor-dances, and indexes arranged in alphabetical order.[5]

When the inquisitors of Languedoc began their work in the 1230s, they did so in an environment in which much thought was being given to the cre-ation and organization of archives and to new ways of presenting texts so as to enhance their intelligibility and searchability. In creating documents that recorded the trials of suspected heretics, depositing those documents in archives, and writing manuals that served as guides to the work of the holy office, the inquisitors were certainly not unique; but they seem to have been unusually skillful in the way they utilized the contents of their archives to help them in their campaign against heresy.

In general, when medieval rulers attempted to sort through the masses of parchment accumulated in their archives, they were usually searching for evi-dence to reinforce their claims to rights of one sort or another.[6] They seldom subjected the contents of their archives to an analytic scrutiny designed to pro-duce not evidence of good title but information that could be used either to formulate or pursue a policy goal. The inquisitors, however, made exactly such use of their records as part of an analytic strategy designed to enable them to act more effectively, to exert power in a more concentrated and efficient way. The inquisitors' activist use of archival material does much to explain the suc-cess they enjoyed in rooting out heresy.

## THE INQUISITORS AND THEIR ARCHIVES

From the early days of the inquisitors' activity in Languedoc, the preservation and protection of their records was a major concern.[7] In 1251 a church council

---

[4] Parkes, "*Ordinatio* and *Compilatio*," p. 115.

[5] Ibid., pp. 115–38; R. Rouse and M. Rouse, "*Statim invenire*"; and Petrucci, "Lire au Moyen Age."

[6] See, in general, Clanchy, *From Memory to Written Record*, pp. 166–72. For an example of the way in which documents were assembled from archives and other sources to reinforce claims to various rights, see the compilation made for the "Great Cause" concerning the succession to the throne of Scotland at the end of the thirteenth century in Stones and Simpson, eds., *Edward I and the Throne of Scotland*, especially 1: 137–62, 2: 296–309.

[7] The surviving records of the Languedocian inquisitors have been described by many scholars.

held at L'Isle-sur-la-Sorgue discussed the proper maintenance of inquisitorial records.[8] In 1255 a council of bishops assembled at Albi decreed that the inquisitors should make duplicate copies of their registers.[9]

At Toulouse it appears that the inquisitors' records were stored in their residence near the Château Narbonnais.[10] At Carcassonne they were kept in a tower in the *cité* adjacent to the inquisitors' residence. A passage connected the tower and the residence, but it was closed with a door to which only the inquisitors had the key.[11] The records stored in these depositories were once fairly extensive. At some point the archives of the Carcassonne inquisition were moved to Montpellier, where they were inventoried in the seventeenth century. At that time the archive contained 115 pieces: nineteen registers, fifty-six books, thirteen *cahiers*, nine rolls, and various other items. Forty-three of these documents had originated in the thirteenth century, the oldest being from 1236. Three registers included material from both the thirteenth and fourteenth centuries. Thirty-six items came from the first half of the fourteenth century. Thus, the period from the thirteenth through the early fourteenth centuries, when the Carcassonne tribunal was most active, was represented by a total of eighty-two items.[12]

Unfortunately, the centuries have been unkind to the archives of the Dominican inquisitors of Toulouse and Carcassonne. At times documents were removed from them. The most striking example of this is the curious fate of the *Liber sententiarum*, or register of sentences, kept by Bernard Gui during his service as inquisitor of Toulouse in the early 1300s. Sometime in the seventeenth century the *Liber* was acquired, possibly by an Englishman of radical Protestant opinions, and taken to England. It found its way into the hands of a Dutchman, Philipp van Limborch, who transcribed it and published it in 1692 as an appendix to his history of the inquisition. Thereafter the manuscript seemed to disappear. Scholars assumed that it had been lost or destroyed. But in the 1970s it was demonstrated that the register had not been lost. Instead, it had been safely residing for several centuries in the British Library as Add. MS 4697.[13]

Other documents from the inquisitors' archives were not as fortunate as Gui's book of sentences. Many registers were broken up and their leaves used to cover other documents. The great bulk of the Dominican inquisitors' records

---

See, among others, Douais, "Les Manuscrits du château de Merville" and "Les Sources de l'histoire de l'inquisition"; *Documents*, 1: vi–ccxciv; and C. Molinier, *L'Inquisition dans le Midi de la France* and "Rapport à M. le Ministre de l'Instruction Publique." Far and away the most interesting discussion of inquisitorial archives is that found in Dossat, *Crises*, pp. 29–55, a work on which I have relied heavily.

8 Mansi, 23: cols. 795–96.
9 Dossat, *Crises*, p. 30.
10 Gui, *Practica inquisitionis*, p. 66.
11 Dossat, *Crises*, p. 31.
12 Ibid., pp. 43–44. The inventory itself is published in Germain, "Inventaire inédit."
13 Nickson, "Locke and the Inquisition of Toulouse."

simply vanished. Much of what survives is known only through the medium of copies made in the seventeenth century by a commission searching for evidence concerning royal rights.[14] Several years ago Yves Dossat, through a painstaking examination of the surviving manuscripts, managed to construct a partial list of the contents of the Dominican inquisitors' archives. According to his findings, the archive at Toulouse at one point must have contained a minimum of sixteen registers of depositions and sentences. Similarly, the Carcassonne archives held a minimum of eighteen registers and books.[15]

Since so much inquisitorial material has been lost or survives only in later copies, we cannot be as precise as we would like about the way in which the inquisitors ordered their records. The surviving originals, however, demonstrate that much effort and thought were devoted to making the contents of the archives readily comprehensible and accessible. We know a good deal about how the depositions given by those interrogated by the inquisitors were transformed from what must often have been a chaotic flow of words into the neatly arranged registers that survive today. Through study of the register kept by Jacques Fournier, bishop of Pamiers, J.-M. Vidal reconstructed the process by which Fournier's notaries worked up witnesses' statements into permanent, written records. During an interrogation the notary made rough notes of the questions posed to the witness and his or her answers. These notes were recorded in a document known as a protocol. At a later date the notary reworked his notes and drew up in Latin a formal act in the official style of the inquisition. This act was written in a paper register. When a suspect's trial was concluded, this version of the act was read to him or her in the vernacular. The suspect, after being given the opportunity to modify the contents of this document, was then asked to confirm it as a true representation of his or her statements. Finally, the act was again transcribed, this time on parchment, and bound up in the book that survives today in the Vatican Library.[16]

## SEARCHABILITY AND RETRIEVABILITY

The process by which the inquisitors' notaries produced the documents that survive today is thus well known. The important thing about archival documents, however, is not so much the mere fact that they exist as the ability of future searchers to find and understand information in them. Unfortunately, we know much less about how the inquisitors tried to make the contents of their records readily retrievable by and comprehensible to future users. Nevertheless, enough original documents survive to let us make some observations about the

---

[14] This material forms the Collection Doat, which is housed in the Bibliothèque Nationale in Paris. See C. Molinier, *L'Inquisition dans le Midi de la France*, pp. 34–40; Omont, "La Collection Doat"; and Kolmer, *"Ad capiendas vulpes,"* pp. 12–15.

[15] Dossat, *Crises*, pp. 37–54.

[16] Vidal, "Le Tribunal d'inquisition de Pamiers," 8 (1903–1904): 386–91.

inquisitors' information retrieval techniques. In this respect, the original manuscript of Bernard Gui's *Liber sententiarum* is particularly valuable. The register
reveals that Gui and his colleagues did not produce anything as elaborate or as
rationalized as the heavily annotated texts emerging from thirteenth-century
schools; but they did make effective use of some of the techniques developed by
the schoolmen to make the contents of their documents more readily accessible.

Since the rediscovery of Gui's register is fairly recent, and its layout long
known only secondhand, it is worth discussing its organization in some detail.[17]
Each page of the register is methodically laid out. In the first part of the manuscript many of the register's pages have been ruled with vertical and horizontal
lines so that the text is enclosed in a double-ruled box. At the top of the page
there is a small box for a running title; at the bottom of the page there is a larger
box, evidently intended for later additions to the text. On both the left and the
right sides of the page, the text is surrounded by large, rectangular boxes designed
to hold marginal annotations. Although in the latter parts of the manuscript the
various parts of the page are not as clearly indicated by means of lines, the same
general page layout is maintained.

The material in the register is organized according to the ceremonies, known
as "general sermons" (*sermones generales*; sing., *sermo generalis*), at which sentences
were imposed on those condemned for heresy. These are grouped chronologically
from the first in 1308 to the last in 1323. The organization of the material in each
sentence is roughly the same. For purposes of illustration, we will use the third
*sermo*, held at Toulouse on 5 April 1310. The text opens on folio 17r with a brief
section noting the place and date, together with the names of the officials involved
in imposing the sentences. The rest of the *sermo* is divided into fourteen sections.
The beginning of each section is signaled by a section heading that is centered
with respect to the left and right margins. These headings are also underlined and
picked out with large paraph marks. The section headings are as follows:

> Oath of the servants of the king's court [oath by royal agents to support the
> inquisition (fol. 17r)]
> The same form of oath for the consuls [a similar oath taken by the consuls of
> Toulouse]
> Sentence of excommunication against those impeding the inquisition
> Grace with respect to crosses [names of those who have previously been sen-
> tenced to wear crosses on their clothing, but who are now allowed to lay
> them aside (fol. 17v)]
> Released from the *mur* [name of a person who had previously been sentenced
> to imprisonment but is now released from captivity]

---

[17] I make no claim to be either a paleographer or a codicologist, and the following discussion
is meant to be not a definitive description of the manuscript but simply some observations on elements of its layout.

Crimes [*culpe*] of those signed with the cross [summaries of the confessions of those who will be sentenced to wear crosses]

Sentence of those signed with the cross [sentence requiring those just named to wear crosses (fol. 19v)]

Crimes of those immured [summaries of the confessions of those who will be sentenced to imprisonment (fol. 20r)]

Sentence of those immured [sentence imprisoning those just named (fol. 33v)]

Sentence of those who died in heresy [orders to exhume and burn bodies of those who had died after receiving the Cathar *consolamentum* (fol. 34r)]

Sentence against the houses in which persons were hereticated [orders to destroy the houses in which the *consolamentum* had been administered (fol. 35r)]

Crimes of the relapsed [summaries of the confessions of those who will be turned over to the secular arm to be burned as relapsed heretics]

Sentence of those relapsed [formal surrender of the relapsed to the secular arm for burning (fol. 39r)]

Sentence against Pierre Guillaume de Prunet, heretic and relapsed

In those sections where the crimes, or *culpe*, of individuals about to be sentenced are summarized, the names of those in question are picked out with paraph marks.[18] In the later sections of the register, the names of those sentenced are not indicated with such marks; instead they are identified by the simple practice of using a very large initial, often five times as large as the rest of the text, for the first letter of each name. The reader of the register is also kept oriented by the consistent use of running titles. Anyone searching through the *Liber* could easily tell whether he was dealing with individuals who had been sentenced to the wearing of crosses, to imprisonment, or to death at the stake. The scribes who drew up the register made effective use of the space they had set aside for marginal annotations. In some cases these are simple corrections of errors in the main body of the text. In other cases they contain important ancillary information. For example, on 25 May 1309 Bernard Aliguer of Mirepoix-sur-Tarn was sentenced to imprisonment in the *mur* (the common term for the inquisitorial prison) at Toulouse.[19] A marginal note indicates that he escaped on 24 April 1310.[20]

An even more interesting marginal note unravels the complicated affair of Adhémar Peyre of Bannières, a village near Lavaur. Adhémar had been deeply

---

[18] The notary who recorded the acts of this particular *sermo* also picked out with paraph marks the individual acts for which an individual was condemned. This, however, was not a practice followed throughout the register.

[19] The use of *mur* to designate the inquisitorial prison was borrowed from monastic usage, in which *murus* was used to describe the punishment room that monasteries were expected to have. See Peters, "Prison before the Prison," pp. 28–29.

[20] *LS*, p. 25.

involved with the Cathar missionaries active in Languedoc in the 1290s and the first years of the fourteenth century. In 1306, however, perhaps feeling that the net was beginning to close on these last Good Men, he presented himself to Bérenger, bishop of Béziers and papal penitentiary. To this dignitary he made a very imperfect and partial confession, abjured all heresy, and swore to hold to the truths of the Catholic Church. However, he subsequently escaped from custody and went back to consorting with the Good Men. On 28 November 1311 he was arrested for the second time. Ordinarily, as a relapsed heretic, Adhémar should have been sent to the stake. What saved him was Bernard Gui's desire to lay hold of Pierre Sanche, a Good Man. As a marginal note to Adhémar's sentence puts it, "This Adhémar Peyre was promised grace concerning his body by the lord inquisitor when he was last arrested, provided he immediately revealed the whereabouts of the heretic Pierre Sanche so that he could be arrested, and fully confessed concerning the involvement of himself and others in heresy; he immediately revealed Sanche's whereabouts, and it was not through his doing that the heretic was not arrested"[21] (see plate 1). This cooperation earned Adhémar the relatively lenient, in the circumstances, sentence of imprisonment *ad murum largum* in Toulouse. Under the terms of such a sentence, prisoners enjoyed a large degree of freedom, often being allowed to wander around the *mur* rather as they wished. As a prisoner, however, Adhémar proved less than exemplary. On 7 March 1316 Gui took the unusual step of sentencing him to the much more severe form of imprisonment known as *murum strictum*, in which a prisoner was kept confined in a cell and could also be burdened with fetters and shackles.[22]

Marginalia were also used to cross-reference entries to other documents. At Toulouse the depositions received by the inquisitors were entered in books referred to as "books of extracts" (*libri extractionum*). Several notes in the *Liber sententiarum* refer readers to these. For example, a note next to the sentence in which Grazide, the wife of Guillaume Géraud of La Garriguette, was required to wear crosses indicates that the "*culpa* of this person is more fully set forth in the second book of extracts, fol. XVI°."[23] All told, such cross-references in the *Liber sententiarum* indicate the existence of at least three of these registers.[24]

Apart from marginalia, Gui's notaries seem to have employed few other special marks to facilitate reference to the *Liber sententiarum* and its allied documents. In a few places we find underlined the names of inquisitors who had previously sentenced people with whom Gui had occasion to deal at a later date. For example, in the section of the *sermo* of 25 May 1309 in which

[21] The entry concerning Adhémar is on fols. 55v–56r of Add. MS 4697, which corresponds to *LS*, pp. 124–25 (incorrectly given as pp. 122–23).
[22] Add. MS 4697, fol. 92v.
[23] *LS*, p. 105; Add. MS 4697, fol. 46v.
[24] On folio 118v, next to the sentence of Raimonde the widow of Guillaume de Mourvilles of Varennes, is the entry *libro tercio cclvi*.

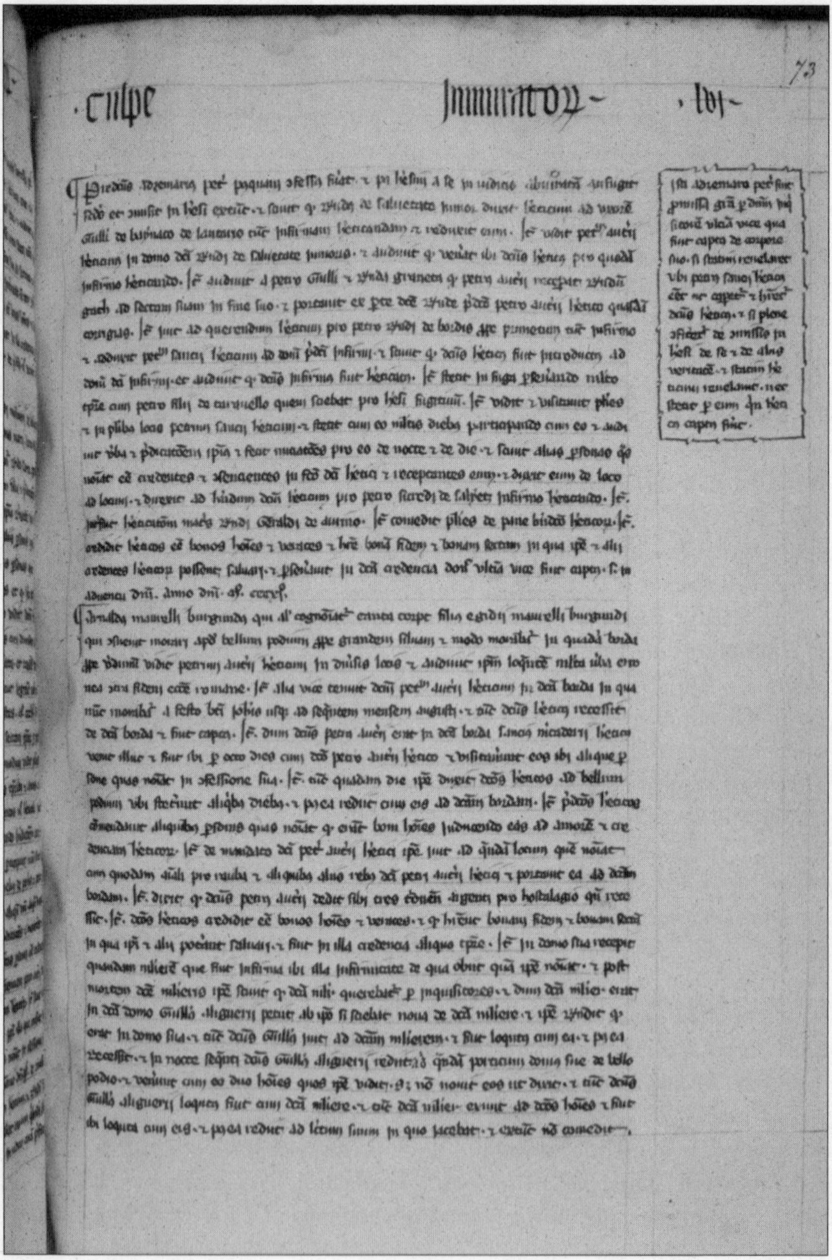

**Plate 1.** Folio 56r of Bernard Gui's *Liber sententiarum*, showing the *culpe* of those sentenced to the mur on 23 April 1312. At the top of the folio is a marginal annotation to the effect that Adhémar Peyre of Bannières was promised special treatment in return for assisting the inquisitors in trying to arrest a Cathar Good Man. Add. MS 4697, reproduced by permission of the British Library.

those who had been sentenced to wear crosses were allowed to lay them aside, we find the following entries:[25]

> Raimonde, widow of Etienne Got of Lagarde, from the time of the inquisitors, Brother Pierre de Pouget and Brother Etienne de Gastine[26]
>
> Guillemette Borrela of Garrigues of the time of the inquisitor, Brother Jean Vigoroux[27]

These marks may have been intended to refer readers, if necessary, to these inquisitors' registers.

Compared to the techniques that contemporary schoolmen were perfecting to facilitate the searchability of their texts, those employed by the inquisitors were not very elaborate. Gui's register lacks many of the ingenious devices used by the schoolmen, such as glosses, interlineations, index symbols, and the highlighting of text through the use of different colored inks and elaborate initials. It should be remembered, however, that the schoolmen had a rather easier task than did Gui and his notaries. The scholastics dealt with works whose content was relatively fixed; they could therefore indulge themselves in the luxury of perfecting elaborate means for enhancing the analyzability and searchability of their limited and predictable texts. The inquisitors, who were required to cope with the chaotic flow of messy reality, had a much more difficult task of organization and representation. Despite the relative simplicity of the means they employed, they seem to have met the challenge reasonably well.

In preparing and preserving documents the inquisitors were certainly not unique. The archives of almost any major European ruler were stuffed full with documents whose layout and organization make just as favorable, if indeed not more favorable, an impression than those of the Languedocian inquisitors. What seems to set the inquisitors apart is the fact that they could at a later date find and use material that had been recorded earlier, often much earlier. In his study of record keeping and literacy in medieval England, Michael Clanchy observes that the making of documents for immediate administrative use, their preservation as a form of perpetual, unfailing memory, and their use again at a later date for reference are three distinct processes that do not logically follow one from another. Most medieval administrative documents, like tax lists and instructions to officials, were intended to be used only at the time at which they were composed. Once they had been used, they had little further function. After they had been prepared and stored away, little active or systematic use was made of them as sources of reference.[28]

---

[25] Add. MS 4697, fol. 4r.
[26] "Pierre de Pouget" is evidently an error for Pons de Pouget, who was active between 1262 and 1264. Etienne de Gastine was active from 1264 to 1276. See *Documents*, 1: clxvii–clxxii.
[27] Vigoroux was active as an inquisitor from 1285 to 1289; ibid., 1: cxxxii.
[28] Clanchy, *From Memory to Written Record*, especially pp. 168–72.

This lack of future reference to old records was due in part to the extraordinary difficulty of locating specific documents in a medieval archive. Some of the best-kept records in medieval Europe belonged to the kings of England. Their servants, however, often found it next to impossible to recover a particular item from the bewildering array of rolls, registers, and files in their possession. Since there were no indexes to the records, it was difficult to find a particular document unless it was of recent origin and its exact date of issue was known.[29] A dramatic illustration of the Crown's inability to make effective use of its archives is provided by Edward I's efforts to discover material to buttress his claims to the superior lordship of Scotland. In 1291, when Edward became concerned to find such material, his first impulse was not to consult the royal archives. Instead, he wrote to English monasteries ordering them to search their own records. Only when this expedient failed to produce much that was helpful to his claims did Edward order a search of chests in the royal archives. This investigation also proved less than useful. In 1300, when the king wished to defend his claims to Pope Boniface VIII, a second effort was made to search the royal archives; this too failed to produce any new information.[30]

English administrators were not alone in their inability to exploit the riches of their record repositories. The archivists of the French crown were also overwhelmed by the masses of parchment in their custody.[31] Even the accomplished administrators of late medieval Florence were often confounded by their archives. One of the most thorough surveys of any medieval state's population and wealth was carried out by Florence in the 1420s and preserved in a document known as the *catasto* of 1427. But, as noted by Herlihy and Klapisch-Zuber, the historians who have unlocked the secrets of this survey, "The enormous data collected on the wealth of the Tuscan population remained largely unused; even the Florentine government did not know how to exploit this mine of statistical riches. The Catasto has remained a vast, unfinished account sheet; its redactors were unable to calculate the final total."[32]

The inquisitors, however, were able to find specific documents housed in their archives. This ability to search their records successfully allowed them to subject those records to analytic scrutiny. The inquisitors could examine the records of their past activity and use the information they thus extracted to exert power in a more concentrated and efficient way. This ability to make effective analytic use of their archives set the inquisitors apart from most of their contemporaries. In mastering their archives the inquisitors faced, of course, a much less daunting task than did the ruler of a large kingdom. The inquisitors had to contend not with a vast array of parchment relating to a

---

29 Ibid., p. 169.
30 Ibid., pp. 152–54.
31 Delaborde, "Les Classements du Trésor des Chartes."
32 Herlihy and Klapisch-Zuber, *Tuscans and Their Families*, p. 361.

huge diversity of matters but with a relatively small amount of material dealing with a tightly delimited area of interest and responsibility—that is, heresy and heretics. The comparatively modest amount of material collected by the inquisitors and its tightly focused nature must, to a large extent, have been susceptible to management by the traditional and well-developed arts of memory, a subject in which the mendicant orders were particularly interested.[33]

The mechanisms that the inquisitors adopted to supply the shortcomings of memory appear to have been simple but effective. In large part the contents of their archives were kept accessible through a process of ceaseless recopying. Not only were the depositions of suspects copied and recopied during their trials, but entire registers were frequently copied so as to prevent the loss of the information in the originals. For example, in the 1240s the inquisitors of Toulouse, Bernard de Caux and Jean de Saint-Pierre, carried out a massive investigation of heresy. The results of this inquiry were consigned to several books. Sometime around 1260, on the orders of the inquisitors Guillaume Bernard and Renaud de Chartres, volumes 4 and 5 of this investigation were copied on paper and placed in a large register of 264 folios, which survives today.[34] Similarly, the original register of the heresy trials conducted in the city of Albi in 1299–1300 was copied on paper. After the death of Bernard de Castanet, who as bishop of Albi had conducted these trials, the manuscript was in 1319 given to Bernard Gui, the inquisitor of Toulouse.[35] Jacques Fournier, when he left the see of Pamiers to become bishop of Mirepoix, had a copy made of the register that contained the records of his inquisitorial work at Pamiers. Thanks to the fact that Fournier later became pope, a part of this register has survived in the Vatican Library.[36]

The principal means adopted by the inquisitors for making the material in their records readily accessible was, however, the relatively simple expedient of arranging or indexing it topographically. In MS 609 from Toulouse, for example, the depositions received in the 1240s by Bernard de Caux and Jean de Saint-Pierre were grouped by village. This is a straightforward and rather obvious use of topography as an ordering principle. To a degree, it simply recognizes the fact that large numbers of people from the same village were often interrogated on the same day.

A much more sophisticated use of topography as an indexing and searching device is provided by Bernard Gui's *Liber sententiarum*. Crucial to the medieval users of Gui's register is the prefatory material inserted before the first *sermo*. This material was omitted from Limborch's 1692 edition and has therefore never been discussed. The register opens with an alphabetical list, labeled "Names of places in alphabetical order" (*Nomina locorum secundum ordinem*

---

[33] On the art of memory as it was understood in the Middle Ages, see Yates, *The Art of Memory*, pp. 50–128, 173–98, and Carruthers, *The Book of Memory*.
[34] This is MS 609. Dossat, *Crises*, pp. 56–57.
[35] Douais, "Manuscrits du château de Merville," p. 172.
[36] Vidal, "Le Tribunal d'inquisition de Pamiers," pp. 389–90.

*alphabeticum*) of the hometowns and villages of those whose sentences are contained in the register.[37] The list takes up three columns spread over two folios. This list is in turn immediately followed by a list of the *sermones generales* contained in the register. For each *sermo* the number of the folio on which it begins is given. The first two entries, which are typical of all of them, read as follows:

> The first sermon of those which are contained in this book was held at Toulouse in the year of our Lord 1307, on the first Sunday of Lent, 5 nones of March [3 March 1308]. i°.
>
> The second sermon was held in Toulouse on the feast of the Holy Trinity, 8 kalends of June in the year 1309 [25 May 1309]. fol. tercio.

After this comes the register's primary finding tool, a "Table of all the persons in the following book" (*Tabula omnium personarum sequentis libri*). This table lists all those whose sentences are recorded in the register. It also gives a brief summary of each individual's sentence (or sentences), the folio number where the sentence is found, and various other information. This material is arranged alphabetically by place of residence. The list begins with the village of Alzon and ends with the village of Vaychis.[38] Under each village individuals are arranged not alphabetically but in the order in which their sentences appear in the register. A typical entry, in this case from Verfeil, looks like this (see plate 2):

> Of Verfeil
>
> Pierre Majoris .†. [a symbol indicating that he is sentenced to wear simple crosses] ____.l°.F.
>
> Michael Mironis to the *mur*. ____.lxxi°.F. Item released from the *mur* with .‡. [a symbol indicating that he is required to wear double crosses] ____ .xcix°.F
>
> Raimond Mironis deceased in heresy. ____ .lxxv°.F
>
> Arnaud Faure would have been immured if he had lived. ____ .cxviii°.F[39]

For the most part it appears that the entries in this index were made at the time that the register was completed and the table drawn up. The presence of notes written in a different hand indicates that some were added at a later date. Some of these later additions record that an individual had completed to the satisfaction of the inquisitors the penances enjoined on him. For example, under the entry for the village of Azas, we find the following entry: "Raimond Vasco to the *mur*. ____ .lii°F. Item released from the *mur* with .‡. ____ .xcix°.F." [Written in a different hand to the left of this entry is: "He has completed." To the right

---

[37] The folios that contain this list do not have Roman numerals; they are 7r and 7v in Arabic numerals.

[38] The list begins on fol. 1r and ends on fol. 8v (10r–17v in Arabic numerals).

[39] Add. MS 4697, fol. 8v (17v in Arabic numerals).

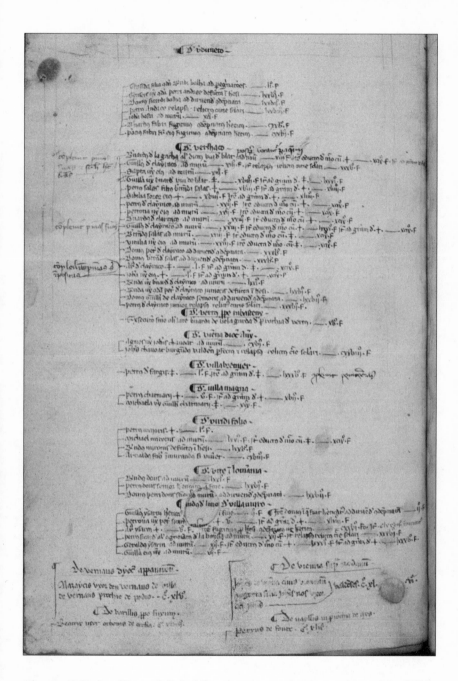

**Plate 2.** Folio 8v of Bernard Gui's *Liber sententiarum*, showing a section of the "Table of All Persons in the Following Book." Add. MS 4697, reproduced by permission of the British Library.

of the entry, apparently in the same hand: "He has completed his penances."][40]

At least one of these later marginal notes attempts to sort out a genealogical matter. Modern historians have long been aware that heresy, particularly Catharism, tended to propagate itself within domestic units such as the family and its servants and dependents. The inquisitors themselves were aware of this. At least in Gui's register a great deal of attention is given to specifying various familial relationships. Under the heading for Saint-Paul-Cap-de-Joux, for example, we find the following entry: "Guillaume Pierre Polier released from the *mur* with .‡. _____ .iiii°.F." [To this entry a later hand has appended the following: "Hugues and Pierre Polier of Verfeil are not of the kindred of the aforesaid Guillaume Pierre Polier of Saint-Paul-Cap-de-Joux."][41]

A topographical system such as this for organizing information may seem exceedingly simple. Indeed, one can imagine that a change of residence by a suspect would have been enough to defeat the inquisitors' classification scheme. In the social and cultural conditions of the late thirteenth and early fourteenth centuries, however, this was probably not a great problem. People certainly moved about a great deal,[42] but clearly only a fraction of a village's inhabitants left home permanently. Many of those who did emigrate also retained a strong sentimental attachment to their kinship groups and home villages. And, in a society where people were connoisseurs of regional accents, emigrants could probably never shake off an association with their home village. This is nicely illustrated by an anecdote told by Arnaud Sicre. Sicre, a native of the county of Foix, had entered the kingdom of Aragon, prepared to feign adherence to Catharism, in an effort to flush out and arrest some of the Cathar Good Men who had taken refuge there. Initially, his search proved fruitless. Feeling exhausted and discouraged, he stopped in the town of San Mateo and hired himself out to Jayme Vital, a shoemaker. One day, as he was working on a pair of shoes, he heard a woman in the street crying out, "Any grain for grinding?" A man named Garaut, who was in the workshop with Sicre, said to him, "Eh, Arnaud, here is a *gannana* [i.e., female worker] from your country." Sicre went out into the street and asked the woman where she was from. She told him that she came from Saverdun. "And since the woman spoke the dialect of Montaillou, he drew her aside and said to her that she was not from Saverdun, but from Prades d'Alion or Montaillou." The woman eventually admitted that she was Guillemette Maury, originally from Montaillou.[43] This chance encounter set in train the series of events that eventually enabled Arnaud to procure the arrest of Guillaume Bélibaste, one of the last Good Men still at large in the eastern Pyrenees. Thus, even if an individual fled

---

[40] Ibid., fol. 1r (10r in Arabic numerals).

[41] Ibid., fol. 7r (16r in Arabic numerals): "Hugo et Petrus Polerii de Viridifolio non sunt de genere predicti Guillelmi Petri Polerii Sancti Pauli de Cadaiovis."

[42] See, for example, the deposition of Pierre Maury of Montaillou, in *Registre*, 3: 110–252.

[43] Ibid., 2: 21–22.

to a different village to escape the inquisition, his or her new neighbors probably acquired and retained a rather good idea of where the fugitive had come from. Given the tenacious association of individuals and their native village, it is not surprising that the inquisitors would have made heavy reliance on geographical origin as a finding tool in their records.[44]

## THE INQUISITORIAL ARCHIVES AS A TOOL FOR THE EXERCISE OF POWER

The ability of the inquisitors to retrieve information from their archives in an efficient fashion was a great aid to their work. It made it possible for them to use their records in an analytical and activist fashion. Unlike the records of most medieval rulers, those of the inquisitors served not merely the immediate purposes for which they were made, that is, to record the trial of arrested heretics; they were also an integral and necessary part of the inquisitors' investigative technology. The inquisitorial registers were thus active instruments not only of knowledge but also of coercion.

Even the most cursory glance at inquisitors in action shows how they were able to make effective use of their records to unravel the affairs of those they investigated. For example, MS 609 of Toulouse records the appearance of 5,518 individuals before Bernard de Caux and Jean de Saint-Pierre in the 1240s. Of these, it is clear that at least 758 (13.7 percent) had appeared earlier before other inquisitors. Bernard and Jean had access to copies of these previous depositions. With tedious frequency one finds at the end of a deponent's statement the notation that his deposition does not agree with the testimony that he had given to a different inquisitor.

For example, on 3 July 1246 Guillaume Bonet the elder of Villeneuve-la-Comptal testified about events that had taken place around thirty years earlier. Although he admitted that he had had contacts with Cathars at a time when the heretics lived openly in Languedoc, he denied that he had ever engaged in the Cathar ceremony known as the *melioramentum*, which the inquisitors understood as an act of "adoration." Indeed, he asserted that he had gone to the Cathar stronghold of Montségur and extracted from it his mother-in-law, Raimonde de Rivali, a Cathar *perfecta*, and forced her to return to the Catholic faith. Unfortunately for Guillaume, he had earlier testified before Guillaume Arnaud. Once this deposition was read to him, Guillaume was forced to admit that he had associated with and "adored" the Cathar heretics.[45] Two or three generations later we find other suspects tripped up by their earlier testimony.

---

[44] Other inquisitorial records contained such topographically arranged tables of deponents' names, among them MS 160 of the Bibliothèque de Clermont-Ferrand, which records the depositions heard by episcopal inquisitors in Carcassonne between 1250 and 1267 (*Documents*, 2: 244 n. 1).

[45] MS 609, fol. 183v. For similar instances of deponents confronted with earlier testimony that contradicted their current statements, see fols. 43v (Guillaume Recort of Montgaillard), 108r (Domina Hylarda of Montesquieu-Villefranche), 168r (Guillaume Isarn of Fanjeaux), 180v

When in February 1325 Bishop Jacques Fournier interrogated Guillaume Delaire of Quié, he had on hand a copy of the testimony that Guillaume had given several years earlier to the inquisitor of Carcassonne. By referring to this deposition, Fournier was able to catch Delaire out in a patent lie.[46]

In addition to discovering contradictory testimony, the inquisitors made other uses of their records during the interrogation process. Normally the inquisitors refused to reveal to suspects the names of those who had testified against them. At times, however, they did produce and use copies of these statements as a means of putting pressure on individuals who were especially obdurate about admitting their guilt. For example, one of the more recalcitrant individuals Jacques Fournier dealt with at Pamiers was Raimonde Guilhou of Vernaux, widow of Arnaud Vidal of Montaillou. Raimonde long held out under interrogation, refusing to acknowledge any personal dealings with the Cathar heretics. Even when she ultimately confessed to contacts with them, she later retracted her confession. Exasperated by her resistance, Fournier at one point, on 27 June 1322, resorted to reading to her a statement given by Jacquette Peregrina of Mirepoix that implicated her in heresy.[47]

Effective record keeping, in addition to making it possible to discover individual lies, allowed the inquisitors to search for and collate material with which they could build a case against a suspect. The original manuscripts from the thirteenth and fourteenth centuries contain indications that inquisitors or their agents have carefully searched them, looking for and marking evidence that could be used against particular individuals. MS 609 of Toulouse contains many marginal notes designed to point out information useful for pending or future investigations. For example, in the margin next to the deposition given by Ermengarde, wife of Pierre Bernard of Le Mas-Saintes-Puelles, on 19 May 1245 is the note: "She is suspected and could say a lot."[48]

To indicate depositions containing information against individuals in whom the inquisitors were particularly interested, notes were made in the margin, taking the form, for example, of *Contra Willelmum de Rocovila*. Three men in whose activity Bernard de Caux and Jean de Saint-Pierre were especially interested were Guillaume de Roqueville, whose family was deeply involved with Catharism, Pons de Latour of Laurac, and the knight, Raimond Bartha.[49] On

---

(Guillemette Rotgeria of Villepinte), 183v (Pierre Borzes of Villeneuve-la-Comptal), 184r (Bernard de la Font and Arnaud Boquet of Villeneuve-la-Comptal), 184v (Dulcia Faure of Villeneuve-la-Comptal), 189v (Asilhana Asilhan of Brom), 192r (Guillaume Vital of Laurac), 194v (Sobranserra, widow of Bernard Raimond of Laurac), 205r (Raimond Géraud of Odars), 242r (Bernarde Trebalha of Saint-Paul-Cap-de-Joux), 242v (Raimond Bernard of Cambon), 251v (Arnaud Martin of Castelnaudary), and 252r (Raimond Muls of Castelnaudary).

[46] *Registre*, 3: 450–51.

[47] Ibid., 2: 230.

[48] MS 609, fol. 20v: "Suspecta est ista et posset multa dicere."

[49] Guillaime de Roqueville: ibid., fols. 44v, 50r–v, 51v, 53v–54r, 56r, 57r. The act of 28 May

folio 75v there appears the testimony, given on 10 July 1245, of Guillaume Rigaut, a leper. According to Guillaume, three years earlier Raimond's concubine had died in the leper house at Laurac. Bartha, at the time a fugitive (or *faidit*) on account of his involvement with heresy, arranged for the Good Men Pierre del Mas and Pons Tholosan to confer the *consolamentum* on her. In the margin next to this entry, the following note was made: "The archpriest of the Lauragais says that Raimond Bartha, knight, hanged two of his sergeants because they captured his mother and six other female heretics."[50]

In the early fourteenth century, someone went through Jacques Fournier's inquisitorial register making note of information against certain individuals. Altogether the register contains thirty-six marginal notations concerning twenty-two people.[51] The annotator showed particular interest in the Clergues of Montaillou, making a total of ten notations concerning the doings of four members of this family.

Other mechanisms were also used to indicate the presence of information concerning particular suspects. At the beginning of the register containing the records of the trials conducted at Albi in 1299 and 1300 by Nicholas d'Abbeville, inquisitor of Carcassonne, and Bishop Bernard de Castanet, we find a table listing the names of individuals implicated in heresy by the testimony recorded in the register. This table is arranged according to the names of the individuals who gave depositions to Nicholas and Bernard. The name of each deponent is followed by a list, arranged by place of residence, of those mentioned in that individual's testimony. The table contains 583 names. The largest number of people implicated by a single witness were the eighty-nine people named in the confession of Guillaume de Landas of Albi.[52]

The inquisitors were well aware of the importance of their records and of the care necessary to make them useful. Bernard Gui noted in his inquisitorial manual that in certain cases it was not expedient to take down all of a suspect's interrogation, since this would lard the record with too much irrelevant detail.

---

1246 condemning Estolt de Roqueville of Montgiscard and Bernard de Roqueville of Les Cassès to perpetual imprisonment in the *mur* is in *Documents*, 2: 20–24. Pons de Latour: MS 609, fols. 39v, 125r. Pons's deposition is on fol. 71v, and the sentence condemning him to perpetual imprisonment is in *Documents*, 2: 42–44. Raimond Bartha: MS 609, fols. 73v, 74v–75v.

50 Ibid., fol. 75v: "Archipresbiter de Lauragues' dicit quod Raimundus Bartha miles suspendit duos servientos suos quia ceperunt matrem dicti Raimundi et alias vi. hereticas."

51 Raimonde the wife of Pierre Cap de Blanc, Simon Barre, Guillaume Rossell, Emersende the wife of Bernard Laurent, Sibille the wife of Pierre Pauc, and Arnaud Carot, all of Ax-les-Thermes; Bernard Clergue of Montaillou, Raimonde his wife, Pierre his brother, and his mother Ermengarde; Arnaud Teisseyre of Lordat; Guillaume Baiardi of Tarascon; Stephania of Château-Verdun; Alazaïs Adhémar; Palharesia of Luzenac; Galharde the wife of Pierre Autier; Guillaume Andorran and Galharde his mother; Sicarde the wife of Bernard Gozini of Pamiers; Guillaume d'Anhaus; Guillemette Bec of Caussou, and Raimond Frézat, rector of Quié (*Registre*, 1: 278–81, 285–86, 290–98, 313–16, 459, 491; 2: 438; MS 4030, fols. 191a, 208b, 308d).

52 This list is printed in Davis, *The Inquisition at Albi*, pp. 103–20.

Conversely, one should not remove too much material from the record, lest it appear truncated. According to Gui, the inquisitor should strive to produce records that could be readily collated without excessive expenditure of time and labor.[53] Writing around 1376, the Aragonese inquisitor Nicholas Eymerich offered some useful advice on how an inquisitor could control the information he received. When the inquisitors began their investigation of heresy in a particular place, they proclaimed a grace period during which people could confess and receive relatively light penalties. Eymerich had observed that confessions received during this period could be so numerous as to make it impossible to follow normal procedures in recording them. To deal with this situation, Eymerich advised that an inquisitor should prepare a small notebook, one per diocese, in which to note the gist of the confessions. In his own hand, so he counseled, the inquisitor should also record the names of those whom the witnesses denounced and who should therefore be summoned for further interrogation.[54]

Not only were the inquisitors' archives useful for ferreting out heretics, they could also be put to more "political" uses. In the late thirteenth and early fourteenth centuries much of Languedoc was disturbed by a major anti-inquisitorial campaign, in which the city of Albi figured prominently. The royal *viguier* of Albi, Guillaume de Pezens, played an important role in this, using the powers of his office to help the anti-inquisitorial party. The inquisitors, however, were able to use information from their archives to bring about his downfall. In 1306 Geoffroy d'Ablis, the inquisitor of Carcassonne, searched his tribunal's records and discovered that the *viguier*'s ancestors had been deeply involved in heresy. His grandmother, Alix, a perfected heretic, had been captured at the fall of Montségur in 1244 and executed. In the 1250s other of his relatives had been condemned for heresy. Since descendants of heretics were barred from public office, this information enabled Geoffroy d'Ablis to secure Guillaume's dismissal.[55]

## THE INQUISITORIAL ARCHIVES IN THE LANGUEDOCIAN IMAGINATION

Given the central importance of the inquisitors' records to their work of repressing heresy, it is not surprising that they became objects of fear and loathing, at times perhaps even more detested than the inquisitors themselves. Critics charged that the inquisitors deliberately altered and falsified their records so as to condemn the innocent. For example, in 1306 the people of Cordes complained to papal commissioners about such fabrication of inquisitorial records.[56]

Bernard Délicieux, a Franciscan who led the anti-inquisitorial campaign of the early 1300s, was convinced that the inquisitorial records were riddled with

---

[53] Gui, *Practica inquisitionis*, pp. 243–44.

[54] Eymerich, *Directorium inquisitorum*, p. 413.

[55] Doat, 34: fols. 104r–7v. See also MS 4270, fol. 266r, and Dossat, "Le 'Bûcher de Montségur,'" pp. 362–65, 374–77.

[56] *Documents*, 2: 335–36.

falsehoods. During his own trial for necromancy and impeding the inquisition in 1319, he rehearsed for his judges the following story. The Dominican friar Jean Martin had complained to the archbishop of Narbonne about the mendacious nature of the inquisitors' records. Martin informed the archbishop that the charges of heresy brought against various inhabitants of Carcassonne were completely false and had been concocted by greedy and power-hungry Dominicans. According to Martin, an unnamed inquisitor, "by birth a Frenchman" (*natione gallicus*) had been unable to find any notable people at Carcassonne whom he could "accuse or bite" (*aruguere [recte: arguere] vel mordere*).[57] He had therefore decided to return to France. This disturbed two Dominicans, Jean de Faugoux[58] and Guillaume de "Maluceriis"; they became worried that henceforth they would be neither honored nor feared by the local people. To ensure their possession of this fear and honor, they invented a host of heretical acts and attributed them to people who were both rich and dead, among them the count of Foix, the marshal of Mirepoix, and the bishop of Carcassonne.

Armed with these falsified records, the Dominicans embarked on a campaign of extortion. According to Jean Martin, the inquisitors and other Dominicans visited many "married ladies" (*dominas maritatas*) from the *bourg* of Carcassonne and the surrounding area, and delivered the following message:

> My lady, it should be obvious to you beyond a shadow of a doubt that we, the preaching friars, love you with all our heart; it should also be obvious to you that your husband's name is written in the inquisitors' books and that there are against him witnesses who say that he was present at the hereticaion of certain deceased individuals. If you wish to look to your honor, and that of your husband and your children, and to save your property, persuade him in whatever way possible to confess this to the inquisitor.[59]

In this way the Dominicans persuaded many women to prevail on their husbands to give false confessions. The accused who could not be manipulated in this fashion were compelled to admit to assorted falsehoods through the application of torture. According to Martin, so full of lies were the inquisitors' books, and so great the danger hanging over the country because of their proceedings, that there was only one solution: the Dominicans should be removed from inquisitorial office, their records should be seized, and totally new records should be composed by new inquisitors not of their order.

---

57 MS 4270, fols. 125r–v. Perhaps Geoffroy d'Ablis is meant.
58 Geoffroy d'Ablis's lieutenant; *Documents*, 1: cxxxiii.
59 MS 4270, fol. 126r: "Domina, constet vobis et pro certo quod nos fratres praedicatores vos diligimus toto corde. Constet etiam vobis quod maritus vester est scriptus in libro inquisitorum et testes habentur contra eum quod ipse interfuit hereticationi aliquorum defunctorum. Si vultis providere honori vestro et suo et filiis vestris et salvare bona vestra, inducatis eum modis omnibus quod confiteatur hoc inquisitori."

According to Délicieux, Martin's words had a powerful effect on the arch-bishop. With the assistance of many wise men, he investigated the inquisitors. Their books were seized and examined. The archbishop also sent an envoy to the pope to ask that the Dominicans be permanently removed from office. The inquisitor of Toulouse and the inquisitor of Carcassonne, Nicholas d'Abbeville, became alarmed. Together they went to the Dominican convent at Prouille. There they put together new registers, transferring into them the contents of their old records but removing anything that might implicate them in wrongdo-ing. To disguise what they had done, they carefully removed the covers from the old registers and used them to bind the new ones they had fabricated.[60]

## THE INQUISITORIAL MANUAL

The thirteenth century was an age not only of record keeping and archive creation, but also of proliferating manuals and how-to books. Across the con-tinent administrators, lawyers, and judges, veterans of years of service in the new bureaucracies of princes and prelates, wrote handbooks designed to educate future administrators in the mysteries of office procedure. Twelfth-century England saw the production of the first of these practical manuals of governance, Richard fitz Neal's *Dialogue of the Exchequer*, which described the operations of the English Crown's chief financial and accounting office, and the law book known as *Glanvill*, which discussed the new procedures followed in royal courts.

The following centuries saw a veritable explosion in the production of such practical handbooks. Interestingly, the Franciscans and Dominicans played an important role in the production of many of these works. The areas to which they directed their primary attention were preaching and confession. Given the friars' commitment to spreading religious instruction among the laity and com-bating heresy, their interest in composing preaching manuals is not surprising. During the thirteenth and fourteenth centuries they produced a large number of treatises designed to help men become effective preachers. All told, between 1200 and 1500 over two hundred *artes praedicandi* appeared.[61] To aid preachers the friars also put together collections of *exempla*: short, memorable stories that could be used to underline a sermon's moral message. Between 1250 and 1350 some forty-six surviving collections were produced.[62]

More relevant to the work of the inquisitors was the great interest that the friars displayed in composing manuals for confessors. Following the Fourth

---

[60] Ibid., fols. 126r–28v. Interestingly, the opponents of the inquisitors were not alone in claim-ing that fabricated or forged registers were in circulation. Bernard Gui charged that during the agitation led by Bernard Délicieux, the inquisition's opponents themselves concocted false regis-ters in which the names of innocent people were recorded (Gui, *De fundatione*, p. 201).

[61] Little, *Religious Poverty*, p. 190.

[62] Brémond and Le Goff with Schmitt, *L'Exemplum*, pp. 58–63. One notable example of this genre was the *Alphabeticum narrationum*, assembled between 1297 and 1308 by the Dominican Arnold of Liège. This contained 800 *exempla* grouped under 555 rubrics, arranged alphabetically and cross-referenced; see Berlioz with Ribaucourt, "Images de la confession," pp. 97–99.

Lateran Council of 1215, the laity was required to partake of communion on certain specified occasions each year. As preparation for the reception of the sacrament, they had to confess to their parish priests. To assist priests who would have to hear these confessions and offer their penitents spiritual and moral counseling, the friars, along with other clerics, produced a large number of treatises. Some of these were massive works, like the *Summa de casibus poenitentiae* of the Dominican Raymund de Peñafort. More usable were the briefer and cheaper confession manuals, designed to give priests the indispensable guidelines for a good confession. As Jean Delumeau notes, "The first preoccupation of the handbook writers was to aid the confessors by explaining how to interrogate the penitent (notably on the Deadly Sins) and so simplify the diversity of special cases. They also explained how to guide the penitent through his or her examination of conscience, how to illuminate motives and circumstances, and thus how to evaluate the magnitude of an offense, and how to overcome obstacles (fear, shame, presumption, despair) to a good confession."[63]

Given this background, it is not surprising that the inquisitors produced their own manuals. Indeed, we can perhaps understand these inquisitorial treatises as a very special form of the manual for confessors. In composing these works the inquisitors were able to draw on the material stored in their archives. This they subjected to a form of scientific scrutiny. Rather like modern historians, they were interested in discovering the exact nature of heretical belief and practice. Accurate knowledge of these subjects allowed them to identify and interrogate heretics more effectively. The earliest inquisitorial manual, the *Processus inquisitionis* (possibly composed in 1248 or 1249), was a very simple affair, being little more than a legal formulary.[64] Thereafter the inquisitors' manuals grew in size, complexity, and sophistication. They contained a great diversity of material. Some were primarily formularies that gave examples of the documents that an inquisitor might have to issue in the course of his work. Some of the texts that, in accordance with the views expressed in Antoine Dondaine's classic essay on this genre, are normally referred to as manuals are in reality works of Catholic apology.[65] Yet, since these described heretical beliefs in order to refute them, they were of use to the inquisitors. The most interesting manuals gave practical advice on how to interrogate suspects. The treatise known as the *De inquisitione hereticorum*, for example, suggests that reluctant witnesses might be persuaded to confess by threatening them with death or telling them that other witnesses had already implicated them.[66]

---

[63] Delumeau, *Sin and Fear*, pp. 199–200. On this genre of literature, see also Bériou, "Autour de Latran IV"; Berlioz with Ribaucourt, "Images de la confession," pp. 95–115; and Berlioz, "'Quand dire c'est faire dire.'"

[64] Dossat, "Le *Processus inquisitionis*," pp. 34–36. This treatise has been edited by Ad. Tardif, "Document pour l'histoire du *Processus per inquisitionem*"; an English translation can be found in Wakefield, *Heresy, Crusade, and Inquisition*, pp. 250–58.

[65] Dondaine, "Le Manuel de l'inquisiteur," pp. 85–194.

[66] Preger, ed., "Der Tractat des David von Augsburg," p. 223.

The most famous inquisitorial manual was written in Languedoc around 1323. This is the *Practica inquisitionis heretice pravitatis* of Bernard Gui, inquisitor of Toulouse. Gui's manual, a virtual *summa* of inquisitorial procedure, as Dondaine has termed it, is divided into five parts.[67] The first two constitute an extensive formulary of the documents that an inquisitor might have to prepare.[68] The third section describes how to conduct one of the great *sermones generales* at which condemned heretics received their sentences.[69] The fourth part, modeled to a large extent on an earlier work, the *De auctoritate et forma inquisitionis* (composed in Italy probably sometime between 1280 and 1292), is a discussion of the powers, rights, and privileges of the inquisitors.[70] The most interesting part of the treatise, however, is the fifth and final section.[71] Here Gui, noting that different types of heresy require different modes of interrogation, discusses the six types of heretics that the inquisitors in Languedoc encountered: the Cathars (referred to as Manichees), the Waldensians, the Pseudo-Apostles, the Béguins, Jewish converts to Christianity who had returned to their old religion, and sorcerers.[72] In subsections devoted to the different heresies, Gui sketches their individual beliefs and practices and offers suggestions on the best strategy to pursue in interrogating representatives of the different sects.

One of the most extensive of these subsections, much of it borrowed from the *De inquisitione hereticorum,* attributed by some to David of Augsburg, deals with the Waldensians.[73] In opening his discussion of how to interrogate a Waldensian, Gui observes that these heretics were unusually difficult to question, given their cleverness at dissimulation and equivocation. To illustrate how they could twist words and their meanings to conceal their true beliefs, Gui gives some sample dialogues, including the following:

> When one of them has been seized and is brought up for examination, he comes as if without a qualm, as if conscious of no wrongdoing on his part, and as if he felt entirely safe. When asked if he knows why he has been arrested, he replies quite calmly and with a smile, "Sir, I should be glad to learn the reason from you." When he is questioned about the faith which he holds and believes, he replies, "I believe all that a good Christian should believe." Pressed as to what he means by "a good Christian," he answers, "One who believes as the Holy Church teaches us to believe and hold." When asked what he calls the Holy

[67] Dondaine, "Le Manuel de l'inquisiteur," p. 116.
[68] Gui, *Practica inquisitionis*, pp. 3–82.
[69] Ibid., pp. 83–171.
[70] Ibid., pp. 173–233. On the Italian work, see Dondaine, "Le Manuel de l'inquisiteur," pp. 113–15.
[71] Gui, *Practica inquisitionis*, pp. 235–355.
[72] Ibid., pp. 236–37.
[73] Mollat's edition of the *Practica* in Gui, *Manuel*, 1: 64–83, indicates the textual borrowings from the *De inquisitione hereticorum* with italics.

Church, he replies, "Sir, what you say and believe to be the Holy Church." If he is told, "I believe the Holy Church to be the Roman Church, over which presides our lord pope and other prelates subordinate to him," then he responds, "That I do believe," meaning that he believes that I believe this.[74]

Gui observed that Waldensians often feigned ignorance, claiming to be simple people unable to answer the inquisitor's questions correctly. Some tried to play on the inquisitor's sympathies, weeping and fawning on him, saying, "Master, if I have done wrong in anything, I will willingly undergo penance. Only help me to be cleared of that infamy of which I am guiltless and with which I have been impugned out of ill will."[75]

This practical advice on interrogation methods reached its fullest development in the *Directorium inquisitorum*, written in the late fourteenth century by the Aragonese inquisitor Nicholas Eymerich. Although Eymerich falls outside both our time period and our region, it is worth considering his views, especially since he seems to have studied Bernard Gui's *Liber sententiarum* at Toulouse.[76] In this treatise Eymerich describes ten ways in which heretics try to hide their beliefs.[77] These include the equivocation and ambiguity in the use of language noted by Gui and other inquisitors. But Nicholas also discusses other deceptions employed by heretics under examination, such as feigned physical problems or insanity.

As a mirror image of the ten deceitful modes of conduct employed by heretics, Eymerich gives a list of ten ruses (*cautelae*) the inquisitor can use to elicit the truth.[78] Some of these are chilling in the frankness with which they advise the use of manipulative and deceptive behavior. Under the heading of his second ruse, Eymerich suggests that a newly arrested heretic should be told by the custodian of the *mur* or by other trustworthy individuals that the inquisitor is a merciful man. When the inquisitor interrogates the suspect, he should tell him that he is ready to show him mercy, since he has been deluded by the person who taught him his errors. This person, so the inquisitor should say, has the greater guilt. Professing his desire to save the suspect's reputation and to release him as

---

[74] Gui, *Practica inquisitionis*, p. 253. Translation from Wakefield and Evans, eds., *Heresies of the High Middle Ages*, pp. 397–98.

[75] Gui, *Practica inquisitionis*, p. 254. Translation from Wakefield and Evans, *Heresies of the High Middle Ages*, pp. 399–400.

[76] In Questio LXXIII Eymerich asks whether the inquisitor can torture those suspected of giving false testimony and whether, if such false witness is proved, he can punish those guilty of it. His answer is that the inquisitor can do so. He then notes: "Concerning this, this event happened in Toulouse in 1312, as I saw in the sentence: For a father had deposed against his son concerning the crime of heretical depravity, and later he revoked his statement" (*Directorium inquisitorum*, p. 622). Eymerich is here referring to the case of Pons Arnaud de Pujols of Sainte-Foy-d'Aigrefeuille, whom Gui sentenced to immuration on 22 April 1312 (*LS*, p. 95).

[77] Eymerich, *Directorium inquisitorum*, pp. 430–31.

[78] Ibid., pp. 433–35. It is interesting to note that the authors of manuals for confessors also advised priests to use various ruses in trying to get their penitents to make good confessions. See Little, "Les Techniques de la confession," p. 95, and the references given there.

quickly as possible, he should urge the suspect to denounce the person who has instructed him in heresy.

Eymerich's fourth ruse is to be used when a suspect, who is not fully convicted by the evidence of the witnesses against him, refuses adamantly to confess his fault. The inquisitor should take the copy of the proceedings and leaf through it, finally saying to the suspect,

> "It is clear that you are not telling the truth, and the true story is what I say it is. Therefore tell me clearly the truth of the matter." Thus he [the suspect] may believe that he is convicted, and that this appears in the proceedings. Or the inquisitor should hold in his hand a schedule or other writing, and, when the suspect or heretic, on being questioned, denies this or that, the inquisitor, as though marveling at his reply, should say: "And how can you deny this? Is it not clear to me?" The inquisitor should then read in his schedule, and turn it around, and read it again. And then he should say, "I have spoken the truth; you should tell me now that you see that I know." Let the inquisitor beware, however, that he not descend to specifics in saying that he knows the truth of a matter of which the heretic is aware, but that he, the inquisitor, is not. Instead, he should stick to generalities, saying, "It is well known where you were, and with whom, and when, and what you said."[79]

Under the heading of his fifth ruse, Eymerich counsels playing on a suspect's fear of prison:

> [The inquisitor] should feign that he has to go on a long journey, and he should say to him [i.e., the suspect], "See, I have felt pity for you, and I wish that you had told me the truth, so that I could have finished your business. Thus you would not have to stay here a prisoner, because you are delicate, and you could easily become sick, since I have to leave you, and go where there is great need of me, and I don't know when I will return. Now, since you have not wished to tell the truth, I must leave you in a dungeon bound in fetters until my return, and this displeases me. This distresses me greatly, since I don't know when I will return." At this point the suspect may begin to beg that he not be left in a dungeon, and little by little he may reveal the truth.[80]

Not only did inquisitors like Gui and Eymerich write inquisitorial treatises, they collected them. Thanks to Yves Dossat's painstaking reconstruction of the contents of the archives of the inquisitorial tribunals at Toulouse and Carcassonne, we have some idea of the treatises on heresy and heretics that they possessed. Not

---

[79] Eymerich, *Directorium inquisitorum*, p. 434.
[80] Ibid., p. 434.

surprisingly, the archives at Toulouse contained a copy of Bernard Gui's *Practica*.[81] We are more fully informed about the holdings of the Carcassonne inquisitors; they seem to have amassed a small library of books on heresy. At one time or another they owned an anonymous anti-Cathar treatise of the late thirteenth century and a copy of Gui's *Practica*.[82] The major item in the collection, however, was a large book of 247 leaves, which Dossat has termed a *véritable corpus de l'Inquisition*.[83] This included a great variety of material: texts of papal bulls, decrees of church councils, and various letters and decrees of the king of France and the count of Toulouse. Also bound into this volume was a collection of treatises on heresy and inquisitorial proceedings that included (a) the directory of Raymund de Peñafort (1242); (b) a consultation by the famous jurist, royal servant, and later pope, Gui Foucois; (c) the treatise *De auctoritate et forma inquisitionis* (ca. 1280–92); (d) a treatise on inquisitorial practice (ca. 1300); (e) a list of pilgrimages imposed on penitents; (f) the section of Etienne de Bourbon's *De septem donis Spiritus Sancti* dealing with the Waldensians; (g) Rainier Sacconi's *Summa de Catharis et Leonistis* (composed ca. 1250); (h) the *Disputatio inter catholicum et Paterinum haereticum* (possibly written by Gregory of Florence, bishop of Fano, d. ca. 1240); and (i) a catalog of heretical errors.

Curiously, the inquisitors seem not to have been interested in collecting books by heretics. Only a few such works have left traces in the inquisitorial archives. The volume of 247 leaves housed in Carcassonne contained a copy of the Cathar text known as the *Interrogatio Joannis*.[84] In the section of his manual devoted to the heretics known as Béguins, Bernard Gui included a copy of a tiny book, the *Transitum sancti patris*, that they were accustomed to read in their assemblies. Its contents consisted of a brief series of comments on the death in 1298 of the Franciscan Pierre-Jean Olivi, a man widely admired in Béguin circles.[85] But this appears to exhaust the known heretical works possessed by the Languedocian inquisitors. However, lack of possession does not indicate lack of interest. When conducting their investigations, the inquisitors showed a lively desire to lay hold of texts owned by heretics. For example, when on 15 December 1246 Bernard de Caux learned from the knight Arnaud de Melglos that he possessed a certain book written in both Latin and Occitan, Bernard extracted a promise from Arnaud to surrender it.[86] Similarly, in 1274 the inquisitors

---

[81] This is MS 388 of the Bibliothèque de la Ville of Toulouse, which was transcribed during the second half of the fourteenth century; Dossat, *Crises*, p. 40. See also Gui, *Practica inquisitionis*, p. viii, and Gui, *Manuel*, 1: xxvi.

[82] The anti-Cathar treatise is in Doat, 36: fols. 91v–203r (Dossat, *Crises*, p. 47); Gui's work is vols. 29 and 30 of the Collection Doat (see Dossat, *Crises*, pp. 48–49; Gui, *Manuel*, 1: xxviii–xxix).

[83] Dossat, *Crises*, pp. 50–52.

[84] This is Doat, 36: fols. 26v–35r.

[85] Gui, *Practica inquisitionis*, p. 287.

[86] Doat, 24: fol. 248v.

of Toulouse, Ranulphe de Plassac and Pons de Parnac, acquired from the Waldensian sympathizer Bernard Raimond Baranhon a Latin life of Saint Brendan and a vernacular book beginning with the words *del segle puent, et terrible*.[87] In the fourteenth century Nicholas Eymerich seems to have been a connoisseur of books of necromancy. In his *Directorium* he says that he had read two books of invocations of demons, one the "Book of Solomon," the other the *Thesaurus necromantiae*. After perusing these works, he burned them.

The fire was undoubtedly the final destination of most heretical works that came into the inquisitors' hands. To a modern scholar, this lack of concern with preserving heretics' books seems a little puzzling. One would think that the inquisitors would have found it useful to have ready access to such works. However, the inquisitors probably felt it unnecessary to preserve most heretical writings. All they needed to know about heresy they could find in works of unimpeachable orthodoxy, like Sacconi's *Summa* or Etienne de Bourbon's *De septem donis*, or in the manuals produced by their fellow inquisitors. Only in unusual circumstances, such as with the Béguins, who were not branded as heretics until the early fourteenth century, did an inquisitor think it useful to preserve and communicate the contents of a heretical work.

The inquisitors of Languedoc, in their production and preservation of documents, were participating in a general trend in medieval society. Everywhere the preparation and storage of documents were becoming fundamental aspects of the art of governance. The inquisitors were certainly not unique in their passion for record keeping, but they seem to have made unusually skillful use of their records. Unlike many of their contemporaries, they successfully solved the vexing question of how promptly and efficiently to retrieve information from their archives. This ability to find useful information quickly, coupled with the analytic skills that the inquisitors applied to the study of that same information, made their archives something more than a mere form of perpetual memory. In the hands of the inquisitors, they were transformed into active tools for the generation of further information and the coercion of suspects.

The care with which the inquisitors prepared and ordered their documents gave them unusual control of the written word, a control that in turn enabled them to diagnose and manipulate the social reality that surrounded them. Perhaps even more important, it gave them effective mastery over the spoken word. The Dominican inquisitors, through their religious training and socialization, were already masters of the hortatory and persuasive word proclaimed during the sermon. But as inquisitors charged with hunting down heresy, they had to deal with a different sort of spoken word: that uttered under interrogation by the suspected heretic. These words, pregnant with danger for those who spoke them, were often veiled, misleading, and obscure. The inquisitors,

---

[87] Doat, 25: fols. 201r–v.

thanks to the knowledge preserved in their archives and set forth in ordered fashion in their manuals, could reshape this oblique discourse so as to reveal the damning "truth" that they believed lay hidden within it. It is clear that few medieval rulers made as constructive and effective use of records and record keeping as did the inquisitors.

# CHAPTER 2

# THE TECHNOLOGY OF
# COERCIVE IMPRISONMENT

A SKILLFUL USE OF documents and archives may have allowed the inquisitors to understand the nature of the heresies they confronted; it may also have allowed them to identify and prosecute specific individuals; and it may have made it possible to outwit suspects in the verbal fencing that took place during interrogation. In the prosecution of many individuals, however, more tangible, coercive measures were needed to extract confessions and cooperation. This brings us to a consideration of one of the most valuable techniques in the inquisitorial tool kit, imprisonment.

The standard generalization about imprisonment in medieval Europe is that it was used primarily to keep people on hand until their trials and was only rarely employed either as a form of punishment or as a means of rehabilitation.[1] On this interpretation, time spent in a medieval prison was for the most part socially and juridically formless, a dead time spent in a dead space between arrest and trial or between trial and execution. But this picture of the restricted role of imprisonment in medieval Europe may be overly simplistic, at least for the thirteenth and fourteenth centuries. The prison and the jail were to be found in almost every medieval landscape. Moreover, it is clear that by the period with which we are concerned, prisons were being used as more than simple holding tanks for those awaiting trial. All over Europe rulers were exploring the different possibilities of imprisonment. Ecclesiastical judges, forbidden by canon law to shed blood, were particularly interested in developing the punitive function of the prison. Bishoprics and monasteries had traditionally maintained prisons and had disciplined errant clerics with incarceration.[2] Therefore, when Pope Boniface VIII declared in 1298 that imprisonment was an appropriate form of punishment for clerics, he was not making a radical break with tradition.[3] The records of papal courts sitting in Avignon in the fourteenth century indicate that papal judges not infrequently used imprisonment as a form of punishment. Secular judges also experimented with the use of imprisonment. Often it was employed to force someone suspected of a crime to submit himself to trial by inquest; but

---

[1] See, for example, Castan, "La Préhistoire de la prison," pp. 20–22.
[2] On monastic prisons, see Pugh, *Imprisonment in Medieval England*, pp. 374–83.
[3] *Corpus iuris canonici*, 2: cols. 1091–92 (VI 5.9.3).

increasingly from the late thirteenth century on, imprisonment was used as a form of punishment for various offenses.[4]

In chapter 3 I shall have more to say on the inquisitors' use of imprisonment as part of their penal strategy. In this chapter, however, we shall be concerned with their use of imprisonment as an interrogation technique. Just as thirteenth-century rulers were discovering that imprisonment could be used to punish offenders, they were learning that it could also be an effective form of coercion and behavior modification. Although the surviving records are not as explicit about the use of imprisonment for this purpose as for others, clear traces of such practices can be found. For example, in the city of Albi the last decades of the thirteenth century were marked by a protracted struggle between the town's inhabitants and their bishop, Bernard de Castanet, over the extent of the former's political privileges.[5] If we can believe the bishop's enemies, he made extensive use of imprisonment in his effort to break his opponents' will. Many of those who aroused the bishop's ire spent time lodged in his jails, places that came to have an evil reputation.[6]

Even peasants, if they had influence with the right people, could use the local lockup to pressure their enemies. In the villages of Montaillou and Prades d'Alion in the county of Foix, Catharism and the inquisition became caught up in the fight for dominance between local strong men. As one move in this complex struggle, Pierre Adhémar persuaded the castellan of Montaillou to imprison Bernard Benet. The two days Benet spent fettered in the lowest parts of the castle were intended to persuade him to go to the bishop of Pamiers and recant as false the testimony he had previously given to the inquisitor of Carcassonne concerning the reception by one of his neighbors of the Cathar *consolamentum*.[7] Thus, it is apparent that the shadow of the prison lay heavily over the social landscape of thirteenth- and fourteenth-century Languedoc.

## IMPRISONMENT IN INQUISITORIAL THEORY

In utilizing imprisonment as a tool for manipulation and coercion, the inquisitors were working with a technique that was no stranger to contemporary rulers. They seem, however, to have been far more purposeful in its use than other thirteenth- and fourteenth-century authorities. Not only was imprisonment for life or for a term of years one of the inquisitors' favorite punishments (see below, chapter 3), it was probably their most effective interrogation technique. The

---

[4] Peters, "Prison before the Prison," pp. 34–45; Pugh, *Imprisonment in Medieval England*, pp. 18–47; Chiffoleau, *Les Justices du Pape*, pp. 229–32; Porteau-Bitker, "L'Emprisonnement," pp. 389–409; Esmein, *History of Continental Criminal Procedure*, p. 72; Harding, Hines, Ireland, and Rawlings, *Imprisonment in England and Wales*, pp. 7–19. See also Geremek, *Margins of Society*, pp. 16–18.

[5] Biget, "Un Procès d'inquisition," pp. 273–341, and A. Molinier, "Etude sur les démêlés."

[6] Collectorie 404, fols. 20v, 29r, 30v, 31v, 33r–34r, 38r–v, 40v, 89r, 94v, 101r.

[7] *Registre*, 1: 406.

Languedocian inquisitors only rarely used torture to extract confessions.[8] Instead, uncooperative witnesses were simply locked away for long periods of time to think things over.

Some inquisitorial manuals devoted extensive discussions to the use of imprisonment as a means for producing useful information. One of the earliest, the *De inquisitione hereticorum*, probably written in the mid-thirteenth century, possibly by David of Augsburg (d. 1271), suggested harsh treatment for reluctant witnesses.[9] The author, who was principally concerned with Waldensians, noted that suspects who had not been deeply involved in heresy could often be led to confess and abjure their errors. All one need do was threaten them with death and then offer them hope of a reprieve, provided they confessed. If a suspect proved obdurate, however, the author recommended that he be imprisoned. Once he had been locked away, his keepers could play on his fears by telling him that other witnesses had testified against him and that, if he was convicted on their testimony, he would be executed. To intensify this pressure, the treatise's author advised reducing the prisoner's food. He should also be denied visitors lest they strengthen him in his resolve to resist or coach him in how to give evasive answers to his interrogators. The only people allowed access to the prisoner should be the inquisitor's agents. These men, feigning pity, were to encourage him to save himself from the stake by confessing. The author concluded his discussion of the manipulation of prisoners with the brutally frank observation: "The fear of death and the hope of life quickly soften a heart that could otherwise hardly be moved."[10]

In his *Practica inquisitionis* Bernard Gui also discussed the role of imprisonment as an interrogation technique. Although not as plainly direct as the author of the *De inquisitione hereticorum*, Gui saw imprisonment as an integral component of the inquisitor's interrogation strategy. Imprisonment—coupled if necessary with hunger, shackles, and torture—could, so Gui observed, loosen the tongues of even the most obdurate.[11] In general, Gui recommended long imprisonment, for years at a time if need be, as a way to extract confessions. For "I have often seen those thus vexed and detained for many years confess not only recent faults but even deeds committed long ago, going back thirty or forty years or

[8] In medieval legal proceedings torture was resorted to in an effort to discover a "full" proof of a suspect's guilt. A full proof required the testimony of two eyewitnesses, the apprehension of the suspect in the act of committing the crime, or a confession. All other forms of evidence constituted only partial proofs. If the judge felt that he had acquired sufficient partial proofs to indicate that the guilt of the suspect was likely, he could endeavor to obtain a full proof by torture. On this see Peters, *Torture*, and Langbein, *Torture and the Law of Proof.* Pennington in *The Prince and the Law*, pp. 156–60, expresses doubt as to whether torture was employed in thirteenth- and fourteenth-century courts as frequently as scholars have believed.

[9] On this work, see Dondaine, "Le Manuel de l'inquisiteur," pp. 104–5, 180–83.

[10] Preger, ed., "Tractat des David von Augsburg," p. 223; Martène and Durand, eds., *Thesaurus novus*, 5: col. 1787.

[11] Gui, *Practica inquisitionis*, p. 284.

more."[12] In some cases, as with the type of heretics known as the Pseudo-Apostles, Gui recommended solitary confinement. If this precaution was not taken, suspects housed together could encourage one another to remain silent. Gui remarked that he had had personal experience with a Pseudo-Apostle who had at first evaded all questions. Nevertheless, after almost two years of detention, evidently in solitary confinement, he finally broke and confessed all.[13]

The fourteenth-century Aragonese inquisitor Nicholas Eymerich also devoted considerable attention to the use of imprisonment as a tool for the extraction of confessions. Even six centuries later, in an age hardened to brutality, some of his recommendations are chilling. To catch out a heretic who persisted in denying the truth, Eymerich did not hesitate to counsel resort to deceit and deception. In some cases a former accomplice could be employed to trick a suspect into confession. This agent was, of course, to be someone who had abandoned heresy and reverted to the true faith, but whom the suspect found personally acceptable. The spy was to visit the prisoner and pretend that although he had abjured heresy, he had only done so out of fear, and that he still adhered to his old beliefs. Once the agent had gained the suspect's trust, he should enter his cell one evening and so prolong the conversation that he would be forced to spend the night there. During the night hours the inquisitor's spy should draw the suspect into a conversation about his heretical beliefs. All this time other agents of the inquisitor were to be hidden nearby, where they could listen to what was said, together with a notary to make an official record of any incriminating statements.[14]

To be sure, there were heretics who confessed their errors but who then clung to them, refusing to recant. According to Eymerich, imprisonment, coupled with psychological pressure, could break such hard cases. He recommended that an impenitent heretic be kept shackled and well guarded. Visits by anyone other than the prison warders were to be prohibited. At frequent intervals the inquisitor and the local bishop should summon the heretic and instruct him on the nature of correct belief. If these exhortations failed, the inquisitor was to choose ten or twelve religious experts, clerics as well as lay jurists, to attempt to persuade the prisoner of his errors. Should he remain obdurate in spite of all this, the inquisitor ought not to be in a rush to turn him over to the secular authorities for execution. (Indeed, Eymerich remarked that since many heretics demand execution, regarding it as a glorious form of martyrdom, one should be in no hurry to oblige them.) Instead, the prisoner should be lodged for several months under extremely severe conditions. If this still failed to break his will, Eymerich advised changing tactics and relaxing the conditions of his detention. In addition to promising the prisoner that he would be treated with

---

[12] Ibid., p. 302.
[13] Ibid., p. 264.
[14] Eymerich, *Directorium inquisitorum*, p. 434.

mercy if he recanted, the inquisitor should see to it that his wife and children tried to persuade him to recant. Only if all these strategies failed should the obdurate heretic be sent to the stake.[15]

The inquisitors were aware that their prisons could be used to detect heresy even among those who were not held captive in them. The author of the *De inquisitione hereticorum* noted that it was easy to discover the supporters (*fautores*) of imprisoned heretics. All one had to do was observe who tried to visit them secretly, who held whispered conversations with them, and who gave them food.[16]

Bernard Gui was particularly impressed by the beneficial effects of holding prisoner a Cathar Good Man, one of that heresy's spiritual elite. Prolonged incarceration, so Gui noted, might lead a Good Man to convert, thereby giving the inquisitors a major victory. Even if the *perfectus* refused to recant, keeping him prisoner instead of sending him straight to the stake could have some benefits. As time dragged on, Gui observed, a Good Man's associates began to fear that he would eventually break down, confess, and denounce them. This often induced them to come forward with confessions. Even if they did not voluntarily confess but had to be cited to appear, their fears made it easy to extract the full truth.[17] In penning this advice, Gui spoke from experience. He had had the good luck to apprehend some of the most prominent of the last Good Men at large in Languedoc in the early fourteenth century. One of these, Pierre Autier, arrested in 1309, had been the guiding force behind this last major Cathar missionary effort in Languedoc. The months that Autier spent in captivity before his execution on 9 April 1310 proved particularly instructive. Not only did he and Amiel de Perles, another Good Man, mutually perform the ceremony known as the *melioramentum* in front of the inquisitors, they produced much incriminating evidence about their followers, both in oral testimony and in writing.[18] The *perfectus* Jacques Autier also fell into the inquisitors' hands. Among those whom Gui condemned in large part on the strength of the Autiers' testimony were Jacques Peyre of Saint-Sulpice-la-Pointe, Géraud d'Artigues of Saint-Jean-des-Pierres, Valencia Mancip and Bernard Mancip of Lugan, Raimonde Maurell of Beaupuy, Arnaud Brin of Prunet, Raimond Dons of Lavit-de-Lomagne, and Arnaud de la Salvetat of Prunet, his wife Bermude, and his sons Arnaud, Pierre, and Raimond, as well as Pierre's wife, Arnaude.[19]

Not only did Pierre Autier provide evidence concerning his followers, he also persuaded at least one individual to confess. This was Perrin Maurell of Beaupuy. Although a native of Burgundy, he, his brothers, and their wives had been living

---

[15] Ibid., p. 514.

[16] Preger, ed., "Tractat des David von Augsburg," p. 221; Martène and Durand, eds., *Thesaurus novus*, 5: col. 1786.

[17] Gui, *Practica inquisitionis*, p. 218.

[18] *LS*, pp. 37, 74. Amiel evidently also put himself into the state known as the *endura*, refusing either to eat or drink.

[19] Ibid., pp. 59, 60, 64, 132, 68, 74–75, 156, 73–74.

at Beaupuy when Autier, hiding from the inquisitors, took refuge with them. The day after Autier left Perrin's farm, however, he was captured. Perrin himself was arrested in short order. At first he refused to reveal the truth of his involvement with Autier. Only after he had spent a long, but unspecified, period in the *mur* in Toulouse, and only after Autier himself had urged him to confess, did he unburden himself.[20] The arrest of Jacques Autier and his fellow Good Men also had a demoralizing effect on their associates. Among those persuaded to confess by the incarceration of these *perfecti* was Isarn Bolha of Verdun-en-Lauragais.[21] Autier's arrest had a similar effect on Raimond Dominici, who was already in custody when Autier was arrested. Raimond had proved a very reluctant witness, refusing to confess to anything for over a year. But once Autier was arrested in September 1305, Raimond abandoned his resistance and made a full confession.[22]

## THE INQUISITORIAL PRISON IN PRACTICE

Thus far I have discussed the use of the prison largely from a theoretical point of view, from the perspective of the authors of the inquisitorial manuals. It is now time to look at the use of the prison in practice. It is worthwhile to begin with some concrete figures. The most extensive surviving register of inquisitorial sentences is that of Bernard Gui, inquisitor of Toulouse, which records his activity between 1308 and 1323. During this period Gui dealt with 637 individuals. Of these, it appears that some 260 (40.8 percent of the total) required a period of incarceration before they made a full confession.

It would be interesting to know how long a term of imprisonment was needed to loosen the tongues of those Gui investigated. Unfortunately, it is not possible to determine this with any accuracy. Nevertheless, it is clear that Gui kept many of his prisoners under lock and key for very long periods in order to extract confessions. Bernarde, wife of Bernard of Sainte-Foy-d'Aigrefeuille, who was condemned to the *mur* on 25 May 1309, had "barely been willing to confess anything" on her first appearance. Only after two years in prison did she make a full confession.[23] Similarly, Bernard Mancip of Lugan, sentenced to immuration on 23 April 1312, required a period of detention exceeding two years before he acknowledged his involvement with heresy.[24] Few people seem to have been as determined as Bernarde and Bernard. A few weeks at most in the cells were enough to persuade many to confess. For example, Pierre Burgada of Saint-Anatholy held out for several months before confessing to the deeds for which he was sentenced to wear crosses on 7 March 1316.[25] Pierre Géraud of

---

[20] His involvement with Catharism must not have been too extensive, since he was only sentenced to wear crosses (ibid., p. 102).

[21] Ibid., p. 15.

[22] Ibid., p. 27.

[23] Ibid., p. 30.

[24] Ibid., p. 132.

[25] Ibid., p. 188 (incorrectly given as p. 190).

Aurin found an imprisonment of a little over a month sufficient to loosen his tongue.[26] In several cases, such as those of Bona Dominica (widow of Guillaume Dominici of Saint-Jean-l'Herm), Pierre de la Salvetat of Prunet, his brother Raimond, and Perrin Maurell, Gui merely noted in their sentences that they were held "for a long time" before they finally confessed.[27]

The fullest data relating to the length of inquisitorial trials come from Bishop Jacques Fournier's register, which covers his inquisitorial activity at Pamiers between 1318 and 1325. The register was kept with great care, and in eighty-seven cases we can calculate exactly how long a trial lasted. The mean length of Fournier's procedures was 54.7 weeks (383 days). The longest procedure required six years (2,201 days), the shortest seven days. Seventy-five percent of the proceedings required 58.1 weeks (407 days) or less, 50 percent 37.4 weeks (262 days) or less, and 25 percent 17.6 weeks (123 days) or less. The most common length of trial (3 cases) was 45.9 weeks (321 days). Two individuals died during their trials. If we subtract these two cases from our sample, we find that the average length of trial was 53.3 weeks (373 days). Once again the longest procedure required 2,201 days, the shortest a mere 7. Seventy-five percent of the trials required 52.6 weeks (368 days) or less, 50 percent 35.3 weeks (247 days) or less, and 25 percent 17.1 weeks (120 days) or less.

These figures are, however, a little misleading. There was often a substantial delay between the end of a person's interrogation and the imposition of sentence. This tends to lengthen artificially the duration of the trials. A better measure of the length of an investigation is the time between the first appearance of a suspect (or the rendering of the first deposition by a witness against the accused) and his or her abjuration of heresy and reconciliation with the church. This figure can be calculated for sixty-nine cases in Fournier's register. The average length of time between the beginning of an investigation and the abjuration of heresy by the defendant was 19.9 weeks (139 days). The longest proceeding required a little over two years (737 days); the shortest a single day. Indeed, the most common length of trial was one day, recorded for thirteen individuals (18.8 percent of 69). In 75 percent of the cases, the trial took 32 weeks (224 days) or less; in 50 percent, 6.6 weeks (46 days) or less; and in 25 percent of the cases, the proceedings required only 11 or fewer days.

In fifty-five cases Fournier imprisoned a suspect during the course of his investigation. In forty-two of these cases, we can determine the length of time an individual spent in custody before his trial was completed and he sought and received absolution. If we exclude those who died during their trials, we find that the average length of time between the detention of an individual and his final confession, absolution, and reconciliation with the church was 24.3 weeks (170 days). The longest period of detention was a little under two years (721 days).

---

[26] Ibid., p. 119.
[27] Ibid., pp. 60, 73–74, 102.

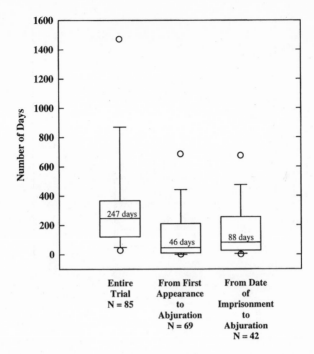

Figure 2.1 Length of Jacques Fournier's Inquisitorial Proceedings, 1318–25
Note: Each box indicates the range between the 25th and 75th percentiles of the data. The solid horizontal lines indicate the 50th percentile. Capped bars indicate the 10th and 90th percentile points. The circles indicate the 5th and 95th percentiles.
Those who died during their trials are not included here.
Source: *Registre.*

The shortest was one day. In 75 percent of the cases, less than 37.3 weeks (261 days) of captivity were required to extract a full confession and repentance; in 50 percent of the cases, 12.6 weeks (88 days) or less were necessary; and in 25 percent of the cases, the suspects confessed and sought absolution after 29 days or less of captivity (see figures 2.1 and 2.2).

Although most people confessed after only a relatively brief period of time in prison, a few displayed a truly heroic determination to hold out. The longest period of imprisonment known from Fournier's register was the 2.5 years endured by Arnaud Teisseyre, a notary and physician from Lordat.[28] Fournier began his investigation of Teisseyre, a relative of the infamous Cathar missionary Pierre Autier of Tarascon, on 22 September 1320, taking the deposition of

[28] Since Teisseyre died without confessing, his period of imprisonment has not been included in the group discussed in the preceding paragraph.

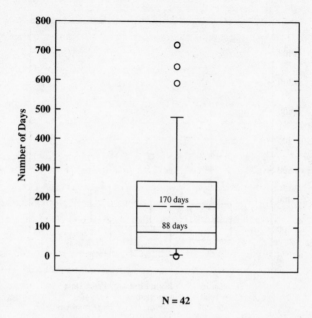

N = 42

**Figure 2.2 Length of Time between Detention and Abjuration of Individuals Tried by Jacques Fournier, 1318–25**
Note: The box indicates the range between the 25th and 75th percentiles of the data. The solid horizontal line indicates the 50th percentile; the dashed line the mean. The capped bars indicate the 10th and 90th percentile points. The circles indicate extreme cases lying beyond the 10th and 90th percentiles.
Source: *Registre.*

Guillaume Castell, the vicar of Verdun.[29] By 27 October Fournier had received the depositions of six more witnesses against the notary. When Arnaud learned of the investigation, he fled from Lordat, getting as far as Limoux, where he was arrested.[30] He was returned to Pamiers on 14 November 1320. Although lodged in the Tour des Allemans, he proved a difficult and recalcitrant witness. His case dragged on until 29 May 1323, when he died, unrepentant and defiant, 2.5 years (926 days) after his incarceration.[31] The other individual who died in Fournier's prison while under interrogation was Jean Rocas de la Salvetat from the diocese of Cahors. Imprisoned by 25 July 1321 for his belief that only one person of the Trinity, God the Father, existed, he refused to recant his errors, dying in prison by 6 September 1322.[32]

[29] The proceedings of this trial are in *Registre*, 2: 194–220.
[30] Ibid., 2: 204.
[31] Ibid., 2: 219–20.
[32] Ibid., 2: 241–54.

Of those who did not die during their imprisonment, the record for endur-
ing incarceration was held by two Waldensians, Jean de Vienne and his wife
Huguette. Imprisoned in early August of 1319, they steadfastly clung to their
beliefs for a little under two years (720 and 721 days respectively) and were finally
burned alive on 2 August 1321.[33] Among other individuals who spent unusually
long periods of time in the Tour des Allemans were Pierre Guillaume the elder of
Unac and Raimonde Guilhou of Vernaux, who spent respectively 1.8 years (646
days) and 1.6 years (590 days) in prison before giving up their resistance.[34]

The inquisitors recognized and employed different regimes of detention for
the suspects they interrogated. In his *Practica inquisitionis* Bernard Gui noted
that an inquisitor should take account of the quality of the person involved, the
nature of his offense, and the evidence against him. In those cases where decisive
proof was lacking and the suspicions entertained as to the defendant's conduct
were not "vehement," the suspect was to be released upon providing suitable
sureties until such time as new, more convincing evidence was found against
him. Such individuals, however, were not given complete liberty. Every day they
were to present themselves at the gate of the inquisition's house in Toulouse and
remain there until supper.[35] From Gui's *Liber sententiarum* we can tell that he
made fairly frequent use of this form of detention. In seven of his sentences, Gui
noted that the individuals in question had been forced to spend time cooling
their heels at the inquisition's gatehouse before making a full confession.[36] But
this form of detention could have its drawbacks. In the *Practica* Gui noted that
gathering together a number of people in this loose form of "arrest" allowed them
to talk together, inform one another about the tribunal's proceedings, and
encourage one another to remain obstinate.[37]

At Pamiers, Jacques Fournier seems to have made use of a variety of forms of
detention short of imprisonment in the Tour des Allemans. When confronted
with reluctant witnesses against whom there was convincing evidence, he
frequently allowed them a delay during which to consider their testimony,
instructing them to remain within the precincts of the city of Pamiers and its
suburb of Le Mas-Saint-Antonin. This he did on thirteen occasions.[38] In a few

---

[33] The proceedings in their trials are in ibid., 1: 508–32.
[34] The proceedings of these trials are in ibid., 2: 221–34 (Raimonde Guilhou) and 3: 331–45
(Pierre Guillaume).
[35] Gui, *Practica inquisitionis*, p. 302.
[36] *LS*, pp. 60 (Bona Dominica), 105 (Jeanne Vital), 107 (Pierre Auros), 108 (Raimonde
Barreria), 114 (Petrona Aribaud), 117 (Raimond Vasco), 127 (Pierre Guilhabert the elder).
[37] Gui, *Practica inquisitionis*, p. 302.
[38] These are the cases of Jacqueline den Carot of Ax-les-Thermes (*Registre*, 1: 154–55), Arnaud
Cogul of Lordat (1: 380), Bernard Benet of Montaillou (1: 408), Arnaud Faure of Montaillou (1:
432), Bernarde Durrieu of Ax-les-Thermes (2: 335), Raimonde Belot of Montaillou (3: 65–66),
Jean Pelicier of Montaillou (3: 78), Guillemette Argelier of Montaillou (3: 89), Raimonde Marty
of Montaillou (3: 105), Pierre Guillaume the elder of Unac (3: 335), Pierre Fornier of Serles (3:
439), Master Guillaume Gautier of Tarascon (3: 441), and Pierre Lombard of Tarascon (3: 443).

cases individuals were detained under closer arrest but were not incarcerated in the Tour des Allemans. Bernard Franque, for example, was lodged in the episcopal palace.[39] Alamande Guilhabert of Montaillou also escaped detention in the Allemans, although her confinement was not as congenial as Franque's; she was kept in a granary attached to the palace.[40]

Those who were imprisoned with a view to persuading them to make a full and complete confession undoubtedly did not enjoy their fate. Imprisonment was, if nothing else, costly. As in all medieval prisons, inmates were expected to pay their own expenses. A protracted stay could put a strain on the financial reserves of even the most well-to-do. Guillaume Marty of Junac, for example, amassed during his seven-week period of incarceration in the *mur* at Carcassonne a debt of fifteen livres of Tours, a sufficiently large sum that he had to sell some land to pay it off.[41] The debts that suspects contracted in prison could work in favor of the inquisitors, loosening tongues that were otherwise tightly tied. A striking example of this is provided by Guillaume Peyre of Belbèse-de-Razès. Arrested on suspicion of being a Cathar believer, he spent a long period detained in the Carcassonne *mur*. Despite the length of his incarceration, he refused to confess. By the time he was released, he had spent some forty sous on his lodging. Once free, Guillaume went to other believers and asked for their help in paying off this sum, but none was willing to assist him. Then, as Pierre Maury told Arnaud Sicre, Fournier's spy, "the devil put himself in his heart," and Guillaume returned to the Carcassonne inquisitor and confessed what he knew about his fellow believers.[42]

For the majority of those detained during interrogation, life does not seem to have been too difficult. For the most part, suspects were apparently not kept under lock and key or isolated from one another. Instead, they were allowed to wander around, almost at pleasure, within the walls of the prison. Just as little was normally done to keep prisoners separate from one another, so was little effort made to isolate them from outsiders. People who had been arrested and were in transit to the *mur* were not kept incommunicado. For example, when Raimond Vayssière of Ax-les-Thermes was being taken to Pamiers, he and his escort halted at Pierre de Gaillac's house in Tarascon. There Vayssière was able to speak to Gaillac, a veteran of many dealings with the inquisitors, and ask his advice on how he should comport himself when questioned. Gaillac advised him to tell the truth. In reply, Raimond blew on his hand, as though making a fire. Gaillac interpreted this to mean that if Raimond told the truth, he would be burned.[43] Even suspects who were ensconced in the inquisitorial prison were still

[39] Ibid., 1: 358.
[40] Ibid., 1: 425.
[41] Ibid., 3: 288. It should be noted that once he had raised the 15 l.t., Guillaume did not return to Carcassonne to pay his debts but instead fled.
[42] Ibid., 2: 57.
[43] Ibid., 1: 273.

allowed visitors. As Guillemette Benet of Montaillou told Jacques Fournier, when she was being held captive in the *mur* at Carcassonne, the priest of Montaillou, Pierre Clergue, was able to visit her and warn her not to say anything against him or other members of his family.[44]

We should not, however, paint too pleasant a picture of life in detention. When the need arose, the grim counsels of the inquisitors' manuals were put into practice. Psychological pressure was exerted on inmates, especially those who were gravely ill. When the notary and physician Arnaud Teisseyre of Lordat, who had endured over two years of confinement, lay near death, the custodian of the prison in the Tour des Allemans, Master Marc Revell, visited him. He urged the dying man to confess, saying, "Master Arnaud, you are in danger. I beg you to tell the truth concerning the heresy and other matters of which you are accused." Teisseyre replied that he had nothing to say. Master Marc then asked him if he wished to confess. When the prisoner said he had no sins to confess, the exasperated jailer burst out, "You who had such abundance and lived so splendidly and had so many temporal delights, how could you be without sin?" All he got in reply was a curt, "*No y sai als*" (I don't know anything else).[45]

More rigorous treatment could also be applied to reluctant witnesses. The conditions under which suspects were held were often made deliberately severe. Uncooperative individuals could find themselves deposited for a time "in strict prison" (*in stricto carcere*).[46] Conditions under this form of imprisonment could be very difficult. For example, in 1263 Raimond Bernard of Flassac, *bayle* of Mazères for the count of Foix, was imprisoned on suspicion of heresy. He confessed, but he did so, he later contended, largely "because of the terrible pain and straitness of the prison and the hunger that I there endured almost continuously for a month and two days."[47] Raimond Peyre, a suspect haled before Jacques Fournier at Pamiers in the early fourteenth century, found himself deposited in a *cachot*, bound with both manacles and shackles. There he spent fifteen days, until his condition came to the attention of Bishop Fournier, who apparently had not ordered such a strict form of confinement. He was liberated from his dungeon and burdened only with leg-irons, so that he could walk about a little. But, so he claimed, his experience of strict confinement had made such an impression on him that he was willing to make a false confession to avoid being sent back to the dungeon.[48]

[44] Ibid., 1: 476.

[45] Ibid., 2: 219–20. "*No y sai als*" is Duvernoy's suggested reading of the corrupt "*Noy seals*" of the text. See his French translation of the register, *Le Registre d'inquisition de Jacques Fournier*, 2: 609 n. 25.

[46] As happened, for example, to Bernard Franque de Goulier of Vicdessos, one of the people investigated by Jacques Fournier (*Registre*, 1: 360).

[47] *HL*, 8: col. 1481.

[48] *Registre*, 3: 430.

In a complaint probably drawn up in 1285–86, the consuls of Carcassonne painted a truly horrific portrait of conditions under the inquisitor Jean Galand in the *mur* at Carcassonne:

> We feel ourselves aggrieved in that you [Jean Galand], contrary to the use and custom observed by your predecessors in the Inquisition, have made a new prison, called the *mur*. Truly this could be called with good cause a hell. For in it you have constructed little cells for the purpose of tormenting and torturing people. Some of these cells are dark and airless, so that those lodged there cannot tell if it is day or night, and they are continuously deprived of air and light. In other cells there are kept miserable wretches laden with shackles, some of wood, some of iron. These cannot move, but defecate and urinate on themselves. Nor can they lie down except on the frigid ground. They have endured torments like these day and night for a long time. In other miserable places in the prison, not only is there no light or air, but food is rarely distributed, and that only bread and water.
>
> Many prisoners have been put in similar situations, in which several, because of the severity of their tortures, have lost limbs and have been completely incapacitated. Many, because of the unbearable conditions and their great suffering, have died a most cruel death. In these prisons there is constantly heard an immense wailing, weeping, groaning, and gnashing of teeth. What more can one say? For these prisoners life is a torment and death a comfort. And thus coerced they say that what is false is true, choosing to die once rather than to endure more torture. As a result of these false and coerced confessions not only do those making the confessions perish, but so do the innocent people named by them. . . .
>
> Whence it has come about that many of those who are newly cited to appear, hearing of the torments and trials of those who are detained in the *mur* and in its dungeons, wishing to save themselves, have fled to the jurisdiction of other kings. Others assert that what is false is true; in which assertions they accuse not only themselves but other innocent people, that they may avoid the above mentioned pains, choosing to fall with dishonor into the hands of God rather than into those of perverse men. Those who thus confess afterward reveal to their close friends that those things that they said to the inquisitors are not true, but rather false, and that they confessed out of fear of imminent danger. . . .
>
> Likewise, and it is a shame to hear, certain vile persons, both defamed for heresy and condemned for false testimony, and, as it is reported, guardians of the dungeons, seduced by an evil spirit, say with a diabolical suggestion to the imprisoned: "Wretches, why do you not confess so that you can be set free? Unless you confess, you will never leave this place, nor escape its torments!" To which the prisoners reply: "My lord, what do we say? What should we say?" And the jailers reply, "You should say this and this." And what they suggest is false and

evil; and those wretches repeat what they have been told, although it is false, so that they may avoid the continuous torments to which they are subject. Yet in the end they perish and cause innocent people to perish as well.[49]

One can suspect that these complaints, coming from opponents of the inquisitors, may be exaggerated. But even individuals whom one might believe to be immune to bias against the inquisitors and their work found conditions in the inquisitorial jails cruel. When in 1306 one of the cardinals charged by Pope Clement V to investigate the complaints of the people of Albi inspected the *mur* at Carcassonne, he discovered that many prisoners whose trials had not yet been completed were being kept shackled and housed in "narrow and very dark prisons." Some had apparently endured these conditions for five years and more. Evidently shocked by what he found, the cardinal ordered that the prisoners should be held under less harsh conditions.[50]

The prison was essential to the repressive campaign of the inquisitors. As noted in chapter 1, the inquisitors were masters of the written and spoken word. The advice given in manuals by men like Bernard Gui and Nicholas Eymerich indicates that they were prepared for almost any verbal gymnastics and histrionics on the part of those they interrogated. Yet it was usually not a display of verbal virtuosity that extracted confessions, but a sojourn in the *mur*. Here the objects of inquisitorial interest could be deposited, often for months at a time. For most the tedium and expense of their confinement were enough to induce them to confess. More determined individuals were subjected to various forms of physical and psychological persuasion. Only a very few were capable of holding out for any length of time against such methods.

All of this may sound banal; it is not. What the inquisitors had done, and they may have been the first in medieval Europe to have done so, was to create a socially delimited space, in which they could isolate individuals from the outer world and subject them without interruption to an enforced and forcible persuasion. Such a planned and active use of imprisonment for behavior modification was possibly without parallel in medieval Europe.

[49] Vidal, *Un Inquisiteur jugé*, pp. 40–41.
[50] *Documents*, 2: 331–32. How conditions of imprisonment in inquisitorial prisons compared to those in other medieval prisons is an interesting question, but one that is difficult to answer. In the late Middle Ages some prisoners experienced very rigorous treatment. One of the harshest regimes known prevailed at the end of the fourteenth century in the dungeon known as the *Fosse* in the Paris Châtelet. The *Fosse* was a room, without light or air, in the shape of an inverted cone. Prisoners were lowered into it by rope through a hatch in the floor. Filled at its bottom with water, it was so small that one could neither stand nor lie down in it (Battifol, "Le Châtelet de Paris," pp. 48–49). With the possible exceptions of the poor wretches who fell into the hands of Jean Galand and Bishop Bernard de Castanet of Albi, few prisoners of the Languedocian inquisitors experienced anything this harsh.

# CHAPTER 3

# THE TECHNOLOGY
# OF PUNISHMENT

ONE OF THE INQUISITORS' most impressive achievements was the elaboration of a complex but flexible system of punishment. Penal systems are intrinsically polysemic; they can simultaneously serve a multitude of ends. Punishment can be part of a strategy of crime control. But it can also perform other functions: therapy or moral instruction for the condemned, the control of labor, and the terrorization of onlookers. Punishment can also have a noninstrumental, expressive aspect, reaffirming deeply held societal notions about personal responsibility and the social order.

It is thus no surprise that the inquisitors' system of penalties served a variety of purposes. Their penal system was intended to be therapeutic, reintegrating penitent heretics into the fold of the church. It was also a system of social control, putting people into an easily identifiable and stigmatized social out-group that was subject to long-term manipulation. Finally, it was a semiotic system, designed to teach the masses a number of salutary lessons: the orthodox nature of the Roman Catholic Church, the damnable nature of dissent, and the terrible majesty of the church, together with its merciful and nurturing disposition. Surprisingly, although judicial institutions constituted one of the primary means by which medieval rulers intervened in the affairs of their subjects, there has been little attention given to medieval techniques and rituals of punishment.[1] In part this may be because there seems at first glance to be little to say about the subject of medieval punishment.[2] Given the lack of scholarship on the subject, one is tempted to conclude that the directors of medieval repressive institutions devoted little thought to the social uses of the penalties they inflicted. The lucky survival of a large number of sentences from the Languedocian inquisitors, however,

---

[1] For example, neither Given in *Society and Homicide* nor Hanawalt in *Crime and Conflict* devote much, if any, attention to this subject. In recent years, however, historians have become more interested in rituals of punishment. See, for example, Edgerton, *Pictures and Punishment*; Cohen, "'To Die a Criminal'" and *Crossroads of Justice*; and the following essays in Chiffoleau, Martines, and Paravicini, eds., *Riti e rituali nelle società medievali*: Zorzi, "Rituali e cerimoniali penali"; Ruggiero, "Constructing Civic Morality, Deconstructing the Body"; and Gauvard, "Pendre et dépendre."

[2] Spierenburg, for example, concludes that there is almost no evidence on how executions were staged in the fourteenth and fifteenth centuries (*Spectacle of Suffering*, p. 44).

gives us a rare opportunity to examine in detail the penal system of at least one medieval tribunal.

Perhaps the most distinctive feature of the inquisitors' penal system was the great flexibility they displayed in punishing those they found guilty. This made their tribunal very different from most contemporary courts. In general, medieval judges who sentenced convicted felons lacked a wide array of options. For the most part custom prescribed quite narrowly what type of punishment could be imposed for a particular offense: execution, mutilation, exile, a fine, and so forth. Beginning in the thirteenth century this rigidity was increasingly felt to be a hindrance to the effective administration of justice. Therefore, legal professionals began to work toward giving judges greater discretion in sentencing.[3]

Probably few medieval judges were as resourceful as the inquisitors in devising a varied and flexible set of punishments. Not only could they make fine distinctions among degrees of culpability, they could alter punishments they had previously imposed if those sentenced proved contrite and cooperative. In effect, they operated something akin to a parole system. The inquisitors' penalties were thus not merely punishments but elements in a system for the long-term manipulation of those who had fallen into their clutches. Taken as a whole, the inquisitors' penalties constituted a veritable political economy of punishment.

## AN INQUISITOR'S PENALTIES: BERNARD GUI AT WORK

The largest body of surviving inquisitorial sentences is contained in the *Liber sententiarum*, or register, kept by Bernard Gui, inquisitor of Toulouse. In 1900 Célestin Douais published a table summarizing the data in this register.[4] His findings have done much to shape subsequent historians' understanding of the operation of inquisitorial tribunals. Working in a period before electronic data processing, however, Douais could discover only the simplest and most obvious patterns in the data. Moreover, his method of presenting his material was occasionally both misleading and erroneous. Since Douais, only Jacques Paul and Annette Pales-Gobilliard have attempted quantitative examinations of Gui's register. Paul's 1981 essay on the "mentality" of the inquisitor makes a number of interesting observations, but it examines only a fraction of the data, that is, the sentences imposed on 5 April 1310. Similarly, Pales-Gobilliard's 1991 paper discusses only a part of the information in the register.[5] I have therefore subjected the data to a fresh analysis.[6]

---

[3] On this, see Schnapper, "Les Peines arbitraires."

[4] *Documents*, 1: ccv. Henry Charles Lea also tabulated the data in the *LS*. Unlike Douais, who counted individual sentences and commutations of previously imposed sentences, Lea evidently used as his unit of analysis the individuals who appeared before Gui. See his *Inquisition of the Middle Ages*, 1: 495.

[5] Paul, "La Mentalité de l'inquisiteur"; Pales-Gobilliard, "Pénalités inquisitoriales."

[6] Not all of the material in Gui's register has been used in the following discussion. Although almost all of the sentences or commutations of sentences in the register relate to single individuals, the *LS* contains two "collective" sentences, a "reconciliation" with the community of the

Gui's register is a complex document, and the terminology that will be used in discussing it needs to be clarified. The register contains 907 different "acts," recorded between 3 March 1308 and 19 June 1323, relating to individuals convicted of heresy. In 633 of these acts Gui imposed some form of penance or punishment on an individual. Of these penances, 544 (85.9 percent) were imposed on those who were alive at the time, 89 (14.1 percent) on those who were deceased. These 633 acts will be referred to as "sentences," "punishments," or "penalties." The other 274 acts consisted of commutations of previously imposed penances into lesser penalties. These will be referred to as "commutations." The 907 acts in the register relate to only 637 individuals. Of these people, 413 appeared before Gui once, and 224 two or more times. In this chapter, they will be referred to as either "individuals" or "cases."[7]

Most of the individuals recorded in the register were tried and condemned by Gui, but some were not. Many of those who appear in the *Liber* had previously been given penances by other inquisitors, penances that Gui, acting as their successor in office, commuted. Some individuals who appear in the register had in reality been tried primarily by someone other than Gui. According to the reforms instituted by Pope Clement V at the Council of Vienne in 1312 (but not put into effect until 1317), inquisitors and local bishops were for certain matters required to act together.[8] Therefore, a number of the sentences recorded in the *Liber* relate to people who were tried primarily by Jacques Fournier, bishop of Pamiers. One individual, the notorious Franciscan Bernard Délicieux, was tried by a specially appointed papal commission; but since Bernard had been extremely active in leading opposition to the inquisitors, Gui made certain to record his condemnation.

All told, Gui's register contains 633 different penalties (see tables 3.1 and 3.2). The least severe punishment in the inquisitor's tool kit was the requirement to perform a number of penitential pilgrimages.[9] This penalty was generally reserved for those whose involvement with heresy had been relatively minor and who readily confessed their misdeeds. Gui recorded a small number of such sentences: only seventeen, or 2.7 percent of the total. For individuals whose involvement with heresy was more serious, there were more severe penalties. When the inquisitors did not think that pilgrimages alone were sufficient, they required the

---

*castrum* of Cordes, and an order for the destruction of copies of the Talmud confiscated from Languedocian Jews. These sentences have been excluded from the following analysis.

[7] Douais's failure to make clear the fact that "acts" do not equal individuals has led into error some of those who have used the table printed in *Documents*. For one example, see Given, "Inquisitors of Languedoc," p. 353.

[8] Lea, *Inquisition of the Middle Ages*, 2: 96.

[9] The inquisitors distinguished between major and minor pilgrimages. Those sentenced to minor pilgrimages had to visit certain churches in the kingdom of France. Those sentenced to major pilgrimages were required to journey to Rome, Santiago de Compostella, Canterbury, and Cologne. Gui, *Practica inquisitionis*, pp. 37–39, 97; and Doat, 37: fols. 111r–v.

wearing of crosses. These were made of yellow cloth and were to be worn at all times on the front and back of a penitent's clothing. Of the 633 sentences in Gui's register, 136 (21.5 percent) took this form. Within this category of punishment, there were gradations. Those who had cooperated and confessed quickly were required to wear only a single set of crosses. Seventy-nine of Gui's sentences (12.5 percent) fell into this category. Those who had not been as cooperative or who were felt to be more deeply involved in heresy had to wear a double set of crosses. Gui recorded fifty-seven such sentences (9 percent of the total).

The next penalty in the inquisitors' hierarchy of punishments, imprisonment, represented a significant increase in severity. Imprisonment was almost invariably for life, and entailed the confiscation of one's property. Of the sentences recorded in Gui's register, almost half (308 or 48.7 percent) were of this type. The inquisitors recognized different types of imprisonment. The normal regime, known by the shorthand term of *murum largum*, was evidently not very harsh; 268 sentences of this type (42.3 percent) were recorded by Gui.

Table 3.1  Acts Recorded in Bernard Gui's Register

| Sentences Imposed | Number | Percentage |
|---|---|---|
| Pilgrimages | 17 | 2.7 |
| Simple crosses | 79 | 12.5 |
| Double crosses | 57 | 9.0 |
| One-year prison term | 1 | 0.2 |
| Perpetual imprisonment, normal regime | 268 | 42.3 |
| Perpetual imprisonment, normal regime, and house destroyed | 8 | 1.3 |
| Perpetual imprisonment, strict regime | 31 | 4.9 |
| Burned alive | 41 | 6.5 |
| Deceased, but would have been imprisoned if alive | 17 | 2.7 |
| Deceased, but would have been burned if alive | 3 | 0.5 |
| Burned posthumously | 52 | 8.2 |
| Burned posthumously; house destroyed | 14 | 2.2 |
| Remains to be exhumed | 3 | 0.5 |
| Condemned in absentia | 40 | 6.3 |
| Ordered on crusade | 1 | 0.2 |
| Reserved for other judgment | 1 | 0.2 |
| SUBTOTAL | 633 | 100.2 |
| **Commutations of Previously Imposed Sentences** | | |
| Released from prison, to wear crosses | 139 | 50.7 |
| Allowed to lay aside crosses | 135 | 49.3 |
| SUBTOTAL | 274 | 100 |
| TOTAL | 907 | |

Note: "Sentences Imposed" sum to more than 100% because of rounding.
Source: Gui, *Liber sententiarum* (Add. MS 4697).

Table 3.2  Individuals and Their Penalties, by Heresy

|  | Cathars (%) | Waldensians (%) | Béguins (%) | Other (%) |
|---|---|---|---|---|
| Penalty |  |  |  |  |
| Pilgrimages | 10  (2.1) | 7  (7.8) | 0  (0.0) | 0  (0.0) |
| Crosses | 107 (22.7) | 19 (21.1) | 1  (5.3) | 7 (31.8) |
| Prison | 249 (52.9) | 36 (40.0) | 13 (68.4) | 9 (40.9) |
| Deceased but would have been imprisoned if alive | 16  (3.4) | 1  (1.1) | 0  (0.0) | 0  (0.0) |
| Burned alive | 30  (6.4) | 7  (7.8) | 4 (21.1) | 0  (0.0) |
| Deceased but would have been burned if alive | 3  (0.6) | 0  (0.0) | 0  (0.0) | 0  (0.0) |
| Burned posthumously | 58 (12.3) | 6  (6.7) | 0  (0.0) | 2  (9.1) |
| Remains exhumed | 3  (0.6) | 0  (0.0) | 0  (0.0) | 0  (0.0) |
| Other | 19  (4.0) | 15 (16.7) | 3 (15.8) | 4 (18.2) |
| TOTAL | 471 | 90 | 19 | 22 |

Note: The unit of analysis in this table is the individual, not the sentence. Since some individuals received more than one sentence, they are counted more than once in this table. Therefore, column totals sum to figures greater than those shown and percentages sum to more than 100%.

Source: Gui, Source: Gui, *Liber sententiarum* (Add. MS 4697).

Imprisonment could either be supplemented with other penalties or intensified. Some individuals, in addition to being imprisoned, saw their houses destroyed. When people had sheltered the Cathar Good Men or allowed the *consolamentum* to be performed in their homes, their houses were torn down and turned into rubbish dumps as a sign of disgrace and a perpetual reminder of the fate of Cathar sympathizers.[10] Eight sentences to the *murum largum* (1.3 percent) involved this additional indignity. Individuals who tried to bend the inquisition to their own ends by concocting false accusations of heresy could expect not only a term in prison but a period of exposure to public obloquy as well. Two individuals who had made false accusations were, before being immured, exposed to public view for several days on specially erected scaffolds, with red tongues sewn on their clothing. One man, who had forged a letter in the name of the inquisitors, was exposed to public view with a red letter attached to his clothing.

For those whom they wished to punish severely, the inquisitors had available a particularly harsh form of imprisonment. Individuals who had been deeply involved with heresy or who had tried to deceive the inquisitors were sentenced to what was known as the *murum strictum*. These unfortunates were locked up

[10] The decrees ordering the destruction of houses were issued separately. However, I have combined them with the other sentences imposed on the individuals in question.

in cells and at times shackled to the walls or floors. Thirty-one such sentences (4.9 percent) were recorded in Gui's register. In one anomalous case a man was sentenced to a one-year prison term. The inquisitors' most severe penalty was death by fire. Technically, of course, the inquisitors, being priests forbidden to shed blood, did not actually condemn anyone to death. They merely "relaxed," or handed over, culprits to the secular authorities, who were expected to carry out the actual executions. Forty-one such relaxations to the secular arm were recorded in Gui's register, 6.5 percent of the total.

Forty sentences (6.3 percent) consisted of condemnations of individuals in absentia. These were people who had either failed to heed citations to appear before the inquisitors to have their beliefs examined or who, having confessed to heretical dealings, failed to appear to receive their sentences or fled without completing the penances that had been imposed on them. The inquisitors also pursued the dead. Gui's *Liber* contains eighty-nine sentences (14.1 percent of the total) imposed on deceased individuals. In sixty-six of the cases (10.4 percent), these sentences consisted of orders to exhume and burn the corpses of the deceased. In fourteen cases the house of the person concerned was also ordered destroyed. In three cases Gui declared that the individuals in question, had they lived long enough to be sentenced, would have been burned. In another three cases the corpses of the deceased were to be exhumed but *not* burned.[11] Finally, in seventeen cases, usually of individuals who had confessed to heretical dealings but had died before penance could be imposed, it was proclaimed that they would have been immured had they lived; therefore, their property was to be confiscated.[12]

## PUNISHMENT AS PROPAGANDA

What sense can we make of this penal system, with its ranked hierarchy of punishments? What purposes did the inquisitors hope their penalties would achieve? What functions, in fact, did their system of penality serve in the campaign against heresy? Unfortunately, the inquisitors rarely engaged in a self-conscious exposition of the purposes of their system of punishment. One who leafs through Bernard Gui's *Practica inquisitionis* finds only scattered comments about the meanings of the punishments he imposed. Uppermost in Gui's mind was the repressive and destructive aspect of the inquisition's work. Thus he discusses how the tasks of the inquisition should be carried out:

> Concerning the order of proceeding, it is to be remembered that the method of any procedure is governed by its end. The end of the office of the inquisition is

[11] These were individuals who had been supporters of heresy, but had not received the *consolamentum* (Gui, *Practica inquisitionis*, p. 123).

[12] We should note two anomalous penalties recorded in Gui's register. In one case an individual was sentenced to take part in the next crusade to the Holy Land, pending which he was to remove himself into exile from Languedoc. In another case an individual was reserved for further deliberation concerning his punishment.

the destruction of heresy; this cannot be destroyed unless heretics are destroyed. Moreover, these cannot be destroyed unless their receivers, fautors, and defenders are destroyed. . . . Heretics are destroyed in a double fashion: first, when they are converted from heresy to the true, Catholic faith, according to Proverbs 12:[7]: Turn the impious, and they will not be such; secondly, when they are surrendered to the secular jurisdiction to be corporeally burned.[13]

Although the inquisitors do not give us much guidance, we need not abandon all hope of understanding the rationales that governed their system of punishment. Sociologists have given much thought to the phenomenon of punishment, and it is instructive to examine how the work of the inquisitors relates to this body of interpretation. One of the most influential understandings of punishment has been that advanced by Emile Durkheim. He argued that the force that holds together a simple society, one that does not have a complex division of labor, is the *conscience collective*, a shared universe of moral values regarded as sacred. A crime violates this sacred order: it shocks and dismays "healthy" consciences. The result is a passionate call from the outraged public for vengeance. Through the act of punishing the offender, the members of a society reaffirm their group solidarity and restore the sacred moral order.

This model, attractive as it may seem, does not fit the work of the inquisitors. Clearly some—certainly many, perhaps most—people in Languedoc clamored for the punishment of heretics and their sympathizers. Nevertheless, the penalties the inquisitors inflicted cannot be understood simply as the inevitable consequences of an offended *conscience collective*, for there was no such unified, monolithic moral order in medieval Languedoc. Indeed, the inquisition existed precisely because the collective consciousness of medieval Languedoc was contested terrain. The Catholic Church and its heretical opponents were engaged in a desperate struggle over the moral constitution of society, a contest that turned on such issues as the relation of the divine to the mundane, the spirit to the flesh, and divine authority to worldly power. Some Languedocians may have hated and loathed those punished by the inquisitors as enemies of God and everything decent, but others saw them as martyrs and saints.

It makes more sense to think of the inquisitors' punishments within a Gramscian problematic: as part of a struggle to impose a cultural and spiritual hegemony on the masses of Languedoc, to win their active assent to the myths that justified the existing distribution of power and authority.[14] The inquisitors may not have been the agents of an outraged collective consciousness, but they were the agents of an outraged ruling bloc. In punishing heretics the inquisitors were not applying sanctions for violating a nonexistent *conscience collective*;

---

[13] Gui, *Practica inquisitionis*, pp. 217–18.
[14] Gramsci, *Prison Notebooks*, pp. 12–14, 244.

instead, they were striving to create such a collective consciousness. They sought to impose their own moral order on a social formation many of whose members were actively opposed to their vision of the right ordering of the world and mankind's relation to the divine. To use James C. Scott's formulation, in punishing heretics and their supporters they were elaborating and defending a public transcript, that is, a rulers' vision of the nature of social, ethical, and power relationships within their society.[15] To accomplish this end, the inquisitors acted as though their penitential system were a species of theater. The imposition of punishment was a performance in which the church's official version of correct spiritual order was acted out in a grandiose and impressive public fashion. The subjects of this performance were as much the members of the audience as they were the people whom the inquisitors sentenced.

In medieval Europe both trials and the infliction of punishment were public occasions, spectacles open to everyone. Inquisitorial trials, however, were secret. Hence most of the work of conveying meaning and reaffirming the values maintained by the church fell on the actual ceremony at which punishment was imposed. At times the inquisitors passed sentence on only one or two individuals in private or semiprivate circumstances; but for the most part they handed out large numbers of sentences on grand occasions, known as *sermones generales*. On 23 April 1312, for example, Bernard Gui imposed sentences on 194 people; he also commuted fourteen previously imposed penances.[16] To enhance the propaganda effects of these general sermons, the inquisitors took care to arrange for impressive and well-attended ceremonies. Gui in his *Practica* devoted considerable attention to describing how to conduct a *sermo generalis*. Once a sufficient number of trials had been concluded and the inquisitor had consulted a council of legal and religious experts on appropriate penalties, he set the date for the sermon on a feast day and summoned the people to attend. The sermon itself was held at a local church or other place suitable for a large gathering. At Toulouse most sentences were imposed at the cathedral of St. Etienne.

When the appointed day arrived, the inquisitor, true to his Dominican vocation, began the proceedings by delivering a sermon. He then received oaths from royal officials, town consuls, and other individuals possessing temporal jurisdiction, all of whom swore to aid the inquisitors in persecuting heretics and their sympathizers. Before the inquisitor imposed sentences on those who had been found guilty, he commuted the penances of people who had previously been condemned. First, those who had been required to wear crosses were allowed to lay them aside. Then those who had been condemned to prison,

---

[15] Scott, *Domination and the Arts of Resistance*, pp. 2–5.
[16] This was the largest number of people Gui dealt with in any *sermo generalis*. But it was not uncommon for him to sentence scores of people at a time. On 25 May 1309 he sentenced 91 people; on 5 April 1310, 110; on 7 March 1316, 74; on 30 September 1319, 160; and on 12 September 1322, 152.

ostensibly for life, were released on condition that they wear crosses, undertake penitential pilgrimages, and perform a number of other pious acts. The message that this action conveyed was that the church was a truly merciful and compassionate mother.

The inquisitor then began the lengthy process of passing sentence on those newly condemned. The inquisitor had previously had drawn up a list of the *culpe*, or faults, of each of those to be sentenced. These lists specified the nature of the condemned's involvement with heresy, stating, for example, how many times he or she had seen Cathar Good Men, heard their preaching, eaten bread blessed by them, received them at home, and so forth. Although composed in Latin, the *culpe* were read out in the vernacular. Not only did this performance justify the punishments imposed by the inquisitors, it also reinforced and restated the nature of orthodoxy. By specifying exactly what illegitimate belief and practice were, the *culpe* firmly circumscribed the sphere of legitimate, orthodox belief and practice. In effect, the reading of these lists of faults was a pedagogic tool. Those in attendance should have gone away from the day's proceedings with no doubt as to what was, and was not, acceptable belief.

Once the *culpe* had been read, those to be sentenced abjured their heresies and swore to obey the church and the inquisitors. The inquisitor then lifted the excommunication they had incurred as a result of their heretical acts. Finally, he proceeded to the imposition of sentences. These were proclaimed first in Latin and then in the vernacular. Gui's practice was to have these read out in a particular order. First he imposed penitential pilgrimages, next the wearing of crosses, and, third, perpetual imprisonment. He then dealt with people who were deceased. The names of those individuals who would have been imprisoned had they lived were announced. As punishment for their errors, their property was confiscated. Then came sentences ordering the "simple" exhumation of those who had been guilty of heretical dealings but had not confessed during their lifetime. The next group Gui sentenced were those who had received the Cathar *consolamentum* on their deathbeds or who had been demonstrated to have died impenitent. The remains of these individuals were not merely exhumed but also burned.

Gui then returned to the living. First he declared excommunicated those who had fled his jurisdiction. And then he imposed the most draconian sentence in his arsenal, relaxation to the secular arm, which meant death at the stake. The first to be sent to the flames were individuals who had relapsed, that is, people who had previously admitted and abjured their errors only to return to them. These people, even if penitent, were handed over to the secular authorities for execution. The next group sent to the fire were the elite members of the various heretical sects—Cathar Good Men, Waldensian priests, and so on—who refused to recant their errors. The last group destined for the stake were those who had confessed, recanted their testimony, and, despite their guilt having been proved by other means, contumaciously persisted in maintaining their innocence. If need be, the inquisitor then excommunicated those fugitives who had refused to answer his citations and fled, but who had not received a definitive sentence terminating their process. Finally, he decreed the destruction of those houses where individuals had received the Cathar *consolamentum*.[17]

Many of the inquisitors' punishments had a highly public, theatrical character. The destruction of houses and their conversion into garbage dumps were intended as perpetual reminders of the fate that awaited heretics. False witnesses who had sought to entrap the innocent with concocted denunciations were, before being imprisoned, exhibited on scaffolds with red tongues affixed to their clothing. Most of those who repented of their heresies and sought reconciliation with the church did not have to endure such intense public humiliation; but the punishments they received were nevertheless eminently public and even more protracted. The yellow crosses affixed to the clothing of many penitents were a concrete, constantly visible sign of both the high cost of involvement with heresy and the merciful nature of the church. And the penitents trudging the roads of western Europe on their compulsory pilgrimages were a dramatic reminder, even to those outside Languedoc, of the ever present danger of heresy.

The most memorable punishment, and that most laden with terror and meaning, was, of course, the burning of relapsed or unrepentant individuals. But sentences to the stake were relatively rare. Between 3 March 1308 and 19 June 1323, Bernard Gui imposed these capital sentences at eleven *sermones*. The largest number he consigned to the flames at a single time was the seventeen Cathars executed on 5 April 1310. All told Gui sent forty-one people to the stake. Less striking than the burning of the living, but still theatrical, were the sentences executed on the cadavers of the deceased. On three occasions Gui ordered the simple exhumation of deceased heretics and their sympathizers. Sixty-six of his sentences, however, involved exhumation and burning.

Executions were dramatic and memorable events. They could form the subject of intense discussion for some time afterward.[18] For example, on 1 May 1320 the Waldensian Raimond de la Côte was burned at Pamiers. The next day his death came up in conversation between a group of people in a tavern in the town of Foix. One man observed that the bishop of Pamiers had deeply regretted having to send Raimond to the stake, since he had been a good cleric. These words prompted one Bérenger Escoulan to say that this was precisely why he had been burned; it was his criticism of the clergy that had earned him a death sentence. Some of the other drinkers pointed out that Raimond had professed heretical ideas, maintaining that it was a sin to take an oath or to condemn men to death. To this Bérenger replied that he agreed with Raimond. As a result of

---

[17] Gui's description of a *sermo generalis* is in *Practica inquisitionis*, pp. 82–86.
[18] See, for example, Doat, 25: fols. 41v–42r, for a conversation concerning a cleric burned for heresy at Toulouse in the early 1270s (testimony of Guillemette, wife of Thomas de Saint-Flour of Toulouse).

these intemperate utterances, Bérenger found himself arraigned four days later before Bishop Fournier. Ultimately he was sentenced to the *mur*.[19]

## THE SPECTACLE OF PUNISHMENT:
## A CONTESTED PERFORMANCE

Many of those present at the *sermones generales* interpreted the day's events in ways that would have pleased the inquisitors. The crowds that attended these great occasions contained many people who had come not merely to witness a ghastly show but to gain instruction about why heretics were being punished.[20] After observing how the condemned behaved, some witnesses went home convinced of the correctness of the inquisitors' actions. For example, Pierre Tort of Montréal attended the execution of a number of Béguins at Pézenas. Because they bore their punishment badly and said many unpleasant things to the inquisitor and the assembled bishops, he decided that they were indeed heretics.[21]

The conclusions drawn by those who attended a *sermo* were not, however, always those the inquisitors intended. After listening to the inquisitor's sermon, hearing the *culpe* and sentences read, and watching how the condemned conducted themselves, many people were convinced that the heretics were right and the inquisitors wrong. This seems especially to have been a problem when Spiritual Franciscans and Béguins were sent to the stake. For example, Pierre Espeyre-en-Dieu, a weaver of Narbonne, was present at the cemetery of St. Felix in Narbonne when two Béguins were burned. Before they were executed, a friar named Bernard Maurini preached a sermon on the subject of their condemnation. Evidently he tried to portray the condemned as pigheaded men who were dying for no good reason. At one point he proclaimed, "These men wish to be burned for barley and for the color brown; these married men are very badly informed."[22] When Pierre heard these words, he thought to himself that it was a

---

[19] *Registre*, 1: 169–73. His release from imprisonment is recorded in *LS*, p. 294. Guillaume Austatz of Ornolac also found himself in trouble for praising Raimond de la Côte. See *Registre*, 1: 200.

[20] Raimond de Buxo of Belpech, a member of the Franciscan Third Order, having taken care to disguise himself, frequently attended the sermons at which Béguins were condemned "to discover what was done or said against the Béguins" (*LS*, p. 301).

[21] Ibid., p. 328. Pierre, a member of the Franciscan Third Order, made a habit of attending the executions of Béguins. How they died determined his view of their orthodoxy. Because the Béguins he had seen executed at Béziers conducted themselves well, he believed them to be martyrs and saints. Concerning the Béguins who had been burned at Narbonne, as well as those executed at Capestang and Lunel, however, he was uncertain as to whether or not they were saved, since he had not been present. Those burned at Narbonne and Pézenas he believed to be heretics, since they had behaved badly.

[22] Doat, 28: fols. 250r–v: "Item, quando frater Maduis, et P[etrus] de Fraxino fuerant condemnati in cimiterio sancti Felicis Narbonae, ipse loquens interfuit. Et a longe audivit frater [sic] Bernardum Maurini tunc praedicantem. Et inter caetera ab eo intellexit haec verba, 'Pour ordi, et pour brun se voulent lassar cremar; aqueste gent marida sont bien mal estrut.'" The meaning of the words that Pierre thought he heard is not altogether clear. However, the preacher was probably referring to the disputes about the type of habit to be worn by the Franciscans and whether

great evil to put good men to death for nothing more than this. He left the cemetery convinced that the Béguins had been treated unjustly.[23] Nor was Pierre the only one to come away from a *sermo* feeling that the inquisitors had acted contrary to justice. Bernard Durban of Lodève was present when his sister Esclarmonde, together with several other Béguins, was burned at Lunel. When her sentence was announced, he could not clearly hear what was said because of the noise of the crowd; but he later learned that she had asked that her confession be read out, a request that the inquisitors refused. Mulling this over, Bernard came to have grave doubts about whether his sister had been justly punished.[24]

How the condemned endured the flames was closely observed. The fortitude displayed by some could make a very favorable impression. When the Waldensian Raimond de la Côte was executed in 1320, people noted with approval that when the flames burned through the cords binding his hands, he joined them together as though in prayer.[25] Bérenger Jaoul, who attended the execution of some Béguins at Lodève, was similarly impressed by the manner of their death. He later told one Maneta Rosa that they had endured their punishment patiently, neither crying out nor even uttering a single word. All in all, he said, it had been "a most beautiful thing to see."[26]

The inquisitors were curiously uninterested in or incapable of policing the execution grounds. Perhaps the fact that they technically did not carry out executions, but entrusted them to secular authorities, played a role in this lackadaisical attitude. Once heretics had been executed, onlookers were free to treat the remains rather as they pleased. Sympathizers with the Béguins burned in the early decades of the fourteenth century were especially interested in acquiring relics of individuals they regarded as holy martyrs and blessed saints. Many a grisly scene was enacted around what remained of their bodies. For example, the morning after a number of Béguins were burned at Lunel a crowd descended on the place of execution. Several of the charred corpses were still relatively intact. Martin Alegre of Clermont-l'Hérault, together with some others, found Esclarmonde Durban's cadaver. They pulled it apart, putting the pieces into sacks. Martin himself made off with a hunk that he thought was either a heart or a kidney.[27]

The pieces of bone and flesh scavenged from execution sites were venerated as holy relics. Bérengère, wife of Guillaume Dominique Veirerii of Narbonne, carried around in a purse a small bone of one of the Béguins burned

---

the friars could keep considerable stores of food in their granaries or cellars. See Moorman, *A History of the Franciscan Order*, pp. 311–17.

[23] Doat, 28: fols. 249v–50v.

[24] Ibid., fol. 12v.

[25] *Registre*, 1: 169.

[26] Doat, 27: fols. 81r–v: "pulcherimum [sic] erat hoc videre."

[27] Doat, 28: fols. 16r–v. The piece of Esclarmonde that Martin made off with was possibly the heart seen at Clermont-l'Hérault by Bernard Peirotas, a priest of Lodève, who was condemned in July of 1323 (fol. 22r).

at Narbonne.[28] Some people were very assiduous in acquiring such relics. Raimond de Niaux of Cintegabelle and his wife Bernarde, both condemned to the *mur* in July 1322, managed to build up a respectable collection, including an assortment of bones and ashes of Béguins burned at Béziers and Lunel. They also acquired a piece of the wood to which either Brother Maduis or Brother Pierre de Frayssenet had been bound when executed. These objects were kept in a pyx, which was stored in Bernarde's chest. From time to time they took these relics out and kissed them. But their trove of sacred treasures was modest compared to the cache they had seen in an unnamed person's house in Narbonne. This individual had acquired the complete head of a woman burned at Lunel (to which was still attached part of the neck, shoulders, and chest), as well as parts of the shins and some other bits.[29]

These macabre stories demonstrate, if nothing else, the inadequacy of a Durkheimian interpretation of inquisitorial punishments. The penalties handed down by the inquisitors were not an expression of an outraged collective consciousness; rather they were a weapon in an ongoing, and hotly contested, ideological struggle. The inquisitors, while ostensibly punishing infractions of a universal and unchanging moral order, were actually trying to impose the sectional moral vision of a dominant elite on an often recalcitrant social formation. Their punishments had as much to do with theater and propaganda as they did with justice or the reconciling of wayward souls.

## PUNISHMENT AS A FORM OF MORAL REEDUCATION

Punishment has often been discussed under the rubric of social control. This interpretation is rather at odds with the Durkheimian conception of punishment that we have already encountered. For Durkheim, punishment had no real, positive effect on those punished. The ones actually affected by a transgressor's punishment were the members of the audience who witnessed the infliction of that punishment; the spectacle of suffering relieved their psychic distress over the infringement of the sacred norms of their society. The moral character of the person punished was, Durkheim maintained, not affected. Hence, for Durkheim punishment had no real deterrent value; it was merely the "professional risk of the delinquent career."[30] Modern societies, however, have generally attributed to punishment a more positive role in reconstructing the character of the sufferer. Since the eighteenth century, imprisonment has usually been regarded as a form of moral education, a therapeutic regime intended not merely to punish the offender but to reconstruct his character and prepare him for a productive life in the community.

---

[28] Ibid., fols. 121r–22r.
[29] *LS*, pp. 310–14.
[30] Durkheim, *Moral Education*, p. 162.

At first glance one might think that there are good grounds for believing that the inquisitors conceived of their system of punishments in just such terms. At the same time as the inquisitors were working out their penal system, church intellectuals were devoting much attention to the sacrament of penance, discussing its practical, legal, and theological aspects.[31] The punishments that the inquisitors decreed were, for the most part, conceived of as penances imposed on repentant sinners. But the situation is more ambiguous than one might at first expect. The place where the inquisitors exercised the most control over their penitents was in the confines of the *mur*. Unfortunately, it is very difficult to determine how many people were languishing at any one time in the inquisitorial prisons of Languedoc. Our best information on the size of the prison population comes from the mid-thirteenth century. For the period from 6 May 1255 to 6 February 1256, there survives an account that gives weekly totals for expenses incurred in housing prisoners at Toulouse (evidently in the prisons of Saint-Sernin and Saint-Etienne). I have summarized these data in figure 3.1. During these nine months the inquisitors incarcerated a large number of people. The smallest number of prisoners was the 85 recorded on 6 May (along with 2 infants); the largest the 219 prisoners (and 18 infants) recorded in January and February of 1256. The average number of prisoners during any one week was 171 (together with 11 infants).[32]

Information on the population of the *murs* at the end of the thirteenth and the beginning of the fourteenth centuries is not as detailed. However, royal accounts reveal that substantial numbers of people were in inquisitorial custody at that time (see figure 3.2). At Toulouse between July of 1293 and June of 1294 the weekly average of prisoners was 144.2; the average weekly total for the same period in 1298 and 1299 was 98.4.[33] In the autumn of 1310 the inquisitors of Toulouse were holding 113 people. Finally, in the late spring of 1322, there were 69 people lodged in the *mur* in Toulouse.[34] Our only information for the *mur* in Carcassonne comes from the year 1312, when there were a total of 162 prisoners there.[35]

Although the inquisitors conceived of imprisonment as a form a penance, the regime they maintained in the *murs* was certainly not that of the Benthamite panopticon. In part this may be due to the fact that inquisitors may not have had great expectations about the ability of imprisonment to effect positive changes in

---

31 On this see Little, "Les Techniques de la confession," pp. 87–99; Michaud-Quantin, *Sommes de casuistique* and "Textes pénitentiels"; Cazenave, "Aveu et contrition"; Delumeau, *L'Aveu et le pardon*; H. Martin, "Confession et contrôle sociale"; and Tentler, *Sin and Confession* and "The Summa for Confessors."

32 These figures are derived from Cabié, "Compte des inquisiteurs," pp. 215–17.

33 *Comptes royaux (1285–1314)*, 1: 465, no. 9703; 2: 559, no. 11754. The total expenses in 1298–99 for the immured were 42 l. 12 s. 10 d.t. I have assumed that the cost of feeding each inmate was 2 d.t. *per diem*, which was the allowance in 1293–94.

34 1310: ibid., 2: 205, no. 17175[2]; 1322: *Comptes royaux (1314–1328)*, 1: 84–85, no. 1348.

35 *Comptes royaux (1314–1328)*, 2: 237–41, nos. 15056–93.

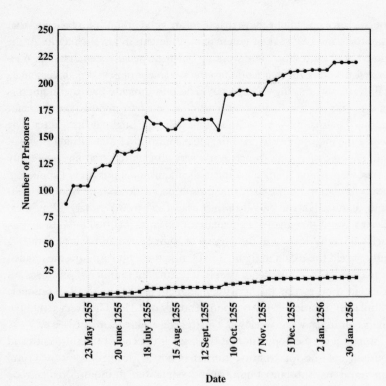

**Figure 3.1  Prisoners at Toulouse, 1255–56, Weekly Totals**
Source: E. Cabié, "Compte des inquisiteurs," pp. 215–17.

their charges' character. Though Bernard Gui has much to say about the way in which incarceration could be used to extract useful information from suspects, he has almost nothing to say about its possible effect on the moral rehabilitation of those sentenced to the *mur*. His few comments are no more than echoes of the provisions of the Council of Toulouse of 1229, which decreed that heretics who converted from the fear of death should be imprisoned to keep them from corrupting others.[36] All in all, the inquisitors seem to have given little thought to the rational organization either of the space in which their prisoners were housed or the time they passed in that space. Some prisoners were detained under vary harsh conditions, bound in shackles, fed on bread and water, and kept in a form of solitary confinement. Most, however, seem to have enjoyed a more congenial

---

[36] Gui, *Practica inquisitionis*, pp. 183, 220. The decree of the Council of Toulouse is in Mansi, 23: col. 196.

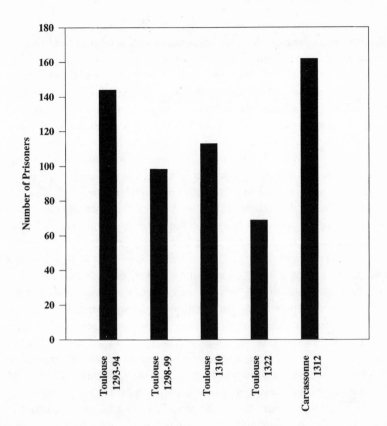

**Figure 3.2** Prisoners in Inquisitorial *Murs*
Sources: *Comptes royaux (1285–1314)*; *Comptes royaux (1314–1328)*.

regime. Indeed, some of the descriptions we have of life in the inquisitorial pris-ons make them sound like the freewheeling jails of eighteenth-century England, where prisoners were largely allowed to construct their own social world.[37] Prison warders were often amiably corrupt. In 1282 Jean Galand, the inquisitor of Carcassonne, felt compelled to instruct the guardian of his *mur* to refrain from exchanging gifts with and making loans to the prisoners and from eating and playing with them.[38] Our best information on prison life comes from Jacques Fournier's register. The bishop's prisoners were housed in a royal prison, the Tour des Allemans.[39] Although it is hazardous to generalize from conditions

[37] See Sheehan, "Finding Solace in Eighteenth-Century Newgate."
[38] Doat, 32: fols. 125r–26r; printed in C. Molinier, *Inquisition*, p. 446 n. 1.
[39] Benad, *Domus und Religion*, p. 51.

in this lockup to those in the *murs* operated by the Dominican inquisitors, nonetheless—given the paucity of our information—it is worth examining the regime maintained in the Tour. Conditions seem to have been rather anarchic. Among those held during the investigation of his conduct was Bernard Clergue of Montaillou. The terms of his detention were sufficiently lax as to allow him ample opportunity to scheme about how to secure the release of himself and his brother, the parish priest of Montaillou, also under arrest but detained elsewhere. Thanks to the gift of four fleeces to one of the prison warders, a man named Garnot, Bernard was allowed to do "whatever he wanted." Garnot's wife, Honors, even gave him a set of keys, so that he could move around at will in the tower, visiting those sentenced to immuration as a punishment for their heretical dealings and busily threatening and cajoling his fellow inmates.[40]

The most striking feature of life in the inquisitorial prisons was its largely unstructured nature. The inquisitors seem to have made virtually no effort to establish a special penitential regime. Unlike prison authorities in early modern and modern Europe, they set up no system of labor. If prisoners worked, they did so of their own volition and on their own schedule.[41] Even more surprising is the lack of any special program of religious education or indoctrination. The *murs* had chapels attached to them, but we do not know much about what went on in them. On at least one occasion, in 1279, an inquisitor, Hugues Amiel, gave a talk (whether it was a sermon is unclear) in the chapel attached to the *mur* of Carcassonne. According to Bernard de Lagarde, a prisoner who was present, Hugues's message was more pragmatic than spiritual. He promised the members of his audience that they would be spared any additional penalties if, within a specified time, they added to their previous confessions.[42] On the whole, religious devotion seems largely to have been a matter of personal choice. The priest Barthélemy Amilhac, for example, during his stay in the Tour des Allemans made his own decisions about when to say his hours and when to fast.[43] Even those sentenced to the *murum strictum* do not seem to have been too closely supervised. Guillemette Tornier of Tarascon, imprisoned "in the *mur's* strict prison" (*in stricto carcere muri*) at Carcassonne in the early fourteenth century, was, thanks to a hole in the wall, able to carry on a lively discussion concerning the merits of the Cathars with the apostate monk Arnaud Majer.[44]

Aside from lodging men and women in separate rooms, no effort was made to keep the sexes apart.[45] Similarly, no effort was made to segregate prisoners awaiting trial from those who had already been condemned. Prisoners who were

---

[40] *Registre*, 2: 277–90; the quotation is from p. 289.
[41] Like Alazaïs Faure of Montaillou, who passed some of her time spinning wool into yarn; ibid., 2: 287.
[42] Doat, 26: fol. 49r.
[43] *Registre*, 2: 283.
[44] Doat, 28: fols. 132r–v.
[45] *Registre*, 2: 278.

under investigation were allowed access to those who had been tried, condemned, and sentenced to immuration.[46] However, at times the prison authorities restricted free access of visitors to prisoners.[47] Writing at the end of the fourteenth century, Nicholas Eymerich noted that inquisitors should be suspicious of the sincerity of penitents who during the initial stages of their investigation doggedly clung to their errors. Such people were rarely genuine converts to orthodoxy. Therefore they should be imprisoned, for life if necessary, to prevent them from infecting others. For the same reason visitors should be restricted. Prisoners should not be allowed visits either by women, who are "weak, and easily perverted," or by simple individuals. Only Catholic men, zealous for the faith and beyond all suspicion of heresy, should have access to them.[48]

Eymerich's Languedocian predecessors may have shared his suspicions about the genuineness of their prisoners' conversion. Yet they seem to have done little to restrict visiting privileges.[49] Spouses had the right to visit their mates.[50] Even visitors who the jailers should have known were suspicious characters had little trouble gaining access to the *murs*. For example, on 2 November 1321, Bernard Clergue, who was under investigation for heresy, was released on surety from the Tour des Allemans. That evening he returned to the prison. He went up to the tower's galleries to find the priest Barthélemy Amilhac, to whom he gave an overtunic. He also walked about in the galleries, saying in a booming voice that could be heard throughout the prison,

> Everyone, however many there are of you, can take an example from me and my brother the priest. Although he was under arrest for a year and three months, nothing came out of his mouth that could harm someone else. And I . . . stuck it out here from last Pentecost; nevertheless, nothing came out of my mouth by which I or someone else could be injured. . . . When I was here, I used to send to my home for ten, or twenty, or thirty sous, and they were immediately sent to me, which would not have happened if the count of Foix had possession of my property. If I had shot off my mouth like Arnaud Cuculli or Arnaud de Savinhan, who are here below, I would not have had as good a *pension* from my house as I have had, because the count of Foix has not given to those immured as good a *pension* as I have had.[51]

---

[46] Ibid., 2: 279–80.

[47] Ibid., 2: 355.

[48] Eymerich, *Directorium inquisitorum*, p. 507.

[49] See, for example, *Registre*, 3: 72.

[50] Doat, 31: fols. 155v–68r (letter of archbishop of Narbonne and other Languedocian prelates to the inquisitors, probably in 1244, printed in *Documents*, 2: 126 n. 1), and 132v–33r (letter of archbishop of Narbonne to inquisitors in his province, 1246).

[51] *Registre*, 2: 289; MS 4030, fol. 177d: "'Omnes quotquot estis potestis accipere exemplum in me et in fratre meo capellano, qui cum per unum annum et per tres menses captus staterit [sic], non exivit aliquod malum per os eius unde alicui persone malum evenire posset. Ego etiam, ut

All in all, it appears that the inquisitors took few concrete steps toward creating a prison regime that would actively reshape a penitent's character and imprint within it a new set of values or behavioral norms.

## PUNISHMENT AS SOCIAL CONTROL

The inquisitors' penal system may not have done much to reshape the character of those who passed through it, but it did function rather well as a form of social control. Once an individual was caught up in the inquisitorial net, it was very hard to escape. The inquisitors kept tabs on their "clientele," often for decades. For most culprits who appeared before a medieval judge, their punishment was a onetime thing. Afterward, their dealings with the tribunal were over, until they committed another offense. This was not the way of the inquisitors, who operated something akin to a parole system. Those who cooperated with the inquisitors could look forward to a relaxation of their sentences. The inquisitors also kept track of them for any signs of feigned penitence or backsliding. The result was that those found guilty of involvement with heresy could expect to reappear time and again at *sermones generales*. Of the 637 individuals recorded in Bernard Gui's register, 178 appeared before him twice, and 46 three times.[52] Also, penitent heretics were not infrequently called on to give depositions against others suspected of heresy. All in all, this extended supervision over convicted offenders was without parallel in medieval Europe.

The inquisitors' flexible system of punishments allowed them to create a new social grouping, that of the penitent heretic or heretical sympathizer. This was a readily identifiable and manipulable subgroup. Its members, once they had passed through the hands of the inquisitors, were not simply reintegrated once-and-for-all into the society of the faithful: they were marked out and set apart from everyone else. This separation was made most dramatically manifest by the physical symbols that many had to wear. Almost all those convicted of heresy but not imprisoned had to wear yellow crosses on their clothing. The vertical arm of these crosses was 2 and one-half palms high while the transverse arm was 2 palms wide. The thickness of each branch of the cross was 2 and one-half fingers. One cross was worn on the chest and one on the back between the shoulders. False witnesses also had to wear red tongues.[53] These symbols were not to be laid aside, indoors or out, or obscured by other clothing. If during their trials suspects

---

dixit, steti hic a festo Penthecostes citra, et tamen per os meum nullum malum egressum fuit per quod ego vel aliquis alter possit dampnificari.' Et addebat: 'Quando ego stabam hic, ego mittebam ad domum meam pro X vel XX [Duvernoy reads XV] vel triginta solidis, et statim michi mittebantur, qui non fuissent michi missi si comes Fuxi bona mea habuisset. Quia si ego tantum extendissem os meum sicut extenderunt ipsum Arnaldus Cuculli et Arnaldus de Savinhano qui sunt inferius, non haberem ita bonam pensionem de domo mea sicut habeo, quia comes Fuxi non dabat aliis inmuratis ita bonam prebendam sicut ipse ha [sic] ipse habebat.'"

52 These figures do not count appearances before other inquisitors.

53 Lea, *Inquisition of the Middle Ages*, 1: 468.

committed perjury, a second transverse arm was added to the cross. Penitents were also required to present themselves at mass at their parish church on Sundays and feast days dressed in a minimum of clothing and carrying rods with which they were beaten by the priest before the assembled congregation.[54] Penitents were also obliged to attend all solemn church processions in similar garb and be scourged at their conclusion.

Those convicted of heresy almost never completed their term of penance. Even if released from prison and allowed to set aside their crosses, they remained ex-heretics or ex–heretical sympathizers. The inquisitors expressly reserved the right to impose new penances or reimpose old ones.[55] Penitent heretics thus entered a special, clearly defined, marginal social status. Marked out from their neighbors by readily apparent physical signs and subjected to public and degrading rituals, they could at any time be saddled with new and heavier forms of punishment.

The wearing of crosses seems to have been regarded as especially humiliating. In the early fourteenth century, at least, people punished in this fashion endured a fairly long period of public shame. Information in Bernard Gui's *Liber sententiarum* allows us to calculate how long 118 people wore their crosses. The mean period of cross wearing was 4.4 years (1,601 days), with the median and the mode both being 2.95 years (1,078 days). The shortest period was a little less than a year, 315 days, the longest 13.3 years (4,858 days). Those marked with crosses seem to have offered a convenient target for abuse and derision. By the 1320s the humiliating treatment of cross-wearers had become such a significant problem that it prompted the archbishop of Narbonne, his suffragans, and the inquisitors to issue a solemn warning to the people of the province not to harass them.[56] Those marked with crosses often found it difficult to make a living. Arnaud Isarn of Villemur-sur-Tarn, for example, found himself forced to take to flight in order to survive. On 25 May 1309 Arnaud was sentenced to wear crosses and perform a number of pilgrimages as atonement for having seen the heretic Jacques Autier at his parents' house. He learned to his sorrow that his punishment made it almost impossible to find work. Finally, after about a year, driven to desperation, he cast aside his crosses while in the town of Gaillac and fled to Moissac. There he became a boatman on the ships traveling up and down the Garonne between Moissac and Bordeaux. For about ten years he managed to keep his past a secret. During this time he was excommunicated in absentia and declared a heretic by the inquisitors. Finally, in June 1321 Arnaud was apprehended at Moissac. While being conveyed to Toulouse, he escaped. But he was recaptured a little before Christmas and lodged in the *mur* at Toulouse. His

---

[54] See the formula in Gui, *Practica inquitionis*, pp. 37–39.

[55] *LS*, 1, 9, 13, 32, 40, 45, 78, 97, 117, 158, 177, 182, 191, 202, 213, 218, 229, 244, 267–68, 295–96, 298, 332, 338, 341, 347, 364.

[56] Doat, 27: fols. 108r–9r.

laying aside of his crosses and his flight from the inquisitors ultimately earned him a sentence of perpetual imprisonment.[57]

The forced adoption of an inferior, degraded social status was a fate not limited to ex-heretics in medieval Europe. Jews and lepers were experiencing similar stigmatization in the twelfth and thirteenth centuries.[58] But the inquisitors both created a stigmatized social group and enlisted its members in the task of repressing heresy. It was not uncommon for ex-heretics and their sympathizers to enter the employ of the inquisitors.[59] Raimond Gros, a Cathar Good Man whose conversion to orthodoxy in 1236 did much to facilitate the work of the inquisitors of Toulouse, spent the rest of his days in the Dominican convent in that city.[60] Another member of this deviant underworld was Bernard de la Garrigue. During the 1260s he had been a Good Man.[61] When he fell into the hands of the inquisitors, Garrigue, unlike many Good Men, did not go to the stake; instead, he confessed, sought absolution, and became a minor functionary of the Carcassonne inquisitors. A similar case is that of Raimond Peyre, a less prominent and devoted heretic from the county of Foix, who had been a mere believer. As a result, he had spent some time in the early fourteenth century lodged in the *mur* at Carcassonne. After his release he occasionally worked for the inquisitors, delivering letters of citation in the county of Foix.[62]

The inquisitors not only used ex-heretics and their sympathizers as minor servants; they also tried to make them a tool with which to catch other heretics. Penitent heretics, as a condition of their absolution and reconciliation with the church, were required to promise to assist in the persecution of heresy. The inquisitors saw to it that this obligation was taken seriously. For example, Guillaume Bérenger of Arzens, who had been allowed to lay aside his crosses, was in 1254 ordered by the bishop of Carcassonne (who had established his own inquisitorial tribunal) to take them up once again for failing to secure the arrest of a fugitive he had chanced upon in the town of Limoux.[63]

[57] *LS*, pp. 350–51.

[58] On the Jews, see Langmuir, "Anti-Judaism" and "The Transformation of Anti-Judaism"; Baron, *Social and Religious History of the Jews*, pp. 96–106. On the lepers, Françoise Bériac, *Histoire des lépreux* and *Des Lépreux aux cagots*; and Moore, *Formation of a Persecuting Society*, pp. 45–60. The only general survey of the symbols that members of out-groups were required to wear seems to be the old monograph of Robert, *Les Signes d'infamie au Moyen Age*. See also Mellinkoff, *Outcasts*.

[59] An inquisitorial account from 1255 reveals that at least two former heretics were serving as *nuncii* for the inquisitors of Toulouse; Cabié, "Compte des inquisiteurs," p. 131. Four other "converted" heretics were also being supported by the inquisitors; ibid., p. 133.

[60] Pelhisson, *Chronique*, pp. 92–96. Gros may have returned to his Cathar faith. At least rumors circulated in the 1240s that he had sought to be hereticated just before his death. Doat, 22: fol. 102v (testimony of Guillaume Garsias, OP, 21 August 1247).

[61] Doat, 26: fols. 46r–v.

[62] *Registre*, 3: 426–27. For more information on Peyre, see Given, "Factional Politics in a Medieval Society."

[63] *Documents*, 2: 215–16.

The most valuable type of penitent was, of course, an elite member of one of the heretical sects, a Cathar Good Man or a Waldensian priest. These people were stuffed with incriminating information about large numbers of people, reaching back dozens, if not scores, of years. The conversion of a Good Man could touch off panic and a virtual frenzy of confession among his former believers. One of the greatest coups of the early days of the Languedocian inquisition was the unexpected conversion of the Good Man Raimond Gros, who had been active in the region around Toulouse for around twenty-two years. On the morning of 2 April 1236 Gros voluntarily presented himself at the Dominican convent in Toulouse. When word of his surrender spread, Cathar believers "were terror-stricken beyond measure."[64] The inquisitors, relying on Gros's information, issued citations to a large number of people. Many did not wait to be summoned but came forward out of fear of arrest. As the Dominican chronicler Guillaume Pelhisson noted, "The Lord then bestowed such favour upon the business of the faith that although the aforesaid Raymond was the one and only witness in many instances, no one challenged his word or contradicted him; on the contrary, a great many said, 'Masters, you may know it is all just as Master Raymond says it is'; and they even asked him to tell them what else should be said in their confessions, because he knew the whole truth."[65]

Most conversions of Good Men were not this spectacular. Yet those who converted often provided the inquisitors with important information. As one example, we can cite the case of Guillaume Raffard of Roquefort, who became a Good Man in the Lombard town of Sermione around 1271. He then returned to Languedoc to preach the Cathar faith. At one point, he was forced for a period of over a year to wander through the country supporting himself through begging, until he found shelter with a poor woman at Latrape.[66] When two years later he was discovered and arrested, he converted to Catholicism, providing his interrogators with much useful information.[67] Indeed, a few converts actively took on themselves the task of hunting down their former colleagues. One of the more interesting examples of this is provided by Raimond Baussan of Lagarde. Raimond had joined the Cathar exodus from Languedoc to Lombardy. After various adventures in Lombardy and Apulia, he found himself, probably in the middle of 1273, at Sermione near Verona. There he witnessed Bertrand Oliba, a Cathar bishop, perform the *consolamentum* on three brothers. He then left Sermione and went to Pavia. There, five weeks later, for reasons that unfortunately are not stated, he presented himself to the local inquisitor, Guillaume de Borga, and sought absolution. To demonstrate his fidelity to the Catholic

[64] Pelhisson, *Chronique*, p. 94 (translation from Wakefield, *Heresy, Crusade, and Inquisition*, p. 224).

[65] Pelhisson, *Chronique*, pp. 94–96 (translation from Wakefield, *Heresy, Crusade, and Inquisition*, p. 224).

[66] Latrape (Haute-Garonne) is a tentative identification for the manuscript's "Trapam."

[67] Doat, 26: fols. 12r–20r.

Church, he procured the arrest of two of his former associates in heresy, Raimond Papier and Pierre de Beauteville. With the permission of the inquisitor, and carrying his letters, Raimond returned to Languedoc to present himself at Toulouse in May 1274.[68]

The damage that a converted Good Man could do became a subject of acerbic commentary among Cathars and their sympathizers. When Bernard dels Plas, who had been a Good Man in the early 1240s, converted, it was said that he had destroyed the town of Gaja-la-Selve.[69] In the early 1270s one man told his acquaintances that those heretics who had converted were "killing the land and its people" by informing on their former believers.[70] In the first half of the thirteenth century the conversion of Cathar *perfecti* and *perfectae* was relatively common. Of the people who in the 1240s appeared before Bernard de Caux and Jean de Saint-Pierre, at least thirty-two were converted *perfecti*.[71] Before the beginning of the Albigensian crusades in 1209, Catharism had been a firmly established, aboveground sect, complete with establishments rather like convents. Indeed, around 1213 there had been about one hundred *perfecti* and *perfectae* living openly in Villemur-sur-Tarn.[72] During this late-twelfth- and early-thirteenth-century zenith of Catharism, it was not uncommon for rather young children—twelve, ten, or even seven years of age—to be induced to become *perfecti* or *perfectae*.[73] It is not surprising that under the pressure of the crusades and the inquisition, the vocation of many of these individuals proved fairly weak. Through the 1270s the inquisitors' records continue to give evidence of converted Good Men. Yet as Catharism became an underground, persecuted religion, only people of a determined and disciplined character were willing to assume the risks of being a Good Christian. In the last decades of Catharism's existence in Languedoc, it was very unusual for a Good Man to convert. Those who were apprehended readily went to the stake as martyrs.

In the late thirteenth and early fourteenth centuries the inquisitors therefore had more success in manipulating the supporters rather than the elite members of the various heresies. In return for a relaxation of their penalties, some heretical followers were willing to contract with the inquisitors to arrange the capture of their former associates. This was a sufficiently common occurrence for Bernard Gui to include in his *Practica* a formula for absolving from punishment someone who had procured the arrest of a heretic.[74] In the mid-thirteenth cen-

---

[68] Doat, 25: fols. 145r–46v.

[69] MS 609, fol. 125r.

[70] Doat, 25: fol. 48r: "interfecerunt terram, et gentes" (testimony of Guillemette, wife of Thomas de Saint-Flour of Toulouse, 4 April 1273).

[71] Information derived from MS 609.

[72] According to the former *perfecta* Bernarde Targueira, who in 1243 said that thirty years before she had stayed in this establishment at Villemur-sur-Tarn (Doat, 22: fol. 2r).

[73] For examples, see MS 609, fols. 20v, 70r, 114v, 143v, 161v.

[74] Gui, *Practica inquisitionis*, pp. 48–49.

tury Amblard Vassal was given license by sergeants in the employ of the inquisitors to consort with heretics and lure them to places where they could be captured.[75] In the early fourteenth century the inquisitors of Toulouse and Carcassonne occasionally released captives on the understanding that they would procure the arrest of suspected heretics or fugitives.[76] In 1305 Guillaume Pierre, a Cathar believer who had abandoned his beliefs, secured the arrest of the Good Men Jacques Autier and Prades Tavernier by luring them to Limoux under the pretext of administering the *consolamentum* to a dying woman.[77]

Unfortunately, what seems to have been the most spectacular example of a former heretical sympathizer laboring for the inquisitors is one about which we are not very well informed. Blaise Boyer, a tailor of Narbonne, had been an associate of the Spiritual Franciscans and the Béguins. In the 1320s he was interrogated by Germain d'Alanh, the episcopal inquisitor for the diocese of Narbonne. In return for a promise that he would not be subjected to any shameful penalties or lose any of his property, he agreed to become a heresy hunter. Armed with a letter from Jean Duprat, inquisitor of Carcassonne, he set off for the east. His travels took him to Sicily, Cyprus, and other places in the eastern Mediterranean. Eventually he returned home with testimonial letters from the inquisitors he had met on his travels. He also brought back an apostate friar, who had been a dabbler in the magic arts. This unfortunate he conveyed at his own expense to the *mur* at Carcassonne. In return for these services, he was in November 1328 given, as a mark of favor, an extremely light penance, requiring only a single pilgrimage to a church in the diocese of Nîmes.[78]

The inquisitors' penalties affected not only those they sentenced but also their descendants. These people, through no fault of their own, could lose their inheritances and be barred from public office. In hopes of escaping the consequences of their ancestors' deeds, some were willing to aid the inquisitors. An example is provided by Guillaume du Puy, a knight from the city of Albi. His father, Pons Bernard, had confessed to Brother Ferrier and sought absolution, sometime probably in the 1240s; however, he died before receiving a penance. His property was seized by the bishop of Albi and Philippe de Montfort, lord of the southern half of the Albigeois. His son Guillaume set out to recover his patrimony. At great expense he searched out heretics and fugitives. Ultimately his labor resulted in the arrest of two active Cathar believers, a deed that greatly assisted the work of the inquisitor Guillaume Raimond. In gratitude, Montfort and the bishop of Albi returned to Guillaume whatever of his father's property was in their possession, an act ratified in May 1264 by the inquisitor Pons du Poujet.[79]

[75] Doat, 25: fol. 186r. These events took place when Etienne de Gastine, active (according to *Documents*, 1: clxix–clxxii) between 1264 and 1276, was an inquisitor.
[76] For examples, see *LS*, pp. 34, 72–73, 258.
[77] *Registre*, 2: 57–58.
[78] Doat, 27: fols. 85r–v, 109v–11v.
[79] Doat, 31: fols. 292v–94v.

One of the more dramatic examples of the use which the inquisitors could make of disinherited heirs is the career of Arnaud Sicre. Arnaud was one of the children of Sibille den Baille, a fervent Cathar from the county of Foix. In the early fourteenth century she was convicted of heresy and burned at the stake; all of her property was confiscated and her children disinherited. Arnaud decided that he might be able to recover his inheritance if he could secure the arrest of a Good Man. A search south of the Pyrenees resulted in his discovery of Guillaume Bélibaste in the town of San Mateo. This Good Christian had escaped from the *mur* in Carcassonne and fled to the kingdom of Aragon for safety. Arnaud brought this information to the attention of Jacques Fournier. With the bishop's permission, he masqueraded as a heretical sympathizer and successfully infiltrated the group of Cathar exiles from Foix who had taken up residence south of the Pyrenees. Eventually Arnaud managed to lure Bélibaste into the diocese of Urgel, where he was arrested.[80]

The inquisitors' penal system is undoubtedly one of the most interesting facets of their work. Their punishments were, to be sure, part of a system of what we might call crime control. Yet to reduce their penal system to a mere mechanism designed to fulfill this purpose would be overly simplistic.[81] This system of punishment was also a means of communication. The great general sermons in which penances were decreed were striking occasions for propaganda, in which the inquisitors sought to teach the assembled crowds the nature of orthodoxy and heterodoxy. Through these grand and impressive ceremonies the inquisitors endeavored to make their own highly contested moral order dominant within Languedoc. This teaching function was also carried on in other venues and by other means. The pilgrimages and crosses imposed on penitent heretics provided a daily reminder of both the costs of heresy and the clemency of the church, a message vividly underlined by the public scourging of penitents on Sundays and feast days.

The inquisitors' penalties also constituted a system of social control. Once caught up in the inquisitorial machinery, a heretic or a supporter of heretics could seldom find a permanent exit from the system. Kept under the protracted surveillance of the inquisitors and subjected to degrading rituals that set the punished off from the rest of society, he or she became part of a permanent, marginalized social group. This creation of a clearly demarcated, easily manipulable out-group was in many ways one of the most impressive achievements of the inquisitors. Punishment in itself may seldom deter malefactors from their deeds, but it would be hard to deny that the inquisitors made intelligent and effective use of it in their work of repressing heresy.

---

[80] Arnaud Sicre's deposition is in *Registre*, 2: 20–81.

[81] I owe my insights about the larger purposes of punishment to Garland, *Punishment and Modern Society*, to which much of this chapter is heavily indebted. See especially pp. 18–22, 58–61.

# SECTION II

# RESPONSES TO
# THE INQUISITORS

T HE PREVIOUS SECTION has examined the Languedocian inquisition from the perspective of the inquisitors. The emphasis has been on the techniques of repression and coercion that they forged during their struggle against heresy. In a sense, the preceding chapters have told a familiar story. The twelfth and thirteenth centuries were a great age in the development of governing institutions. All across Europe governance was becoming the province of the bureaucrat and the professional. Everywhere office routines were being consolidated, archives created, and professional administrators recruited. The Languedocian inquisition was but one example of this phenomenon.

The exercise of power, however, is a dialectical process. Power is not simply the inevitable and automatic consequence of the deployment of ever more professional and well articulated bureaucratic forms of government. The impressive techniques of the Languedocian inquisitors were applied to a society that was anything but an inert and plastic mass. Medieval Languedoc was a complex and sophisticated social formation possessed of an intricate array of social and political organizations. To gain a full understanding of how the inquisitors operated, we must therefore examine how the people of Languedoc responded to their efforts.

The three chapters in this section attack this problem under what are essentially two headings. Two of the chapters are devoted to resistance: chapter 4 deals with its individual, covert forms and chapter 5 with collective, overt, and primarily violent resistance. Chapter 6 examines some of the ways in which Languedocians sought to exploit the resources of the inquisition to serve their own ends. Together, they seek to penetrate the shadowy world of nonelite politics. With some exceptions, this section deals not with the political practices of the ostensible masters of medieval society but with those of the subordinated groups within that society—that is, peasants, artisans, women, and so on. In the ideology of the rulers, these people were political ciphers, mere subjects whose political role was reduced to obedience and the provision of the material resources needed to support the existing array of power relationships. The political practices of these subordinate groups are today extraordinarily difficult to ascertain. The dominant elites were uninterested in them, and ordinary people were for the most part illiterate and hence incapable of leaving a direct record of how they conducted their political affairs. What we know about the political practices of the dominated must be painfully reconstructed from the often recalcitrant records generated by their rulers.

The question is made even more difficult by the fact that we shall often be examining practices that people fervently wanted to keep hidden. The chapters in this section concern what James C. Scott has called "the infrapolitics of subordinate groups," the "wide variety of low-profile forms of resistance that dare not speak in their own name."[1] By their very nature such forms of political activity depend for their effectiveness on disguise, secrecy, and anonymity. If successful, they leave almost no traces in the records. In the case of the Languedocian inquisition, we generally know only of acts of resistance and manipulation that failed, when the veil of secrecy and deception designed to delude the inquisitors was pierced, leaving resisters and manipulators fully exposed to their pitiless gaze. At the distance of seven centuries, it is impossible to fully penetrate this shadow world of resistance and manipulation, but enough can be learned to make our efforts, uncertain as they necessarily must be, worthwhile.

---

[1] Scott, *Domination and the Arts of Resistance*, p. 19.

# CHAPTER 4

# FORMS OF INDIVIDUAL
# RESISTANCE

**M**Y GOAL IN EXAMINING opposition to the inquisitors is not to offer a series of narratives of individual acts.[1] Instead, I will try to categorize the different forms that resistance to the inquisitors could take and to examine how that opposition was organized and conducted. A very simple way of categorizing resistance is to divide it into individual and collective. Since human beings seldom operate in true isolation, the boundary between these two forms is rather fluid; still, this rough-and-ready distinction is not without utility.

## THE ARTS OF EVASIVE DISCOURSE:
## SUSPECTS UNDER INTERROGATION

Concerning certain forms of individual resistance, we are very well informed. A central aspect of the medieval inquisitor's work was the questioning of frightened and reluctant witnesses. Over the years the inquisitors developed a great deal of insight into the ways in which heretics and their supporters sought to protect themselves while under interrogation. The fruits of their experience were passed on in the manuals that some of them wrote. Bernard Gui, drawing on the work often attributed to David of Augsburg, discussed extensively the ways in which various types of heretics sought to evade admitting their errors. But the most elegant treatment of the stratagems employed by heretics to avoid detection was that of the Aragonese inquisitor Nicholas Eymerich. In his *Directorium inquisitorum*, written at the end of the fourteenth century, he included an illuminating discussion of the "ten ways in which heretics seek to hide their errors." Although Eymerich was not Languedocian and his career falls outside the time frame with which we are principally concerned, he was shaped in the traditions first elaborated by his Occitanian colleagues. It is therefore worth quoting his discussion at length.

> The first way [of concealing their errors] is by equivocation. For example, if they are questioned concerning the true body of Christ, they reply concerning the

---

[1] Some incidents of opposition have received extensive treatment. See, for example, the discussions of the resistance movement led by Bernard Délicieux in Dmitrewski, "Bernard Délicieux," and Hauréau, *Bernard Délicieux*.

mystical body of Christ. For example, if it is said to them: "Do you believe that this is the body of Christ?," they reply, "I believe that this is the body of Christ." By this he means a stone that he sees there, or his own body, which is the body of Christ, meaning that all corporeal bodies are Christ's, since they are God's, and Christ is God. . . .

The second way of evading a question or misleading a questioner is by adding a condition. For example, if it is asked: "Do you believe in marriage according to the sacrament?," he replies, "If it pleases God, I certainly believe it to be so," understanding by this that it would not please God that he believe this. . . .

The third way of evading a question or misleading a questioner is through redirecting the question. For example, if it is asked: "Do you believe that the Holy Spirit proceeds from the Father and the Son?," he replies, "And what do you believe?" And when he is told, "We believe that the Holy Spirit proceeds from the Father and the Son," he replies, "Thus I believe," meaning, "I believe that you believe this, but I do not. . . ."

The fourth way of evading a question is through feigned astonishment. For example, if it is asked: "Do you believe that God is the creator of all things?," he replies with astonishment, and as if confused, "What else should I believe, should I not believe this?," meaning that he ought not so to believe. . . .

The fifth way of evading a question is through twisting the meaning of words. For example, if it is asked: "Do you believe that it is a sin to swear to tell the truth in court?," he replies, shifting the meaning, "I believe that he who tells the truth does not sin." He thus does not reply concerning the oath about which he was questioned, but about telling the truth, about which he was not asked. . . .

The sixth way of evading a question is through an open changing of the subject. For example, if it is asked: "Do you believe that after his death Christ descended into Hell?," he answers, "O my lord inquisitor! How much should everyone contemplate in his heart the fearful death of Christ! And I, a poor wretch, do not? For I am poor on account of Christ, and I have to beg for my food." And thus they switch to talking about their poverty, or that of Christ. . . .

The seventh way of evading a question is through self-justification. For example, if it is asked: "Do you believe that Christ ascended into heaven?," or something else concerning the faith, he replies, justifying himself, "O my lord, I am a simple man, and illiterate, and in my simplicity I serve God, and I know nothing about these questions, or these subtle matters. You can easily trick me, and lead me into error; for the sake of God, do not ask me about these things. . . ."

The eighth way of evading a question is through feigned illness. For example, if someone is interrogated concerning his faith, and the questions having been multiplied to the point that he perceives that he cannot avoid being caught out in his heresy and error, he says: "I am very weak in the head, and I cannot endure any more. In the name of God, please let me go now." Or he says, "Pain has overcome me. Please, for the sake of God, let me lie down." And, going to his bed, he lies down. And thus he escapes questioning for a time, and meanwhile thinks over how he will reply, and how craftily he will conduct himself. Thus they conduct themselves with respect to other feigned illnesses. They frequently use this mode of conduct when they see that they are to be tortured, saying that they are sick, and that they will die if they are tortured, and women frequently say that they are suffering from their female troubles, so that they can escape torture for a time. . . .

The ninth way of evading a question is by feigning stupidity or madness. For example, if they are questioned concerning the faith, fearing lest they be caught out in their errors through the efforts of the inquisitor, they act as if they were mad, and out of their minds, as did David before Achish, lest he be caught out. And thus, when answering questions, they laugh, and insert many irrelevant, ridiculous, and foolish words. They thus reveal their heresies and errors, but in such a way that they seem to say whatever they say in jest. This mode of behavior they frequently adopt when they realize they are going to be tortured, or handed over to the secular arm, in the hope that through such deceit they may avoid torture or escape death. I have had much experience with such people, who at times constantly act out of their minds, but at other times have lucid intervals. . . .

The tenth way of avoiding detection is through a way of life that is apparently holy. For heretics differ from the ordinary way of life of the faithful in their behavior, dress, and speech. For they commonly go about without shoes, or with only sandals. They wear cast-off clothes, some white, others brown, some only a cloak, others a long and broad undershirt. They do not use belts but ropes. Some wear drooping hoods; others have long hair, according to their sect. Some go about looking down at the ground; others with their faces raised to heaven. They speak words of humility and have the outer appearance of sanctity, like sepulchers that outside are gilded and whitewashed but inside are full of the cadavers of the dead. For within, in many cases, they are full of pride, wantonness, gluttony, *accidia*, and vainglory, as those who know them realize. Through this appearance of sanctity they mislead and deceive many people, and escape from the inquisitor's judgment.[2]

Although at the end of this passage Eymerich has evidently slipped from the realm of analysis into that of fantasy and propaganda, the rest of his description seems well grounded in reality. The archives of the Languedocian inquisitors provide material with which to illustrate several of his observations. More than one inquisitor encountered people who feigned illness or madness to escape condemnation. Pierre Dominici of Narbonne, a Béguin belonging to the Third

[2] Eymerich, *Directorium inquisitorum*, pp. 430–31.

Order of St. Francis, tried such a ploy on Bernard Gui. Pierre had originally been tried by the archbishop of Narbonne. At that time he had recanted his errors and been condemned to wear crosses. Once free of the archbishop's clutches, Pierre repented his weakness in renouncing his beliefs and laid aside his crosses. Ultimately, he fell into Gui's hands. After two months of questioning, he once again recanted his errors. As a relapsed heretic, the only fate he could look forward to was death at the stake. Perhaps to escape execution, he faked lunacy. Praising as holy individuals heretics whom the church had condemned, he composed a litany in which he inserted the names of some seventy heretics among the ranks of the holy martyrs, virgins, and confessors of the true church. He went about his prison in Toulouse reciting this litany, sometimes in a loud voice, sometimes in a low one. At one point he read his litany over in the presence of Gui himself. If this folly was calculated, it failed to save Dominici; he was relaxed to the secular arm on 12 September 1322.[3]

Prisoners simulated physical as well as mental illness. An example is provided by Jacquette Amorosa of Lodève, condemned at Carcassonne on 1 March 1327. Jacquette and her husband were sympathizers with the Béguins. Jacquette herself had given alms to a fugitive Béguin, Guillaume Serrallerii of Lodève. Although her husband was arrested and imprisoned, he managed through an intermediary to warn her not to confess. Thanks to an ailment that made her hard of hearing, she contrived for a long time to escape interrogation. When she was finally arraigned before the inquisitors, she continued to claim that she was afflicted by her hearing problem, underlining her point by bursting into tears.[4] In a similar but slightly different fashion, the old and inveterate opponent of the Carcassonne inquisition, Guillaume Garric, claimed that he could not clearly remember his involvement with heretical matters because of his advanced age.[5]

## THE INTIMIDATION OF WITNESSES

Eymerich's list of the wiles employed by deceitful heretics deals only with the behavior of those interrogated by the inquisitor. It is not hard, however, to find other types of individual resistance. Many people resorted to the simple expedient of threatening those who might testify against them. On 13 June 1245 Bernard Cogota of Le Mas-Saintes-Puelles, who had already testified to inquisitors on two other occasions, appeared before the inquisitors of Toulouse. He informed them that he had fled his home with his entire *familia* after hearing Pierre Gauta publicly say to the lord of Le Mas-Saintes-Puelles, "Bernard del Mas, is it a good thing that someone who may have denounced you goes about alive on the face of the earth?"[6] A similar example is provided

---

3 *LS*, pp. 383–86.
4 Doat, 28: fols. 233v–35r.
5 *LS*, p. 283.
6 MS 609, fol. 2v: "Bernarde del Mas, est ne bonum quod aliquis qui detexerit vos eat vivus super terram?"

by the testimony given to the same inquisitors by Pierre Terreni, originally of Fanjeaux but at the time of questioning a resident of Toulouse. He admitted that he had previously concealed from the inquisitor Brother Ferrier his knowledge of the involvement of Pierre Record and his family with the Cathars. He had done so because Pierre had told him he could lose his head if he did not keep his mouth shut.[7]

Some people preferred blandishments to threats. The deposition given on 12 January 1284 at Toulouse to the inquisitor Hugues Amiel by Bernard de Villeneuve-la-Comptal, *domicellus* of Pech-Luna, provides an interesting illustration. As a youth in the early 1250s, Bernard had often acted as a guide for the Cathar Good Men on their clandestine journeys through the Lauragais. Sometime around 1254–55 a knight named Pons de Villeneuve-la-Comptal contracted an illness from which he eventually died. His *bayle*, Adhémar de Bordes, sent Bernard to find a Good Man who could give the dying man the *consolamentum*, directing him to Pons Magrefort, a knight living in Gudas. In turn Pons sent Bernard to Pierre de Mas of Fajac-la-Relenque at Molandier. Pierre told Bernard to present himself the next evening at the mill at Bélesta. At the appointed time and place Pierre de Mas appeared, along with his brother Pons and two Good Men, Guillaume Raimond and Guillaume Alboara. Bernard then conducted them to his parents' home in Villeneuve-la-Comptal. Although the heretics remained there for some days, they never managed to hereticate the dying knight. A couple of years later Bernard, again acting as a guide, was present during a night meeting at Dreuilhe where he saw two heretics in the company of a number of people, including Guillaume Bermundi of Salles, who was staying with the witness's uncle. They all performed the ceremony known as the *melioramentum*; Guillaume then entrusted the heretics to Bernard, who guided them beyond Puivert.

A quarter of a century later, when the inquisitors were settling accounts with the heretical sympathizers of the Lauragais, people began to worry about what Bernard might have to say. Accordingly, Pons de Mas of Fajac twice sought Bernard out, once at Belpech and once at Pech-Luna, to ask him not to reveal what he knew about Pons's involvement with the heretics. Pons also offered Bernard some advice on how to conduct himself before the inquisitors: he should only denounce people from Fajac who had already been burned. Pons also promised to pay whatever expenses Bernard incurred during his trip to see the inquisitors. Guillaume Bermundi and Gausbert Olric, Guillaume's brother-in-law, also begged him not to reveal Guillaume's dealings with the heretics. When Bernard refused to promise this, they at first threatened him with death. But Gausbert thought better of this, later giving him forty sous in money of Tours on the understanding that he would conceal what he knew about Guillaume.[8]

---

[7] Ibid., fol. 166v.
[8] Doat, 26: fols. 73r–76r.

## FEIGNED COOPERATION

One of the paramount goals of the inquisitors was to lay hold of a member of the elite groups of the various heresies they persecuted—a Cathar Good Man or a Waldensian priest. To do so, they were willing to go to great lengths. A few people who had fallen into the inquisitors' hands exploited this desire in order that they themselves might escape from custody. For example, Pierre Bernier of Verdun-en-Lauragais, a Cathar believer whom Bernard Gui sentenced to be burned on 25 May 1309, apparently had been arrested and imprisoned in Carcassonne sometime in early 1305. There he promised the inquisitor that he would endeavor to secure the arrest of some heretics. He was released and, in the company of some of the inquisitor's agents, sent off to hunt down his former comrades. However, he gave his companions the slip, alerted the heretics, and took to his heels.[9]

Bertrand Raimond, a tailor of Saint-Papoul, made use of the same ruse. Bertrand was deeply involved with Catharism. His brother Pierre was a Good Man; Bertrand himself had spent some time in the Cathar zones of refuge in Lombardy. When he was arrested and imprisoned in the *mur* at Carcassonne, he secured his release by promising to search out and capture some of the heretics still at large. Then, as the sentence Bernard Gui imposed on him in absentia on 30 September 1319 put it, he not only failed to procure the capture of any heretics, but, like a dog returning to its vomit, he alerted those whom he was supposed to arrest and then escaped.[10]

Another man who tried to elude the inquisitors in this fashion was Pierre de la Salvetat of Prunet. Pierre had served as a guide for the Good Men Pierre Autier and Amiel de Perles. When he was arrested, he agreed to procure the arrest of Adhémar de Bannières, a Cathar believer whom the inquisitors believed might be able to lead them to the Good Man Pierre Sanche.[11] Persuaded by Pierre de la Salvetat's arguments, the inquisitors released him. Almost immediately, indeed on the evening of the very day he was set free, Pierre located Adhémar. However, instead of arresting him, he told him to escape. Adhémar got away, but Pierre was not so lucky; he was seized as he fled, and on 5 April 1310 he was condemned to perpetual imprisonment.[12]

A few years later Géraud de Vincendat of the Bordal del Forç de Pausadier in the Gascon parish of Laveraët tried a similar maneuver on Gui. A Waldensian sympathizer, he at first refused to reveal what he knew about heresy until he had been implicated by others, arrested, and detained in prison. In an effort to exculpate himself he claimed that he had kept silent because he wished to arrange for the capture of some Waldensian priests before making a full confession. Gui easily saw through this rather pitiful ruse. In concocting his tale, Géraud stated

---

[9] *LS*, p. 34.
[10] Ibid., p. 258.
[11] Ibid., p. 124.
[12] Ibid., pp. 72–73.

that he had intended to secure the arrest of the Waldensians through the agency of two sergeants. But as Gui discovered, one of these men had been dead for three years; the other had left Gascony two years earlier. When confronted with this information, Géraud admitted that he had made up his story in the hopes that he might somehow win his release.[13]

## PLAYING ONE INQUISITOR OFF AGAINST ANOTHER

The fact that there was no regionally unified Languedocian inquisition, but merely a set of independent tribunals—some run by Dominican inquisitors, some by local bishops in cooperation with the inquisitors—opened the possibility that suspects could play one tribunal off against another. When relations between inquisitors were strained, as Jean Duvernoy claims they may have been in the early 1320s between the Carcassonne inquisition under Jean de Beaune and the Pamiers tribunal under Bishop Jacques Fournier, the space for strategic maneuver could become relatively large.[14] The onetime *bayle* of Montaillou, Bernard Clergue, had been deeply involved in Catharism. This, however, did not prevent him from trying to use the inquisitors to destroy his enemies within the village. At one point he prevailed on a fellow villager, one Bernard Benet, to go to Carcassonne to inform the inquisitor that certain other inhabitants of Montaillou had been present at the deathbed heretication of Guillaume Guilhabert. When Guillaume Autier, Arnaud and Alazaïs Faure, and Alamande, the late Guillaume Guilhabert's mother, learned of this, they hastened off to Pamiers to deliver their own testimony to Bishop Fournier. They did so, as Alamande explained, in the belief that they would find greater clemency with the bishop than with the Dominican inquisitor in Carcassonne.[15]

The most manic, if not perhaps the most successful, example of individual resistance that we can find in the records consists of Bernard Clergue's efforts to save himself and his family. Among Bernard's many machinations was an effort to set one inquisitorial tribunal against another. For a long time Bernard and his brother Pierre, the priest of Montaillou, had been able to deflect attention away from their involvement with Catharism. However, their luck eventually ran out and they were both haled before the inquisitors. But Bernard was a tough and determined individual. During the two years that the bishop of Pamiers investigated his conduct, he clung obstinately to a strategy of admitting as little as possible.[16] Even when lodged in the prison of the Tour des Allemans, he made

---

[13] Ibid., p. 232.

[14] Duvernoy's reasons for suspecting strained relations between Pamiers and Carcassonne are given in his French translation of Fournier's register (*Registre*, 2: 518).

[15] *Registre*, 1: 424.

[16] All together, the proceedings against Bernard Clergue took up a little over three and a half years. The most active period of the investigation, when information was actually being collected against Bernard, lasted only a little over two years. See Benad's chronology of the proceedings against Bernard and Pierre Clergue in *Domus und Religion*, pp. 331–37.

good use of his time to browbeat and intimidate other prisoners who had testified against his family.[17] Bernard was particularly interested in getting Alazaïs Faure, one of his brother's former mistresses, to retract her testimony. Bernard wanted her not only to revoke the confession in which she had implicated Pierre, but also to tell Fournier that she had been prevailed on to perjure herself by an enemy of the Clergue family, Pierre Adhémar. If she did this, Bernard promised that he would bribe the guardian of the inquisitorial *mur* of Carcassonne to release Alazaïs's husband, who was a prisoner there.[18]

If Bernard's boastful words to his fellow prisoner, the priest Barthélemy Amilhac, can be believed, he also used his influence to get the inquisitor of Carcassonne to arrest the two men he regarded as the chief architects of the troubles that had befallen his family, Pierre Adhémar and Pierre de Gaillac. Furthermore, he claimed that he could ensure that the conditions of their imprisonment would be anything but pleasant: "Now they are arrested and put in an evil place; and they will not leave it, no matter how many friends they have; and I know this because Master Jacques, the guardian of the *mur* [of Carcassonne], is such a good friend of mine that it will go ill with those prisoners in the *mur* of Carcassonne."[19]

## FLIGHT

Some individuals made use of the rather obvious expedient of flight, which seems to have been relatively common. Of the 603 individuals sentenced by Bernard Gui during his period of service as inquisitor of Toulouse, 39 (6.5 percent) were at one time or another condemned in absentia. The register recording Jacques Fournier's inquisitorial work in the diocese of Pamiers gives evidence of an even greater propensity to flight. Of the eighty-eight living individuals against whom Fournier initiated proceedings, twelve (13.6 percent) were fugitives at one time or another.

Escape from the inquisitors may not have been too difficult. The inquisitors themselves had only a very small staff of full-time agents. To search out and arrest suspects they had to rely largely on the assistance of other jurisdictions. Both the competence and motivation of those called on to assist the inquisitors seem at times to have been limited. The unreliability of the inquisitors' assistants is revealed even in the midst of what otherwise seems to be a dramatic instance of inquisitorial power and authority. In the late summer of 1309, the inquisitor of Carcassonne carried out an arrest of virtually the entire population of the village of Montaillou.[20] Such mass arrests, although uncommon, were not unheard of;

---

[17] *Registre*, 2: 285, 290–94.
[18] Ibid., 2: 287–88.
[19] Ibid., 2: 281.
[20] I follow Benad in dating this event to the late summer of 1309, rather than to 1308 as do other historians; see his *Domus und Religion*, pp. 146–49, 328.

and they testify to just how heavily the hand of the inquisitors could lie on the Languedocian countryside. Nevertheless, the net that the Carcassonne inquisitor drew around Montaillou was fairly porous. Emersende Marty escaped through a very simple ruse. Early in the morning she balanced a loaf of bread on her head, picked up a sickle, and walked out of the village. When she encountered men who had been set to guard the passes in the hills around Montaillou, she told them that she was a stranger who had come to the village to help with the harvest. By means of this quickly improvised (and, it would seem, transparent) deception, she avoided arrest.[21]

Even after someone had fallen into the hands of the inquisitors, escape from custody does not seem to have been extraordinarily difficult. In the first decade of the fourteenth century, the custodians of the *mur* at Toulouse had considerable difficulty in maintaining effective security. In 1309 and 1310 eight men escaped.[22] April 1310 was a particularly bad month. On the 19th Guillaume Falqueti escaped; five days later, on the 24th, there was a mass breakout, when five prisoners made off.[23] After this escape, security was evidently improved. Nevertheless, one other person, Pierre Gilbert the elder of Ferrus, escaped—not from the *mur* itself but from the looser form of detention at the prison's gatehouse.[24]

Bernard Gui's register contains the story of a man who escaped from the inquisitors not once, but twice. This was Pierre Bernier of Verdun-en-Lauragais. As noted above, Pierre had been arrested by the inquisitor of Carcassonne in 1305. At that time he succeeded in getting loose by promising to help the inquisitors arrest some other suspects, an opportunity he used to flee. He was recaptured, this time by the inquisitor of Toulouse. On 13 March 1306 he confessed to his involvement with Catharism and abjured. Subsequently he once again escaped, this time from the *mur* in Toulouse, and returned to his association with the Cathar heretics. After being at large for about three years, he was arrested for the third time. Tried by Bernard Gui, who had no sympathy to spare for this relapsed heretic, he was handed over to the secular authorities to be burned on 25 May 1309.[25]

Of course, not all efforts to escape from inquisitorial prisons were successful. Sometime between April and September of 1319 Perrinus Faure, a Waldensian

---

[21] *Registre*, 1: 344.

[22] These escapes are recorded in *LS*. The escapees were Guillaume Falqueti of Verdun-en-Lauragais (pp. 13, 256), Raimond de Verdun-sur-Garonne (p. 14), Pierre Usabe of Verdun-en-Lauragais (pp. 19, 177), Bernard and Guillaume Aliguer of Mirepoix-sur-Tarn (p. 25), Hyspanus Faure of Vacquiers (pp. 29, 255–56), Pierre Bernier of Verdun-en-Lauragais (pp. 34–35, 77), and Raimond Bertric of La Rabinia (p. 261).

[23] Falqueti (ibid., p. 13), Raimond de Verdun-sur-Garonne (p. 14), Bernard and Guillaume Aliguer of Mirepoix-sur-Tarn (p. 25), Hyspanus Faure of Vacquiers (p. 29), and Raimond Bertric of La Rabinia (p. 261).

[24] Ibid., p. 127.

[25] Ibid., pp. 34–35. Gui's register also contains a reference to an individual, not sentenced by Gui, who escaped from the *mur* at Toulouse. This was Vital Sanche; pp. 42, 187.

sympathizer from Pallanne in the diocese of Auch, hatched an escape plot with some other prisoners in the *mur* at Toulouse. They acquired material with which to make a rope and a ladder, but their scheme was uncovered before they could execute it. Similarly, Barthélemy des Vignes, sentenced to the *mur* by Gui on 12 September 1322, was also apprehended trying to escape.[26]

Although flight was both a common and an obvious form of resistance, the vast majority of those tried by the inquisitors in the late thirteenth and early fourteenth centuries did not try to flee. It is therefore worth reflecting on the factors that went into the decision to become a fugitive. Running away from the inquisitors might save one from the stake or the *mur*, but it also meant surrendering one's wealth and social position. Thus much agonized thought was often required before a suspect decided to decamp, as we can see in the case of Béatrice de Lagleize of Varilhes, a member of the petty nobility of the county of Foix.

Béatrice had a great deal to answer for. At one time she had believed that the Cathar *perfecti* were good Christians in whose faith one could be saved. She had also dabbled in magic. In the spring of 1320 Jacques Fournier began taking testimony against her from various witnesses. Béatrice got wind of this and realized that she would undoubtedly be cited to appear. In a quandary as to what to do, she consulted her lover, Barthélemy Amilhac, a stipendiary priest at Mézerville. Amilhac came to Varilhes, where he spoke to Béatrice outside the town. Béatrice asked him whether, if she were summoned by the bishop, she should appear or flee. Barthélemy asked her if she felt herself guilty of anything that savored of heresy. To this Béatrice replied in the negative, telling Barthélemy that had she had any dealings with heresy, she would certainly have told him, since she loved him so passionately. Reassured, Barthélemy advised her to appear, since Bishop Fournier would undoubtedly deal fairly with her.[27]

Béatrice appeared before the bishop on 26 July 1320. At that time she denied any contacts with the Cathars. Fournier, unconvinced, ordered her to return on the 29th.[28] Béatrice was profoundly disturbed by her interrogation, especially by the fact that Fournier knew that her father had also been suspected of heresy. She bundled up her clothes, told one of her daughters that she intended to appear before Fournier on the 29th, and fled to Belpech in the diocese of Mirepoix. From there she sent for Amilhac. When the priest arrived and saw the large amount of clothing she had brought with her, he asked her what she was up to. Béatrice told him that Fournier had interrogated her about her beliefs concerning the Eucharist, her dealings with Pierre, Guillaume, and Jacques Autier (all Cathar Good Men), and her consultations with a witch. Frightened by all this, she had decided, despite what she claimed was her innocence, to flee to her sister in Limoux. Barthélemy was irate; he reprimanded her

[26] Ibid., pp. 231, 356.
[27] *Registre*, 1: 246.
[28] Ibid., 1: 216–17.

and told her she must testify. To this Béatrice replied that she would never go back to Pamiers, even if Fournier offered to give her the entire diocese. Barthélemy, before returning to Mézerville, where his presence was required for the celebration of the upcoming feast of the invention of St. Stephen, gave her some money. Evidently his resolve had been weakened by Béatrice's charms, for he also agreed that once the feast was over, he would conduct her to Limoux. Until then, he advised her to go to Le Mas-Saintes-Puelles, which he felt was an out-of-the-way place where no one would look for her.[29] Béatrice agreed and Barthélemy thereupon conducted her to Le Mas-Saintes-Puelles. However, he was wrong in his surmise that no one would look for Béatrice there. Within a few days agents of Bishop Fournier had tracked her down. She was arrested and returned to Pamiers on 1 August.[30]

More complex motives than a simple desire to escape the consequences of one's acts could also be at work. At least two people became fugitives out of concern for their children. These were Pierre Raimond Dominici of Le Born and his wife, Petrona. In 1309 they evidently came under suspicion of involvement with Catharism, for in that year Petrona made a deposition before the inquisitors. A year later she gave further testimony, at which time she apparently abjured all heresy. But when her husband was summoned to testify, the couple fled. Only after spending eleven years in hiding did they surrender to Bernard Gui. When they were asked why they had fled, they replied that they had done so out of fear that if they were imprisoned, their seven small children would die of starvation.[31]

In some cases people fled because they could not bear the social and economic consequences of the penances imposed on them. For example, sometime in the early fourteenth century one Bernard Servel, a blacksmith from Tarascon, was condemned to wear crosses. His wife, Asperta, was also given some form of penance. Since all of their property, including Asperta's house, was confiscated, they were reduced to penury. Because of his crosses, Bernard could find no one willing to hire him. Indeed, he felt that he was an object of universal mockery. He and his wife therefore decided to leave the county of Foix and go south over the Pyrenees. When they reached a pass leading into the kingdom of Aragon, Bernard removed his crosses and hid them. When Asperta told him that he would be punished if this was discovered, he assured her that he had put the crosses in a place where he could find them again if he ever crossed back into Foix.[32]

Whatever motives may have impelled someone to take to his or her heels, the decision was probably facilitated by the belief that flight could end success-

[29] Evidently Barthélemy was unaware that Le Mas-Saintes-Puelles had had a lengthy history of involvement with Catharism, 422 of its inhabitants having appeared before the inquisitors Bernard de Caux and Jean de Saint-Pierre (figure derived from MS 609).
[30] *Registre*, 1: 246–47. This is Béatrice's version of events. For Amilhac's version, which differs slightly, see pp. 256–58.
[31] *LS*, pp. 347–50. Both were sentenced to perpetual imprisonment on 12 September 1322.
[32] *Registre*, 2: 465.

fully. Until the middle of the thirteenth century, there were within Languedoc itself certain places where heretics could find safety; but with the destruction in the 1240s and 1250s of the Cathar strongholds of Montségur and Quéribus, the last local zones of refuge were eliminated. Thereafter anyone seeking safety from the inquisitors had to go into exile. In the late thirteenth and early fourteenth centuries the safest goal for fugitive Cathars was Italy, above all Lombardy, where there were large, active cells of Cathar *perfecti* and *credentes*. In the Lombard cities Languedocian exiles could find refuge, support, and religious instruction.[33] In the early fourteenth century, however, many fugitives, especially those from the county of Foix, chose to cross the Pyrenees into the kingdoms of Aragon and Valencia, the last newly acquired from the Muslims. Here the local inquisitors do not seem to have been as active or as zealous as those in Languedoc.[34]

Another factor that seems to have been important in persuading people to flee was the presence of a support network that could sustain fugitives until they reached safety. In the early days of the Languedocian inquisition, in the 1230s and 1240s when Cathar strongholds still existed and the Cathars numbered many members of the local aristocracy among their adherents and sympathizers, such networks appear to have been relatively large and active. When Pierre de Mazerolles, the lord of Gaja-la-Selve, was a fugitive in the 1240s, he could count on the help of his *bayles*, Guillaume Faure and Adam Vital of Plagne. These men not only personally supplied him with food but compelled others to do so as well.[35]

Fugitives of less exalted rank could not expect such extensive support, but the aid they did receive was often key to a successful escape. Condors Marty of Junac, for example, was able to reach Catalonia thanks to the financial help of an unnamed rich man of the Sabarthès.[36] Even less generous acts, such as the delivery by Arnaud Maury of Montaillou of a shirt to one of his brothers who had made a halt during his flight into Catalonia at the Pyrenean town of L'Hospitalet, could be a help.[37] Some people, like Rixende de Miraval de Gralhet, a resident of Saint-Paul-Cap-de-Joux, could draw not only on relatives but also on other individuals with whom they had forged strong ties. On 6 August 1274 Rixende told the inquisitor Pons de Parnac that when she fled to Arles (where she was later arrested), she persuaded her son to escort her there. She was also helped with a

---

[33] For some references, see Doat, 25: fols. 131r–34r (testimony of Pierre Guillaume of Roqueville), 298r–331v (testimony of Pierre de Beauteville of Avignonet); and *Registre*, 2: 403–4 (testimony of Sibille Peyre).

[34] Life in exile in these regions is discussed frequently in Fournier's register. See the depositions collected by the Aragonese inquisitor, Bernard of Puigcercos (*Registre*, 2: 441–68), and the depositions of Arnaud Sicre (2: 20–81), Jean Maury (2: 469–519), and Pierre Maury (3: 110–252).

[35] MS 609, fols. 85r–v.

[36] *Registre*, 2: 518–19.

[37] Ibid., 3: 34.

gift of six sous of Toulouse from Guillaume, *domicellus* of Lassereuille, whom she had nursed as an infant.[38]

As the thirteenth century drew to a close, however, both zones of refuge and support networks shrank as the inquisitors in southern France, northern Italy, and northern Spain became more vigilant and effective.[39] Flight became a more difficult prospect. By the 1270s witnesses were beginning to regale the inquisitors with stories about the difficulties of life on the run. For example, on 2 June 1273 Petronilla, the wife of Deide Debras of Villefranche-en-Rouergue, told the inquisitor Ranulphe de Plassac that a man called Guillaume, from near Albi, had fled to Lombardy after his sister and her husband were imprisoned by the inquisitors. However, he had eventually returned to Languedoc, to tell Petronilla that "he had found a wicked people in Lombardy; they had treated him badly and therefore he had come back."[40] That one's problems could begin even before reaching Lombardy appears in the testimony given to Ranulphe and his colleague Pons de Parnac in 1274 by Raimond Hugues of Roquevidal. Sometime in the winter of 1272/73

> Aymeri [de Toulouse], dressed magnificently, passed through Roquevidal with an Englishwoman. A few days later Aymeri returned to the witness's house, completely destitute. He explained that while he was on his way to Lombardy with the aforesaid woman and another woman, while they were resting in a certain house, he was robbed of both women, all his money, and his clothes. He was almost caught, but he escaped by running.[41]

Life as a fugitive could be so difficult that many people returned to their homes—like Pierre Maurs, who fled to Catalonia when the people of Montaillou were arrested en masse in 1309, only to return to Montaillou sometime around 1321.[42] A few individuals found the fugitive's life so hard that they eventually surrendered to the inquisitors. This is revealed most clearly in the pathetic tale that Arnaud Cimordan de Gasconia told the inquisitor Pons de Parnac in 1276. Arnaud had fallen into the hands of the inquisitors as early as the 1240s, when

---

[38] Rixende claimed that Guillaume was not aware that she intended to flee to Arles (Doat, 25: fols. 176v–77r).

[39] For a recent discussion of the papacy's efforts to persuade Italian towns to foster the persecution of heretics, see Diehl, "Overcoming Reluctance to Prosecute Heresy."

[40] Doat, 25: fol. 4v: "dictus Willelmus in Lombardia invenerat malam gentem, et quod eum male receptaverant, et quod ideo redierat."

[41] Ibid., fols. 104v–5r: "Item idem Aymericus optime indutus transivit alias per Rocavidal cum quadam muliere anglica. Et post paucos dies idem Aymericus totus spoliatus fere rediit ad domum ipsius testis, narrans quod dum iret in Lombardiam cum praedicta muliere et quaedam aliae [sic], fuerunt ablatae in itinere dum iacerent in quadam domo ambae mulieres, et peccunia tota, et vestes quas portabant. Et fere ipse fuerat captus sed evaserat per forsam de corer."

[42] *Registre*, 3: 76.

he had appeared before Bernard de Caux. Imprisoned in the *mur* at Toulouse, he found conditions there intolerable. Most prisoners were supported by the king, since it was he who benefited from the confiscation of their property consequent on their condemnation. However, in Arnaud's case his property had passed to the bishop of Toulouse, who did not prove as generous as the king. Although royal agents made regular deliveries of food to the inmates of the *mur*, Arnaud was expected to obtain his bread by sending a messenger to the bishop's palace. Arnaud had trouble securing the services of such a messenger, so he often had to do without. When he did receive his ration, he found the bread so hard as to be inedible. Not only did Arnaud not get enough to eat, he also lacked clothes and other necessities. He therefore escaped.

Queried by the inquisitor as to the identities of those who had been aware of his fugitive status, he replied with a depressing tale of suffering and exploitation. His wanderings took him through Gascony, into Bigorre, and back into the region around Toulouse; he evaded arrest on at least one occasion, married, and worked as a common laborer. Most interesting from our point of view are the dealings he had with various churchmen. Many of these used their knowledge of his fugitive status to exploit him. When Arnaud first escaped, he went to the abbey of Gimont's grange at Aiguebelle. There he kept the story of his escape from the *mur* secret. However, when he left Aiguebelle and went in search of work harvesting grain and grapes, he told of his escape to one Pierre Binhac, the prior of Minhac.[43] Not only did Pierre not pay him for his labor, but Arnaud wound up giving the prior ten sous of Toulouse so that he would intercede for him with the bishop of Toulouse and the inquisitors. The prior took the money without living up to his end of the bargain.

Arnaud seems to have had better luck at the abbey of Feuillant. Here he at least got paid during the seven years he spent working for the monks. To this new set of employers Arnaud once again revealed that he had escaped from the *mur* and beseeched them to intercede on his behalf with the inquisitors. He gave two sous *morlanos* to one of the monks, named Raimond Sanche, in the hopes that he would persuade the abbot, a man named Auger, to take up his cause. To Abbot Auger himself Arnaud offered fifteen sous *morlanos*. A more honorable man than the prior of Minhac, the abbot refused to take his money, telling Arnaud that he saw no other remedy for him than to return to the prison from which he had escaped. Yet Arnaud persisted. His final effort to get a churchman to help him was an interview, arranged by his wife, with the parish priest of Gasconia, Arnaud Escoulan. Arnaud gave the priest five sous of Toulouse to arrange his long-sought reconciliation with the inquisitors. If the priest succeeded, Arnaud told him he would give him another ten sous, as well as some

---

[43] This is a tentative identification of "Benito." Minhac was a grange that belonged to the Cistercian abbey of Bonnefont. See Higounet, "Granges et bastides." Another possible identification would be Saint-Béat (Haute-Garonne).

linen. The priest took the money but did nothing. Unable to find an intercessor, Arnaud ultimately surrendered himself directly to Pons de Parnac.[44]

Although many fugitives are encountered in the inquisitorial records, it is difficult, given the scattered and fragmentary nature of the references, to use this information to develop a quantitative picture of those who fled from the inquisi- tors. The material that best lends itself to quantification comes from Jacques Fournier's register. As noted above, twelve of the eighty-eight living individuals investigated by Jacques Fournier can be classified as fugitives. This is not a very large group; and seven of the twelve were originally from the village of Montaillou. Therefore the reader should be cautious about overgeneralizing from the remarks that follow.

A large number of the fugitives eventually tried by Fournier, six in all, fled well before formal investigations of their conduct had begun.[45] All of these were male; four were from the village of Montaillou, one from Junac, and one from Esplas-de-Sérou. With the exception of Pierre Acès of Esplas-de-Sérou, who fled a very short distance (less than ten kilometers from Ganac to Foix), and was at large for a relatively short time, all the rest spent many years in exile in Catalonia and Aragon. Three others fled during their trials.[46] One, Arnaud Teisseyre of Lordat, took to his heels while Fournier was interrogating witnesses concerning his behavior, but before he had been summoned to appear. Raimonde Testanière of Montaillou fled after the conclusion of her trial, but before the imposition of sentence.[47] In one case, that of Sibille Peyre of Arques, it cannot be determined at what stage of her investigation she decided to decamp.

Men, who possibly had a wider network of social connections outside their home villages, and who probably had better prospects of finding gainful employment in exile, showed a greater propensity than women to flee. The nine male fugitives constituted 16.7 percent of the fifty-four living males investigated by Fournier, while the three female fugitives made up only 8.8 percent of the thirty-four living women tried by Fournier. Determining the social status of these twelve fugitives is difficult. Nevertheless, there seems to have been something of a bimodal distribution with respect to their social status. On the one hand, three people were of fairly high but not exalted rank: Béatrice de Lagleize was a member of the petty aristocracy of the county of Foix, Arnaud Teisseyre

---

[44] Doat, 25: fols. 220v–25r; a transcript is printed in *Documents*, 1: lxxxi, n. 1.

[45] These were Guillaume Maurs, Guillaume Bayle, Pierre Maury, Jean Maury, all of Montaillou; Bernard Marty of Junac; and Pierre Acès of Esplas-de-Sérou. Sibille Peyre of Arques should possibly be included in this group, although the information is not sufficient to allow a precise determination.

[46] These were Bernard Benet and Bernard Clergue, both of Montaillou, and Béatrice de Lagleize of Varilhes.

[47] It should be noted that Raimonde claimed she left her village of Montaillou not to avoid Fournier, but because of her poverty (*Registre*, 1: 470). The fact that only one person fled after trial but before the imposition of sentence makes an interesting contrast to the pattern at Toulouse, where several people tried by Gui fled before he could assign them penances.

of Lordat was a notary and physician, and Bernard Clergue was at one time the *bayle* of the village of Montaillou. These people probably had enough resources and enough knowledge about the wider world to be able to regard flight as a reasonable alternative. At the same time, they were not of such distinguished position that the prospect of flight was unthinkable. On the other hand, people of relatively modest status were also well represented among the fugitives. Almost half of the group, five in all, were shepherds;[48] Pierre Acès of Esplas-de-Sérou was an agricultural laborer. The ties that bound these people to their home villages were possibly weaker than those of more prosperous individuals. In the case of the shepherds, they had skills that were in relatively high demand among employers and, thanks to the existence of an elaborate pattern of transhumance in the Pyrenees, they were aware of what at least part of the larger world was like.

Aside from the shepherds, who spent many years at large in Catalonia and Aragon, most fugitives did not elude capture for very long. Béatrice de Lagleize, for example, fled sometime after her appearance before Jacques Fournier on 26 July 1320, getting as far as Le Mas-Saintes-Puelles, approximately forty kilometers away. But within a matter of days she was located and arrested, since she appeared before Fournier again on the first of August. Sometime between 7 and 19 April 1321, Bernard Benet was released from the Tour des Allemans for the coming Easter holidays, on condition that he remain within the confines of Le Mas-Saint-Antonin, adjacent to the city of Pamiers. Bernard violated his parole and fled; but by 20 June he was back in custody.

Similarly, with the exception of those who spent long years in exile in Spain, fugitives did not get very far. If one measures the straight-line distance between the places where our fugitives started and where they were captured, one finds that almost all covered distances of less than 80 kilometers. As already noted, Béatrice de Lagleize managed only about 40 kilometers from Varilhes to Le Mas-Saintes-Puelles. Raimonde Testanière traveled about 25 kilometers from Montaillou to Saurat; Arnaud Teisseyre about 55 kilometers from Lordat to Limoux; Sibille Peyre about 65 kilometers from Arques to Mazères; and Pierre Acès a scant 7 or 8 from Ganac to Foix. The record—a not very impressive one—was held by Bernard Benet, who, in his flight from Pamiers, got as far as Puigcerda in Catalonia before backtracking to Ax-les-Thermes, for a total distance as the crow flies of about 110 kilometers.

Because this chapter has tried to penetrate what is most definitely a twilight world, characterized by deceit, deception, and flight, its lessons are rather difficult to encapsulate. It is tempting to characterize the behavior that we have

---

[48] These were Guillaume Maurs, Guillaume Bayle, Pierre Maury, and Jean Maury, all of Montaillou, and Bernard Marty of Junac.

examined as an example of what James C. Scott has characterized as the "weapons of the weak."

To do so, however, would be a mistake. The subterranean war described by Scott, with its anonymous acts of small resistance, foot-dragging, tool breaking, and other forms of petty sabotage, operates in a specific social and ideological context: one in which the rulers and the ruled, the exploiters and the exploited, share a common normative scheme. The "weapons of the weak" work only if the poor are careful always to play the role of the "respectable" poor, entitled by the community's normative system to at least a minimum of decent treatment by the rich and powerful.[49] But in the struggle waged by inquisitors against heretics and their sympathizers, there was no shared normative universe. The inquisitors could not be manipulated by the sort of appeals to common, universal values employed by Scott's peasant resisters. By definition, there was no such shared ground between the inquisitors and the heretics. In a sense, then, we have in this chapter looked at what we might call the "weapons of the *truly* weak."

Our resisters may have been weak, but they were not completely defenseless. Yet assessing the effectiveness of the forms of individual resistance that we have encountered in this chapter is difficult. We can view these acts only through the distorting mirror of the inquisitors' own records. But there are indications that such resistance could be successful. The inquisitors themselves felt that they faced a formidable challenge in unmasking heretics. Authors of inquisitorial manuals, from the pseudo-David of Augsburg to Bernard Gui to Nicholas Eymerich, commented on the skill with which heretics could twist words and play with their meanings in order to deceive unwary inquisitors. The problem of fugitive heretics was thought sufficiently grave for Bishop Jacques Fournier to put up a fair amount of money to subsidize a spy to hunt down Cathar refugees in northern Spain.[50]

Indeed, the heretics and their supporters felt that their techniques of evasion and deception could shield them from detection. A conversation reported by Fournier's spy, Arnaud Sicre, illustrates this last point. One night as Sicre sat around the fire with the Good Man Guillaume Bélibaste and a number of Cathar believers in the Aragonese town of Morella, Bélibaste called on Condors Marty of Junac to tell the company how she had deceived "that *bacalar*," Geoffroy d'Ablis, the inquisitor of Carcassonne. Condors obligingly said that

> when she appeared in Carcassonne before the lord inquisitor, she had confessed to some things concerning herself and heresy and she had behaved humbly. The inquisitor, receiving her testimony graciously, touched her with his hand lightly on the shoulders. She then embraced his leg, begging him to show mercy to her. The inquisitor told her that she should not be afraid, for he would do her

---

[49] Scott, *Weapons of the Weak*, pp. 22–26, 278–80, 284–89.
[50] See the testimony of this agent, Arnaud Sicre, in *Registre*, 2: 20–81.

no harm. Later the inquisitor released her, although, as she then said in the presence of the aforesaid heretic, she had not confessed the half of what she had done and what she knew about others; because, as she said, had she confessed fully, evil mischance would have happened to some others.[51]

Perhaps the best indication of the effectiveness of these forms of individual resistance is the fact that some types of heresy did survive persecution. The Waldensians, unlike the Cathars, persevered throughout the Middle Ages. To do so, they paid a high price. They had to abandon their early emphasis on preaching and their hopes for the general reform of the church, and turn inward, perfecting a form of church organization and a pastoral life directed toward sustaining individual believers in their faith.[52] But the fact that they survived until the sixteenth century, when most were absorbed into the new Protestant churches, is a tribute to what could be accomplished through the mechanisms of subterranean resistance examined above.

---

51 Ibid., 2: 71–72.
52 See Gonnet and Molnár, *Les Vaudois*, pp. 163–210, and Audisio, *Les Vaudois*, pp. 224–58, 275–78. Cameron, however, in *The Reformation of the Heretics*, pp. 15–24, is skeptical about the importance attached by other scholars to the "clandestine church organization" of the late Waldensians and the role in that organization of itinerant preachers known as *barbes*.

# CHAPTER 5

# FORMS OF
# COLLECTIVE RESISTANCE

T HIS CHAPTER DEALS with an important, but obscure, phenomenon: the nature of collective, popular political activity in medieval Europe. The history of the political activity of the medieval masses survives only as transmitted to us in the records kept by the rulers of society, who were not necessarily interested in understanding the political behavior of their subalterns. Moreover, we can usually only study a fraction of popular, collective behavior, primarily large-scale uprisings or rebellions. Some of these, such as the 1378 revolt of the *Ciompi* in Florence or the English Peasants' Rebellion of 1381, have generated a vast and often illuminating literature.[1] But these major rebellions were the mere tip of an iceberg. And this much larger world of collective, popular political action remains a shadowy one. As a result, medievalists have written little that can be placed beside the highly detailed studies produced by historians of early modern and modern Europe, such as George Rudé on riots, E. J. Hobsbawm on "primitive" forms of rebellion, or Charles Tilly and Edward Shorter on French strikes.[2] That Tilly, a sociologist with a strong historical bent, found little to say about the premodern era in his study of forms of collective action in European history is symptomatic of the lack of progress that has been made in fleshing out a sociological analysis of collective action in the Middle Ages.[3]

The detailed records of the inquisitors, however, allow us to examine certain aspects of the resistance movements that they provoked. Collective resistance to the inquisitors could take many forms. To begin with, we must distinguish between covert resistance and open challenges. Undoubtedly most collective resistance was covert, taking the form of guiding, sheltering, and feeding the elites of the heretical sects active in Languedoc. But these forms of resistance do not demand much analytical acumen of their interpreters. In many ways they are not very different from those discussed in chapter 4 under the heading of individual

---

[1] Interesting recent discussions of these uprisings can be found in Stella, *La Révolte des Ciompi*, and Justice, *Writing and Rebellion*.
[2] Rudé, *The Crowd in History*; Hobsbawm, *Primitive Rebels*; and Shorter and Tilly, *Strikes in France*.
[3] Tilly, *From Mobilization to Revolution*.

resistance. The more interesting and problematic phenomenon is that of open challenges to the inquisitors. Thus the following discussion will be primarily devoted to the phenomenon of open, collective challenges to the inquisitors, their agents, or their allies. Unfortunately, here as in the preceding chapter most of the evidence concerns unsuccessful resistance efforts. Bearing this caveat in mind, we can nevertheless discern some interesting things about this form of opposition.

## THE PATTERN OF VIOLENT OPPOSITION

To give the reader a feel for the dimensions of open, collective resistance to the inquisitors, I have constructed a table that records incidents of one particular type of this activity: acts that involved violence. I chose such incidents because their status as acts of resistance is relatively unambiguous and because they probably stood a better chance of being recorded than other types of collective resistance. Table 5.1 lists every act of violent resistance to the inquisitors that I have been able to find.[4] In gathering data for this table, I have cast my net very widely. I have included violent acts directed not only at the inquisitors or their immediate agents but also against informers, members of the Dominican order, and other churchmen who, without being formally in the employ of the inquisitors, were participating in the search for heretics.

Some obvious conclusions can be drawn from this table. One is the relative paucity of violent challenges to the inquisitors and their work. In all, for a period covering almost ninety years, I was able to find only forty-four cases of violent resistance. Even more striking is the extreme rarity of assaults on the inquisitors themselves. All told, there were only eight events in which inquisitors were physically assaulted or confronted by their opponents. And one of these eight cases consisted of no more than a projected attempt on the life of Bernard Gui, an assault that never took place.[5] Violent challenges were concentrated within two time periods (see figure 5.1). In the 1230s and 1240s, twenty-three incidents took place, and in the last decades of the thirteenth century and the first two of the fourteenth, eighteen incidents occurred. In part, of course, this pattern may be a mere artifact of the survival of the records. Nevertheless, the bimodal distribution fits well with what we know about the history of the inquisition and of heresy in Languedoc.

That the first inquisitors encountered much resistance in the 1230s and 1240s is hardly surprising. The inquisition itself was new and very unpopular. Heresy, both Catharism and Waldensianism, was still widespread. Catharism in

---

[4] This table undoubtedly underestimates violent opposition to the inquisitors. Inevitably, I must have missed a few incidents. In one case, involving the deposition given by Guillemette Amiel on 20 November 1245 in which she said that two of her relatives, including her husband, had been killed by Cathar believers some time after the Treaty of Paris, the events were described in such a cursory fashion that I found myself unwilling to categorize them as open, violent opposition (see MS 609, fol. 94r).

[5] *LS*, p. 228.

Table 5.1 Violent Acts of Resistance

| Date | Act | Location | Object | Number Involved | Source |
|---|---|---|---|---|---|
| 1233 | Two female heretics rescued from messenger of abbot of Sorèze | Roquefère | Agent | Mob | Doat, 26: fols. 39v–40v |
| 1234, March | Mob frees suspect arrested by Ferrier | Narbonne | Inquisitor | Mob | Emery, *Heresy and Inquisition*, p. 77 |
| 1234, March | Mob thwarts arrest of suspect by the archbishop and viscount of Narbonne | Narbonne | Bishop/ viscount | Mob | Emery, *Heresy and Inquisition*, p. 77 |
| 1234, 15 June | Riot against inquisitor Arnaud Catalan | Albi | Inquisitor | Mob | Pelhisson, *Chronique*, pp. 112–23 |
| ca. 1234–35 | Jean Teisseyre rescued from burning | Toulouse | Count of Toulouse's *viguier* | Mob | Pelhisson, *Chronique*, p. 52 |
| ca. 1234–35 | Stoning of Dominicans | Toulouse | Dominicans | Mob | Pelhisson, *Chronique*, p. 52 |
| 1235, spring | Murder of Arnaud Dominic | Aigrefeuille | Informer | ? | Pelhisson, *Chronique*, p. 66 |
| 1235, spring | Rescue of Cathar believer from abbot of St. Sernin and comital *viguier* | Toulouse | Inquisitorial agents | ? | Pelhisson, *Chronique*, pp. 66–68 |
| 1235, 15 Oct. | Guillaume Arnaud expelled from Toulouse by consuls | Toulouse | Inquisitor | Small mob | Pelhisson, *Chronique*, pp. 72–74 |
| 1235, autumn | Priests citing heretics expelled from Toulouse | Toulouse | Inquisitorial agents | ? | Pelhisson, *Chronique*, pp. 76–78 |
| 1235, Oct.–Nov. | Boycott of Dominicans | Toulouse | Dominicans | ? | Pelhisson, *Chronique*, p. 78 |
| 1235, 2d half | Dominican convent attacked | Narbonne | Dominicans | Mob | Emery, *Heresy and Inquisition*, p. 81 |
| 1235, 4 or 5 Nov. | Dominicans making citations roughed up | Toulouse | Agents/ Dominicans | 2 | Pelhisson, *Chronique*, pp. 80–82 |
| 1235, 5 or 6 Nov. | Dominicans expelled | Toulouse | Dominicans | Mob | Pelhisson, *Chronique*, pp. 82–86 |

Table 5.1 Violent Acts of Resistance (*cont.*)

| Date | Act | Location | Object | Number Involved | Source |
|------|-----|----------|--------|-----------------|--------|
| 1237 | Murder of Raimond Bru | Tarabel | Heretic desiring to convert | ca. 2 | MS 609, fol. 55v |
| 1240 | Murder of nephew of priest of Saint-Paul-Cap-de-Joux | Saint-Paul-Cap-de-Joux? | Relative of agent | ? | MS 609, fol. 223r |
| 1241 | Effort to rescue heretics held by abbot of Saint-Papoul | Saint-Papoul | Abbot | ca. 18 | MS 609, fols. 31v–40v passim |
| 1241–42 | Murder of Pierre Capellanus's clerk | Caraman | Agent | 10 | Doat, 23: fols. 313r–14r |
| 1242, 28 May | Murder of Guillaume Arnaud by men from Montségur | Avignonet | Inquisitor | ca. 60 | Dossat, "Massacre d'Avignonet," pp. 350–51 |
| 1244 | Priest's house attacked | Beauteville | Priest | Mob | Doat, 25: fol. 194v |
| 1245 | Two sergeants who had arrested 7 female heretics hanged | ? | Agents of archpriest of the Lauragais | Small group | MS 609, fol. 75v |
| 1245 | Imprisonment of Emersende Viguier and her son | Cambiac | Informer | 6 | MS 609, fol. 239v |
| 1247 | Messenger and clerk of inquisition killed and records stolen | Caunes | Agents | ? | Doat, 31: fols. 105v–7r; *HL*, 8: col. 1239 |
| 1268 | Murder of Pestilhacus, inquisitorial sergeant | Between Roquefère and Sallèles-Cabardès | Agent | 4 | Doat, 25: fol. 191v |
| 1283–84 | Plot to steal inquisitorial registers | Carcassonne | Records | 14 | Doat, 26: fols. 195v–216v, 250r–54r, 261v–65v, 267v–71v |
| ca. 1295 | Nicholas d'Abbeville attacked | Carcassonne | Inquisitor | Mob | Doat, 30: fol. 94r |
| 1296 | Inquisitors attacked at Franciscan convent | Carcassonne | Inquisitor | Mob | MS 4270, fols. 231r–32v, 238r–v |

Table 5.1 Violent Acts of Resistance (*cont.*)

| Date | Act | Location | Object | Number Involved | Source |
|------|-----|----------|--------|-----------------|--------|
| ca. 1297–98 | Dominicans boycotted | Carcassonne | Dominicans | ? | Gui, *De fundatione*, p. 102 |
| 1302, 11 Feb. | Riot against Bishop Castanet | Albi | Bishop/ inquisitor | Mob | Gui, *De fundatione*, p. 202 |
| 1302, 2 Dec. | Riot against Dominicans | Albi | Dominicans | Mob | Gui, *De fundatione*, pp. 201–3 |
| 1302 | Murder of Guillaume Dejean | Larnat | Agent ? | 5 | Pales-Gobilliard, *Geoffroy d'Ablis*, pp. 152–54 |
| 1303, 10 Aug. | Riot against former consuls | Carcassonne | Consuls | Mob | MS 4270, fols. 194r–95v |
| 1303, Aug. | Dominican convent stoned | Carcassonne | Dominicans | Mob | MS 4270, fol. 291r |
| 1303, late Aug. | Assault on *mur* | Carcassonne | *Mur* | Mob | MS 4270, fols. 228v–30v |
| 1303, early Sept. | Attack on Dominican convent | Albi | Dominicans | Mob | AM Albi, FF17 |
| 1303, late Nov. | Jean de Recoles arrested | Castres | Agent | 100+ | Hauréau, *Bernard Délicieux*, pp. 176–87 |
| 1309 | Tongue of Mengarde Maurs cut out | Montaillou | Potential informer | ? | *Registre*, 2: 222 |
| 1310 | Arnaud de Sobrenia of Tignac drowned | Ax-les-Thermes | Potential informer | Small group | *Registre*, 1: 281 |
| 1310 | Murder of brother of Guillaume Peyre | Quié ? | Cathar believer | ? | *Registre*, 2: 57 |
| 1310 | Murder of unidentified man | Ax-les-Thermes | Potential informer | ? | *Registre*, 2: 333 |
| 1310 | Murder of Pierre Marty | Junac | Potential informer | ? | *Registre*, 3: 276–77 |
| 1311 | Murder of Arnaud Lezerii | Montaillou | Potential informer | ? | *Registre*, 3: 65 |
| 1319 | Plot against life of Bernard Gui | Toulouse | Inquisitor | 3+ | *LS*, p. 228 |
| 1320, Sept. | Murder of Brother Raimond de Ponte of Mérens | Bouan | Agent ? | ? | *Registre*, 1: 271 |

Note: Most dates are only approximate.

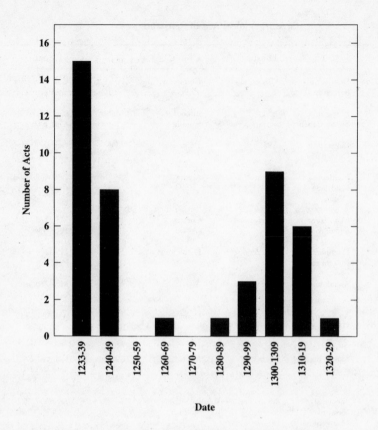

**Figure 5.1  Date of Violent Acts of Opposition to the Inquisitors**

particular commanded a large following among the local nobles, who were pre-pared to use their influence to protect it. Although the Albigensian crusades had ended in the 1220s and the French royal government was engaged in solidifying its authority in Languedoc, the region can scarcely be described as effectively paci-fied. In 1240 and 1242 there were two major rebellions against French rule. Large numbers of banished nobles—*faidits* as they were known—remained at large. And the Cathar heretics possessed strongholds at Montségur and Quéribus. This first period of violent resistance also produced the largest number of direct assaults on the persons of the inquisitors. At both Albi and Narbonne, inquisitors were confronted by rioting mobs. The town authorities in Toulouse expelled first the inquisitor Guillaume Arnaud and then the entire Dominican convent. The most spectacular violent assault on an inquisitor was, of course, the assassination of Guillaume Arnaud and his assistants at Avignonet. Guillaume was the only

Languedocian inquisitor to perish at the hands of his enemies, but in the 1230s and 1240s a number of other inquisitorial agents were also assaulted and killed.

Once the rebellions of the 1240s had been put down and the castles of Montségur and Quéribus captured, evidence of violent, open opposition to the inquisitors becomes relatively rare. Yet at the same time that it apparently became more difficult for opponents of the inquisition to organize violent resistance, the inquisitors were having considerable difficulties. Diplomatic factors connected with the papacy's Italian policies often made papal support for the inquisitors uncertain. Indeed, from 1238 to 1241 the inquisition was, in effect, suspended.[6] And from 1249 to 1255 the Dominicans, angered by papal interference, abandoned their work as inquisitors, leaving the task of prosecuting heretics to local bishops.[7] From the 1250s until the 1280s the inquisitors also seem to have become less active; fewer records of their activities have survived. Thus during this time the inquisitors may have done less than in previous decades to arouse violent resistance.

Only in the 1290s did the inquisitors' work once again stimulate significant outbreaks of violence. Two obvious facts stand out from an examination of these incidents. The first is the great importance of the urban riot. The period from 1295 through 1302 saw no less than eight anti-inquisitorial riots in either Albi or Carcassonne. The second is that most acts of physical violence against individuals were directed against defectors, real or imagined, from within the ranks of the heretics rather than against the inquisitors or their agents. This is a significant change from the 1230s and 1240s, when most acts of violence against individuals had been directed against the inquisitors, their agents, or churchmen assisting in the hunt for heretics. In contrast, between 1290 and 1320 four of the seven individuals whose murders are recorded in our sources were Cathar believers slain by other adherents of their sect to keep them silent. At Montaillou a woman was silenced by the radical expedient of cutting out her tongue. This pattern is clear and dramatic evidence of the difficulties experienced by Catharism during its last decades of existence in Languedoc, when it had become a hunted, underground church, afflicted with paranoia and declining into a self-destructive pattern of internal violence.

## STRUCTURES OF RESISTANCE: THE HERETICAL SECT

One of the more curious conclusions that emerges from an examination of the data is that the sectarian structures of the various heresies tended not to be focal points around which open, collective resistance was organized. When heretics and their sympathizers mounted overt challenges to the inquisitors, they seem to have usually coordinated their efforts around networks provided by other social institutions, such as the family, the village, or the lord-client relationship.

---

[6] Dossat, *Crises*, pp. 137–45.
[7] In some places the Dominicans seem not to have gone back to work until 1259 (ibid., pp. 173–88).

Most efforts to organize resistance through the institutions of the sects them-selves appear to have been passive rather than active, more concerned with deceiving the inquisitors than with challenging them. One of the few incidents in which believers, brought together for a Cathar religious ceremony, acted con-frontationally is known to us from testimony that Etienne Vital of Varagne gave to Ranulphe de Plassac and Pons de Parnac on 25 September 1274. Etienne tes-tified that when the Lady Brunisende lay on her deathbed at Beauteville around 1244, he was sent to fetch Cathar heretics to perform a *consolamentum*. He brought the heretics to Beauteville and introduced them into the sickroom. He then left, but as he went out of the house, he heard the Lady Raimonde, the wife of Bernard Pons of Beauteville, crying out that there were heretics in the house. Hearing this, the knights Pons and Arnaud de Villeneuve, the dying woman's sons, armed themselves; many others also seized their weapons and rushed out to protect the heretics. A crowd descended on the local priest's house. To keep him or any of his *familia* from leaving the building, they threw stones and sticks into the upper story of the house.[8]

In the period between 1275 and 1325, the best-documented challenge to the inquisitors, even if it was rather covert in nature, was the effort made in the 1280s to destroy the inquisitorial archives at Carcassonne. By the middle of the 1280s the inquisitors of Carcassonne had compiled a great deal of information about the career of the Good Man Guillaume Pagès, active between 1269 and 1284. From the surviving remains of this material, it appears that many of the leading citizens of Carcassonne—among them consuls of the *bourg*, royal *vigu-iers*, professors of law, canons of the cathedral of Saint-Nazaire, the bishop's official, and the archdeacon of Carcassonne—had had intimate dealings with Pagès. In the mid-1280s these people began to fear for their safety. To protect themselves, they decided to strike not at the inquisitors but at the source of their dangerous knowledge, their registers. One of the inquisition's employees, a former Good Man named Bernard de la Garrigue of Lados, was recruited to steal the registers and burn them. However, he lacked a major qualification for the job: he did not know how to read. He was therefore assisted by a professional copier of manuscripts. But when the two penetrated the inquisition's headquar-ters, they discovered that the inquisitor, Jean Galand, had gone to Toulouse and taken with him the key to the chest in which the registers were kept. Before a second attempt could be mounted, Galand got wind of the plot and began to arrest, interrogate, and convict members of the conspiracy.[9]

---

[8] Doat, 25: fols. 193v–95r.

[9] The depositions extracted by the Carcassonne inquisitors concerning this plot are in Doat, 26: fols. 195v–216v (Bernard Agasse of Carcassonne), 250r–54r (Bernard de la Garrigue), 261v–65v (Arnaud Mata of Carcassonne), and 267v–71v (Guillaume Serra of Carcassonne). Excerpts have been published by Mahul, ed., *Cartulaire et archives*, 5: 638–43. The plot is discussed in Lebois, "Le Complot des Carcassonnais."

This is a pretty story, but there is grave doubt about whether it ever happened. Galand, the inquisitor, was a controversial figure in Languedoc, widely hated and feared. The people of Carcassonne accused him of all kinds of malfeasance in office.[10] Jean-Marie Vidal, one of the most thorough and careful early historians of the Languedocian inquisition, was convinced that the plot existed only in the inquisitors' imagination and that the depositions concerning it were completely false.[11] At this distance in time, one may not feel warranted in being as categorical about the falsity of this plot as was Vidal. Nevertheless, it is clear that a great deal of uncertainty hangs over the reality of these events. If we set this plot aside, we are left with very little evidence that believers *qua* believers ever mounted any direct challenges to the inquisitors after the middle of the thirteenth century.

For the most part, heretical believers cooperated, *qua* believers, largely by trying to coordinate their testimony to the inquisitors. Documents generated by the campaign launched in the early fourteenth century to track down the Béguins yields some information on this point. When Pierre de Mazères was condemned on 5 July 1322, his sentence noted that the Béguins imprisoned in the Tour des Allemans in Pamiers had gotten together and discussed how to concert their answers to the inquisitor. They had agreed that they would not answer any questions except those relating directly to their own beliefs, nor would they take any oaths except those relating to those same beliefs.[12] Another Béguine, Amoda de Limoux, sentenced on 1 March 1327, told of attending a meeting with several Béguines and two Béguins at which they discussed how they should reply to the inquisitors.[13]

The Cathars, with their longer experience of the inquisitors and their ways, were capable of cleverer subterfuges. Some Cathar *credentes*, at least, seem to have been aware in one fashion or another that Romano-canonical law required for proof of guilt the testimony of more than one witness. One of the Cathar exiles who had grouped themselves around the Good Man Guillaume Bélibaste told Arnaud Sicre, Jacques Fournier's spy:

> Many *credentes* are unwilling to see the lords, that is, the heretics, in the company of more than one or two other *credentes* at most. They do this lest, if they are detected, they can be implicated by several witnesses. For, as it was said, one

---

[10] Vidal, *Un Inquisiteur jugé*, pp. 39–43.

[11] His arguments are set out ibid., pp. 26–31. H. C. Lea waffled a bit on the question of the existence of this conspiracy. Observing the differences in the accounts given by the alleged conspirators, he concluded that little weight could be put on their testimony. His final judgment was that "the whole has an air of unreality which renders one doubtful about accepting any portion, but there must have been some foundation for the story" (*Inquisition of the Middle Ages*, 2: 59). Other historians, such as Auguste Molinier, Guiraud, and Douais have accepted the veracity of the documents relating to this plot. See Lebois, "Le Complot des Carcassonnais," p. 159.

[12] *LS*, p. 302.

[13] Doat, 28: fol. 239r.

or two witnesses can easily be discredited, because one can say immediately that such are one's enemies. Thus, they greatly prefer to see the lords, that is, the heretics, either alone or with one other *credens*, rather than with two, lest they be convicted.[14]

At first it may seem puzzling that heretics and their sympathizers made little use of the institutions of their sects in organizing challenges to the inquisitors. But most heretical sects did not have much in the way of formal organization. In the case of the Cathars, this was in part due to their ecclesiology. The Cathars recognized as members of the church only the *perfecti* and *perfectae* who had received the *consolamentum*, the purifying baptism of the holy spirit, and who lived lives of strict asceticism. Thus the ordinary believer, the *credens* still embroiled in the sins of the world, was not a member of the church at all. The Cathar *perfecti* have been criticized by modern scholars for failing to produce a code of ethical conduct for the *credentes*, who were in their eyes still steeped in the sins that kept them prisoners of the flesh. They could, perhaps, also be criticized for failing to create an institutional framework that would allow their believers to organize effective challenges to the inquisitors.

An even more serious impediment to developing institutions around which resistance could be organized was the underground life that the heretical sects were forced to lead. At the beginning of the thirteenth century, the Good Men and Good Women had had a more elaborate set of religious institutions, complete with bishops and their assistants, a network of convents, and regular meetings. We are not as well informed about Waldensian organization, but we do know that the Lombard wing of the sect was capable of holding important conferences. In Languedoc, however, as a result of the Albigensian crusades, heresy was driven into hiding. It became impossible to support any but the simplest forms of organization. During the thirteenth century what organization the Languedocian branch of the Cathar church had crumbled away. Convents disappeared, as did the Cathar diocesan structure. The last Good Men who tried to revive the sect in the early fourteenth century were essentially independent entrepreneurs, who cooperated among themselves on only an ad hoc basis. Without an authority to impose discipline, relations among these missionaries were often less than cordial. Some of the Good Men resented the efforts of the brothers Pierre and Guillaume Autier to lord it over them; and disputes about the distribution of gifts from the faithful led to strained relations.[15]

It is therefore not surprising that many of our examples of heretics cooperating with one another to orchestrate responses to the inquisitors through sectarian-related forms of organization should involve the Béguins. In the

---

[14] *Registre*, 2: 74. Perhaps this exile was Arnaud Maury, although Sicre could not remember exactly if he was the person in question.

[15] Ibid., 3: 144–45.

second and third decades of the fourteenth century, when this group became of interest to the inquisitors, they were quite different from the other heretics. Indeed, they were a group that, until Pope John XXII decided to settle affairs with the Franciscans over the issue of Christ's poverty, had been regarded as orthodox. The Franciscan Third Order to which many belonged was also relatively highly organized; it possessed a rule, elected officers, and held regular meetings.[16] These attributes provided a ready-made structure around which resistance could be organized.

## STRUCTURES OF RESISTANCE: KINSHIP

Kinship ties were important in organizing resistance to the inquisition. In chapter 4 we have already encountered the frantic efforts made by Bernard Clergue to save his brother Pierre from the inquisitors. In addition to browbeating his fellow prisoners and trying to use his influence in Carcassonne to harm his brother's enemies, Bernard expended vast sums of money trying indirectly to buy influence on Bishop Fournier. To the lord of Mirepoix, a marshal of France, he gave 300 livres during a visit by the marshal to the papal curia. He also entrusted another 150 l.t. to his brother-in-law, who was accompanying the lord of Mirepoix, to spend on defraying the costs of the marshal's trip. The lord of Mirepoix's wife also benefited from Clergue's largesse, receiving a mule—all in the hopes of persuading the marshal to speak favorably to Fournier about Pierre Clergue. Although the lord of Mirepoix seems to have had no success with Fournier, he persuaded some cardinals and other members of the Roman curia to send the bishop four letters asking that Pierre be released. Bernard also gave money to Loup de Foix, a relation of the count of Foix. More cash went to the reeve of Rabat, a friend of the bishop's; to the archdeacon of Pamiers, German de Castelnau; and to Fournier's spy, Arnaud Sicre. All told, Bernard claimed that he laid out 14,000 sous, but to no avail. As Bernard lamented to the priest Barthélemy Amilhac, "The lord bishop is a hard case, and in vain is he supplicated, because he does nothing at anyone's entreaty. And the more he is asked, the less it accomplishes."[17]

In general, resistance efforts organized around kinship ties were rather modest affairs. At times relatives arranged with one another to give as little incriminating evidence as possible. For example, in 1321 Guillaume de Bayssanis of Le Born confessed to Bernard Gui that eighteen years earlier, when he had been nine years old, he had seen Pierre Autier and various other Cathar Good Men. When Gui asked him why he had delayed so long in coming forward to confess, he said that his father had ordered him not to. When his father was summoned to appear at the *sermo generalis* at which he was to receive his sentence,

---

[16] On the Franciscan Third Order, see Moorman, *A History of the Franciscan Order*, pp. 42–45.

[17] *Registre*, 2: 282–83; MS 4030, fol. 176b. Where Duvernoy reads *Carcassonam*, thus having the marshal make a trip to that city, I read *curiam*.

he took his son aside and said, "Son, I don't know if I will ever see you again; but take care that as long as I or your mother are alive, you don't tell anyone the things you know or have seen concerning heresy."[18]

Most resistance to the inquisitors by kinship groups was covert and defensive. On occasion, however, kinship ties provided a network around which more open challenges could be organized. Bernard Gui's register provides an instance of one such move toward open opposition. On 23 April 1312 Gui sentenced Raimonde, the widow of Martin Barreria of Saint-Papoul, to wear crosses. According to her sentence, she had entered into a kin-based conspiracy to rescue her brother from the custody of the inquisitors of Carcassonne. Sometime in late 1303 or early 1304 she had met twice with another brother, Pierre Raimond of Saint-Papoul, a Cathar Good Man, to discuss freeing their brother Bertrand from the inquisitors. Altogether she had received about twenty-five livres from Pierre for this purpose, along with another twenty sous, evidently for her own use.[19]

A clearer example of an overt challenge offered to the inquisitors by a group of kinsmen comes from the register of Geoffroy d'Ablis, inquisitor of Carcassonne. This is a particularly interesting story, since it shows that the ties of family loyalty were strong enough to involve seemingly good, indeed committed, Catholics in an effort to thwart inquisitorial activity. On 13 June 1308 Guillaume de Rodès of Tarascon appeared before d'Ablis's lieutenants, Géraud de Blomac and Jean de Faugoux. According to Guillaume's testimony, he had on a Wednesday just before Pentecost about nine years earlier received a letter from his brother Raimond, a Dominican friar living in Pamiers. His brother asked him to come immediately to Pamiers, "because there was danger in delay." The next day Guillaume arrived in Pamiers. His brother took him aside and told him that a Béguin (at this time the Béguins were still regarded as orthodox) named Guillaume Dejean had informed Raimond de Rodès's fellow Dominican, one Guillaume Pons (or perhaps Raimond de Lacourt), that he had stumbled across some Cathars up in the mountains of the county of Foix. When Dejean arrived in the village of Mérens, a man named Pierre Amiel had asked him if he would like to meet the heretics Pierre and Guillaume Autier and hear their preaching. Dejean had replied in the affirmative and Amiel had introduced him to the Good Men, with whom he had had a long conversation. Dejean had then brought word of his discovery to Pamiers, intending to arrange the Autiers' arrest. One of the things Dejean had learned from the Good Men was that Guillaume de Rodès had received the heretics in his house in Tarascon. The Dominican to whom Dejean had spoken passed this information on to his fellow friar, Raimond de Rodès. This alarming information had impelled Raimond to write to his brother.

---

[18] *LS*, p. 343. His father was probably the same Pierre de Bayssanis condemned by Gui to perpetual imprisonment on 23 April 1312 (pp. 119–20).

[19] Ibid., p. 108.

Once Guillaume de Rodès arrived in Pamiers, his brother asked him if he had indeed had dealings with the heretics. Guillaume assured Raimond that the Béguin was a liar and that he had never received the Autiers. But, armed with his brother's information, he went to Ax-les-Thermes to warn Raimond Autier, the heretics' brother, of what was afoot. Word spread; and one day Guillaume Delaire of Quié, another Cathar sympathizer, spotted Dejean in the plaza at Ax-les-Thermes. He went up to him and asked if he was looking for the heretics. When Dejean said that he was, Delaire offered to guide him to Larnat, where Pierre and Guillaume Autier could be found. However, when they reached Larnat and were on the bridge of Alliat, Pierre, together with Philippe de Larnat, a local *domicellus*, seized the Béguin, striking him so that he could not call out for help. They took him into the hills above the town and questioned him about what he was up to. When he admitted that he was trying to arrest the heretics, they threw him off a high cliff into a ravine or cave, where his body was never discovered.[20]

Although kinship networks provided nodes around which resistance could be organized, it was rare for these groups to offer open challenges to the inquisitors. Indeed, the two examples cited above can be classified as overt only if we assume that rescuing a Cathar sympathizer from prison and murdering an informant would inevitably become publicly known facts. This rarity is not as puzzling as it at first might appear. Kinship groups can be tough, durable units. In many societies and at many times they have served as a means to organize political activity. As political action groups, however, kinship organizations present some distinct problems of mobilization and deployment.[21]

A kinship group is strong because the ties that unite kinsmen are multiple and intertwining, involving many aspects of human existence: economic cooperation, ritual fellowship, and so on. Most societies, and especially those of medieval Europe, regard the fulfillment of duties to kinsmen as a moral imperative. A would-be leader who wants to use his kin for a political purpose thus has the advantage of being able to minimize the transaction costs of mobilizing a political action group because he can appeal to the moral imperatives of kinship. Yet he also faces some significant drawbacks. Leadership roles are often relatively undefined.[22] Most decisions that the leaders of families make are matters of routine, determined by traditional norms and practices. Anyone who attempts to lead the kin group into a new area of activity must be seen to be acting for the greater good of the group in accordance with the moral code that governs relations among kinsmen. Failing this, he can easily forfeit the allegiance of his kinfolk. These constraints, inherent in the nature of the kinship group, can make it difficult to mobilize kinsmen to respond effectively to intervention by a new,

---

[20] Pales-Gobilliard, ed., *Geoffroy d'Ablis*, pp. 150–54, 158.
[21] My argument is indebted to Bailey, *Stratagems and Spoils*, pp. 50–51.
[22] Indeed, this seems to have been particularly true of peasant families in some regions of Languedoc. See the discussion of this point in chapter 7.

outside political organization such as the inquisition, especially if that organization has at its command effective means of coercion.

In the case of Catharism, the ideology of the sect itself tended to work against family ties. For the Cathars the world was a prison in which souls stolen from heaven were incarcerated, the body was a mere tunic fashioned by the devil to make souls forget their angelic origin, and procreation was a way to produce new bodies in which souls were held captive. The complex networks of social ties that united individuals in this world were seen as affairs of the flesh and hence of no moral worth. The ties of blood were no real ties at all: they were merely an artifact of the devil's strategy to conceal from those imprisoned in this world their true, celestial identity. The only real kinship was that which existed within the sect itself.[23] As the Good Man Guillaume Bélibaste told Pierre Maury, once a man had the understanding of the true faith, that is, Catharism, "he should do good only to the good, that is, the heretics or the believers of heretics."[24] Given this ideology, it is not surprising that Cathars may have experienced difficulties mobilizing resistance to the inquisitors around the networks of kinship.

## STRUCTURES OF RESISTANCE: LORDSHIP

If the kin group only rarely functioned as the nodal point around which open challenges to the inquisitors were organized, one might expect that that other pillar of medieval social organization, the lord-client tie, would offer a more useful institutional framework for resistance. In the late twelfth and the first half of the thirteenth centuries, Catharism had attracted a significant following among the nobility of Languedoc, particularly in the region known as the Lauragais, lying to the east of Toulouse. Noble families produced many Cathar *perfecti*, as well as some of the most devoted believers. Moreover, as Michel Roquebert has observed, Cathar nobles drew their clients, retainers, and servants, all members of what medieval society understood as the *familia*, into sympathy with the heretics.[25]

Yet, by the late thirteenth and early fourteenth centuries it is very difficult to find evidence of any challenges to the inquisitors that were organized around a seignorial clientage group. One of the very few occasions when such a group took steps to hinder the inquisition is recorded in Jacques Fournier's register. On 4 July 1324 Bernard Marty of Junac, whose family had been deeply involved with Catharism, appeared before the bishop and told the following story. Around 1310, when Bernard had been living in Aigues-Juntes, his father had died. When Bernard finally managed to get to Junac and asked his sister Raimonde what had happened, she told him that their father's death had been suspicious. He had been ill, but had recovered, only to die suddenly and unexpectedly. When she

---

[23] *Registre*, 3: 242.
[24] Ibid., 3: 185.
[25] Roquebert, "Le Catharisme comme tradition," p. 222.

discovered his body, she noted that his windpipe had been crushed immediately below the chin. This observation had led her to believe that men from the castle of Junac had killed him to keep him from revealing what he knew about their involvement in heresy. When Bona Femina, the illegitimate daughter of Junac's priest, voiced the same suspicion, Bernard decided that the women must be right, since his father had been "very talkative."[26] On the whole, however, such incidents were rare. Indeed, one is more likely to find evidence in this late period of inquisitorial pressure causing splits between lords and followers, a subject that will be discussed in chapter 7.

At least two factors contributed to preventing open challenges from being organized around the lord-follower tie. First, noble lineages devoted to Catharism suffered heavily in the early thirteenth century. War, rebellion, and the attentions of the first inquisitors all took their toll.[27] By the late thirteenth and early fourteenth centuries, members of the Languedocian nobility, with the exception of some families in the county of Foix, seem to have lost their taste for heresy.[28] Second, there was a general loosening of such ties following the assertion of French hegemony in Languedoc. The growing influence and authority of the royal government gradually came to offer a more attractive and more rewarding focus of loyalty for the individuals who had made up the *familia* of local Languedocian nobles. At the same time the nobility became more self-conscious and exclusive. The growing importance of royal taxation in Languedoc, which spared those members of the nobility who could argue that they were bound to personal military service to the king, made the members of this group ever more conscious of their separate class identity.[29] All in all, noble houses and their networks of clients and dependents became progressively more unlikely to serve as the centers of opposition to the inquisitors.

## STRUCTURES OF RESISTANCE: THE VILLAGE

Many open challenges to the inquisitors were organized around and through the communal institutions of the village and the town. The twelfth and thirteenth centuries in Languedoc saw much development of horizontal social ties that united inhabitants of the same residential community to one another. This phenomenon is best known for the region's major cities and towns, which often gained a large measure of political autonomy, created their own legal systems, and formed organs of self-administration, the most important being boards of elected

---

[26] *Registre*, 3: 276–77.

[27] Roquebert, "Le Catharisme comme tradition," pp. 239–41.

[28] On Catharism and the nobility of the county of Foix, see Duvernoy, "La Noblesse du comté de Foix," pp. 123–40.

[29] Given, *State and Society*, pp. 195–96. In light of the importance of royal taxation as a wedge that split the nobility off from the rest of society, it is interesting to note that the county of Foix, where we have detected the traces of a challenge to the inquisitors organized around a seignorial clientage group, was normally exempt from direct royal taxation in the late thirteenth and early fourteenth centuries.

consuls. Indeed, in the early years of the thirteenth century the city of Toulouse came close, for a time, to fashioning something like an independent city-state.

Similar organization around ties of coresidence went on among the peasantry. In parts of Languedoc, a major reorganization of settlement patterns took place during the eleventh and twelfth centuries. This phenomenon has been best studied by Monique Bourin-Derruau in the region around the city of Béziers. In the earlier Middle Ages settlement had been relatively scattered. In the eleventh and twelfth centuries, however, the inhabitants of the Biterrois grouped themselves into compact, densely inhabited, fortified settlements known as *castra*. In the late twelfth century the inhabitants of these *castra* began to organize politically; in the thirteenth century many acquired self-governing consulates modeled on those of the larger towns.[30]

Virtually all the evidence for resistance organized around village institutions comes from the mid-thirteenth century, before the period with which we are primarily concerned. It is nevertheless worth considering. Much of this resistance, not surprisingly, was fairly covert. In the 1240s Bernard de Caux and Jean de Saint-Pierre carried out a massive investigation in the region around Toulouse, interrogating scores, if not hundreds, of people from a single village.[31] They discovered several cases in which an entire village colluded to conceal the truth. For example, on 30 May 1245 Guillaume de Guzens told the inquisitors that the people of Saint-Martin-Lalande had several years previously been summoned to appear at Castelnaudary before the inquisitor Guillaume Arnaud. On the journey there, the villagers had discussed their situation and agreed that they would all lie.[32] Evidence of similar concerting of testimony came from the villages of Auriac and Les Cassès.[33]

The investigations of Bernard de Caux and Jean de Saint-Pierre also revealed more active measures of resistance. It was not uncommon for villagers, at times at the forceful urging of a local magnate, to impose taxes on themselves to assist Cathar Good Men. Such an event took place in Cambiac in the 1240s. When the Good Man Guillaume Fort was arrested, the villagers, partly at the prompting of the local lord, Guillaume Sais, raised money with which to bribe the *bayle* of Caraman to release him.[34] The inhabitants of Caraman also taxed themselves in an effort to fend off the consequences of their involvement with heresy. On 19 February 1245 Bertrand d'Alamans de Saint-Germier of Caraman appeared before the inquisitors. According to his testimony, about two years earlier two Cathar heretics had been liberated from captivity while being taken from Caraman to Toulouse. The entire population of Caraman, with two exceptions,

---

[30] Bourin-Derruau, *Villages médiévaux en Bas-Languedoc*, 2: 145–80.
[31] MS 609, which preserves what remains of this investigation, indicates that some fifteen villages each produced more than a hundred witnesses.
[32] MS 609, fol. 31r.
[33] Ibid., fols. 94, 223r.
[34] Ibid., fols. 238r, 239r, 240r.

had asked Bertrand to approach the local *bayles*, Aribert and Pons Guillaume, and request that they not conduct an investigation into this affair. The *bayles* agreed, on condition that they each be paid 100 sous of Toulouse. Bertrand conveyed their demand to the villagers. All but two of the *castrum*'s inhabitants agreed to this bargain. Caraman's consuls took on themselves the task of collecting the money, each inhabitant paying according to his or her ability. In all, 150 sous were collected, of which 100 went to Aribert and the rest to Pons Guillaume.[35]

On occasion villagers also organized violent resistance. One very interesting story comes from the earliest days of the inquisition. On 31 August 1278 Guillaume Raffard of Roquefère ("Ruppeforti"), a converted heretic, told the following story to the inquisitors. About forty-five years before (therefore sometime around 1233) Pierre Boissa, the abbot of Sorèze's messenger, had arrested two female Cathar heretics. As he was taking them to Sorèze, the women of Roquefère assaulted him with sticks and stones and rescued the heretics. Pierre, having escaped from the harpies of Roquefère, made his way to Sorèze and denounced them to the abbot. The abbot, collecting Roquefère's lord, one Jourdain, descended on the *castrum*. There he assembled the local women, their husbands being at work in the fields, and queried them about these events. The women replied that Boissa

had not found or arrested any heretics there [in Roquefère]; but he had arrested two good, married women from the *castrum*, who, like an idiot, he had claimed were heretics. It was these women they had liberated, and no others. They produced two married women from the *castrum*, saying that these were the women he had arrested, an assertion that the two women also repeated. The messenger replied that these were not the women whom he had arrested, and who had been taken from him; he had arrested two women who were most certainly heretics, whom the women had rescued. He would certainly recognize them were they present, which they were not. Because the messenger could produce no other proof of his contention, he was reduced to an object of derision.[36]

In early 1245 Pierre Fogasset of Caraman told the inquisitors a less amusing tale. In either 1241 or 1242 Master Pierre Capellanus of Vallègue ("Vihrac") and Cessales had been persecuting the inhabitants of Caraman. Some ten men got together with the local *bayle* and decided to frighten him into abandoning his

---

[35] Doat, 23: fols. 69r–70r.
[36] Doat, 26: fols. 40r–v: "responderunt quod nuntius ille non invenerat nec ceperat ibi haereticas, sed ceperat duas bonas mulieres de castro maritatas quibus sicut stultus imponebat quod erant haereticae, et quod illas abstulerunt ei et non alias. Et ostenderunt eis duas mulieres de castro maritatas, dicentes quod illas ceperat, quod ipse duae mulieres similiter asserabant. Dictus vero nuntius ex adverso dicebat quod non erant ille mulieres quas ipse ceperat, et abstulerant ei, sed procul dubio ceperat duas haereticas quas abstulerant ei. Et non videbat eas ibi quia bene cognosceret eas. Et quia dictus nuntius non potuit aliter factum suum probare, fuit reductus in trufam."

activities. Among his other responsibilities, Master Pierre was collecting the tithes in Caraman; one of his associates in this enterprise, Jean Bérard, volunteered to lure him to a place where he could be effectively terrorized. The other conspirators armed themselves and set up an ambush at the pass of "den Auger." A short time later Bérard led Master Pierre and his clerk into the pass. The bushwhackers leaped out of concealment and assaulted their unsuspecting prey. Master Pierre managed to escape, but his clerk was killed and his body thrown down a well.[37]

Such incidents in which open defiance of the inquisitors was organized around the social networks of the village or the *castrum* seem, however, to have virtually vanished after the 1240s. One obvious explanation for this is the growth of a more hostile environment for heresy and its sympathizers. But there may also have been some structural factors at work. Languedocian villages and *castra* had experienced a major phase of internal organization in the twelfth and thirteenth centuries, but they had not become closed, corporate communities. Unlike some of the common-field villages found in parts of northern Europe, especially the Midlands of England, they did not practice a closely integrated form of communally regulated cultivation. Moreover, villages were not hermetically sealed off from the outside world. Villagers were tied to outsiders by bonds of kinship, economic exchange, and patronage. All of this tended to break down any sense of solidarity among them. Without the leadership, and perhaps the coercive authority, of members of the local nobility, it appears that it was difficult to mobilize villages to offer open resistance. As we have seen, by the late thirteenth century such outside leadership was rare.

## STRUCTURES OF RESISTANCE: THE TOWN

The most effective challenges to inquisitorial activity occurred in the towns, whose inhabitants had the necessary combination of wealth, organization, and political connections to mount serious resistance. The early years of the inquisition in Languedoc were marked by a number of spectacular confrontations between inquisitors and townspeople. In 1234 the inquisitor Ferrier tried to arrest one of the inhabitants of the *bourg* of Narbonne. A mob quickly gathered at the suspect's house and set him free. When the archbishop and the viscount of Narbonne entered the *bourg* the next day to arrest the suspect, they were forced to withdraw by the assembled citizens.[38]

In June of that same year at Albi, an attempt by Arnaud Catalan to exhume and burn the remains of a woman named Boyssene set off a riot that almost cost him his life. When Catalan ordered the woman's exhumation and cremation, the bishop of Albi's *bayle*, frightened by the unsettled mood of the city, refused to carry out his order. The inquisitor therefore went himself to the cemetery and delivered the first mattock blows to Boyssene's grave. Leaving the bishop's servants

---

[37] Doat, 23: fols. 313r–14r.
[38] Emery, *Heresy and Inquisition*, p. 77.

to finish the job, he set off for the cathedral, where a synod was being held. But he was overtaken by the bishop's terrified servants, who reported that they had been ejected from the churchyard. Catalan went back to the cemetery to confront those who had defied his orders. There Guillaume du Puy seized him, crying out, "Get out of the city, you villain." The inquisitor was beaten and dragged out of the graveyard and through the city streets toward the River Tarn, with the mob crying out after him, "Away, rid the earth of this fellow! He has no right to live." A local priest, one Isarn, who was following the crowd in the expectation of witnessing the inquisitor's martyrdom, was also seized and beaten. The two were finally rescued by some sympathetic Albigeois. As they made their way to the cathedral, the aroused townspeople shouted after them, "Death to the traitors!" and "Why don't they cut off the traitor's head and stuff it in a sack and throw it in the Tarn?" Once safely back at the cathedral, Catalan excommunicated the entire city.[39]

The best known of these early urban challenges to the inquisitors was the determined resistance mounted by the townspeople of Toulouse. This episode was vividly described by the Dominican Guillaume Pelhisson, an eyewitness to and participant in some of the events. When the inquisitor Guillaume Arnaud cited twelve leading citizens of Toulouse to appear before him, he touched off a firestorm of opposition. The suspects, with the backing of the local authorities, ordered him to leave town or cease his investigations; Arnaud persisted. The consuls therefore physically ejected him from the city on 15 October 1235. Retiring to Carcassonne, Arnaud instructed some of the city's clergy to issue a second citation to those suspected of heresy. When they did so, they were in turn expelled. The consuls also inaugurated a boycott of the Dominicans, the bishop of Toulouse, and the canons of the cathedral. The bishop, unable to acquire the necessities of life, abandoned the city. The Dominicans managed to hang on, despite the armed guards posted at their gates, thanks to the support of sympathetic citizens who in the middle of the night threw loaves of bread and pieces of cheese over the convent's wall. Three weeks into the boycott, Guillaume Arnaud tried once again to issue citations. This time he entrusted the task of delivering them to his fellow Dominicans. Expecting to be martyred, a small band of friars went about the city. Although they were abused and roughed up, they completed their task. The consuls, thoroughly exasperated, expelled all the Dominicans from the city in the first week of November 1235.[40] They, and the inquisitor Guillaume Arnaud, were not able to return until August 1236, ten months later.[41]

After the 1230s, however, we find little in the way of open resistance offered by the towns of Languedoc. On the one hand, this may have been because by the

[39] Pelhisson, *Chronique*, pp. 112–22. The translations are from Wakefield, *Heresy, Crusade, and Inquisition*, pp. 226–28.

[40] Pelhisson, *Chronique*, pp. 70–88.

[41] Wakefield, *Heresy, Crusade, and Inquisition*, p. 148, who discusses the problems of dating the Dominicans' return.

1240s the activities of the inquisitors, combined with the propaganda of the new mendicant orders, had rooted heresy out of the major cities and confined it largely to rural zones of refuge.[42] On the other hand, it may have been because the inquisitors had learned to behave with circumspection when investigating urban heresy. Wakefield, at least, believes that after the return of Guillaume Arnaud and the Dominicans to Toulouse in 1236, the inquisitors acted more cautiously. And, because of the Franciscans' reputation for comparative mildness, a Friar Minor, Etienne de Saint-Thibéry, joined Guillaume Arnaud as a co-inquisitor.[43] For whatever reason, it is clear that the inquisitors' activities did not again arouse concerted opposition in Languedocian cities until the last decades of the century. But when urban opposition returned, it constituted one of the gravest challenges the Languedocian inquisitors ever faced.

Opposition first surfaced in Carcassonne. In the early 1250s, when the Dominicans were refusing to act as inquisitors, heresy hunting there had been left to the local bishop, Guillaume Arnaud (1249–55). Guillaume seems to have conducted his investigations in a relatively clement fashion. Penalties were relaxed in return for money payments and prisoners were allowed temporary leaves from incarceration.[44] In the 1260s, however, matters began to change. The Dominicans once again took charge of the inquisition. Equipped with a new prison built at royal expense and a permanent headquarters for their tribunal, the inquisitors set about laying local heretics by the heels. They eventually amassed a great deal of information implicating many prominent Carcassonnais in dealings with Catharism.[45]

By the mid-1280s the people of Carcassonne were beginning to agitate against the inquisitors. They appealed to both King Philip III and Pope Honorius IV.[46] Efforts were made to enlist other towns in the opposition movement. People who had appeared before the inquisitors were called on to retract their confessions.[47] It was also around this time that the (somewhat doubtful) plot to destroy the inquisitors' archives would have been hatched. In the early 1290s the Carcassonnais enjoyed some success in winning a sympathetic hearing from the king. In 1291 Philip IV issued instructions to the seneschal of Carcassonne to the effect that henceforth no one was to be arrested on the order of the inquisitors unless he was a self-confessed heretic or held to be a heretic by *fama publica*. In this last case, the seneschal should first obtain the counsel of various people

---

[42] See the argument for the rapid destruction of Catharism in Toulouse in Mundy, *Repression of Catharism at Toulouse*, pp. 45–50.

[43] Wakefield, *Heresy, Crusade, and Inquisition*, p. 148.

[44] C. Molinier, *L'Inquisition dans le Midi de la France*, pp. 275–76, 299–304, and Poux, *La Cité de Carcassonne*, 2: 154–55.

[45] Guiraud, *Histoire de l'inquisition*, 2: 295–302; Mahul, *Cartulaire et archives*, 5: 635–36; Doat, 26: fols. 153v–54r, 255r–57v; 28: fols. 166v–70r.

[46] Doat, 30: fol. 97v; *HL*, 9: 334.

[47] MS 12856, fol. 13v., cited by Vidal, *Un Inquisiteur jugé*, p. 6 n. 3; Doat, 26: fols. 270v–71r.

"worthy of trust" before making an arrest. These orders were renewed in late 1295 and early 1296.[48]

Perhaps as a result of this royal support, opposition to the inquisitors began to turn violent in the mid-1290s. Sometime around 1295 the inquisitor Nicholas d'Abbeville was driven from his pulpit when he tried to preach and was stoned through the streets. Other Dominicans were insulted and beaten up, and the order was boycotted.[49] In this tense atmosphere the local Franciscans took the side of the Carcassonnais. In 1296 the inquisitor's lieutenant, Foulques de Saint-Georges, accompanied by a royal judge and twenty to twenty-five sergeants, came to the Franciscan convent to cite several people from the *bourg* of Carcassonne who had taken refuge there. The Franciscans locked the gates against them. Angry words were exchanged, the convent's bell was rung, and a column of smoke sent up to summon the townspeople. A mob shouting "At the traitors" (*Als trachors*) poured into the streets. Stones and crossbow bolts were showered on the inquisitors and their assistants, who had to fight their way to safety.[50]

The king's support, however, proved short-lived. Once Philip IV had settled the disputes over clerical taxation that had in the late 1290s led to a falling out with Pope Boniface VIII, he returned to the traditional royal policy of cooperation with the inquisitors. In September 1298 he ordered his officials to carry out the arrest of suspected heretics at the direction of the inquisitors.[51] The Carcassonnais appealed to Boniface VIII, but found him unwilling to intervene.[52] Unable to attract the permanent support of the king or the pope, the Carcassonnais were left to the mercies of Nicholas d'Abbeville. Nicholas, in addition to prosecuting various individuals on charges of heresy, excommunicated the consuls and the inhabitants of the *bourg*. By 1299 he had so ground the consuls down that they were willing to acknowledge a degree of collective guilt and, as penance, build a chapel in honor of St. Louis.[53]

For the moment the *bourg* of Carcassonne's opposition to the inquisitors had been quelled. However, events were to take place in Albi that would revive opposition on a new and greatly expanded scale. The bishop of Albi, Bernard de Castanet, had been locked for some time in a struggle with the people of his

---

[48] *HL*, 10: *Preuves*, cols. 273–75.

[49] Gui, *De fundatione*, pp. 102–3; Doat, 30: fol. 94r; and Lea, *Inquisition of the Middle Ages*, 2: 68–69.

[50] Dmitrewski, "Bernard Délicieux," p. 194; MS 4270, fols. 231r–32v, 238r–v. The dating of this incident is a problem. The depositions in MS 4270 place this event after the *vidame* of Amiens's removal of prisoners from the Carcassonne *mur*, which occurred in 1303. However, Foulques de Saint-Georges was active as an inquisitor in the 1290s (see *Documents*, 1: cxxxii). Foulques was accompanied by Etienne Auriol, a judge of the royal criminal court in Carcassonne, whom Strayer in his *Les Gens du justice du Languedoc*, p. 106, indicates as being active in 1299–1300. Dmitrewski gives the date as 1296, and I have followed him.

[51] *HL*, 10: *Preuves*, cols. 276–77. See also Lea, *Inquisition of the Middle Ages*, 2: 67.

[52] Lea, *Inquisition of the Middle Ages*, 2: 69; MS 4270, fols. 119v–20v.

[53] The negotiations over this settlement produced a number of documents, which are in Doat, 32: fols. 283v–88r, 299r–308r.

cathedral city over the limits of their respective political authority. In late 1299 Castanet, perhaps as part of this struggle, decided to embark on a heresy investigation.[54] He arrested twenty-five inhabitants of Albi, following up these arrests with another seven a year later. Those seized were among the leading citizens of the town, seventeen of them having previously served as consuls. With the assistance of Nicholas d'Abbeville, Castanet tried these men very rapidly between 2 December 1299 and 30 March 1300. The penalties he and Nicholas imposed were among the harshest possible. Twenty-four people were sentenced to imprisonment, with attendant confiscation of property; they were removed from Albi and incarcerated in Carcassonne.[55]

Many of the people of Albi were convinced that the charges against their fellow citizens had been trumped up by Castanet and d'Abbeville and that the innocent had been forced to confess through the liberal application of torture. Their suspicions were reinforced by the misadventures of one of Castanet's jailers, the priest Jean Fresqueti. According to testimony gathered by a papal commission in 1307, Fresqueti had participated in torturing the suspects.[56] Apparently repenting his involvement in the affair, he fled to the Franciscan convent in Albi, having the prescience to take with him copies of the depositions collected by Castanet and d'Abbeville. From there he made his way to the Franciscan house in Lautrec. Unfortunately for Fresqueti, Castanet bribed the viscount of Lautrec to extract him from the convent. Jean was returned to Albi, imprisoned by Castanet, and quickly murdered to prevent the Franciscans from securing his release.[57]

In trying to organize resistance to Castanet and the inquisitors, the Albigeois made contact with a Franciscan friar, Bernard Délicieux. Délicieux had long been an opponent of the Carcassonne inquisitors and he undertook to help the townspeople.[58] Two royal *enquêteurs*, one of whom was the *vidame* of Amiens, Jean de Picquigny, had just arrived in Languedoc. The complaints of the Albigeois were delivered to them.[59] In the autumn of 1301 Délicieux and a delegation of Albigeois went north to Senlis for an interview with the king.[60] Philip IV was once again at loggerheads with the pope and thus ready to entertain complaints about the inquisitors. As a result of this meeting, the king seized the temporalities of the see of Albi and saddled the bishop with a huge fine. He also imposed a variety of restraints on the Languedocian inquisitors.[61] In the aftermath of this interview, the situation in Albi drifted toward open war. Local nobles took

[54] Biget, "Un Procès d'inquisition," p. 325.
[55] Ibid., pp. 295, 298, 311, 283–84.
[56] Collectorie 404, fol. 172v.
[57] Ibid., fol. 83v.
[58] On his earlier involvement in resistance, see Dmitrewski, "Bernard Délicieux," pp. 195–96.
[59] AM Albi, FF15.
[60] MS 4270, fols. 123r–24v.
[61] Compayré, *Etudes historiques et documents inédits*, pp. 239–40; Lea, *Inquisition of the Middle Ages*, 2: 79–81; Dmitrewski, "Bernard Délicieux," p. 208; *HL*, 10: *Preuves*, cols. 379–84.

advantage of Castanet's discomfiture to begin seizing tithes that had been recovered by the bishop or his predecessors. On 11 February 1302 Castanet, returning to Albi from Toulouse, was greeted by a mob that issued out of the city gates crying, "Death! Death! Death to the traitor, death!"[62]

If his enemies can be believed, Castanet himself embarked on a campaign of terror and assassination. According to the complaints collected by papal commissioners in 1307, Castanet disposed of anyone who might be able to tell the truth about his condemnation of the supposedly heretical citizens of Albi. Castanet's *bayle* was poisoned and, in addition to Jean Fresqueti, two other individuals who had assisted in torturing the suspects were imprisoned and murdered.[63] The Albigeois replied in kind, directing much of their anger against the local Dominicans. During Advent in 1302, Dominican preachers were driven from their pulpits and harried through the streets. According to Bernard Gui, the Albigeois boycotted the friars for the next six years, refusing to give them alms, attend mass in their convent, or allow their dead to be buried there. On one occasion in 1303, a mob assaulted the Dominicans' convent and did considerable damage.[64]

It was the *bourg* of Carcassonne, however, that flirted with open rebellion. In the summer of 1303 the *vidame* of Amiens, the king's *enquêteur*, visited Carcassonne. Bernard Délicieux used this opportunity to secure a copy of the agreement that Nicholas d'Abbeville and the *bourg*'s consuls had negotiated in 1299. The exact terms of this agreement had been kept secret and Bernard proceeded to put the darkest possible interpretation on them. In a fiery sermon preached in early August he roundly denounced the pact. In it, so he said, the consuls had admitted that the entire *bourg* was guilty of heresy; they had thus saddled with guilt all the descendants of the *bourg*'s inhabitants to the fourth generation. This meant, Bernard contended, that if in the future the inquisitors proceeded against inhabitants of the *bourg* on suspicion of heresy, they could send them to the stake as relapsed heretics.[65]

The current inquisitor, Geoffroy d'Ablis, tried to present a more palatable interpretation of the agreement. On 10 August he held a meeting at the bishop's palace. Here he announced that in 1299 the consuls had not confessed to any complicity in heresy, that they had not asked absolution for their misdeeds, and that the people of the *bourg* had not been absolved since they had never been excommunicated in the first place.[66] But as the agreement was being read aloud, a man stood up and cried out, "Behold this lying document; ah traitors, at the

[62] Gui, *De fundatione*, p. 202.
[63] These were Pierre Milhani, *bayle* of the bishop's bastide, and Raimond de Brinh and Guillaume Revelli. See Collectorie 404, fols. 7v, 18v, 37v–38r, 51r, 53v, 56v–57r, 63r, 70r, 76r, 83v, 85v, 87v, 94v, 98r, 99r.
[64] Gui, *De fundatione*, pp. 201–3; AM Albi, FF17.
[65] MS 4270, fols. 135v–36v, 160r–v, 193v–94r, 223v, 267r, 281r–v, 286r–v, 292r–v.
[66] Doat, 34: fols. 21r–24v.

traitors!" At this, the crowd stood up and rushed out of the church. Rioting soon began in the *bourg*; in the ensuing uproar the houses of several of those consuls who had agreed to the 1299 pact were destroyed.[67] After the riots the *bourg* remained in a virtual state of insurrection. A mob stoned the Dominican convent, shattering its windows.[68] Sympathizers of the inquisition were assaulted. Crowds followed Dominicans through the streets, crying out derisively, like crows, "*Cohac, cohac.*"[69] Some friars were attacked and the order was boycotted. Royal agents patrolling the *bourg* were disarmed; in effect, the townspeople had usurped royal jurisdiction.[70] Under the leadership of one Elie Patrice, the townsmen also organized their own militia.

The *vidame* of Amiens, who had left Carcassonne before the riot, now returned. He was presented with a demand that he remove those convicted of heresy from the inquisitorial *mur*. Eighty men from Albi concealed themselves in the Franciscan church, ready to attack the *mur* if the *vidame* failed to act.[71] Picquigny surrendered to the pressure. Accompanied by a mob, he went to the *mur*. As the crowd milled about and the inquisitors tossed copies of an appeal to the pope out of one of the prison's upper windows, he demanded entry. Initially the jailers refused; but when Picquigny prepared to force his way in, they opened the doors. The *vidame* transferred the inmates to the royal prisons in the *cité*. There the members of the anti-inquisitorial party collected statements in which the prisoners asserted that they had been tortured into giving false confessions.[72]

Armed with this material, Délicieux embarked on a propaganda tour. In some places, such as Rabastens, Gaillac, and Cordes, he succeeded in getting promises of cash to support the struggle against the inquisitors.[73] He also presided over the formation of a formal confederation linking the towns of Albi, Carcassonne, and Cordes in a single alliance to prosecute the campaign against the inquisitors.

At Christmas of 1303, King Philip arrived in Languedoc, but his trip to the Midi did not help resolve the region's problems. Instead, his visit became itself a source of further discontent and unrest. Philip's old enemy, Boniface VIII, had died in October, to be succeeded by a Dominican pope, Benedict XI. With a new pontiff in Rome, Philip was less disposed to curry favor with his subjects by opposing the inquisitors. Nevertheless, his initial acts boded well for the inquisitors' enemies. Philip's entry into Toulouse was greeted by a demonstration of the

---

67 MS 4270, fols. 194r–v, 199r–v, 206v, 224v, 287r–v. The quotation ("Ecce falsum instrumentum; ah proditores, ali proditores") is from fol. 194v.

68 Ibid., fol. 291r.

69 Ibid., fols. 221v–22r, 281v. Evidently they were mocking the black and white, "crow-like" garb of the Dominicans.

70 Doat, 64: fols. 320r–23v; MS 4270, fols. 222r–v.

71 MS 4270, fols. 49r–v, 59r–v.

72 Ibid., fols. 155v–56r, 228v–30v, 237r–38r, 288r–v, 298v–300v.

73 Ibid., fols. 47r–48v; Dmitrewski, "Bernard Délicieux," p. 471.

wives of the Albigeois prisoners, who cried out to him, *Justicia! Justicia!*[74] The king entertained complaints about the inquisitors and issued orders designed to ameliorate the treatment of those held in their custody and to expedite their trials.[75] On 25 January, Philip entered Carcassonne, where the townspeople had sumptuously decorated their houses to welcome him. Delegations from Albi and Cordes were also present to swell the reception. The high hopes that the inquisitors' enemies had for the king's visit were soon dashed, however. As the king was about to mount the stairs leading into the royal stronghold, he was accosted by Elie Patrice, the leader of the *bourg*'s militia. Gesturing toward the *bourg*, Patrice said to the king, "Lord, lord, have mercy on this town of yours which is treated so harshly." Annoyed by Patrice's effrontery, Philip had his bodyguards remove him. Patrice, disheartened, rode through the streets of the town calling on his fellow citizens to take down their decorations.[76]

When the king left a disappointed Carcassonne, Délicieux and a number of townsmen followed him to Béziers. There the king's councilor, Guillaume de Nogaret, told them that Philip had a great many matters to settle with the new pope, and that Benedict, himself a Dominican, would certainly not be kindly disposed to a wholesale recall of the inquisitors. He therefore urged them to await more favorable circumstances to prosecute their case.[77] Philip himself gave the Carcassonnais a clear sign of his displeasure. The consuls of the *bourg* had presented two silver vessels to the king and the queen. Not only did the king refuse his, but he also made the queen return the one she had received.[78]

This act convinced some of the Carcassonnais that they could hope for no real help from the king. As Elie Patrice put it, they confronted two choices: either to burn the *bourg* and flee the wrath of the inquisitors or to find a new lord who would be able to protect them.[79] They therefore sought out a member of the royal house of Majorca, Prince Ferrand, the son of King Jayme. Ferrand proved interested in their proposals. Accordingly, around Easter a number of the *bourg*'s consuls agreed to renounce their fealty to Philip and call upon Ferrand to become

---

[74] MS 4270, fol. 214r.

[75] *HL*, 10: *Preuves*, cols. 428–31; MS 4270, fols. 139v–40r.

[76] MS 4270, fols. 233r–33v: "Domine, domine, sit vobis cordi ista misera villa vestra quae ita male et dure tractatur." This is the story told by Bernard Audegerii at Bernard Délicieux's trial in 1319. Arnaud Marsindi, also interrogated during this trial, gave a slightly different account of what took place. According to Arnaud, the confrontation between the king and Elie Patrice occurred during the royal procession through the city's streets and involved an explicit threat to the king. Arnaud claimed that Patrice said to the king: "My lord, do us justice quickly, for we can go to another lord" (*Domine, faciatis nobis ius breve, quia nos possumus ire ad alium dominum*). Philip, not surprisingly, was outraged by these words. The two parted company in the street, Patrice saying: "Now I return to my people; may you, my lord, go with God" (*Nunc revertor ad populum meum, ad Deum, domine, sitis*). Marsindi's testimony is given on fols. 226r–26v.

[77] Ibid., fols. 112v–13r.

[78] Ibid., fols. 103r–v.

[79] Ibid., fol. 104r.

their lord.[80] An effort was made to enlist the people of Albi in the plot; wisely, as it proved, they refused.[81]

Délicieux was given the task of transmitting the offer to Ferrand. Together with the guardian of the Franciscan convent of Carcassonne, he left to seek out the prince. During his journey Bernard took the precaution of destroying the incriminating documents he was carrying, tearing them up, burying them in a small hole, and urinating on them.[82] Bernard located the prince, who was in attendance at his father's court, at Saint-Jean-Pla-de-Corts near Perpignan. Délicieux had a long interview with him. King Jayme, however, became suspicious about the friar's visit and summoned Bernard to explain his presence. The king found his replies unsatisfactory and called on Ferrand to explain. After a royal outburst of rage, in which the king struck his son, pulled clumps of hair out of his head, and was barely restrained from beating him with a rod, Ferrand revealed the entire plot. Jayme promptly ordered Délicieux and his companion out of the kingdom.[83]

Fairly quickly thereafter, information about this attempted treason reached the French royal court. Informed of this, Délicieux led another embassy from Carcassonne and Albi north in the hopes of averting the king's wrath. This embassy failed in its purpose; indeed, Délicieux was arrested and imprisoned in the Franciscan convent in Paris.[84] Ultimately, fifteen inhabitants of the *bourg* were tried, condemned, and hanged, along with forty people from Limoux, who, in a manner that is not at all clear from the surviving sources, had become involved in the conspiracy. The *bourg* of Carcassonne was deprived of its consulate and saddled with a fine of 60,000 l.t.[85]

Opposition to the inquisitors did not end with this execution. With the death of Pope Benedict XI and the election of Clement V (1305–14), Bernard Délicieux (who had been released from arrest) and the people of Albi returned to the fray. The new pope was besieged with complaints, including some delivered to him personally by prisoners' wives. Bribes were also distributed among the cardinals. The inquisitor of Carcassonne, Geoffroy d'Ablis, found it necessary to visit the pope at Lyon to defend his conduct. In March 1306, the pope, at the request of the people of Albi, Carcassonne, and Cordes, dispatched two cardinals to investigate. For the duration of this commission, the inquisitors were instructed that they could neither torture nor subject to harsh terms of imprisonment anyone without first securing the cooperation of that person's bishop.

[80] Ibid., fols. 75v–78v, 103v–4v, 113r–16r, 195r–96v, 207r–v, 219r–v, 250v–51v, 284r–v, 293v–96r.

[81] Ibid., fol. 78v.

[82] Ibid., fols. 105r, 117r–v.

[83] Ibid., fols. 197v–98r; Finke, ed., *Acta aragonensia*, 3: 131–34.

[84] MS 4270, fols. 225v–26r, 80r–81v, 251v–53r, 296v.

[85] Mahul, *Cartulaire et archives*, 6.1: 10–11; *HL*, 9: 277–80; 10: *Preuves*, cols. 461–63; Hauréau, *Bernard Délicieux*, pp. 126–27; Gui, *De fundatione*, p. 105; Doat, 64: fols. 47r–v; Lea, *Inquisition of the Middle Ages*, 2: 90.

After visiting Carcassonne and Albi in April, the cardinals took steps to ameliorate the conditions under which prisoners were being held.[86]

After such upheaval and conflict, this may seem a rather paltry outcome. Nevertheless, it is clear that these events constituted the gravest challenge that the Languedocian inquisitors experienced in the late thirteenth and early fourteenth centuries. Inquisitors and other Dominicans were manhandled and boycotted. Restrictions were placed on the inquisitors' activities. For a time investigations may have come to a virtual halt. Indeed, this period of tumult and confrontation may have helped facilitate the last outburst of Cathar preaching in Languedoc: the mission of Pierre Autier and his fellow Good Men. At least Bernard Gui, writing several years later, commented, "During this persecution of the inquisitors and interference with their office, many heretics came together, and their numbers began to multiply and heresies sprouted up and infected many people in the dioceses of Pamiers, Carcassonne, and Toulouse, and around Albi."[87]

It is not surprising that towns presented such a grave challenge to the inquisitors. Townsmen had resources that were beyond the reach of other enemies of the inquisitors. One of these was the mob. The ordinary routines of daily life in the town brought together large numbers of people, to sell their goods in the marketplace and to hear sermons preached in the churches. These large groups could be quickly mobilized to oppose the inquisitors. As we have seen, the riot played a major role in the anti-inquisitorial campaign. As was typical of the better studied riots of early modern and modern Europe, such actions were largely reactive and defensive.[88] The rioters assembled spontaneously to block the efforts of the agents of the inquisitor, as when Foulques de Saint-Georges in 1296 tried to arrest suspects at the Franciscan convent in Carcassonne. What is striking, however, is that anti-inquisitorial riots could also be proactive and aggressive. In the right circumstances—with the intervention of a charismatic speaker such as Bernard Délicieux and with the connivance of the town authorities—mobs could be motivated to carry out violent assaults. The riot at Carcassonne directed against the consuls who had approved the 1299 pact with the inquisitor Nicholas d'Abbeville, as well as the riot at the gates of the city of Albi that almost cost Bishop Castanet his life, are good examples of this pattern.

Linked to the riot was the demonstration. When Philip IV came to Languedoc, he was greeted at Toulouse by the wives of the prisoners from Albi, who cried out for justice. At Carcassonne he was treated to the somber and ominous sight of the people of the *bourg* solemnly removing the decorations they had hung out for his entry.

The towns' campaign against the inquisitors was also greatly aided by their wealth and by their ability quickly to mobilize that wealth. Using some of the

---

[86] Lea, *Inquisition of the Middle Ages*, 2: 92–94.
[87] Gui, *De fundatione*, p. 204.
[88] See Tilly, *From Mobilization to Revolution*, pp. 184–88.

same mechanisms they employed to levy taxes, the townsmen were able to raise substantial amounts of money. The towns of Albi, Cordes, and Carcassonne pooled their resources and paid Bernard Délicieux a regular salary to conduct the campaign against the inquisitors.[89] When the *vidame* of Amiens was excommunicated for removing the inquisition's prisoners from the Carcassonne *mur*, these three towns provided him with 3,000 livres to prosecute an appeal at the papal court.[90]

The wide network of social and political ties established by the urban elites as a result of their mercantile activity and their participation in the political structures of the French kingdom also helped them establish alliances with other groups. First of all, it made it possible for them to organize on a regional scale. Unlike participants in village-based opposition, they were able to transcend the limits of a single locality. The commercial and political links that united the leading elements of the various Languedocian towns were thus put to good use in fashioning opposition to the inquisitors. Second, the political experience of the towns' ruling elites enabled them to enlist as allies a number of royal agents. At critical junctures royal servants intervened on the side of the townsmen. As we have seen, the *vidame* of Amiens removed prisoners from the *mur* in Carcassonne. When he was excommunicated for this, at least one royal official took steps to block publication of the sentence. A priest of the church of Notre-Dame-de-la-Platée of Castres, one Jean de Recoles, who tried to publish the sentence of excommunication in November of 1303, was promptly arrested by the lieutenant of Albi's royal *viguier*.[91] This same *viguier*, Guillaume de Pezens, also took steps to further the organization of opposition to the inquisitors. When the leaders of Albi's anti-inquisitorial party tried to collect money to fund their efforts, many people refused to contribute. However, Guillaume, together with a royal judge, Master Galhard Etienne, intervened, compelling the reluctant to pay up.[92]

Moreover, towns had propaganda resources available that other opponents of the inquisitors lacked. The ability of the Carcassonnais and the Albigeois to attract the sympathy of the Franciscans gave them access to skilled rhetoricians, able to sway the emotions of the mob. As we have seen, at certain critical moments the preaching of Bernard Délicieux was of vital importance to the campaign against the inquisitors. Indeed, the hold of this eloquent speaker over the masses of the *bourg* of Carcassonne seems to have been hypnotic. Raimond Arnaud, a Dominican who attended one of Bernard's sermons, reported that when Délicieux left the pulpit, people in the crowd tried to kiss his hands and clothing, while others cried out, "This is an angel whom God has sent us!"[93]

[89] MS 4270, fols. 133v–34r.
[90] Ibid., fols. 154r–55r.
[91] The text of the inquisitor's investigation of this affair is published in Hauréau, *Bernard Délicieux*, pp. 176–87.
[92] MS 4270, fol. 266r.
[93] Ibid., fol. 235v: "Iste est angelus quem Deus misit nobis."

Townsmen also proved skilled at the use of other forms of propaganda. After being removed from the Carcassonne *mur*, the inquisitors' prisoners were interviewed in their new lodgings in the royal jails. Rolls containing the names of the people whom the prisoners claimed they had been forced to denounce as their accomplices were drawn up. These documents were sent around Languedoc to stir up opposition. Brother Bernard de Linac, a Franciscan, took one roll to Toulouse and showed it to citizens of that town. At Lautrec the guardian of the Franciscan convent had another roll read to the people who came to hear mass in his church.[94] And pictures were as important as words. In the fourteenth century it was common for towns to be decorated with representations of good and bad government and with likenesses of paragons of virtue and vice.[95] At Albi the townspeople put art to work to make a clear, symbolic point. The town gate next to the Dominican convent had been adorned with images of St. Dominic and the murdered Italian inquisitor, Peter Martyr. During the anti-inquisitorial campaign these images were expunged. In their place were depicted the royal *enquêteurs*, Richard Leneveu and Jean de Picquigny, and two local leaders of the opposition, Pierre Probi of Castres and Arnaud Garsia of Albi.[96]

The record of open resistance to the inquisitors seems to have been something of a mixed bag. Challenges to the inquisitors can be found throughout the thirteenth and early fourteenth centuries, although they were most common in the 1230s, 1240s, 1290s, and the first two decades of the fourteenth century. However, it does seem that such behavior was relatively rare, as several factors militated against widespread collective resistance to the inquisitors. In premodern Europe, collective action often grew out of the daily routines of the population.[97] The grain riot, for example, required as an enabling condition the presence of a regular market in grain and a population dependent for its sustenance on that market. Market days brought together large numbers of people who could, without much organization, react violently to the perception of unfair prices. Little in the routine of daily life in medieval Languedoc brought together large numbers of people who were exclusively heretics or their sympathizers. Indeed, in the late thirteenth and early fourteenth centuries, meetings of Cathars and their sympathizers were rare and clandestine events.

In premodern Europe, popular collective action also usually grew out of preexisting social networks, not specially formed interest or action groups. Yet in medieval Languedoc the most widespread heretical sect—Catharism, a radical, world-rejecting religion—was hostile to most of the preexisting social networks that could have served as the basis for collective resistance. For the Cathars, the

---

[94] Ibid., fols. 27r–v; Dmitrewski, "Bernard Délicieux," pp. 484–85.

[95] I know of no study of this that discusses Languedoc directly. For an interesting discussion of some of this art, see Edgerton, *Pictures and Punishment*.

[96] Gui, *De fundatione*, p. 203.

[97] Tilly, *The Contentious French*, p. 10.

world and everything in it was the product of the devil. The flesh and the social ties created after the flesh were simply snares designed to delude souls about their true, heavenly nature. The Cathar religion denied any religious or moral value to those social ties around which collective resistance to the inquisitors could most readily have been fashioned. Prevailing standards of right and justice as well tended to work against the organization of collective resistance. Many people in Languedoc were sympathetic to heretics of one sort or another; but many were not. Even in villages with a high representation of Cathar or Waldensian sympathizers, there were many committed Catholics. This deep ideological division within the Languedocian population made the organization of large-scale, collective resistance difficult.

Finally, the nature of inquisitorial pressure worked against the mobilization of large-scale, collective action. In the early days of the inquisition in the mid-thirteenth century, the inquisitors had often swept up vast numbers of people in their investigations. By the end of the thirteenth and the beginning of the fourteenth centuries, however, such wholesale actions were over. The inquisitors' efforts were much more focused and targeted. Even in villages that seem to have been hotbeds of heretical activity, the inquisitors' attentions were directed to only a part of the population, many of whom were connected by kinship ties.[98] The tendency for the inquisitors to select for investigation and punishment only some of a settlement's inhabitants meant that they seldom offended more than a fraction of that locality's population. With some people in the clutches of the inquisitors, others relieved that they had been passed by, and still others undoubtedly pleased at the difficulties of their neighbors, it was difficult to organize resistance on a large scale.

It was thus only in unusual circumstances that the conditions for open, collective opposition to the inquisitors came together. This conjunction of forces occurred most frequently in towns. Here the maladroit actions of a Bishop Bernard de Castanet, who offended the ruling elite of Albi, and of a Nicholas d'Abbeville, who raised the specter of guilt over the entire *bourg* of Carcassonne, simultaneously offended large segments of the local population. In the towns of Albi and Carcassonne, the daily routines of public life—attendance at market, attendance at the sermons of the Franciscans—brought large numbers of people together. Once assembled, these crowds could be persuaded, in a time-honored form of political protest in the cities of southern France, to riot against the inquisitors and their allies. Hence it is no surprise that the inquisitors found that the most serious challenge to their work came from the towns of Languedoc.

---

[98] Of the 637 people who appear in Bernard Gui's *LS*, 395 (62 percent) can be identified as kin to one another.

# CHAPTER 6

# MANIPULATION

I N THE ARENA of Languedocian politics, the inquisitors and their institution constituted both new players and a new resource. They were hardly unique in occupying such a role in thirteenth- and early-fourteenth-century Languedoc. This period witnessed a significant reshaping of the Languedocian political arena: the assertion of royal overlordship, the consolidation of political authority by many local potentates, the spread of communal forms of organization among the region's villagers, and, at the end of the period, the growing influence of the Avignon papacy.[1] Nevertheless, in the changing context of Languedocian politics, the inquisition was a new resource of an unusual nature. It was equipped with a novel and, at times, exceptionally thorough set of investigating techniques; it was far more coercive in its operations than most other governing institutions; and the sanctions it employed were unusually varied and flexible.

It was thus a tempting tool for ambitious politicians, whether great or small. Those who could figure out how to ally with or manipulate the inquisitors found themselves in possession of a valuable mechanism with which they could further their own ends. As we shall see in this chapter, the inquisition could be put to work to destroy one's enemies, protect one's friends, or fatten one's moneybags. Indeed, the late thirteenth and early fourteenth centuries seem to have been a period when efforts to manipulate the inquisition were particularly frequent.[2] By this time the inquisition had become something of a known factor in Languedocian society. Dominican tribunals had long been established in Toulouse and Carcassonne. Thousands of individuals had passed through their hands. Over time many people must have acquired a fairly sophisticated understanding of how the inquisitors operated, what evidence they found convincing, and what types of heterodoxy attracted their interest.

---

[1] See Given, *State and Society*, passim.

[2] One indication is the frequency with which inquisitors imposed penances on individuals whose chief fault was bearing false witness against the innocent (see below). For example, on 13 August 1324 at Pamiers, nine people were condemned as false witnesses (Doat, 28: fols. 71r–86r); at Narbonne on 11 December 1328, four such people were sentenced (27: fols. 134r–35v); and at Carcassonne on 10 September 1329, seventeen false witnesses were penanced (27: fols. 241r–45r).

But the inquisition was also a dangerous institution with which to involve oneself. Most efforts to manipulate it depended on deceit and deception and on controlling the flow of information to the inquisitors. And as we have seen, the inquisitors had unusually effective means for discovering that which people wished to keep secret. Manipulating the inquisition may have given some Languedocians access to a new and unusually effective political resource. Yet there was always the danger that the inquisitors might discover what was afoot. The price paid by an unlucky schemer for access to this particular resource could be very high.

## FALSE TESTIMONY BY ISOLATED INDIVIDUALS

In this chapter we shall examine some of the better-documented efforts to manipulate the Languedocian inquisition. We shall begin by looking at some cases where individuals acting on their own tried to involve their enemies in the toils of the inquisition. Certainly many an individual must have felt a strong temptation to try to even the score with an old adversary by delivering him to the inquisitors. Yet such incidents have left relatively faint traces in the records. One of the few well-documented cases comes from Bernard Gui's tenure at Toulouse. On 22 April 1312 Gui sentenced Pons Arnaud de Pujols of Sainte-Foy-d'Aigrefeuille to perpetual imprisonment. In the list of his *culpe*, it was stated that Pons had, without being summoned, presented himself to Gui. He had told the inquisitor that about twenty years earlier he had fallen ill. His son Pierre had brought two Cathar heretics to him and urged him to be received into their sect. Gui, assuming that a father would not falsely denounce his own son, began an investigation. Pierre, however, steadfastly denied all the allegations against him. Gui grew suspicious. He summoned Pons and made him repeat his charges in his son's presence. Pierre persisted in his denials; Gui thereupon arrested Pons. Further investigation revealed that at the time when Pons claimed to have been ill, he was in fact in perfectly good health. Moreover, there had been almost no heretics at large in the area where he lived. When Gui confronted Pons with this information, he broke down and admitted that hatred for his son (unfortunately not explained in the record) had led him to invent the entire story.[3]

Another individual who tried to dupe Bernard Gui with a false denunciation was Jean de la Salvetat of Prunet. On 31 December 1311 he made a deposition in which he accused several people of having had contacts with the Good Man Jacques Autier. These people were duly arrested. Under interrogation, however, they maintained their innocence, even when Gui confronted them with their accuser. In the course of these proceedings, on 23 April 1312 Jean de la Salvetat was sentenced to perpetual imprisonment.[4] Lodged in the

---

[3] *LS*, pp. 95–96. For a case from the 1250s in which a wife's hatred for her husband may have led her to give false testimony against him, see *Documents*, 2: 214–15.

[4] *LS*, p. 140.

*mur,* Jean continued to insist for the next two and a half years on the truth of his accusations. Yet Gui's doubts grew. The testimony of other witnesses indicated that on the dates when Jean had claimed to see certain individuals in the company of Jacques Autier, the heretic had actually been elsewhere, in the company of entirely different people. Gui therefore called on Jean to tell the truth. When Jean once again reiterated his story, Gui had him placed in what seems to have been a form of solitary confinement.[5] Jean broke almost immediately; on the same day, or the day after (1 July 1314), he admitted that he had fabricated his accusations. As punishment, he was sentenced on 6 March 1316 to a strict regime of imprisonment; he was also required to wear red tongues on his clothing and to undergo public exhibition.[6]

When Arnaud Raimond of Douzens, a clerk, tried to manipulate the inquisition, he was not seeking to settle an old score; he merely wanted to make some money. On 2 December 1291 Arnaud, who had been detained in the *mur* in Carcassonne, appeared before Guillaume de Saint-Seine. According to Arnaud, about three years earlier, while he was directing the destruction of a stone wall in a building belonging to the Templars, he had discovered a clay pot hidden in the wall. He broke open the pot and found within it many pieces of parchment, so decayed that he could barely read them. When Arnaud finally deciphered them, he realized that he had chanced on wills leaving bequests to Cathar Good Men and on bonds recording debts owed to the heretics. Arnaud discussed his find with Guillaume Raynes, the *bayle* of Comigne. The *bayle* observed that Arnaud could acquire many friends and benefactors if he returned these incriminating documents to the relatives of the people who had had them drawn up. To Arnaud this seemed like a good way to gain some *lucrum temporale.* Since the fragments he had found were so deteriorated that he feared no one would give them any credence, he copied them over in his own hand, transferring the wax he had found on the originals to his copies. To make the copies look more authentic, he put them in a small window next to a cooking fire, so that the smoke could discolor them. He then set out to blackmail the heirs of those named in the documents. All told, he got seven people in a number of villages near Capendu in the Minervois to give him a total of 129 sous and some wheat.

Once he had rehearsed this tale, he was sent back to prison. A little more than two weeks later, on 17 December, he appeared again. The time he had spent in prison had led him to reconsider his story. He now testified that he had not found the documents but had forged them in their entirety. He had gotten the idea from an authentic will in his possession, which recorded a bequest left by his uncle Armanch, a knight of Aigues-Vives, to the heretics. Since he and his wife were very poor, he had decided that he could make some money by forging similar documents. He had picked out local men whom he thought

[5] Ibid., p. 181.
[6] Ibid., pp. 180–83.

would be able to help him and forged wills and bonds in which he put the names of their ancestors. He used these forgeries to obtain money from the descendants of those named in them. At some point he had fled to Catalonia. When he learned that the inquisitors, who had evidently been apprised of the contents of his forgeries, were taking them seriously, he returned to clear up the matter (or at least so he claimed).[7]

It is hard to evaluate the degree of success that individuals like these had in attempting to play on the inquisition. Evidence of very few such cases exists in the records. This might, of course, indicate that individuals acting on their own were relatively successful, since so few were discovered; but in fact the odds were against them. Although the inquisitors were prepared to begin an investigation on the evidence of a single witness, they were reluctant to convict unless his or her evidence could be corroborated by others.[8] And, as we have seen in the cases of Pons Arnaud and Jean de la Salvetat, the inquisitors' possession of an institutional memory, preserved in their archives, enabled them to spot weak points in a mendacious confession. These considerations lead me to believe that isolated individuals enjoyed little success in using the inquisitors to gain some personal advantage.

## THE INQUISITORS' SERVANTS

Successful manipulation of the inquisitors required either collective action or special knowledge of the inquisitors and their operations. One group that had this special knowledge consisted of the inquisitors' own servants and assistants, who were not always very well supervised. The Languedocian inquisition was anything but a modern police bureaucracy, with an elaborate system of training and examination of candidates for advancement within its ranks. True, the inquisitors themselves experienced a form of vetting before they came to their posts. At least they had been through the training system of the Dominicans and their superiors had had an opportunity to evaluate their character and ability; but their servants underwent no such evaluation process. Moreover, in many cases the inquisitors had to rely on servants of other masters, kings and great lords, to carry out many of the tasks of hunting down heretics. If these people worked for an unobservant or complacent inquisitor, they had ample opportunity to make their positions serve their own ends.

The inquisitors' notaries were particularly well placed to profit from their association with the holy office. Their job was crucially important to the day-to-day functioning of the inquisition. Not only did the notaries produce the documents recording the inquisitors' work, they were often entrusted with the task of carrying out various aspects of an investigation.[9] Some were unable to resist the temptation to enrich themselves through a little corruption.

[7] Doat, 26: fols. 143r–47v.
[8] Eymerich, *Directorium inquisitorum*, p. 614.
[9] For examples, see *Registre*, 1: 468–69, 3: 421.

Undoubtedly the most notoriously venal notary to serve the inquisitors was Menet de Robécourt.[10] A native of the diocese of Toul, Menet became attached to the inquisitors of Carcassonne around 1320. During his two decades of service, he amassed a record of brutality, corruption, and avarice that is almost without parallel in the history of the Languedocian inquisition. His penchant for brutality is illustrated by his conduct in the affair of Pierre de Tournemire, a priest of Montpellier. In 1325 Menet, along with the Dominican Raimond Pelat, was sent by the inquisitor of Carcassonne, Jean Duprat, to investigate heresy in Montpellier. One of the individuals on whom Menet focused his attention was Tournemire. In his youth this priest had briefly been a Béguin, an offense for which he had subsequently sought and received pardon. Despite the offer by Pierre's friends to provide a bond in the impressive sum of 25,000 livres to guarantee his later appearance at Carcassonne, Menet and his companion arrested the priest, who was gravely ill. Spirited away from Montpellier in the middle of the night, Tournemire barely survived the journey to the *castrum* of Loupian, falling off his horse three times. When Pierre and his captors reached Béziers, physicians declared that Pierre was not fit to travel. Nevertheless, he was brought, more dead than alive, to Carcassonne. There, harassed to his very last breath by Menet, he expired, still maintaining his innocence. Pierre was denied burial in consecrated ground. His relatives asked Jean Duprat for copies of his confession so that they could undertake the defense of his memory. But Duprat refused, a refusal repeated by his successors in office. Only after thirty years of effort did Tournemire's friends and heirs manage to secure the appointment of a papal commission. In 1357 it cleared the priest of all charges of heresy.[11]

Not only was Menet zealous and brutal, he was also corrupt. Sometime, evidently in the late 1330s, Aymon de Caumont, inquisitor of Carcassonne, began an investigation of Jean de Lombers, a converted Jew. Seven witnesses were summoned to give testimony. Their evidence led the inquisitor to cite Lombers himself. He failed to appear, but he did bribe Menet to try to clear his name. The notary had the witnesses against Lombers arrested and incarcerated. In the inquisitorial prisons they were tortured to persuade them to revoke their depositions. When the statements that Menet wrung from his victims did not suit his purposes, he made alterations to them in his protocols. Ultimately the witnesses were released from captivity. Apparently, they began to tell the truth about what had happened to them, for Aymon de Caumont had them rearrested on 25 December, probably in 1342. However, the prisoners managed to get the ear of Pope Clement VI, who in 1343 ordered an investigation. The results of this inquiry are not known.[12]

---

[10] The following paragraphs draw heavily on Vidal, "Menet de Robécourt."
[11] Ibid., pp. 447–49; *Bullaire*, pp. 293–94.
[12] Vidal, "Menet de Robécourt," pp. 445–47; *Bullaire*, pp. 288–90.

Menet was finally done in when his path crossed that of the formidable Jacques Fournier. In the 1330s Menet was sent, along with some others, to investigate heresy in the city of Albi. If we can believe the charges later levied against them, these agents made good use of this opportunity to extort money from the townspeople.[13] In 1334 some of Albi's consuls complained of this to Jacques Fournier, then a cardinal at the papal curia. Fournier was disturbed by the fact that notaries were being allowed to carry out investigations without the presence of an inquisitor, a practice he had carefully avoided when he had been bishop of Pamiers. The consuls asked him to intercede with the pope. Before much could be done, John XXII died and Fournier himself was elected pope in December 1334, taking the name Benedict XII. Menet attempted to quash the accusations against him by beginning a heresy investigation of Géraud Coll, one of the consuls who had complained to Fournier while he was cardinal. Informed of this, the new pope ordered an investigation. Benedict's agents found against the notary. In 1340 Géraud Coll was declared free of any taint of heresy; Menet was deprived of his office and ordered to pay damages to Coll.[14]

Among the inquisitors' other servants were sergeants, often in royal or seigniorial employ but on loan to the inquisition. Although these people were not as influential as the notaries, there is evidence that some were able to put the inquisition's authority to use for their own purposes. Guillaume Maurs of Montaillou, for example, told Jacques Fournier an interesting story about two such sergeants. Guillaume's father and brother had been incarcerated in the *mur* at Carcassonne on suspicion of heresy. Through a contact he had made while living in Saint-Louis, he got in touch with one Bernard de Saint-Martin, a notary of Limoux. This Bernard assured Guillaume that he was so influential that he could free Guillaume's relatives from the *mur*, even if they were Cathar Good Men.

This proved, of course, to be an empty boast. Nevertheless, Guillaume went with the notary to Carcassonne. There he found lodging in the *bourg* near the bridge leading over the Aude to the *cité* where the inquisition's *mur* was located, and he waited for the notary to deliver on his promises. One day two royal sergeants, who were issuing citations to appear before the inquisitor, came to the house. They ate dinner with Guillaume and his friends. During the meal they asked Guillaume to identify some people, whom they described, who were from Prades d'Alion, a village that neighbored Guillaume's own Montaillou. After taking an oath to tell the truth, he said that the men they were interested in were Pierre Jean and Prades Aymeri.

The sergeants then revealed that these men had assaulted them. To revenge themselves, they wanted to cite them to appear before the inquisitor. They pro-

13 Vidal, "Menet de Robécourt," p. 439.
14 Ibid., pp. 437–45; *Bullaire*, pp. 230–32, 266–72, 277–78. For another case of an inquisitorial notary, Barthélemy Adalbert, condemned for malfeasance in office on 24 November 1328, see Doat, 27: fols. 112v–18r.

ceeded to ask Bernard de Saint-Martin to draw up a letter of citation. If he did this, they would remove the inquisitor's seal from one of the authentic letters they had in their possession and attach it to the forgery. Bernard obligingly wrote out a letter. For some reason, unfortunately not specified, the sergeants had also conceived a hatred for Pierre Clergue, the rector of Montaillou. They therefore asked Guillaume Maurs if he knew anything about the rector's involvement with heresy. Maurs obliged them with some anecdotes about Clergue's dealings with the Cathars. The sergeants then had the notary draw up another letter, this one citing Clergue to appear. In his deposition to Fournier, Maurs did not say that any of the parties to this forgery intended to profit financially from it. Yet, when Guillaume was sentenced to perpetual imprisonment on 5 July 1322, it was specifically stated in his sentence that he and his fellows had intended to extort money from their victims.[15]

This particular effort to manipulate the inquisitors seems to have gone off the rails rather quickly. In targeting Pierre Clergue of Montaillou, the conspirators had made a serious mistake. Pierre, along with his brother Bernard, was, as we shall see, a master of the art of manipulating the inquisitors. When Guillaume Maurs returned to Montaillou, he discovered that Clergue had managed to get the sergeants arrested for forgery. He also learned that he was being sought in connection with the affair. He therefore took to his heels and fled south toward Catalonia.[16]

## CONDITIONS FOR SUCCESSFUL MANIPULATION

In attempting to put the inquisition to their own use, individuals not affiliated with the institution confronted a more difficult task. On the whole, if a conspiracy wished to have a chance of success, it needed to satisfy several conditions. First, it was necessary to recruit several people willing to give false testimony against the intended victim. Second, it was advisable to enlist individuals of relatively high social standing, whose testimony would be well received and who could handle the expenses involved in mounting a conspiracy. And third, it helped if the intended victim was someone who had offended important members of the local political establishment and thus made himself vulnerable to attack.

We can see all of these factors at work in a plot hatched by some inhabitants of Pézenas to do in their common enemy, the notary Raimond Berleti. In 1325 Berleti's enemies made accusations concerning his alleged involvement with the Béguins to the court of the bishop of Béziers, but nothing seems to have come of them.[17] In 1329 the plotters approached the Dominican inquisitors. On 19 May Bernard Pastour, a merchant of Pézenas, presented himself, without having

[15] *LS*, p. 297.
[16] *Registre*, 2: 172–73.
[17] Doat, 27: fols. 211r–v, 212r.

been previously cited, to the inquisitor of Carcassonne, Henri de Chamayou, who was at the bishop's palace in Béziers. Bernard gave the inquisitor a note, written on paper, concerning Berleti's alleged heretical activities.

According to the note, the *domicellus* Imbert de Roquefixade and Jean Maurand had been in Pézenas when a number of Béguins were executed. Afterward they had come across Raimond Berleti at the place where the heretics had been burned. They saw him bowing before their remains as though he were worshiping them. They also observed him take some bones and wrap them up in cloth, as though they were the relics of saints. When the bystanders asked him what he doing, he replied, "I am gathering up the bones of these burned people, who are true martyrs. Certainly their faith was sounder than that of those who burned them, and this I believe. They were the best Christians. It was with great prejudice and injustice that they were burned; I believe that they are martyrs, I praise their faith, and I believe that they are in paradise."[18] The bystanders rebuked him, pointing out that the church would not have burned the Béguins if they had not been heretics, but he would not change his opinion.

Upon receipt of this missive, Chamayou opened an investigation. Pastour informed the inquisitor that his note had been written by Master Guillaume Lombard of Pézenas, a cleric and a procurator, and by Pierre, the clerk of a Pézenas notary named Arnaud Vascon. It had been drawn up at the urging and under the supervision of the apothecary Guillaume Mascon, also of Pézenas. The information in the note had come from Jean Maurand, Imbert de Roquefixade, Durand du Puy, and Guillaume de Cazouls. Chamayou summoned these individuals to give depositions. When they appeared, however, the conspiracy began to unravel. Jean Maurand alone claimed that he had been an eyewitness of the events described in Pastour's note. The others at first denied any knowledge of the affair. Only after being directly confronted with Bernard Pastour did Imbert de Roquefixade reluctantly support his story.

His suspicions aroused, Chamayou arrested Pastour, Imbert, Maurand, and Guillaume de Cazouls. After further interrogation in Béziers, they were removed to the *mur* at Carcassonne. Ultimately they all broke under questioning and admitted that they had fabricated the charges against Berleti. The reasons why these men wanted revenge on the notary are not very clear. The only conspirator whose motives we know is Raimond Caplieu, a Pézenas dealer in skins, who contributed sixteen deniers to the expenses of composing the denunciation. He admitted that he hated Berleti because Berleti had accused his uncle, Pons Montréal, of receiving fugitive, apostate members of the Franciscan order.[19]

---

[18] Ibid., fol. 205v: "Ego colligo de ossibus istorum combustorum vere martirum, quia pro certo ipsi erant sanioris fidei quam illi qui eos fecerunt comburi. Et de hoc habeo fidem meam. Et ipsi erant optimi Christiani et cum magno praeiudicio et contra ius sunt combusti. Et credo martires et eorum fidem laudo et credo quod sint in Paradiso."

[19] Ibid., fol. 215v.

To judge by the conspirators' occupations, it appears that this group of plotters was of fairly distinguished background. Imbert de Roquefixade was a member of the local nobility. The mercantile sector of Pézenas society was represented by three individuals: an apothecary, a dealer in skins, and a man described simply as a merchant. The legal profession contributed a procurator and a notary's clerk. The conspirators were a relatively sophisticated group, and they tried very hard to make their accusations sound plausible. They were careful to recruit several potential witnesses whose stories would corroborate one another.[20] They also took care to make sure that their statements would sound convincing. When the plotters were drawing up their denunciation, both Jean Maurand and Guillaume Mascon wanted it written down that they had seen Berleti after dark, wrapping up the heretics' bones in either a white cloth or some green sendal (a kind of silk fabric). Master Guillaume Lombard, who was helping compose the note, said, "You shouldn't say that he was putting them in a white cloth, or green sendal, but simply say that it was sendal; similarly, you shouldn't name a suspicious hour, or say it was at night, because this would make everything suspect, since at night one couldn't tell if it was a white cloth or green sendal."[21]

Berleti also seems to have been particularly vulnerable. For reasons that are not specified, the notary had gained the enmity of the bishop of Béziers. The plotters believed that if Berleti was found guilty of favoring heresy, the bishop would see to it that he received a severe punishment.[22] All in all, these conspirators displayed a degree of foresight and planning that was, in a perverse way, admirable. Had some of them been less pusillanimous in the presence of the inquisitor, they might have succeeded in delivering their enemy to the not-so-tender mercies of the bishop of Béziers.[23]

## MIDDLEMEN AS MANIPULATORS

Among those well placed to appropriate and exploit the resources offered by the inquisition were those individuals who occupied the role of "middleman" in Languedocian society. Whenever local communities are being brought under the control of larger, outside political and cultural organizations, middlemen play an

[20] Ibid., fol. 208v.
[21] Ibid., fol. 210v: "Magister Guillelmus Lombardi dixit, 'Non ponatis nec dicatis quod poneret ea in panno albo vel cendato viridi sed in cendato simpliciter, nec de hora suspecta vel de nocte, quia totum esset suspectum cum de nocte non posset discerni an esset pannus albus vel cendatum viride.'"
[22] Ibid., fol. 209v.
[23] My description of this plot is drawn from ibid., fols. 204r–10r (*culpe* of Bernard Pastour de Marcel of Pézenas), 210r–12r (*culpe* of Guillaume Mascon of Pézenas), 212r–v (*culpe* of Guillaume Benedict of Cazouls), 212v–14r (*culpe* of Jean Maurand of Pézenas), 214r–15r (*culpe* of Imbert de Roquefixade of Pézenas), and 215r–16r (*culpe* of Raimond Caplieu of Pézenas). Their sentences are given in Doat, 27: 241v–45r. Pastour's *culpe* are printed in *Documents*, 1: cxviii–cxxii.

important social and political role.[24] What gives the middleman his opportunity is the gap in communications between the local community and the outside organization. Sometimes this gap is cultural: when the two groups have very different notions about normatively appropriate behavior, the middleman acts as a cultural translator between those two incompatible normative realms. Frequently the gap is institutional: in this case, the directors of the outside organization are not able to develop a field administration with which they can effectively penetrate the local community. Often they find it difficult to gain direct, unmediated knowledge of what is happening there. Conversely, inhabitants of the local community remain ignorant of how the outside, directing organization operates and are often uncertain about how to deal with it.

Such an institutional gap existed in much of Languedoc in the late thirteenth and early fourteenth centuries. The church, the crown, and the local princes were in the process of constructing more elaborate administrative mechanisms, but these did not as yet penetrate too deeply into the region's villages and towns. The gulf between local society and the new governing institutions offered an opportunity to those members of local communities who could develop contacts with these outside governing structures and mediate the outsiders' interactions with their communities. These mediators were in a good position to exploit the mutual ignorance of insiders and outsiders.

The most spectacular example of how occupation of the middleman's role could facilitate manipulation of the inquisition is provided by the Clergue family of Montaillou. At times in the early fourteenth century, Pierre Clergue and his brother Bernard almost completely monopolized the channels of communication between their village and the power structures of the larger world. Pierre was the village priest. With what seems to have been a near monopoly on literacy in the village, he was Montaillou's chief cultural mediator, the prime conduit through which the norms of the international church should have been disseminated among his parishioners. But Pierre was hardly the best agent of cultural assimilation—in addition to being a Catholic priest, he was a Cathar believer. His brother Bernard was at times Montaillou's *bayle*, the chief local representative of the village's lord, the count of Foix.[25] As long as the directors of Languedoc's governing organizations did not interest themselves too much in what was happening in Montaillou, the Clergues were free to manipulate their strategic position in the interstices between the outside world and the local community. Bernard, the representative of seignorial authority, was particularly well situated to use that authority to bolster his influence among his neighbors. As

[24] The middleman and/or cultural broker has received much attention from anthropologists. See, for example, Bailey, *Stratagems and Spoils*, pp. 167–76; Adams, "Brokers and Career Mobility Systems"; Geertz, "The Javanese Kijaji"; Silverman, "Patronage and Community-National Relationships"; and Wolf, "Group Relations in a Complex Society."

[25] On the duties of Languedocian *bayles*, see Dognon, *Les Institutions politiques et administratives*, pp. 50–51.

custodian of the property confiscated by the count following someone's condemnation for heresy, he was able to take advantage of the villagers by offering to help them recover land that their families had lost. Bernard also had other opportunities to exploit his office. One of his duties as *bayle* was to collect the tithes and turn them over to the village priest. Since he and his brother Pierre controlled both ends of this operation, they were able to divert tithe revenue to their own projects. At least one resident of Montaillou believed that Bernard had used the tithes to support the Cathar Good Men.[26]

When the inquisitors began to take an interest in the inhabitants of Montaillou, the Clergues were at first able to protect their friends and deliver their enemies into the inquisitors' clutches. Pierre Clergue, the local representative of the church and hence a figure without whose cooperation the inquisitors found it difficult to operate effectively, was able to shield some of his fellow Cathar sympathizers. For example, he kept one Guillemette Benet out of the inquisitorial prisons. Guillemette had confessed her involvement in heresy to the inquisitor of Carcassonne. The inquisitor sent a letter to Clergue, probably in 1309, ordering him to cite Guillemette to come to Carcassonne to hear her sentence. Pierre promptly sent one of his brothers to Guillemette with a scheme to keep her out of the *mur*. She was to take to her bed and claim that she had been injured in a fall from a ladder. Thus, when Pierre came to summon her to attend the *sermo generalis*, he would be able to report that she was too ill to do so. The inquisitor at Carcassonne accepted this excuse and, by this expedient, Guillemette was able to stay out of prison for almost twelve years.[27] Similarly, according to Pierre Maury, it was Pierre Clergue's indulgence that on one occasion spared him from arrest. One day when the priest came to the house of Maury's father to collect the tithes, he happened on Pierre, who was at that time a fugitive. Although Clergue knew this, he did not have Maury arrested.[28] Not only did Pierre use his position to protect his clients, he also used it to pursue his own, often unsavory, interests. Raimond Vayssière of Ax-les-Thermes believed that Clergue had free access to the sexual services of several women in Ax-les-Thermes because they feared he would turn them in to the inquisitors.[29]

The most detailed evidence of how the Clergue brothers could use their middleman role to manipulate the inquisition comes, ironically, from the period when their position was disintegrating. The bishop of Pamiers, Jacques Fournier, was sufficiently interested in rooting out heresy to make the effort necessary to penetrate behind the screen that the Clergue brothers had erected; he thus discovered the extent of their involvement with Catharism. Pierre was arrested and incarcerated. In an effort to save his brother, Bernard made full use of the resources he had accumulated over the years in his role as a middleman.

[26] *Registre*, 1: 316–17.
[27] Ibid., 1: 476; Le Roy Ladurie, *Montaillou*, pp. 91–92.
[28] *Registre*, 2: 187; Le Roy Ladurie, *Montaillou*, p. 92.
[29] *Registre*, 1: 279.

The testimony of Bernard Benet of Montaillou, despite its contradictions, provides a dramatic glimpse of Bernard Clergue's machinations. When Benet first appeared before Fournier on 25 March 1321, he already had a long history of unhappy dealings with the inquisitors. His father had been condemned for heresy and his lands confiscated. Bernard himself had been sentenced to wear crosses.[30] The tale (or rather tales) that he told the bishop is a complex one of intrigue, perjury, and deception, all of it set afoot by Bernard Clergue. Early in Lent, so Benet claimed, Bernard had approached him with a proposition. Clergue wanted Benet to go to Carcassonne to testify to the Dominican inquisitor. He was to say that some sixteen to twenty years earlier Guillaume Guilhabert of Montaillou had received the *consolamentum* on his deathbed. Present at this ceremony had been Guillaume Autier of Montaillou, Arnaud Faure and his wife Alazaïs, and Guillemette, the dying man's sister. In return for this testimony, Clergue promised that he would use his influence with the inquisitor to get Benet permission to lay aside his crosses; he would also turn over to Benet a meadow confiscated from his father. Clergue also promised to pay all of Benet's expenses on the journey to Carcassonne. Applying a stick as well as a carrot, Clergue threatened to have Benet burned as a relapsed heretic if he did not cooperate.

Benet, unwilling to perjure himself, at first refused. Ultimately, however, Clergue's mixture of blandishments and threats won him over. Not long after this Bernard Clergue, his wife Raimonde, and Pons Gary de Laroque d'Olmes, Clergue's nephew, set off for Carcassonne. Benet followed after, catching up with them at a place called Brenac. There he had second thoughts about perjuring himself and turned back toward Montaillou. Pons Gary pursued him, overtaking him at Coudons. If Benet did not come along quietly as originally agreed, Pons Gary promised to rouse the country against him as a fugitive heretic and have him conveyed to Carcassonne as a prisoner. Benet, faced with the prospect of going to the stake as a relapsed heretic, acquiesced and directed his steps to Carcassonne. Once there, he told the inquisitors the story concocted by Clergue.

Benet testified that he knew of the heretication of Guillaume Guilhabert only by hearsay. After giving his deposition, he reported back to Clergue. Bernard told him that his deposition was worthless unless he stated that he had been an eyewitness. He therefore gave Benet a revised story to tell the inquisitor. Benet was to say that when Guilhabert fell ill, he had gone with one Guillaume Belot to find a Good Man to perform the *consolamentum*. After much searching, they had found either Guillaume Autier or Prades Tavernier and brought him to Montaillou. Benet was to say that he had been present at the heretication. He was also to add to the list of those in attendance the names of Guillaume Belot and Alamande Guilhabert, the dying man's mother. Finally, he was to testify that everyone present had performed the *melioramentum*, eaten bread blessed by the heretic, and agreed to receive the *consolamentum* on his or her deathbed. Benet

30 Ibid., 1: 395–96.

dutifully returned the next day to the inquisitor to add these details and corrections to his original story.[31]

Now, however, on 25 March at Pamiers, Benet informed Jacques Fournier that everything he had said at Carcassonne had been a lie. Bernard Clergue had concocted the entire story to discredit Guillaume Autier of Montaillou, Arnaud Faure, and his wife Alazaïs and to revenge himself on them. These were the people whose testimony Clergue believed had led to his brother's arrest. When Benet had returned from his trip to the Carcassonne inquisitor, he had told the truth of the matter to the subchaplain of Montaillou and to Pierre Adhémar, an enemy of the Clergues. He had then decided to come to Pamiers to inform the bishop. Not surprisingly, Fournier arrested Benet and detained him in prison.[32] On the 30th, Benet was again called to testify: he said that his statement on the 25th had been false.[33] The next day he appeared yet again and reaffirmed the truth of what he had said in Carcassonne. The story he now told ran as follows. About two weeks before Lent, Bernard Clergue had informed him that the Carcassonne inquisitors had received testimony indicating that Benet had been present at Guilhabert's heretication. At first Benet claimed that he did not remember anything at all about the affair, since he had been a child when Guilhabert died. Eventually he did recall the incident and told everything to Clergue. Clergue urged him to go to Carcassonne, offering to pay all his expenses. As in Benet's first tale, Clergue was represented as offering to use his influence to persuade the inquisitors to let Benet set aside his crosses. About two weeks later, Alazaïs Faure, the sister of the deceased Guillaume Guilhabert, accosted him and tried to persuade him not to testify, promising to give him twelve sheep or anything else he wanted.[34] Guillaume Autier also tried to bribe him.

Just as he had related in his first deposition to Fournier, Benet told of setting off for Carcassonne and catching up with the Clergues and Pons Gary at Brenac. But now Benet claimed that Bernard Clergue there changed his mind about the wisdom of Benet testifying and told him to go home. Benet replied that he intended to tell his story to someone, whether to the inquisitor of Carcassonne or the bishop of Pamiers, and left. Once again Pons Gary was represented as pursuing him. But this time his message was that Bernard Clergue, after giving more thought to the matter, had decided that Benet ought to go to Carcassonne after all, since some of those who had been present at the *consolamentum* might already have confessed to Fournier. So Benet finally made his way to Carcassonne and

[31] Ibid., 1: 395–99.
[32] Ibid., 1: 400–401.
[33] Ibid., 1: 401–2.
[34] In her own testimony Alazaïs Faure gave a different account of this incident. According to her, Benet tried to blackmail her. If she gave him some sheep, he promised that he would not testify and that he would leave the country, going either to Narbonne or Puigcerda. Alazaïs claimed that she refused his offer, reasoning that once he had sold the sheep and used up the money, he would demand more and better sheep from her (ibid., 1: 412).

delivered his deposition.[35] When he returned to Montaillou, he came under pressure from one of the Clergue family's enemies, Pierre Adhémar. Adhémar was also a middleman, having been both consul and *bayle* of the village of Prades d'Alion. Since he had some sort of relationship with the bishop, he felt that this would give him a particular advantage in pursuing his own ends.[36] After reproaching Benet for giving what he maintained was a false confession to the inquisitors, Adhémar encouraged Benet to go to Pamiers to tell Bishop Fournier that he had lied to the Carcassonne inquisitors and that he had been persuaded to perjure himself by Clergue.

To convince Benet to take these actions, Adhémar employed the resources afforded to him by his middleman role. While Benet had been absent in Carcassonne, Adhémar had already seized all of his animals. Benet threatened to complain to the current *bayle* of Prades d'Alion. Adhémar thereupon promised to return his beasts the next day. However, the following day Adhémar appeared not with Benet's animals but with Raimond Trilhe, the subchaplain of Montaillou, and Bernard Marty, the consul of Montaillou. Again Adhémar demanded that Benet go to Pamiers to retract his confession about the heretication of Guillaume Guilhabert. Adhémar also prevailed on the lieutenant of the castellan of Montaillou to imprison Benet. Benet spent two days in irons before Adhémar removed him from the castle and took him to Lordat. On the journey there, Adhémar made it clear that if Benet did not retract his confession, he would have him incarcerated in the castle at Lordat and ultimately hanged. These threats, so Benet now told the bishop, had induced him to present himself on 25 March and revoke the true confession he had made in Carcassonne.[37]

Further evidence about how the middlemen of Montaillou and Prades d'Alion tried to manipulate the inquisition comes from the testimony of Raimonde Testanière of Montaillou. Raimonde appeared before Fournier's tribunal on 13 April 1321. At that time she offered testimony damaging to the Clergue family.[38] By the autumn of 1322, however, Fournier was receiving reports that Raimonde was spreading the story that she had lied to the bishop. Fournier proceeded to cite her to appear. On receipt of this summons, Raimonde excused herself by claiming to be ill. When Fournier summoned her again, he discovered that she had fled. Ultimately she was found hiding in the village of Saurat and was brought as a prisoner to Pamiers.

---

[35] Ibid., 1: 402–5.

[36] At one point Adhémar stated: "as long as the bishop lives, I will be of his household and I will be able to do many good things" (ibid., 3: 366–67). Le Roy Ladurie (*Montaillou*, p. 53) believes that Adhémar was here claiming to be a member of the bishop's kindred. Benad (*Domus und Religion*, p. 28) argues that it is more likely that Adhémar was not claiming to be one of Fournier's kinsmen, but to be a member in some fashion of his household, or *familia*.

[37] *Registre*, 1: 405–6.

[38] Ibid., 1: 455–63.

When she appeared on 23 December 1322, Raimonde reaffirmed the truth of her 1321 deposition. She admitted, however, that she had been telling people that, at the urging of Pierre Adhémar, she had lied. It was, she informed the bishop, fear that had led her to do so. When she had returned to Montaillou after testifying in 1321, Bernard Clergue's wife, also named Raimonde, had visited her and bitterly reproached her. She told Raimonde Testanière that the Clergues would ultimately settle accounts with her and the others who had testified against them. This threat so terrified her that she told Raimond Trilhe, the sub-chaplain of Montaillou, that Pierre Adhémar had persuaded her to make a false confession concerning Pierre Clergue. Raimonde believed that Trilhe must have passed this story on to Raimond Clergue, one of Bernard's brothers. At any rate, when Hugues de Polignac, a royal sergeant, passed through Montaillou on his way to the baths at Ax-les-Thermes, Raimond Clergue brought him to see her. It is possible that this Hugues was a relative of Jacques de Polignac, the guardian of the *mur* at Carcassonne, and a good friend of the Clergue family. In his presence she repeated her story about how she had perjured herself.

Even the arrest of Bernard Clergue by the bishop did not put an end to the Clergue family's efforts to intimidate Raimonde. When Bernard was first arrested, he was kept under a form of house arrest in Montaillou by agents of the count of Foix. The conditions of this detention were evidently not too strict, since Bernard managed to persuade two sergeants to escort him to Raimonde's house. There he gave vent to his anger, declaring, "I shall defend myself against you, and make you stand on one foot, since there is no one else who will testify against me, and I will easily refute your testimony!" Later Raimonde learned from Fabrissa den Rives that Clergue had also threatened her. Eventually, out of fear of the Clergues, Raimonde had decided to make up the story about Pierre Adhémar persuading her to make a false confession. When the inquisitor of Carcassonne had visited Montaillou, she had told this story to his notary. To the bishop, however, she affirmed that her original confession had been true and that she had not been suborned by Pierre Adhémar to make a false statement.[39]

## MANIPULATION BY THE INQUISITORS' "CLIENTELE"

One group that seems to have been particularly well placed to put the resources of the inquisition to work for its own benefit was composed of those tried and condemned for heresy. At first this may seem rather surprising. Yet penitent heretics were well positioned to manipulate the inquisitors. On the one hand, having had firsthand, and often prolonged, contact with the system, they knew better than most what the inquisitors' procedures were, what questions they were likely to ask, and what motivated them to display severity or clemency. On the other hand, such people were familiar with the beliefs, practices, and personnel of the heresy with which they had been involved. If they decided to bring a false

[39] Ibid., 1: 464–70; the quotation is from p. 467.

accusation against someone, they were able to make up a very convincing story.[40] Moreover, as we have seen above, it was not unheard of for penitent heretics, once they had been processed through the inquisitorial machinery, to become low-level servants of the inquisitors and hence be in a good position to influence their masters' views.

The most striking example of such behavior is provided by the multifold machinations of the notary Pierre de Gaillac. Gaillac came from a family of Cathar believers from the Fuxéen town of Tarascon. If his testimony to the inquisitors of Carcassonne can be believed, his contacts with Pierre Autier and his fellow heretics began around 1300 when he was a student at Toulouse. In 1308 and 1309 he testified before Geoffroy d'Ablis's tribunal in Carcassonne.[41] It is possible that he was sentenced to a term of imprisonment.[42] If he was imprisoned, the consequences of this do not seem to have been too great, for in the 1320s he was actively practicing as a notary in the courts of the county of Foix.

Gaillac's testimony to Geoffroy d'Ablis and his lieutenants was the beginning of a long and at times rewarding relationship. Gaillac made a practice of denouncing various neighbors, acquaintances, and rivals to the inquisitors. In April 1309 he informed on one Pierre de Niaux of Tarascon. According to Gaillac, Pierre had tried to persuade him to convey to the inquisitor some inaccurate information about the heretication of Jourdain de Rabat.[43] In May 1309 Gaillac made yet another appearance at Carcassonne, this time to report on Guillaume Tron, another notary from Tarascon. According to Gaillac, one day as he and Tron were returning to Tarascon from the assizes held at Alet-les-Bains, they fell into a discussion of the inquisition. Tron criticized Gaillac for confessing so readily and so easily after only a short term of incarceration. In addition to relaying these remarks, Gaillac provided information concerning Tron's unorthodox religious opinions. Gaillac told Jean du Faugoux, the inquisitor's lieutenant, that Tron had talked about some of his experiences as a student at Toulouse. There Tron had shared rooms with a clerk who had been something of a freethinker. This man had maintained that it was contrary to nature and therefore impossible for bread to be turned into the body of Christ during the mass. According to Gaillac, Tron indicated that he was to some degree sympathetic to this opinion.[44]

Thereafter Gaillac frequently intruded himself into the workings of the inquisition. When Jacques Fournier began investigating heresy in the diocese of

[40] This is a point made by an unidentified legal expert who in the 1330s was called on by the papacy to examine some of the records of the Carcassonne inquisition. His remarks about the skill ex-Cathar believers could display in concocting false accusations against the innocent is in Doat, 32: fols. 171v–72r.

[41] Gaillac's deposition is printed in Pales-Gobilliard, ed., *Geoffroy d'Ablis*, pp. 332–61. Interestingly, and most unusually, he was allowed to write out in his own hand a summary of his testimony, which was included in d'Ablis's register.

[42] Ibid., p. 52.

[43] Ibid., pp. 352–55.

[44] Ibid., pp. 358–59.

Pamiers, Gaillac appeared before him at least three times as a witness against various people suspected of heresy.[45] In addition, he was free in offering advice to people concerning what they ought to say when questioned by the bishop.[46] It seems that it was in this period that he began trying in earnest to use the inquisition to settle scores with old enemies. Although we unfortunately have no evidence to explain his animosity, he was active in the effort to entangle the Clergues of Montaillou with the inquisition.[47]

It is about his efforts to destroy his old acquaintance, Guillaume Tron, that we are best informed. Gaillac, operating in conjunction with some other enemies of Tron, concocted a story that Tron had been a Cathar believer. He and his fellows were so successful that Tron was not only arrested and interrogated, but also sentenced to immuration in Carcassonne. When this conspiracy was discovered, the investigation into it produced what is without doubt the fullest documentary record of any effort to manipulate the inquisition. It is therefore worth considering in some detail how this plot was constructed and how it unraveled.

It seems that the inquisitors learned only by accident that they had been maneuvered into condemning an innocent man. On 14 August 1324 one Bernard Mineur, a weaver, appeared before Jacques Fournier's tribunal to report a suspicious conversation he had overheard. On the evening of the preceding Friday, Bernard and a friend, Guillaume d'Alion, had visited the Pamiers residence (apparently a tavern) of a woman named Gauzia Desplas. As they sat drinking in front of her house, Bernard saw four men seated at a table in front of a neighboring building. Three of them he recognized as Pierre den Hugol, Pierre Peyre, and Jacques Tartier of Quié. Bernard heard Pierre den Hugol say to one of the others, "If you tell the truth, all of us are lost!" To this his interlocutor, whom Bernard did not know, replied, "If I don't tell the truth, the bishop will know it, and misfortune will come to all of us."[48]

Given the atmosphere in Pamiers under Fournier's episcopate, Mineur suspected that this little group was talking about heresy. He therefore tried to get his companion to pay attention. Nudging Guillaume with his elbow, Mineur hissed, "Listen to what those peasants are talking about." Guillaume, who had not been paying much attention to anything, since he was suffering from a fever, roused himself from his stupor and looked at the four men. Realizing that their conversation had been overheard, the four got up to leave. As they hastened off, Hugol shrugged his shoulders and said to the man he had been urging to remain silent, "Well, then, say what you want to say." Later that same day, Bernard again ran into Hugol and the others. When the four men spotted him, they began mut-

[45] On 24 October 1309 he gave testimony against both Raimond Vayssière of Ax-les-Thermes and Arnaud Teisseyre of Lordat; on 3 April 1321 he testified about the late Simon Barre of Ax-les-Thermes (*Registre*, 1: 273, 2: 196–97, 1: 299).

[46] Ibid., 2: 434–35.

[47] Ibid., 2: 281–82, 295.

[48] Ibid., 3: 372.

tering among themselves, "That's him!"[49] A few days later Mineur encountered Hugol and his friends yet again, this time as they were drinking wine at another tavern. Bernard approached Hugol and asked him if he had indeed said the words that Bernard had overheard. Pierre made no reply; instead he turned pale, paid posthaste for his wine, and scuttled off with his companions as fast as he could.[50] This behavior prompted Bernard to bring his information to the bishop.

Fournier, after he had interrogated Mineur and Guillaume d'Alion, decided that the matter was serious enough to warrant further investigation. On 9 September Pierre den Hugol was arraigned before the bishop. He was only the first of a parade of suspects in this affair to pass before Fournier's tribunal. Between 9 September 1324 and 11 June 1325, nine individuals were questioned. Six were from the town of Quié, above Pamiers on the Ariège river: Pierre den Hugol, Pierre Peyre and his brother Raimond, Jacques Tartier, Pierre de Laurac, and Guillaume Delaire. Two, Pierre Lombard and Guillaume Gautier, were from Tarascon, and one, Pierre Fournier, was from Serles. The story wrung out of these reluctant witnesses was an unpleasant one of rivalry and revenge. At the center of the affair stood Pierre de Gaillac and Guillaume Tron, men who had become inveterate enemies. When Fournier began his investigation, Gaillac was dead. But it was his passionate hatred for Tron that had involved all the others in a plot to deliver their common enemy into the hands of the inquisitors.

Over the years Tron had done little to ingratiate himself with Gaillac. An irascible individual, Tron was ever ready with an insult. Since the two were both notaries and residents of Tarascon, their legal work brought them into close and often unpleasant association. In the law courts of Foix, the past dealings of Gaillac and his family with the Cathars proved a liability. It was an easy matter for Tron to put him at a disadvantage by alluding to his heretical past. As Gaillac told Pierre Peyre:

> I want to confound completely Master Guillaume Tron of Tarascon because I cannot be in any court where he is without him vilifying me; and because of this I would like to see him destroyed or hanged. Therefore, even if I knew that because of this my soul would go to one hundred thousand devils, I intend to revenge myself on him, by accusing him of heresy, whether truly or falsely, so that I can confound and destroy him.[51]

To Peyre's brother Raimond he explained that with Tron out of the way he and his friend Guillaume Gautier would dominate the county's courts and grow rich.[52]

[49] Ibid., 3: 374, 373.
[50] Ibid., 3: 373.
[51] Ibid., 3: 389.
[52] Ibid., 3: 413.

One of Gaillac's first steps toward mobilizing the resources of the inquisition involved a chance meeting in 1318 with Raimond Peyre of Quié. Like Gaillac, Raimond Peyre had passed through the investigative machinery of the inquisition of Carcassonne. During the time when Geoffroy d'Ablis supervised this tribunal, Raimond had spent some time in the inquisitors' *mur*.[53] On his release from prison, he had entered the inquisitors' employ. In 1318, when he was recruited by Gaillac, he was living in Carcassonne and carrying out various minor tasks. One of his jobs was to deliver letters summoning individuals to appear before the inquisitors. Shortly before he met Gaillac, Raimond had been dispatched on such an errand to Tarascon. There, at one of the town gates, he encountered Guillaume Tron. Tron immediately showered abuse on him: "Eh, Raimond Peyre, will you do nothing else other than carry the Carcassonne inquisitor's little notes to these parts?" To which Raimond replied, "And you call the letters of the lord inquisitor little notes? Is there not a good man in these parts who would not gladly carry the lord inquisitor's letters if he wished it?" Tron replied, "You scum; you are so proud with your little notes, it seems as if you came from Santiago." The last words of this exchange were Raimond's: "Master Guillaume, you are so proud; yet you will be glad someday if a man puts water in your hands."[54]

Full of wrath, Raimond returned to Carcassonne. There he promptly called on the inquisitor, Jean de Beaune, and informed him about his conversation with Tron. The next day Raimond's business brought him back to the inquisition's building. In the great hall he encountered Tron once again, this time in the company of Bernard Augé of Tarascon. Not at all inhibited by his surroundings, Tron resumed where he had left off at Tarascon: "You traitorous scum, who should have been burned up with the letters you're carrying into the Sabarthès, you destroy and beat down the entire land. You do ill, and you sow discord between the men of the land and the lord inquisitor; because of this misfortune will come to you."[55] While Tron berated Peyre, Augé was overcome with a fit of laughter. With this laughter ringing in his ears, Raimond hastened back to the refectory to report this new exchange to the inquisitor.

Raimond, having delivered his denunciation, made his way toward his lodgings. As he was walking through the *bourg*, he encountered Pierre de Gaillac standing in the doorway of the house where he was then living.[56] Still angry about Tron, Raimond poured out the story of what had transpired between himself and the notary. Pierre, who had undoubtedly been waiting for just such an opportunity, suggested that he and Raimond put their heads together and work out a scheme for putting Tron and his wagging tongue into the prisons of the

[53] Ibid., 3: 435–36.
[54] Ibid., 3: 426–27.
[55] Ibid., 3: 427; MS 4030, fol. 307a–b. (Where Duvernoy reads *portatis*, I read *aportatis*.)
[56] *Registre*, 3: 418.

inquisition. Gaillac's proposal was that Raimond denounce Tron as a Cathar believer.[57] Raimond, as he later told Bishop Fournier, felt some reservations about perjuring himself; but Pierre told him he need not worry about retribution since it was the inquisitors' practice not to reveal to the accused the names of those who had informed against them. He also promised to help Raimond, whether in legal or other matters, if he testified against Tron. With these reassurances, Raimond agreed.

The next morning the two visited the inquisition's headquarters. Gaillac, who may not have completely trusted either Raimond's fortitude or his theatrical skills, himself told the notary assigned to record Raimond's deposition the story they had concocted. He assured the notary that he was simply repeating what he had heard from his companion. The story that Gaillac put into Raimond's mouth ran as follows. About fourteen years earlier Raimond had one evening visited the house of Guillaume Delaire in Quié. There he had found the Good Men Guillaume Autier and Prades Tavernier. While he was talking to them, Guillaume Tron arrived. Tron asked Raimond to leave so that he could speak in private with the heretics. Raimond went into the part of the house known as the *foganha*, where the cooking fire was located. From there he had been able to see Tron sitting and talking with the Good Men.[58] When the two schemers finished their business and were leaving the building, Gaillac said to Raimond, "Now misfortune will come to Guillaume Tron, because he will be arrested by the lord inquisitor and detained in the *mur*." He also warned, "See to it that you stand firmly by the testimony you have given, because if you contradict yourself or revoke the deposition, great misfortune will come to you, because the lord inquisitor will arrest you."[59]

Gaillac, having set his plot in motion, began casting about for other allies. One of the first he found was Raimond Peyre's brother, Pierre. Pierre still lived in the brothers' ancestral village of Quié. Like Raimond, he too had had previous dealings with the inquisition. His wife had testified before Geoffroy d'Ablis and at some time he himself had been a prisoner in the *mur* at Carcassonne.[60] Not only was Pierre bound to his brother by kinship ties, but he also hated Guillaume Tron. Tron, in addition to being a notary, was a usurer. Sometime around 1316 he had lent money to Pierre, taking as security a cape worth three sous in money of Toulouse. Pierre had repaid the sum, but Tron had refused to return the cape. Pierre had accordingly conceived a profound hatred for the man.

When Raimond arrived in Quié to visit his brother, Pierre regaled him with complaints about the cape and the insults that Tron had heaped on him. He

[57] Ibid., 3: 427–28.
[58] Ibid., 3: 421–23. Every time Peyre appeared before the inquisitors he altered the details of Tron's alleged visit to Delaire's house. See 3: 408–9 and 428 for slightly different versions of what happened there.
[59] Ibid., 3: 423.
[60] Ibid., 3: 387, 400.

ended his tirade by declaring that he wished to revenge himself on the notary. To this Raimond replied that his brother would probably never be able to gain any satisfaction through the count of Foix's courts. Jeanne of Artois and Marguerite of Béarn, both widows of deceased counts, were at this time engaged in a pro-tracted dispute over who had the best claim to be guardian of the new count, Gaston II, until he came of age. With the county's political leadership in such turmoil, it was very unlikely that Pierre could expect justice from the count's courts in Tarascon. Therefore, so Raimond counseled his brother, he should have recourse to the Carcassonne inquisition. Raimond also informed Pierre that he and Gaillac had already spoken to the inquisitors about Tron. Taken aback by the audacity of this, Pierre asked Raimond if he could in good conscience bear false witness against someone. To which Raimond replied, "What's it to you as long as we put Master Guillaume in a tight spot by testifying against him?" When Pierre replied that he was pleased that his brother and Gaillac had denounced Tron, Raimond suggested that he go to the inquisition with his own false testi-mony. Pierre demurred, stating that he could not spare the time for a trip to Carcassonne. Later that same day Pierre went to Tarascon and there fell afoul of Tron, with whom he had a violent argument about the cape.[61]

One evening later that same week Pierre ran into Gaillac in the marketplace at Quié. Gaillac invited the man to accompany him to Tarascon. During their walk there, Gaillac tried to persuade Pierre to go to Carcassonne to testify against Tron, even promising to pay his traveling expenses. Pierre replied that he approved of what Gaillac and his brother had done, but that he would not him-self go to Carcassonne because of the state of his affairs and because he had never seen Tron in the company of heretics.[62] By the time the two reached Tarascon, the sun had set. In the marketplace they found Master Guillaume Gautier and Raimond Peyre. Gaillac suggested that they all go to a place just outside town called the Champ de Foire. Fearful of watchful eyes, he insisted that they leave town one by one. As they were sneaking out of Tarascon, some of the company encountered Pierre Lombard, Gaillac's brother-in-law, who decided to tag along. When the group had reassembled in the fields, everyone vented his particular grievances against Tron. Strengthened in their hatred of the notary by this recita-tion of past injuries, the men agreed to cooperate in lodging false accusations. They concluded the meeting by swearing to keep the plot a secret.[63]

Gaillac took it on himself to recruit other members for the conspiracy. As the meeting in the Champ de Foire was breaking up, he told Raimond Peyre that he intended to go further into the mountains to Ax-les-Thermes and Montaillou. On this trip he hoped to enlist Guillaume de Celles in the plot. When Raimond testified before Fournier's tribunal, he said that he did not know for certain whether Celles was successfully recruited. But several days after the meeting at

61 Ibid., 3: 395–96.
62 Ibid., 3: 389–90, 396–97.
63 Ibid., 3: 390–91, 396–99, 414–15.

Tarascon, Raimond again encountered Gaillac. Pierre then said to him, "By my faith, Raimond, in the matter of Guillaume Tron we have found what we wanted." From these words Peyre deduced that Gaillac had managed to find other people willing to serve as witnesses against Tron. But because someone came at that moment to fetch Gaillac away, he was not able to pursue the matter.[64]

Similarly, a conversation that Raimond had with Gaillac a few years later indicated that the notary had enlisted in the conspiracy yet another person, Bernard de Lourde of Foix. When in September 1324 Raimond helped Gaillac thresh some millet, Gaillac told him, "See how the whole world hates Master Guillaume Tron! For Bernard de Lourde of Foix has given me two large measures of cloth so that I can see to it that Guillaume Tron is well guarded in the *mur* at Carcassonne!"[65] Gaillac also secured the cooperation of Guillaume Delaire of Quié, who testified against Tron on 9 April 1318.[66] If what Delaire told Jacques Fournier seven years later can be believed, Gaillac also obtained the assistance of Jacques Tartier of Quié and Guillaume Cavatier of Tarascon. At least Cavatier on one occasion joined Gaillac in trying to persuade Delaire to go to Carcassonne to testify. And, after Delaire had gone to Carcassonne and returned to Quié, he was accosted by Jacques Tartier, who asked him if he had done as Gaillac had instructed.[67]

Ultimately, of course, this conspiracy unraveled. Yet the plotters enjoyed a considerable measure of success, managing to get Tron lodged in an inquisitorial prison. Had Bernard Mineur not happened to overhear a tavern conversation, the notary might have died there. Unfortunately, not much is known about what befell the members of this conspiracy. When Fournier began his investigation, Gaillac was dead. Pierre Peyre was sentenced to immuration;[68] sentences do not survive for the other conspirators. However, it is probably safe to assume that they were dealt with severely. About the same time as Fournier was dealing with the plot against Tron, he was finishing up the investigation of yet another conspiracy. The ringleader of this second group of plotters was a cleric from Verdun named Guillaume de Travier. Guillaume had gone in for deceit on a large scale, falsely accusing six men of heresy. Fournier had arrested all six and detained them in prison for more than a year. Had one of these prisoners, Pierre Merenges, been found guilty, he would have gone to the stake as a relapsed heretic. In his machinations against Pierre and the others, Travier had managed to involve as his assistants a total of eight people. In this case the surviving records do reveal what befell the plotters. All nine were required to make good any losses their victims had suffered as a result of the proceedings against them. With the exception of

---

[64] Ibid., 3: 416.

[65] Ibid., 3: 431.

[66] Ibid., 3: 447–48 (MS 4030, fol. 310d), 450. (I read the date of Delaire's testimony against Tron as 1318, rather than Duvernoy's 1319.)

[67] *Registre*, 3: 454.

[68] Doat, 27: fol. 148v.

Travier, all were sentenced to be exposed to public obloquy: they were to be displayed on a pillory in clothing adorned with double yellow crosses and red tongues, a punishment that was to be repeated in every significant town in the entire diocese of Pamiers. In addition, all but one were condemned to perpetual imprisonment. Of these, four were sentenced *ad strictissimum carcerem*, that is, to be kept bound in chains and fed on nothing but bread and water. Travier, who was one of these four, was also degraded from the priesthood, and Fournier specified that Travier was never to have any hope of release in the future nor were the conditions of his imprisonment ever to be ameliorated.[69] It is unlikely that Fournier displayed greater clemency to the enemies of Guillaume Tron.

Efforts to manipulate governing institutions like the inquisition were unique neither to the inquisition nor to Languedoc. Wherever the records allow us to examine the workings of medieval governing institutions, which were under construction in this period, we discover people busily at work influencing and exploiting them for their own ends. Manipulation of these organizations for purposes other than those for which they had been created was perhaps more the rule than the exception.

In a social formation like medieval Europe, where the political arena was composed of a complex web of crosscutting ties of allegiance, the men who staffed the new governing institutions of the thirteenth and fourteenth centuries often had important bonds of loyalty to politicians or rulers who were not the ostensible masters of these institutions.[70] Their overall careers, and often even their appointments to office, depended less on the patronage of the master of the institution they formally served than on the favor of someone else whose influence secured that appointment.[71] That there might often be a divergence between their interests and those of the institution they staffed is hardly surprising. Historians of medieval administration have long noted the grasping venality of almost all royal servants, who were often far more concerned with enriching themselves than in furthering the interests of their master.[72] In addition to finding governing institutions staffed by administrators who were either venal or divided in their loyalties, we also find the populations they governed busily at work colonizing and exploiting these institutions for their own purposes.[73]

The efforts of various Languedocians to exploit the resources offered by the inquisition were thus not unusual. And the inquisition was vulnerable to

---

[69] Doat, 28: fols. 76v–83v. The sentence was imposed on 13 August 1324.

[70] For some examples from Languedoc, see Given, *State and Society*, pp. 176–77.

[71] As Raymond Cazelles has observed, some of the French king's servants were as much a species of ambassador from great regional magnates as they were royal employees. See his *La Société politique*, pp. 267–68.

[72] See, for example, Hilton, *The West Midlands*, pp. 243–48.

[73] Recent work on the institutions of English criminal justice in the late Middle Ages has shown how these were often used by people for almost any and all purposes other than the repression of crime. See, for example, Maddern, *East Anglia*, especially pp. 135–225.

manipulation. For one thing, its staff was open to the temptations of sloth and corruption. Like virtually every other medieval governing institution, the inquisition did not exercise very tight control and supervision of its staff. They were certainly not part of a modern civil service, with a clearly demarcated career path, standards for promotion, and regular review of candidates for promotion. Inquisitors themselves were selected on an ad hoc basis, and the church provided no formal training for them. Those men who had studied law before becoming inquisitors would have received a general orientation in canon and Roman law, but no specific training in the procedures of the inquisition of heretical depravity. Those who served as inquisitorial lieutenants before themselves becoming inquisitors did receive a form of apprenticeship training, but many inquisitors were evidently appointed to their posts without much prior, direct contact with the institution. Inquisitors were subject to review by the papacy, which was not as infrequent as one might believe, given that appeals from inquisitors' decisions were supposedly not allowed.[74] Nevertheless, they were not subject to close oversight as were the Spanish inquisitors of the early modern period, whose sentences were reviewed by a central body.

At the same time, those who wanted to exploit the inquisition may have faced an unusually tricky challenge. Despite the factors just mentioned, it appears that the Languedocian inquisition enjoyed a much higher degree of relative autonomy vis-à-vis the structures of its surrounding society than did most medieval governing institutions. That is, the inquisition was able to become a social actor in its own right, pursuing its own interests apart from those of any particular social class within its society.[75] In general, medieval states and governing institutions tended to have relatively limited autonomy. Medieval kingdoms, for example, were headed by kings who were members of a particular social class, the land-owning aristocracy. Monarchs thus shared the interests of this dominant class in a direct and personal fashion. Moreover, they were bound to the other members of the aristocracy by many personal ties, including those of marriage. They participated in an aristocratic culture that was largely closed to members of other classes. Finally, their governments were staffed in large part by members of that same aristocracy.

In contrast, the inquisitors were not deeply involved in the complex webs of affection, loyalty, and dependence that usually bound the directors of governing institutions to the people whom they sought to rule. Instead, most of them belonged to an elite institution within the Catholic Church, the Dominican order. The order chose its members with relatively great care and put them

---

[74] See below, chapter 8.

[75] On the subject of "relative autonomy," a concept to which various meanings can be attached, see Skocpol, *States and Social Revolutions*, pp. 24–33; Krasner, "Approaches to the State," pp. 230–40; Carnoy, *The State and Political Theory*, pp. 54–55, 108–9, 200–202; and Poulantzas, *Political Power and Social Classes*, pp. 255–321.

through an elaborate apprenticeship and education system.[76] It was also an institution that in the late thirteenth and early fourteenth centuries was still imbued with much of the missionary zeal of its founder, St. Dominic. The inquisitors were far more ideologically motivated and goal-directed team players than most medieval administrators. Moreover, many of them were not natives of Languedoc and hence had a particularly thin web of connections to local society. This unusual degree of relative autonomy made the inquisition peculiarly resistant to exploitation by outsiders for purposes other than stamping out heresy. Clearly those best placed to do so were members of the ruling elite. The extreme case of how a member of the power elite could hijack the inquisition and use it for his own purposes is, of course, King Philip the Fair, who used and abused inquisitorial procedures to destroy the Knights Templar. But politicians less well connected faced a much harder task in trying to appropriate some of the resources offered by the inquisition. As we have seen, many of those who tried to do so, despite some temporary successes, were ultimately destroyed.

The material considered in this chapter indicates that those who worked together rather than individually had a greater chance of success. If we look at the types of collective entities that were involved in efforts to manipulate the inquisitors, we find an interesting pattern. Collective efforts at manipulation were often organized differently than collective forms of resistance. In chapter 5 we saw that much collective opposition to the inquisitors was organized around the preexisting structures of Languedocian social institutions: the kinship group, the village, and the town. Efforts at manipulation did at times involve some of those same social groups, primarily kinship groups. For example, the conspiracy that Pierre de Gaillac put together against Guillaume Tron involved a number of kinsmen. And it was clearly the close-knit cooperation of the Clergue brothers that allowed them to use the inquisition to establish something akin to a reign of terror in their home village. However, many of the groups that sought to manipulate the inquisitors were what social anthropologists would call factions.[77] Like the factions studied by anthropologists in modern societies, the conspiracies we have examined were small in size. They had limited goals, usually the destruction of a particular individual. They had no formal structure and they gave rise to no long-lasting forms of organization or association. What leadership they had was informal. Finally, as is illustrated by the ease with which some seem to have unraveled, they were inherently unstable.

The inquisition was, for those who sought to manipulate it, a rather crude, blunt instrument. It was primarily an engine of destruction. If successfully deployed, it could be used to destroy one's enemies. But it was hard to build on it positively, to use it to accumulate resources for oneself and one's allies and clients. It lent itself far more effectively to predation than to construction.

[76] On this, see Douais, *L'Ordre des Frères Prêcheurs*.

[77] See Bailey, *Stratagems and Spoils*, pp. 51–55; Nicholas, "Factions"; and Pocock, "Faction in Gujerat."

# SECTION III

# THE SOCIAL AND POLITICAL CONTEXT

I N THE PREVIOUS sections we have examined what could be called matters of agency and contingency. We have looked at how the inquisitors went about trying to identify, prosecute, and punish heretics and their sympathizers. We have also examined how the people of Languedoc reacted to the inquisitors, how they sought to resist or manipulate them. Each of these behaviors was, in some sense, willed by those who engaged in it.

But history is more than the mere summation of a host of individuals' consciously willed actions. All activity takes place in the context of a predetermined set of social, economic, and political structures. These structures, often unacknowledged and unperceived by those embedded in them, play a major role—at times perhaps even a determining role—in deciding the success or failure of any course of action. No one expressed this more pithily than Karl Marx when he wrote, "Men make their own history, but they do not make it just as they please; they do not make it under circumstances chosen by themselves, but under circumstances directly found, given and transmitted from the past. The tradition of all the dead generations weighs like a nightmare on the brain of the living."[1]

In this section we will turn to a consideration of some of the factors that, although unacknowledged and unperceived by our protagonists, helped control and shape the work of the inquisitors. In chapter 7 we will look at factors that facilitated the inquisitors' work; in chapter 8, those that hindered them.

---

[1] K. Marx, *The Eighteenth Brumaire*, p. 595.

# CHAPTER 7

# THE ROLE OF SOCIAL
# STRESS AND SOCIAL STRAIN

I N MANY WAYS the success of the Languedocian inquisitors in com-
bating heresy is surprising. A relative handful of Dominican heresy hunters,
assisted by a few bishops, confronted the task of policing an extensive region
inhabited by well over a million people.[1] Yet in the course of a few generations
they rooted out Catharism and successfully contained the other heretical sects. In
part this was due to the skill and determination with which some inquisitors
applied themselves to their work. Nevertheless, there must have been forces at
work within Languedocian society that facilitated their efforts. The nature of
these factors is the subject of this chapter.

My argument is a simple one. Many of the techniques employed by the
inquisitors involved the systematic social isolation of those they investigated, a
goal pursued through, inter alia, imprisonment both of suspects and penitents
and the permanent insertion of individuals into the readily recognizable and stigmatized category of penitent heretic. In short, the inquisitors sought to extract
the people they prosecuted from the social networks in which they were embedded. Their efforts were assisted by the cleavages and conflicts that marked certain
important Languedocian social organizations. To borrow some terminology from
the anthropologists, we can say that these social organizations displayed characteristic strain systems,[2] to which the inquisitors applied, in the form of their
investigations, a novel and threatening outside stress. Under the right conditions
this external stress could so exacerbate an already existing strain system as to cause
social conflict and breakdown, thus aiding the work of the inquisitors.

## LORDSHIP

Lordship is probably one of the first social bonds that springs to mind when we
think about medieval social solidarities. It is a complex phenomenon, embracing

---

[1] Wolff, ed., *Histoire du Languedoc*, p. 217.

[2] My concept of strain and strain system is derived from that of Beals and Siegel, who argue
that "strain has to do with those areas of life in which culturally induced expectations tend to be
frustrated most frequently" (see *Divisiveness and Social Conflict*, pp. 68–69; the quotation is from
p. 68). It should be noted that my understanding of "strain system" has less to do with notions
of culturally induced expectations, the focus of Beals and Siegel, than with the existence in any
social organization of certain fundamental conflicts of interests.

a wide variety of relationships. These range from the intimate, informal, face-to-face ties of a master and his household retainers to the highly formalized, and often emotionally distant, relationships of a great prince and his subjects. Material to illustrate my theme is most easily culled from relationships of the latter sort. Therefore, we will first direct our attention to the strains that afflicted the ties between great lords and their subjects in thirteenth- and early-fourteenth-century Languedoc.

In many ways the thirteenth century was a great age of lordship in the south of France. After the end of the Albigensian crusades, lords—whether the Capetian kings, newly implanted aristocrats of northern French extraction, or native Languedocians—everywhere perfected their means of governance and consolidated their lordships. This process has been best studied in ecclesiastical lordships, especially that of the bishops of Albi.[3] In this diocese the bishops took advantage of the upheaval caused by the Albigensian crusades and the imposition of Capetian overlordship to enhance their secular authority. The crusades eliminated the Trencavel family, viscounts of Carcassonne and Albi, as their rivals for political power in the diocese. Through the first half of the thirteenth century, the bishops conducted a long and relatively successful struggle against the pretensions of the French kings, who had fallen heir to the Trencavels' rights. In this contest the people of the city of Albi were initially allied with the bishops. In return, the bishops granted the townspeople various privileges. Although it cannot be said that the bishops took a benevolent attitude toward heresy, their alliance with the townspeople may have something to do with the fact that the inquisitors—after their early, occasionally unpleasant, experiences with trying to ferret out heretics in Albi—left the city largely alone until the 1280s.[4]

In the second half of the thirteenth century, however, relations between the bishops and their subjects became strained. And with the promotion to the see of Bernard de Castanet in 1276, political life in Albi became truly envenomed. Castanet set about reducing the powers that the townsmen had arrogated to themselves during the long vacancy that had preceded his arrival. He tried to exert greater control over the town's judicial affairs and he may have attempted to infringe on the citizens' right to elect their own consuls. The townspeople responded by trying to foster the development of royal authority, evidenced most concretely by a growing number of appeals from the bishop's courts to those of the king. In 1297 matters came to a head when the bishop arrested thirteen townsmen for cutting down trees and vines. Before the bishop's *bayle* would release them, he demanded what they asserted were excessive guarantees for their subsequent appearance in court. The prisoners, claiming that the customs of the city had been violated, appealed to the king. The royal *viguier* took custody of

---

[3] See Biget, "Un Procès d'inquisition"; Biget, "La Restitution des dîmes"; and A. Molinier, "Etude sur les démêlés."

[4] Biget, "Un Procès d'inquisition," pp. 274–78.

the accused, allowed them to offer what they claimed were the customary sureties, and released them. This action began a dispute between Castanet and the royal authorities that dragged on for years.[5]

In this agitated atmosphere Castanet seems to have relied heavily on the inquisition as a tool for intimidating his opponents. One of his goals was the recovery of church tithes that were in lay hands. Some of the relatively impecunious petty lords of the Albigeois were understandably disinclined to part with these valuable supplements to their income.[6] On at least one occasion the bishop used a threat of heresy prosecution in an effort to pry tithes out of reluctant hands. In 1307 the notary Pons Sivalh told the following story to papal commissioners. Several years before, some *domicelli* who had been excommunicated by the bishop for refusing to hand over the tithes in their possession had come to Sivalh. They asked him to draw up appeals to the archbishop of Bourges, Albi's metropolitan, and the pope. But Castanet's official, Guillaume de Saint-Jean, forestalled this. He informed Sivalh that if he drew up the appeal, the bishop would have him arrested and turned over to the inquisitors as a supporter of heretics.[7]

The bishop also used heresy accusations to punish those who defied his authority. When Pope Boniface VIII held his great jubilee in Rome in 1300, a number of Albigeois wished to attend. When they applied to Castanet for permission, they were met with refusal. One of the witnesses later interviewed by the papal commissioners believed that Castanet did this to prevent his subjects from taking advantage of a visit to Rome to denounce him to the pope.[8] However, a number of people defied Castanet and went to Rome. When they returned, they were arrested, ostensibly on the grounds of involvement with heresy. Yet many Albigeois believed that their only fault was defiance of the bishop.[9]

The most spectacular use that Castanet made of inquisitorial proceedings was the series of trials he held in 1299 and 1300. His decision to embark on these investigations may have been linked to the disputes that had grown out of the felling of trees and destruction of vineyards and the subsequent appeal to the king.[10] Castanet arrested several leading citizens of Albi. With the assistance of the inquisitor of Carcassonne, he tried these men very rapidly between 2 December 1299 and 30 March 1300. Twenty-four people were sentenced to imprisonment; they were removed from Albi and incarcerated in the *mur* in Carcassonne.[11] This touched off major protests, as the people of Albi loudly

---

[5] The best guide to these events is ibid., pp. 273–341.

[6] On the tithe issue in the diocese of Albi, see Biget, "La Restitution des dîmes."

[7] Collectorie 404, fol. 104r.

[8] Ibid., fol. 130r.

[9] Ibid., fols. 35r, 53r, 62v, 85r, 113r, 134r, 139r, 159v.

[10] Biget, "Un Procès d'inquisition," pp. 325–26.

[11] Ibid., pp. 283–84, 295, 298, 308, 311. The records of these proceedings have been published by Davis, ed., *The Inquisition at Albi*. See above, chapter 5.

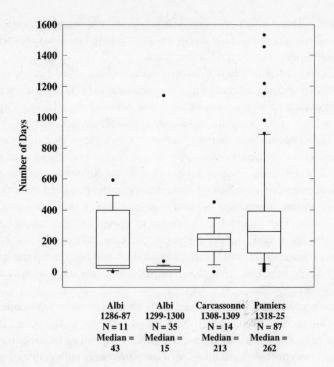

**Figure 7.1 Length of Trials at Selected Sites in Languedoc**

Note: Each box indicates the range between the 25th and 75th percentiles of the data. The solid horizontal lines indicate the 50th percentile. Capped bars indicate the 10th and 90th percentile points. The dots indicate cases lying beyond the 10th and 90th percentiles.

Sources: Albi, 1286–87: BN Lat. 12856; Albi, 1299–1300: Davis, ed., *The Inquisition at Albi*; Carcassonne, 1308–09: Pales-Gobilliard, ed., *Geoffroy d'Ablis*; Pamiers, 1318–25: *Registre*.

asserted the innocence of their fellow citizens and the mendacity and tyranny of the bishop. Whether the people whom Castanet condemned were guilty or innocent is a question that vexed contemporaries and continues to vex modern historians.[12] Evaluating the truth of these charges after almost seven centuries is difficult, but some quantitative evidence may throw some indirect light on this question. We can calculate the length of trials for four inquisitorial tribunals sitting in Languedoc between the 1280s and the 1320s. Figure 7.1 gives a graphical representation of the length of the trials conducted by these tribunals.[13] It is clear

[12] Biget, who has studied these trials more thoroughly than anyone else, is convinced of the reality of the charges against the inhabitants of Albi. See "Un Procès d'inquisition," pp. 291–92; "L'Extinction du Catharisme urbain"; and "Autour de Bernard Délicieux."

[13] Of the eleven trials at Albi in 1286–87, the median length of time required was 43 days; of the thirty-five trials of those arrested at Albi in 1299–1300, 15 days; of the fourteen trials

from this figure that the trials of those arrested in Albi in 1299 and 1300 were unusually rapid. They were, as a group, concluded even more quickly than the proceedings that Castanet had held in the mid-1280s. This tends to lend some credence to the claims of Castanet's enemies that he used liberal application of torture to extract confessions. All in all, one cannot help but suspect that Bernard de Castanet was one bishop who did not shrink from invoking the fearsome processes of the inquisition to deal with matters quite unrelated to heresy.

Albi was not the only diocese where political tensions between a bishop and his subjects produced an increased interest in heresy hunting. Something similar happened in the diocese of Pamiers under Jacques Fournier. Fournier, a zealous pursuer of heretics who was nevertheless punctilious about the niceties of inquisitorial procedure, was clearly cut from a different cloth than Bernard de Castanet. No one ever accused Fournier, a future pope, of the sort of misdeeds alleged against the bishop of Albi, who was denounced by his enemies as a brutal and cynical power politician. Nevertheless, although Fournier may not have been corrupt, he does seem to have surrendered to the temptation to use the inquisition to help resolve an old and contentious issue in his diocese, the tithe obligations of the people of the region known as the Sabarthès.

When in the early fourteenth century Fournier became bishop of Pamiers, a see that embraced most of the county of Foix, he entered an arena that had long been agitated by tithe disputes. Indeed, these quarrels had begun as early as the 1250s and 1260s, well before the see of Pamiers existed. When in 1261 the abbot of Saint-Volusien in the town of Foix tried to enforce his claims to the right to collect tithes in the archdeaconry of the Sabarthès, his efforts were greeted with rioting.[14] Opposition to tithes in the late thirteenth century became so determined that the church was forced to moderate its demands. Many towns and villages won exemptions of one sort or another. Around 1300, however, church authorities resumed the struggle, as the see of Pamiers, carved out of the sprawling diocese of Toulouse in 1295, found itself short of income.[15] Claiming a right to larger tithes, the diocesan clergy brought suit against the people of the Sabarthès. A particular point of disagreement were the *carnelages*, tithes collected on animals. In an area like the Sabarthès, whose agrarian economy gave an important role to animal husbandry, these were particularly lucrative and particularly detested.

In 1311 an attempt was made to settle the quarrel. With the count of Foix, the inquisitor of Carcassonne, and the official of the archbishop of Narbonne acting as arbitrators, an agreement was worked out between the diocesan clergy

---

recorded at Carcassonne in 1308–9, 213 days; and of the eighty-seven trials recorded at Pamiers in 1318–25, 262 days.

[14] Llobet, *Foix médiéval*, pp. 28–31.

[15] See Vidal, "Les Origines de la province ecclésiastique," 15 (1903), pp. 310–28.

and the tithe payers that included an elaborate schedule of dues on various goods.[16] This arbitration, however, did not end the dispute. The difficulty may have arisen because the agreement required the nobility of the diocese to pay the *carnelages* at a rate only half that of commoners. When Fournier became bishop of Pamiers, he found it necessary to excommunicate the people of the Sabarthès and put the country under an interdict. In this charged atmosphere he was eager to uncover any antitithe sentiments that seemed to savor of heresy. Of the individuals who passed before his tribunal, four were accused of uttering inflammatory comments about tithes.[17] Indeed, in the case of two of these men, Raimond de Laburat of Quié and Pierre Guillaume of Unac, hostility to tithes seems to have been the principal charge against them. Both paid a heavy price for their opinions.

Pierre Guillaume's troubles began with a chance encounter.[18] On 23 November 1322 Barthélemy Hugues of Saverdun was on the road from Caussou to Unac, where he was a student at the priory. His trip was interrupted by a heavy rainstorm. To get out of the downpour, he ducked into the workshop of Pierre Guillaume, a cobbler. There he fell into a conversation with Guillaume and one Simon Géraud, a mercer from Ax-les-Thermes. The discussion turned into an argument, in part because Guillaume would not lend the wet student a pair of shoes. As one subject led to another, Guillaume proclaimed that the diocese's clergy were behaving in an evil manner by demanding that tithes be paid on goods that had always been exempt. Losing his temper, he said to Barthélemy, "Leave me alone, you other clerics, you greatly want to lord it over us, and you inflexibly strive to deprive us of our rights."[19] He went on to declare that all of the clergy should be driven out of the country. If the old count of Foix, Roger Bernard, were still alive, the county's inhabitants would have so arranged matters with him that no cleric would dare set foot beyond the Pas de la Barre, which divided the uplands of Foix from the lowlands.[20] These words, spoken in the heat of an argument, probably won Pierre Guillaume a sentence of perpetual imprisonment.[21]

Raimond de Laburat of Quié also ran afoul of the bishop over the tithe issue. In late 1321 Fournier became interested in Raimond's conduct.[22] At that time he

[16] The text of this agreement is printed in *Registre*, 3: 337–41. The dispute is discussed by Llobet, *Foix médiéval*, pp. 49–54.

[17] These four were Raimond de Laburat, Pierre Guillaume of Unac, Guillaume Austatz of Ornolac (*Registre*, 1: 200–201, 209) and Bernard Clergue of Montaillou (2: 284).

[18] The records of Fournier's investigation of Pierre Guillaume are in ibid., 3: 331–45.

[19] Ibid., 3: 336–37.

[20] Ibid., 3: 331.

[21] There is no record of Pierre Guillaume's sentence. However, his case was discussed by the board of experts assembled by Fournier on 14 January 1329 to advise the bishop concerning the sentences of a number of people whom he proposed to imprison. As Vidal suggests, this is a good indication that Pierre was subsequently imprisoned ("Le Tribunal d'inquisition de Pamiers," pp. 429–30).

[22] The records of Fournier's investigation of Raimond de Laburat are in *Registre*, 2: 308–29.

learned that Raimond had said many inflammatory things not only about tithes but also about Fournier himself. Around Easter of 1321 a group of men in the plaza of Quié got into a discussion of the bishop's excommunication of those who refused to pay the tithes. Raimond was reported to have said, "We made the churches for the priests, and the doors of the churches, and then the priests close the churches' doors in front of our eyes! . . . I wish that we had a book box in some furrow or some field and that mass was celebrated on that box; if this were so, the priests would not be able to close the doors so that we can't see or hear mass!"[23] He went on to claim that although God had not instituted excommunication, priests quickly and easily excommunicated their flocks.

On Palm Sunday Raimond found another occasion to vent his dislike of the clergy. When the rector of Quié, Raimond Frézat, informed his parishioners that the bishop had ordered them to provide fifteen to twenty pounds of wax to make a great candle for Easter, Raimond was infuriated by what he saw as a violation of custom.[24] To Frézat, he said, "What power does your bishop have that he orders us to provide this paschal wax? Who is this bishop of yours who orders us to provide this paschal wax, since we have not previously been accustomed to make a waxen candle of this kind?" The rector replied that Fournier was so impressive a man that even if he were not a bishop, "you would think him a lord. And he has the power to make you provide this paschal wax." Raimond answered, "If the bishop has the power to order us to provide this paschal wax, it's up to us how much wax we use, a pound, a half pound, a quarter pound, or even a plain candle. And he can't compel us to use a specific quantity of wax."[25] After Frézat's brief reply,

> Raimond said that he wished that all the priests and clerics in the world were dead, or that all other men were in paradise. Thus the priests and clerics would have to plow and dig in the fields. And he added that he wished he were with the bishop in a certain pass that he named. And there "we could fight out between him and me this issue of the *carnelages*. Then I could see what sort of guts this bishop has."[26]

These and similar remarks (along with a slight suspicion of involvement with Catharism) resulted in Raimond's condemnation *ad murum strictum* on 19 June 1323.[27]

These events in the dioceses of Albi and Pamiers make it clear that the strains involved in the consolidation of lordship could function in a way that facilitated

[23] Ibid., 2: 309.
[24] Ibid., 2: 324–25.
[25] Ibid., 2: 314.
[26] Ibid., 2: 314–15.
[27] *LS*, p. 393.

the work of the inquisitors. Not only were some lords unwilling to protect their subjects from the attentions of the inquisitors, but some ecclesiastical lords were even willing to mount their own inquisitorial investigations. Although a bishop like the zealous Jacques Fournier was probably genuinely concerned with the threat of heresy, one is tempted to believe, as did many of his contemporaries, that Bernard de Castanet made a cynical use of inquisitorial techniques to crush men whose only fault was opposition to his will.

It is relatively easy to discover strains between lord and follower in the highly institutionalized types of lordship, like that of the bishop of Albi. Trying to examine the strains that afflicted more informal, less institutionalized, and hence less well documented forms of lordship is more difficult. It is possible, however, to identify several factors that were weakening the ties between lords and followers in the thirteenth and fourteenth centuries. In the early thirteenth century many of the Languedocian nobility experienced severe difficulties.[28] Many suffered greatly during the Albigensian crusades, as well as in the revolts of the early 1240s. Some became *faidits*, that is, outlaws and fugitives. Others managed to come to terms with the French monarchy and regained part, if not all, of their lands; still others lost everything. These people were certainly not as well fitted as their ancestors to be the leaders of extensive clientage groups. In the area around Carcassonne there was a sizable replacement of native lords by a new aristocracy, primarily recruited from northern France.[29] The ties of lordship that bound these new masters to their Languedocian subjects and clients may have been relatively fragile.

Other developments reinforced a sense of separateness and social exclusiveness on the part of the Languedocian nobility. In the late Middle Ages, the importance of vertical social ties uniting members across class and status boundaries generally tended to wane as the horizontal ties uniting individuals within a single class or status group strengthened. All European nobilities became increasingly more clearly marked off from other status groups and more self-conscious. This process was promoted in Languedoc by the fiscal policies adopted by the royal government and the church. Royal taxation was especially important in creating aristocratic self-consciousness and exclusivity. As in many Mediterranean countries at the beginning of the thirteenth century, the nobles of Languedoc had been deeply involved in the life of the local towns. Many had lived in urban areas and participated in civic affairs, providing members of the governing consulates. However, during the thirteenth century they began to withdraw from civic life. In large part this was due to taxation, which became increasingly frequent in the late 1200s, as the kingdom found itself involved in ever more expensive wars. The growing tax burden caused many nobles to

[28] For a brief summary of the fate of the Languedocian nobility in the thirteenth and early fourteenth centuries, see Given, *State and Society*, pp. 105–8.
[29] See Timbal, *Un Conflit d'annexion*.

distance themselves from involvement in town affairs. Since royal taxes were justified as being necessary for the king's wars, nobles claimed to be exempt because of their personal liability for military service. Disputes about the validity of these claims became common. To escape taxation, some nobles physically abandoned the cities. Those who did not often asserted that they formed a community legally distinct from that of the bourgeoisie.[30] In places the demands of the church played a similar role in setting the nobility clearly apart from other social groups. As we have seen, when an effort was made to settle the dispute over the *carnelages* in the county of Foix, nobles were allowed to pay at half the rate of commoners. The sense of social separateness engendered by these developments may well have worked to loosen ties between lords and followers.

Hence it would not be surprising if the bonds that united lords and their clients were prone to fray under pressure from the inquisitors. Indeed, it is possible to find evidence of this in the inquisitorial records. Even in the 1240s, when heresy was more widespread in Languedoc and the inquisition was relatively new and its work more frequently contested, we can find servants turning against their masters. For example, on 23 February 1246 Arnaud de Bonahac, a servant of Pierre de Resengas of Lanta, a member of the nobility of the Lauragais, appeared together with his wife Raimonde before the inquisitors of Toulouse. Arnaud reported that around Easter of 1245 he had heard four men enter his master's house in the middle of the night. Since he had heard rumors that Pierre's wife, Austorga, was a Cathar believer, he suspected that these men were heretics.[31] His wife Raimonde seconded these suspicions. One day Raimonde happened to glance through a hole into the house's cellar and saw four men come out of one room and go into another. On another occasion, a different servant, a woman named Jordana, was in the cellar making bread when four men suddenly emerged from a subbasement. These strangers, whom Arnaud believed to be heretics, remained in the house for over two weeks. Austorga, her son Pierre, her daughter Orbria, and two other men frequently visited them. Armed with this information, Arnaud went to Pierre Dellac, the *bayle* of Caraman. He told Dellac that he could easily arrest the heretics. The *bayle* put off immediate action, saying that he needed to consult his brother. Finally, on the Saturday before Easter, Dellac appeared in Lanta. The heretics, however, had left the day before.[32]

Jacques Fournier's register contains several anecdotes that let us see how the ties that united a lord and his clients could unravel under the stress of inquisitorial investigations. Arnaud de Sobrenia of Tignac was the *bayle* of Simon Barre, a member of the nobility of the county of Foix. One day his body was found floating in the Ariège river. Since Arnaud had known the "secrets" of his master,

---

[30] See Given, *State and Society*, pp. 195–96.
[31] Austorga de Resengas was condemned to perpetual imprisonment on 25 March 1246 (*Documents*, 2: 4–5).
[32] MS 609, fols. 200r–v.

the people of Tignac decided that Simon must have had the *bayle* drowned to keep him from testifying to the inquisitors.[33]

Another illustration of tension between lord and client is provided by the career of Aycred Boret of Caussou. Boret was a thug, one of the specialists in personal violence who gravitated around the nobility of the county of Foix. Indeed, at the time that Jacques Fournier became interested in him, he was incarcerated in the castle of Foix, awaiting execution for murder.[34] Boret had long been associated with the Planissoles, a local aristocratic family. His ties with this family had been intimate, to say the least. Boret admitted to one of his acquaintances that he had helped Raimond de Planissoles murder and secretly bury in his father's garden a man named Pierre Plani.[35] However, taxation turned Boret against the Planissoles. When *tailles* were levied in Caussou, Boret blamed Guillaume de Planissoles and another member of the local nobility. In the presence of his neighbors, he openly referred to Planissoles as a devil. He was so enraged that, as he told one Vital Record, "he would go to the seneschal of Foix, or the bishop of Pamiers, or to the devil, in order to get Guillaume de Planissoles and Raimond Aurus of Caussou put in an evil place." Boret's words were not mere bluster, for he went to Bishop Fournier and denounced Planissoles as a Cathar believer.[36]

## KINSHIP

The vertical bonds that united lords and clients were not alone in being subject to social strain. Horizontal bonds, such as those uniting kinsmen and the inhabitants of the same town or village, were also afflicted by characteristic patterns of friction and conflict. These strains too played into the hands of the inquisitors. In discussing the strains that afflicted kinship ties, I will focus on the diocese of Pamiers and the county of Foix. Thanks to the unusual detail in the inquisitorial register of Jacques Fournier and the researches of Le Roy Ladurie, we are relatively well informed about the nature of kinship ties in this part of Languedoc.[37]

One might at first think that kinship ties would present a significant problem for the inquisitors. In many ways, the family was the basic unit of medieval society, the center not only of biological reproduction but of economic, cultural, and to an extent political reproduction as well. As Le Roy Ladurie has made clear, among the relatively well documented peasants of the Ariège, the kinship unit, incarnated in the household (conceived of both as a domiciliary unit and a network of relatives), not only was central to their social life but was the object of

---

[33] *Registre*, 1: 281.
[34] Ibid., 3: 354.
[35] Ibid., 3: 347.
[36] Ibid., 3: 349–51, 353–54; quotation on p. 349.
[37] But see Benad's criticisms of Le Roy Ladurie in *Domus und Religion*.

considerable emotional investment.[38] Moreover, as students of heresy have noticed, Catharism tended to propagate itself along family lines.[39]

Yet there were countervailing forces at work. The evidence concerning the kinship system of the Fuxéen peasantry, mainly derived from Fournier's register, is not always as clear about the nature of that system as we would like it to be. To understand it we often have to make reference to what we know about peasant kinship organization in other parts of the Pyrenees. However, it does seem that these kinship groups were characterized by certain strains that could facilitate the work of the inquisitors. For one thing, the rules for determining membership or leadership in the kinship group seem to have been fluid. Indeed, the kinship groups we find in Fournier's register, organized around the physical *ostal*, appear to have had some of the characteristics associated with cognatic, or bilateral, kindreds.[40]

Throughout the Pyrenees the primary focus of the kinship group appears to have been the household: the *domus* of Fournier's register, the *ostau* of the central Pyrenees, and the *etxe-ondo* of the Basques. The *ostal*'s perpetuation across the generations was the paramount goal of the kinship system. To guarantee this, in the western Pyrenees the eldest child, whether male or female, inherited the entire household. In some places it was held improper for a female heir and a male heir to marry, since this would extinguish one of the households. Thus, only younger children, whether male or female, could marry an inheritor. Among the Basques, when a male younger son of one *etxe-ondo* married the female heir of another *etxe-ondo*, he had to provide a dowry. Once the marriage had been consummated, he moved into his wife's household and assumed her name, which was borne by their children.[41] The county of Foix was not Basque, of course. People in this region tended to stress the principle of patrilineal descent.[42] But the matrilineal principle was not totally obliterated. The chief goal of the family remained the preservation of the *ostal*, which could be passed through both males and

---

[38] Le Roy Ladurie, *Montaillou*, pp. 51–107.

[39] See Roquebert, "Catharisme comme tradition."

[40] For this terminology, see Fox, *Kinship and Marriage*, pp. 146–74. See also Goody, *Family and Marriage*, pp. 222–39. For discussions of kinship in Toulouse and in Catalonia, which abutted on Languedoc just south of the Pyrenees, see Mundy, *Men and Women at Toulouse*, pp. 27–41, 88–112; Freedman, *Peasant Servitude in Medieval Catalonia*, pp. 45–50; and Bonnassie, *Catalogne*, 1: 258–82. These studies show a general tendency for inheritance customs to move away from equal division of property among heirs to a system that favored a single heir. They also indicate a relatively advantaged status for women, able to control their dowries and at times exercising a fair degree of personal autonomy.

[41] Poumarède, "Les Coutumes successorales," pp. 25–26. See also Goyheneche, "Basque Economic and Political Structures," p. 6; Frank and Lowenberg, "The Role of the Basque Woman," p. 15; and Frank, Laxalt, and Vosburg, "Inheritance, Marriage, and Dowry Rights," pp. 22–24.

[42] Immediately on the other side of the Pyrenees, in Andorra, early modern and modern inheritance customs gave the head of the household, or *cap de casa*, complete freedom in designating the heir to his holding. The heir could be any child, regardless of sex or birth order. See Platon, "Du Droit de la famille," pp. 153–54.

females.[43] The adoption by children of their mother's family name rather than their father's seems to have been not uncommon. It was also not unheard of for a man to adopt his wife's family name if he took up residence in her *ostal*.[44] The kinship system of the Ariège thus seems to have had a definite cognatic aspect.

Cognatic descent groups can be divided into those with an ancestor-focus and those with an ego-focus.[45] In descent systems with an ancestor-focus, people reckon kinship by tracing a line of descent from a common ancestor, say a paternal great-grandfather.[46] In descent systems with an ego-focus, individuals reckon their kin by working outward from themselves, first counting ascendants among both their maternal and paternal kin, and then working downward from these ascendants to determine their collateral kin. In such a system kindreds are essentially personal, as each individual, with the exception of full siblings, has a different kin group.

The kin groups of the county of Foix seem to a certain extent to have combined the two principles. They had an ancestor-focus, in that what mattered most to members of the family in reckoning kinship was the *ostal* to which they belonged. But these kinship groups also had something of an ego-focus. At least there always seems to have been a certain amount of ambiguity surrounding the reckoning of kinship ties. Indeed, individuals appear to have had a degree of freedom in choosing the *ostal* and the kinship group with which they wished to affiliate. For example, Arnaud Sicre, Jacques Fournier's spy, preferred to attach his fortunes to his mother's kindred and *ostal* in Ax-les-Thermes rather than to that of his father's kindred in Tarascon.[47] The upshot of all this is that the moral bonds that attached one member of a kinship group to another could often be fairly loose.

Not only did the kinship system of the county of Foix provide no firm rules for determining the membership of a kin group, it also provided no clear-cut rules for allocating leadership roles. Age seniority alone was not decisive.[48] Among members of the same generation there was often conflict over who would exercise effective leadership. Within the *ostal* one brother did not necessarily exercise complete control over his siblings. Fournier's register, for example, reveals

---

[43] For Le Roy Ladurie's views on inheritance and descent, see *Montaillou*, pp. 64–66.

[44] *Registre*, 2: 129; Le Roy Ladurie, *Montaillou*, p. 64.

[45] Fox, *Kinship and Marriage*, p. 164.

[46] These cognatic descent groups with an ancestor-focus seem very similar to the form of kinship system that Herlihy and Klapisch-Zuber argue was the norm in western Europe before lineage forms of kinship organization appeared in the late tenth and early eleventh centuries (*Tuscans and Their Families*, pp. 337–42).

[47] *Registre*, 2: 21.

[48] For example, Bernard Rives of Montaillou found himself forced to cede effective leadership of his *ostal* to one of his sons. When his daughter Guillemette, who had married and moved out of the household, tried one day to borrow a pack animal from her father, he told her that he neither could nor dared give her an animal without his son's approval (ibid., 1: 340; see also Le Roy Ladurie, *Montaillou*, p. 65). Interestingly, Bonnassie has detected much tension between different generations of the same family in Catalonia shortly after the year 1000 (*Catalogne*, 2: 545–47).

brothers from the Clergue *ostal* in Montaillou seemingly working at cross-purposes. Although Bernard Clergue of Montaillou tried to persuade Bernard Benet to testify against the Faure and Guilhabert families, his brother, Raimond Clergue, approached Martin Guilhabert with a scheme for bribing Benet to keep his mouth shut.[49] If age was not a sure criterion for establishing leadership within the kin group, neither was gender. For example, Sibille den Baille of Ax-les-Thermes, a Cathar adherent ultimately burned at the stake, clearly assumed leadership in her household (see below).

It is thus clear that there were several sources of potential strain within the kinship structures of the Fuxéen peasant family. The pressures that the inquisitors exerted as they pursued their investigations exacerbated these strains. In effect, there was added to the preexisting strain system that was characteristic of the peasant family a new stress—a novel, externally applied pressure that could not be dealt with through the routine devices offered by local society.[50] This new stress so inflamed strains already present within some kinship groups that it produced unregulated, divisive, and disruptive conflict.[51]

Fournier's register contains several examples that illustrate how the new stress constituted by inquisitorial activity could cause family groups to shatter along just such lines as our analysis would predict. In a kinship system such as that in the Sabarthès, where age by itself did not constitute a clear-cut title to positions of leadership, we would not be surprised to find that inquisitorial pressure generated conflicts between parents and children. One particularly vivid instance of such conflict comes from the deposition of Bernard Marty. Bernard's father, Pierre, was a blacksmith in the town of Junac. His son Arnaud was an ardent Cathar believer who was frequently away from home guiding Good Men around the countryside. One day, when Arnaud returned from a night journey to Quié, his father questioned him about his activities. Arnaud refused to explain. That night at dinner Pierre upbraided his son, "Arnaud, your ways do not please me, because you go out by night and you come back by night." Arnaud replied, "Be quiet, father; sometime bad luck will come to you." To which his father replied, "You speak to me like this?" Arnaud retorted, "Unless you shut up, your head will wind up at your feet one of these days." Enraged by this, his father threw a container of salt at Arnaud. Arnaud seized it and lunged at his father, but he was restrained by one of his friends, Pierre Talha, who was also sitting at the table. As Arnaud again told his father that bad luck would come to him, Pierre picked up the bench on which he was sitting and threw it at Arnaud. He also proclaimed that Arnaud was no son of his and that he would see to it that he experienced an evil *aventura*; this was evidently a threat to inform on him to the inquisitors. Arnaud stormed out of the house. Thereafter,

[49] *Registre*, 1: 431.
[50] Beals and Siegel, *Divisiveness and Social Conflict*, p. 91.
[51] I roughly follow Beals and Siegel in their classification of types of conflict (ibid., p. 22).

according to Bernard Marty, there was for a long time bad blood between Arnaud and his father.[52]

Most differences of opinion between parents and children were not so violent. Nevertheless, Fournier's register makes it clear that Catharism frequently divided the generations. Guillemette Dejean of Prades, for example, was a Cathar believer. Indeed, her brother, Prades Tavernier, was one of the last *perfecti* in the Ariège. However, her son, Pierre Prades, was a Catholic priest. He was sufficiently suspicious of his mother that he made her move to Joucou, where he was living, evidently to keep an eye on her.[53]

Inquisitorial activity could also turn spouses against one another. Sibille den Baille of Ax-les-Thermes was a dedicated Cathar adherent, who ultimately died at the stake. Yet her husband, Arnaud Sicre, was hostile to the heretics. Therefore she threw him out of her house, forcing him to move to Tarascon. Subsequently, Arnaud became an inquisitorial agent, searching out fugitive heretics and participating in the mass arrest of the inhabitants of Montaillou.[54] And in the next generation, Arnaud and Sibille's son, also named Arnaud, became a spy for Jacques Fournier in the hopes of recovering his mother's property, confiscated for heresy.[55]

Ties between siblings, especially brothers, were beset by a host of potential tensions over matters of inheritance, marriage, and so forth. It is therefore not surprising that we find the issue of Catharism turning one brother against another. For example, when Guillaume Escaunier of Ax-les-Thermes was living in Arques, his mother fell gravely ill. It was decided that she should receive the *consolamentum*. Guillaume was dispatched to find the necessary heretic. He made his way to Ax, where he lodged with his brother Raimond, who was not a believer. There he contacted Sibille den Baille. When she learned that Guillaume was searching for a Good Man, she told him to meet her that night at the cemetery. Together with his brother and Pierre Montanier, a believer, Guillaume went to the cemetery. There they waited a long time. When it was pitch dark, and rain had begun to fall, Raimond Escaunier, who was evidently growing suspicious, asked, "What are we doing here?" Guillaume told him that they were waiting for Sibille, who was bringing a man who would accompany them to Arques. Raimond's suspicions now fully aroused, he said, "And who is this man?" Guillaume replied, "I don't know." At that moment Sibille appeared with the

---

[52] *Registre*, 3: 261–62, MS 4030, fol. 276c: "'Arnalde, non placeret [sic] michi vie tue, quia de nocte vadis et de nocte reverteris,' cui respondit dictus Arnaldus: 'Pater, taceatis, aliquando mala fortuna veniret vobis [Duvernoy reads nobis].' Et cum dictus pater respondisset: 'Et michi hoc dicis?' dictus Arnaldus respondit quod: 'Nisi taceatis, capud vestrum ponetur ad pedes aliqua dierum.'" For another example of inquisition-induced stress between generations of the same household, see *Registre*, 2: 186–87.

[53] *Registre*, 1: 336.

[54] Ibid., 2: 9, 28, 170–71. I find Duvernoy's argument (2: 171 n. 299) that Arnaud did not take part in the arrest of the people of Montaillou unconvincing.

[55] Ibid., 2: 20–81.

*perfectus* Prades Tavernier. Sibille entrusted Tavernier to them and advised them to leave Ax-les-Thermes not by the road that went by the baths, but to go through the old town lest they be seen. As they left, Raimond once again asked his brother who was the man whom Sibille had produced. This time Guillaume told him that Prades was one of the people known as heretics.

> And then his brother said that if this was known, it would go badly for him. Then he [i.e., Guillaume] replied that he wanted to take this man to their mother so that he could receive her into their sect. His brother told him that he would not go with him, but that he would reveal this to the priests. When the witness heard this, he replied that he should in no way tell the local priests, because they would be lost if this got out. His brother told him that he would not go with them. And he [Guillaume] said to his brother, "Don't you want to see your mother, who is dying?" And then his brother went with them, muttering to himself, and following behind.[56]

The way in which inquisitorial pressure could exacerbate the strains inherent in Fuxéen peasant families is nicely illustrated by the internal quarrels that afflicted the exile community that took shape in the early fourteenth century in the kingdom of Aragon. One member of this group was Emersende Marty of Montaillou, who had fled with her daughter Jeanne to the village of Beceite in Catalonia. There Jeanne married Bernard Befayt, also a devotee of Catharism. In Montaillou Jeanne had been a good Cathar; but in Catalonia she became, if not a good Catholic, at least a good hater of Cathars. She came to loathe the sight of the Cathar *perfecti*. On one occasion, she drove the Good Man Guillaume Bélibaste out of her mother's house; she told him that if he ever came back she would kill him.[57] She constantly harassed her mother, calling her "a little old heretic" and threatening to have her burned. On occasion the two came to blows. One day Emersende and Jeanne argued during dinner and Jeanne began to beat her mother. Bernard Befayt was summoned to administer husbandly correction, which he did with great zest, throwing Jeanne down the stairs and out of the house, a commotion that brought the neighbors to watch.[58]

Eventually Emersende and the other Cathar exiles began to fear that Jeanne would betray them. They met to discuss how they could prevent this. Among other things, it was proposed to take her to a distant town and abandon her there. Not surprisingly, this was judged to be an inadequate measure, as was returning her to Montaillou, since there would be nothing to prevent her from going to the inquisitors once she had been abandoned. Finally, it was decided that the best solution was murder. Lengthy discussions then followed as to the

---

[56] Ibid., 2: 13–15.
[57] Ibid., 2: 63–64.
[58] Ibid., 3: 178.

best person and method to carry out the deed. The techniques considered included throwing Jeanne off various cliffs and bridges, stabbing her with an assortment of lances and swords, and poisoning her. After much discussion the plotters settled on poison as the best method. However, the apothecary from whom they tried to buy some poison (under the guise of treating sick donkeys) refused to sell it, suspecting the purpose for which it might be used; Jeanne thus escaped with her life.[59]

This circle of exiles also hatched another plot that set one kinsman against another. This time they planned to kill Jean Maury of Montaillou, Emersende Marty's nephew. Jean Maury had fallen ill and was expected to die. His fellow Cathar sympathizers therefore approached him about receiving the *consolamentum*. Since any sins, which included the eating of flesh or cheese, that were committed after the reception of the *consolamentum* canceled out its effects, steps were taken to keep the dying from eating any unclean foods. To guarantee that sufferers would die in a sanctified state, they were placed in what the inquisitors called the *endura*, in which they were deprived of all food except water. Of course, the *endura* helped guarantee not only a good death and ultimate salvation, but also a sharply reduced chance of recovery. Maury, unwilling to commit what would in effect be suicide, refused to have anything to do with the *consolamentum*. Moreover, he threatened to have those who had raised the matter arrested. When he recovered from his illness, the exiles, fearing that he would disclose them, contemplated killing him. To his credit, Jean's brother Pierre refused to have anything to do with the plot and told Jean what was afoot. Subsequently Jean's enemies repented of their scheme and asked him to forgive them. Jean did so; but prudent man that he was, he thereafter tested his food by first giving some of it to a dog.[60]

There is a difficulty with the argument that I have been making up to this point. Although it can be said without too much hesitation that Languedocian family life was marked by certain strains and that inquisitorial pressure helped to exacerbate them, it is hard to point to concrete instances where such strains played directly into the hands of the inquisitors. There are, however, a number of such cases preserved in the records. One of these involves the family of Sibille den Baille. The frictions generated by the adherence of this devout Cathar believer to heresy not only led to the breakup of her marriage but seem ultimately to have turned her husband and her son into agents of the inquisition.

Another example comes from the 1240s and the Lauragais. Although this case is outside the time period and geographic region of our focus, it is worth considering. Emersende Viguier of Cambiac was married to a fervent Cathar believer, but she came to detest the heretics. Her hostility stemmed from an incident that occurred around 1222, well before the Dominican inquisitors had

[59] Ibid., 2: 55–57, 3: 172–78, 247.
[60] Ibid., 2: 484–85, 3: 114–15.

set up shop. At that time she was still a young woman; she was also pregnant. One day her aunt took her to Auriac to see two Cathar Good Women. Emersende listened to their sermon and performed the ritual known as the *melioramentum*. The *perfectae* then told her that she was carrying a demon in her womb. This struck the others who were present as a good joke and they all laughed at her. Thereafter, despite her husband's admonitions, and some beatings, she refused to show any reverence to the heretics. Indeed, when the inquisitors became active in the Lauragais, she began working to secure the heretics' arrest. In the summer of 1245, for example, she found a sack full of twenty-three fresh eels, a man's shirt, and some other things in a ditch in the woods near Cambiac where heretics were accustomed to hide. She immediately took this to the priest of Auriac, Martin Casel, and told him that he could find some heretics if he searched the area.

In June 1245 some Cathar sympathizers tried to intimidate her into silence. A group of men, including her husband and the lords of Cambiac, Jordan Sais and his son Guillaume, paid her a visit. They ordered her to hold her tongue and under no circumstances to tell the inquisitors what she knew. She replied that she would tell the inquisitors nothing but the truth. Guillaume Sais thereupon had her shut up in a barrel. Her son tried to defend her. Saying "Boy, you want to help this little old woman who wants to destroy us all?," Sais put him in the barrel with her.[61] The two spent a night in these cramped quarters before they were released, after giving three sous and four deniers to Sais. Yet this episode failed to deter Emersende. In August 1245 Guillaume Sais persuaded some of Cambiac's villagers to collect grain for the Good Men. When Emersende learned where the grain was stored, she informed Martin Casel, who seized it. Sometime later money was raised in Cambiac to help free the Cathar deacon, Raimond Fort, from captivity. Among those who contributed was Emersende's husband. Emersende later saw a woman named Fabrisse Vassaro carrying bread and wine toward a thicket located between Cambiac and Maurens. She informed Casel of this and the priest went to investigate. In the thicket he found a hut inhabited by a number of heretics. He relieved them of the money they had, but since he had only two men with him, he did not dare arrest them.[62]

## VILLAGES AND TOWNS

Another important horizontal bond in Languedocian society, that of coresidence in a local community, also reveals a pattern of preexisting strains being exacerbated by the added stress of inquisitorial activity. As we have seen above, towns

[61] MS 609, fol. 239v: "Et tunc dictus Willelmus Saicius cepit ipsam testem et posuit in quadam tonella et filium ipsius testis similiter quia manutenebat eam, dicendo ei, 'Garcifer, vultis vos juvare vetulam istam que vult nos destruere omnes?'"

[62] Ibid., fol. 240r. See also Martin Casel's deposition on fols. 237v–38r. Interestingly, Casel does not mention the incident in which he took the heretics' money. A cynic might think Casel had been more interested in the Cathars' funds than in bringing them to justice.

and villages, communities that were self-conscious and highly organized, could present serious difficulties for the inquisitors. Yet at the same time they contained strains that resulted in inquisitorial opportunities. Some of these stemmed from the economic growth that Languedoc experienced in the thirteenth century, which in many towns produced a widening gulf between rich and poor. The development of institutions of self-government also created political rivalry between groups of "ins," who attempted to monopolize control of these institutions, and "outs," who wanted to force their way into the charmed circle of governmental power. Many of these issues were exacerbated by the growing weight of taxation, which produced disputes over apportionment.[63] The rich, who tended to dominate town governments, favored regressive taxes, while the poor just as adamantly demanded progressive taxes.[64]

These tensions between "ins" and "outs" and rich and poor could, under the right circumstances, facilitate the work of the inquisitors. The troubled affairs of Aycred Boret are a case in point. We have seen above how the issue of the levying and collection of *tailles* in Caussou turned him against the Planissoles family. Taxation also turned Boret against other inhabitants of Caussou. Vital Record told Fournier that one day he encountered Boret and some other men discussing the *tailles*. When he heard Boret criticize members of the Rauzi Spesa and Vidalens households, he asked him what he had against them. Boret answered that the people of those households had taken "the part of the devils and thus cast down us poor people."[65] More information on why Boret hated these two families was provided by his sister, Gauzia Polier. She heard Boret say that

> those Vidalens and Rauzis have destroyed us; for they involved in the levying of this tallage that devil, that is, Guillaume de Planissoles. He is not our peer; nor did he pay anything toward the tallage, since he is of the nobility, which contributed nothing to the tallage. But Guillaume has destroyed and confounded these men. Vital Record, who was a little further down the road, said to Aycred, "And why are you complaining about the Vidalens and the Rauzis?" Aycred replied, because they had joined to themselves in the tallage those who were neither their peers nor paid anything toward the tallage, but beat down the other poor men.[66]

To revenge himself, Boret decided to accuse these men (who were evidently innocent) of heresy. In the hearing of his sister, Gauzia, he said that he intended to get Raimond Rauzi and Guillaume Vidalens lodged in either the inquisitor's

---

[63] On the development of social tensions in Languedocian cities, see Wolff, "Les Luttes sociales."
[64] Ibid., pp. 81–83; Pélissier, "La Lutte des classes"; Wolff, ed., *Histoire de Toulouse*, pp. 169–71; and Wolff, "Réflexions sur l'histoire médiévale," p. 341.
[65] *Registre*, 3: 350.
[66] Ibid., 3: 351.

*mur* or Bishop Fournier's prison, just as he had done to his neighbor, Raimond Bec. To this his sister said, "If you have unjustly caused Raimond Bec to be lodged in the prison of the Allemans, may God justly set him free." To this Aycred replied, "Be quiet, good woman. Sometimes the devil is more powerful than God. And I must help myself out with either God or the devil."[67]

Fournier's register provides another illustration of how disputes about taxes could lead people to contemplate informing on their neighbors. On 31 October 1324 Pierre Peyre of Quié testified before Fournier's tribunal. He said that in early February about two years before, he and Pierre Fornier de Serles of Ornolac had been bringing two loads of wine to Tarascon. When they reached the caves near Ornolac, Fornier said that Arnaud Martelli of Tarascon, the town consul, had done him a serious injury when Tarascon had been tallaged. Therefore he wanted to see Martelli arrested on a charge of heresy. Arnaud, so he claimed, was an evil heretic and, indeed, worse than a heretic. To this Peyre said, "Do you know anything involving heresy that relates to Arnaud? Because . . . if you know anything about him . . . and you can prove it, we can certainly find a way to harm Arnaud; for, on account of the injuries he did me, Master Guillaume Tron now lies ill." Fornier mulled this over a little and then said, "If you know about heresy, you can help me accuse him so that Arnaud Martelli will lie ill in the *mur* as a heretic. I would give you a quarter of the wheat called *trimestre*, which you could sow."[68] Peyre replied that he would not help Fornier. Fornier then upped his offer, telling Peyre that he would give him ten sous of Toulouse if he helped him incriminate Arnaud and expel him from the Sabarthès. According to his testimony, Peyre righteously refused this offer; but he did assure Fornier that he would support him if his denunciation were indeed true.[69] Nothing seems to have come of this discussion, but it illustrates how the social dynamics of the levying of taxes could assist the inquisitors in their work.

An even better demonstration of the way in which social tensions among neighbors facilitated the work of the inquisitors is the series of events that took place in Carcassonne. In the early years of the fourteenth century, Carcassonne, together with Albi and a few other towns, formed an anti-inquisitorial league. The key figure in this resistance movement was Bernard Délicieux, a Franciscan friar. He assumed much of the work of coordinating the efforts of the people of Carcassonne and Albi, he led the embassies that sought the assistance of King Philip IV, and it was his eloquence in the pulpit that aroused the masses of the *bourg* of Carcassonne to action. Yet expedients that Délicieux and his associates adopted in order to stir up opposition reveal how social and political rivalry could aid the work of the inquisitors. Délicieux succeeded in enlisting the bulk of the

---

[67] Ibid., 3: 348.

[68] Ibid., 3: 399. On Guillaume Tron, see above, chapter 6.

[69] Ibid., 3: 399–400. Fornier himself denied that he had expressed a desire to entangle Martelli with the inquisitors; ibid., 3: 438–39.

population of the *bourg* of Carcassonne against the inquisitors; but to do this he had to exacerbate tension in the town.

In 1299 the consuls of the *bourg* and the inquisitor Nicholas d'Abbeville had reached an agreement settling the disputes between the inquisitors and the community. Although its terms were kept secret, in the summer of 1303 Délicieux secured a copy of this pact.[70] Once he got possession of the document, he put the darkest possible interpretation on it. In a fiery sermon he denounced the agreement. By its terms, so he claimed, the consuls had admitted that they and all the people of the *bourg* had aided and abetted heresy. This admission tainted even infants in their cradles. If the inquisitors thereafter proceeded against any of the *bourg*'s inhabitants, they could treat them as relapsed heretics and consign them to the flames. According to one witness, Délicieux pointed out some of those in the congregation and denounced them as traitors.[71] Another witness said that Bernard explicitly called for their death, saying,

> My lords, against those who have sold out this *bourg*, who have concocted this false instrument through which the entire town is found guilty of favoring heretical depravity, so that there remains no future for the people of this town other than the fire, and against those who have bound everyone in the town even unto the fourth generation, we ought to take action, arresting them, killing them, and eradicating them and all their race, so that henceforth neither they nor any of their kindred will exist in this *bourg*.[72]

An attempt by the incumbent inquisitor, Geoffroy d'Ablis, to provide a more palatable exegesis of the terms of the 1299 agreement only succeeded in touching off a riot, in which the houses of several of the consuls of 1299 were destroyed.[73] Délicieux thus succeeded in mobilizing the bulk of the town against the inquisitors, but at the cost of setting one part of the population against the other. Some of the former consuls whose houses were destroyed during the rioting were driven into exile and, seemingly, into the arms of the inquisitors.[74] The friar preached other equally divisive sermons. On one occasion, according to the Dominican Raimond Arnaud, he proclaimed from the pulpit of the church of St. Vincent in the *bourg* of Carcassonne, "In our counsels we have some hidden traitors who reveal everything we say and decide to our hidden enemies." Elie

---

[70] MS 4270, fol. 287r.

[71] Ibid., fols. 281r–v.

[72] Ibid., fol. 223r: "Domini, contra illos qui vendiderunt istum burgum et fecerunt falsum instrumentum per quod totam istam villam obligaverunt ad fautoriam hereticae pravitatis, ita quod non restat nisi ignis hominibus istius villae, et obligaverunt omnes de villa usque ad quartam generationem, deberemus procedere, eos capiendo et occidendo et destruendo ipsos et totam radicem eorum, ita quod de caetero nullus ipsorum nec de eorum genere essent in isto burgo."

[73] Ibid., fols. 194r–v, 199r–v, 206v, 211r–12r, 224v, 287r–v.

[74] Ibid., fols. 199r–v, 212r, 223v–24v, 286v–87v.

Patrice, the leader of the town's militia, then got up and said, "My lord, Brother Bernard, tell us who these traitors are who are revealing these things; for by the body of God we will cut out their tongues."[75]

The chronic conflicts that pitted rich against poor also hampered the anti-inquisitorial party's search for allies. In those towns where the consuls favored joining the alliance, the poor were often hostile. This hostility stemmed not so much from Catholic bigotry as from resentment against the taxes levied to defray the expenses of the campaign against the inquisitors. Thus Délicieux's efforts to raise money in Cordes and Rabastens aroused opposition. Certain people insisted that any money collected should be used only for the good of the towns themselves. Even at Albi the consuls' attempts to fund their exertions on behalf of their imprisoned fellow citizens met with resistance; the recalcitrant had to be compelled to pay up. At Limoux it seems that the poor favored Délicieux while the rich opposed him. When the consuls proved unwilling to take any action against either the king or the inquisitors, the friar's response was to compare them to ignorant pigs who liked nothing except lying in the mud. He appealed over their heads to the town's poor. These, he claimed, lacking the connections and influence of the rich, would not be able to protect themselves from the inquisitors. The poor of Limoux apparently took Bernard's words to heart; his visit was followed by rioting.[76]

This chapter has argued two points: that various forms of Languedocian social organization were marked by certain characteristic forms of social strain and that these patterns of strain helped the inquisitors to pry apart social organizations that might otherwise have effectively resisted them. The first point is relatively obvious. It would be a rare social organization that was not characterized by conflict of some sort. The strains that we have perceived in the network of ties that united lords and followers, fellow kinsmen, and inhabitants of the same community were certainly not unique to Languedoc. Similar strains can be found everywhere in medieval Europe, although their precise nature varied from place to place.

The second point is more hypothetical. There is much that we would like to know, both about Languedocian social organization and about the operations of the medieval inquisitors, that—given the vagaries of record survival—will forever be beyond our grasp. The sort of connection between preexisting strain systems and the effects of inquisitorial pressure for which I have argued here is often hard to establish unambiguously. At the most, I can claim that the evidence I have

---

[75] Ibid., fols. 235r–v: "'In consilio nostro habemus aliquos proditores et mascaratos qui omnia quae dicimus et tractamus revelant mascaratis inimicis nostris.' . . . 'Domine frater Bernarde, dicatis nobis qui sunt illi proditores qui ista revelant, quia, per corpus Dei, nos abscidemus eis linguas.'"

[76] Ibid., fols. 212r–v (Limoux), 243r–v (Albi), 265v–66r (Limoux and Albi), 301r–2r (Limoux).

assembled is consonant with my argument, though clearly it in no way consti-
tutes irrefutable proof of that argument. Nevertheless, the interpretation I have
proposed here makes it easier to understand how the inquisitors, despite their
small numbers and their lack of a large staff of assistants, succeeded as well as they
did in eradicating heresy.

# CHAPTER 8

# STRUCTURAL CONSTRAINTS

THE INQUISITORS OF Languedoc were in many ways some of the more successful wielders of power in medieval Europe. The techniques they developed for the manipulation of the objects of their investigations were among the most advanced and ingenious of their day. However, I do not want to leave the reader with an exaggerated impression of their effectiveness. Above all, I do not want to suggest that the exercise of power is a matter of pure technology, that those who are clever enough to develop the sort of techniques discussed in section I of this book will inevitably prevail in the arena of political conflict. Such an argument would be tantamount to reducing political history to a species of intellectual history.

Technologies of power are deployed in a concrete social situation, and the correlation of forces present in that situation plays a large role in determining how effective or ineffective those techniques will be. In the previous chapter we looked at the ways in which certain aspects of social and political organization facilitated the work of the inquisitors; in this chapter we will examine the structural factors that hindered it. Aspects of the inquisitors' self-organization as well as features of Languedocian social and political organization restrained heresy hunting.

## STRUCTURAL CONSTRAINTS IN THE ORGANIZATION OF THE INQUISITION

Although the inquisitors may have operated the most effective police institution in medieval Europe, it was far from being a fully developed bureaucracy.[1] The only qualification specified for an inquisitor, decreed by Clement V at the Council of Vienne, was that he be forty years old.[2] Though many displayed skill and determination, the men who became inquisitors in Languedoc received no special training for their posts, neither in the idiosyncratic legal or administrative traditions of the inquisition nor in the nature of heresy and heretics. Dominican inquisitors had, of course, been through the order's schools. The education received there, designed to acquaint members of the order with theology and make them effective preachers, was undoubtedly useful to future inquisitors. The

---

[1] Kieckhefer, *Repression of Heresy in Medieval Germany,* pp. 3–6, and "The Office of Inquisition."
[2] *Corpus iuris canonici,* 2: cols. 1182–83 (Clem. 5.3.2).

Dominicans' facility with the intricacies of theological debate and familiarity with the propaganda uses of the spoken word were helpful in the interrogation of heretics, especially those who, like the Waldensians, were given to equivocation. Some men, before becoming inquisitors in their own right, experienced a form of apprenticeship by serving as inquisitorial lieutenants. Yet for the most part inquisitors were self-taught. What they knew about heresy or the operations of the holy office they learned on the job or by studying some of the available antiheretical tracts and inquisitorial manuals.

What factors led to a particular Dominican's selection as inquisitor are, unfortunately, almost impossible to discern. Surprisingly enough, chance may have played a major role in the appointment of the most famous medieval inquisitor, Bernard Gui. Gui joined the Dominicans in 1280 and labored in the order for over twenty-five years before becoming an inquisitor. Although he displayed aptitude for administration and historical research, little in his career would have led one to suspect that he would become a hunter of heretics.[3] Bernard Guenée has suggested that Gui's appointment in January 1307 as inquisitor of Toulouse might have been due in part to a chance visit in April 1306 by Pope Clement V to the convent of Limoges, of which Gui was then prior.[4]

Gui's career also illustrates how many inquisitors, once they had taken up their positions, were distracted by other duties. He was forced to interrupt his work at Toulouse for three years between 1316 and 1319. In August 1316 he was named procurator general of the Dominicans and by September he was in attendance on Pope John XXII at Lyon. In January 1317 the pope sent Gui and another man as legates to northern Italy and Tuscany to try to restore peace there. Gui and his companion were unsuccessful, but this legation kept Gui in Italy until the spring of 1318. Once finished in Italy, Gui was sent north in September 1318 to try to arrange peace between the king of France and the count of Flanders, a task at which he once again failed.[5] It was only in 1319 that he returned to Toulouse, handing down 160 acts at a great *sermo generalis* held on 30 September.

Once a man was appointed inquisitor, he was supervised in only the loosest fashion. Since there was no career path in the inquisitorial office, no ranking of ever more responsible posts to which one advanced after a period of probation and examination, there was no way in which the incompetent and the lazy could be easily weeded out and the active and effective rewarded. As a result, some inquisitors, like Bernard Gui, appear to have been models of zeal. Others, like Jean de Beaune, who left important business to his notaries, or Geoffroy d'Ablis, who seems to have been overly genial in interrogating suspects, were comparatively slack in the way they conducted themselves.[6] Some, if we can believe their

---

[3] There is a brief summary of Gui's career in Amargier, "Un portrait de Bernard Gui."

[4] Guenée, *Between Church and State*, p. 48.

[5] Ibid., pp. 51–57.

[6] See respectively *Registre*, 3: 421, where Jean de Beaune, after receiving a witness's oath, let his notary carry out the actual interrogation, and 2: 71–72.

enemies, were venal in the extreme. We may better understand the lack of zeal displayed by some Languedocian inquisitors, and the corruptibility of others, when we realize that becoming an inquisitor was not a particularly good career move for an ambitious ecclesiastic. It is difficult to reconstruct the careers of the Dominicans who staffed the inquisitorial tribunals of Carcassonne and Toulouse,[7] but it seems that few inquisitors were true highfliers. Only a few became bishops. One exception was Bernard Gui, who was appointed bishop of Tuy in Galicia in 1323; however, he continued to serve as inquisitor of Toulouse until he was transferred to the see of Lodève in 1324. Similarly, Jean Duprat, inquisitor of Carcassonne, became bishop of Évreux in 1328.[8] Despite the success of these two inquisitors, the impression remains that serving as an inquisitor did not provide a stepping-stone to higher office. The episcopal inquisitors of Languedoc had better luck: Bernard de Castanet, despite all his troubles at Albi, eventually became a cardinal, and Jacques Fournier of Pamiers became pope. However, it seems that their successful careers were due to other accomplishments than their work as inquisitors.

The Languedocian inquisition was thus clearly not a fully developed bureaucratic entity. The lack of both specialized training for would-be inquisitors and effective supervision meant that the level of activity and competence displayed by individual inquisitors was highly variable. In addition, the inquisitors were also hindered by the fact that their tribunals did not constitute a unified, coherent institution directed by a clearly designated central authority. For all practical purposes each inquisitorial tribunal was independent. In Languedoc the Dominican inquisitors of Toulouse and Carcassonne did cooperate with one another. Despite some frictions, they usually worked well with the inquisitorial tribunals set up by the bishops of Albi and Pamiers. Cooperation with tribunals outside Languedoc, however, often necessitated papal involvement. In 1289 several heretics, natives of the kingdom of France, were apprehended in the diocese of Verona. The intervention of Pope Nicholas IV was required for the transfer of these fugitives to the Languedocian inquisitors.[9] Similarly, in 1323 a letter had to be dispatched from Pope John XXII before the bishop of Lérida and the inquisitor of Aragon would turn over to the inquisitor of Carcassonne several fugitives from the diocese of Pamiers.[10]

Perhaps one of the gravest impediments to the inquisitors was their total dependence on external sources for financing. The money that clothed and fed

---

[7] The most thorough work on the careers of Languedocian inquisitors has been done by Vidal and is to be found scattered through the notes in his *Bullaire*.

[8] Ibid., p. 124.

[9] Doat, 32: fols. 155r–56r.

[10] *Bullaire*, pp. 90–91. Surprisingly, one factor that does not seem to have incommoded the inquisitors was their being at once papal judges and members of the Dominican order. Although the order at times tried to legislate how the inquisitors should conduct themselves, these injunctions seem to have had very little impact. See the discussion in Dossat, *Crises*, pp. 101–4.

the inquisitors, furnished their *scriptoria* with paper, parchment, and ink, paid their servants, and maintained their prisoners all came from outsiders. When the inquisitors imposed a penance entailing the confiscation of property, that property passed into the hands of the condemned person's lord. In turn, the lords were expected to use the revenues from these confiscations to defray the inquisitors' expenses.[11] Even the prisons used by the Dominican inquisitors were built at royal expense and the prisoners lodged there supported out of the royal coffers.[12] And these financial needs could be great. For the period between May 1255 and February 1256 there survives an account detailing the expenses of the inquisitors of Toulouse, Jean de Saint-Pierre and Renaud de Chartres. The total laid out amounted to a little more than 830 livres, no small sum.[13] Regrettably, information from the end of the thirteenth and the beginning of the fourteenth centuries is not as full. However, in 1293–94 royal accountants recorded the transfer to the inquisitors of Toulouse, their jailers, and those charged with administering confiscated property a sum of 310 l. 12 s. 6 d.t. In 1298–99 the royal government laid out for the same purposes 290 l. 12 s. 6 d.t. Finally, in 1302–1303 the royal government gave the inquisitors of Carcassonne a pension amounting to 150 l.[14]

The *sermones generales* at which the inquisitors imposed penances could be costly events. A tally of expenses is available for only a single *sermo generalis*, that held in Carcassonne on 24 April 1323[15] (see table 8.1). For this occasion the king's government spent over a hundred sous on wages and other expenses for the messengers and sergeants who attended the inquisitors. Entertaining the counselors who met to offer advice concerning the sentences to be imposed cost a hundred sous. Construction of the platform on which the ceremony took place added yet another hundred sous to the bill. But the single largest expense was incurred in the burning of four individuals relaxed to the secular arm, with the executioner receiving twenty sous a head for his services. When the cost of the wood and cordage used in the conflagration were added in, the total bill for the execution came to 8 l. 14 s. 7 d. The exhumation and burning of three corpses on the following day was almost as expensive, costing 5 l. 9 s. 6 d. All told, the royal government spent 31 l. 4 s. 10 d. on what was a fairly modest *sermo*.

How successful the inquisitors were in balancing their books is difficult to determine. Though we are not nearly as well informed as we would like to be about their ability to collect the moneys due to them, we know that at times they were criticized for their spending. In the mid-thirteenth century Innocent

[11] *Bullaire*, p. xxxix.

[12] *Documents*, 1: ccxxiv–ccxxvi; *HL*, 8: cols. 1206, 1435–36.

[13] Figures derived from Cabié, "Compte des inquisiteurs." The account itself gives a total (inaccurate) of 832 l. 19 s. 3 d. (p. 220).

[14] *Comptes royaux (1285–1314)*, 1: 463, nos. 9681–88; 1: 559, nos. 11747–52; 1: 613, no. 12771.

[15] *Comptes royaux (1314–1328)*, 1: 517–20, nos. 8648–701.

Table 8.1 Royal Expenses for a *Sermo Generalis* in Carcassonne, 24 April 1323

|  | Livres | Sous | Deniers | Percent of Total Cost |
|---|---|---|---|---|
| Messengers | 2 | 10 | 10 | 8.1 |
| Erection of platform | 5 | 0 | 3 | 16.0 |
| Wages and expenses of sergeants | 2 | 12 | 6 | 8.4 |
| Cloth | 1 | 17 | 6 | 6.0 |
| Counselors | 5 | 0 | 0 | 16.0 |
| Burning of 4 individuals | 8 | 14 | 7 | 27.9 |
| Exhumation of 3 deceased | 5 | 9 | 6 | 17.5 |
| TOTAL | 31 | 4 | 10 | 100.0 |

Note: The exhumation of the deceased occurred on 25 April 1323.
Source: *Comptes Royaux (1314–1328)*, 1: 517–20.

IV complained that Jean de Saint-Pierre and Renaud de Chartres were maintaining too large a staff.[16] In 1269 Alfonse de Poitiers, who as count of Toulouse had to finance much of the inquisitors' work, also complained about their spending.[17] The very diligence of the inquisitors in stamping out heresy may ultimately have reduced their revenue stream. As the number of heretics gradually shrank and as heresy's social base became more and more restricted to the peasantry, the opportunity for lucrative confiscations declined. Whether this inconvenienced the inquisitors of Languedoc, we cannot say. Yet Nicholas Eymerich, writing late in the fourteenth century about conditions in Aragon, noted that the decline in confiscations had made temporal lords reluctant to pay the inquisitors' stipends.[18]

The inquisitors' lack of a secure and independent source of income meant that they could maintain only a relatively small staff of permanent servants. In the 1250s the inquisitors of Toulouse employed on a regular basis about twenty-seven individuals. Thirteen were described as members of the inquisition's *familia*. These included four men labeled as masters, who were probably the inquisitors' notaries, one man described as a *scriptor*, one sergeant, a cook, and a doorkeeper. The inquisitors also paid eleven named messengers and up to three jailers. This is not a very large group with which to police an area that must have numbered several hundred thousand inhabitants.[19] Nevertheless, these permanent servants could form the core of a shock troop for the hunting down and arrest of heretics

[16] Doat, 31: fols. 81r–82r.
[17] *HL*, 8: col. 1584.
[18] Eymerich, *Directorium inquisitorum*, p. 653.
[19] For an estimate that puts the population of the *sénéchaussée* of Toulouse-Albigeois at about 600,000 in 1328, see Given, *State and Society*, p. 150.

and their sympathizers. Bernard Gui seems to have made extensive use of messengers (*nuncii*) and sergeants in his effort to apprehend the last batch of Cathar *perfecti* at large in Languedoc, Pierre Autier and his colleagues.[20] Other inquisitors also used these men for especially difficult or important tasks. For example, Guillaume Pierre Cavalherii, a *nuncius* of the inquisitor of Carcassonne, spent two weeks in the early 1320s pursuing fugitive heretics from Carcassonne to Avignon to Marseilles.[21] Similarly, when fugitive Béguins were reported to be hiding in Narbonne, it was members of the inquisitorial *familia* who were charged with guarding the exits from the city.[22] And when the inquisitor of Carcassonne decided to arrest the inhabitants of the village of Montaillou, he entrusted the task to the guardian of his *mur*, Jacques de Polignac.[23]

The members of the inquisitorial *familia* were thus of great importance in the task of hunting down heretics. They were, however, often not the most satisfactory instruments. Not only were their numbers small, but they were generally ill supervised and often ill disciplined. Many inquisitorial servants seem to have pursued their own agendas without much concern for their masters' wishes. For example, the guardian of the prison in which Jacques Fournier detained those he was investigating evidently felt that he could treat prisoners pretty much as he pleased. When Raimond Peyre was arrested, the jailer, acting on his own authority, loaded him with chains and deposited him for two weeks in a dungeon. When this came to the bishop's attention, he ordered that most of Raimond's chains be removed and that he be allowed some freedom to move about in the prison.[24] In the 1260s two sergeants in the employ of the inquisitor Etienne de Gastine, apparently acting on their own, gave Amblard Vassal permission to associate with heretics so that he could arrange their arrest. This arrangement backfired, since Amblard used this opportunity to flee.[25]

Like most medieval government employees, the inquisitors' agents were rather poorly paid. In a period of little more than nine months in 1255 and 1256, the inquisitors of Toulouse spent only 45 l. 9 s. 4 d. on the salaries of the thirteen members of their *familia*. Over the same period they provided their *nuncii* with only 10 l. 5 s. The combined cash bill of the inquisitors for wages thus amounted to only 55 l. 14 s. 4 d., a mere 6.7 percent of their total outlay

---

[20] *LS*, pp. 47, 88, 137, 146, 174. On this group of Cathars, see Vidal, "Les Derniers ministres" and "Doctrine et morale."

[21] Doat, 34: fol. 229v.

[22] In this case, the Béguins managed to get away. They were being hidden in the home of Bérengère Donas. When she learned that the city exits were being watched, she guided the Béguins to a vineyard of hers that lay within the city. This abutted on the town wall and gave access to the open fields beyond. There the Béguins hid for a day and part of the following night. Then, following Bérengère's instructions, they climbed over the wall and made their escape (Doat, 28: fols. 220v–21r).

[23] *Registre*, 3: 91

[24] Ibid., 3: 430.

[25] Doat, 25: fol. 186r.

of 830 l. 10 s. 4 d.[26] This modest recompense may help explain the propensity of inquisitorial agents to corruption. We have already encountered Menet de Robécourt, whose peculation and abuse of office finally brought him to the attention of Pope Benedict XII (see chapter 6). Menet was not the only inquisitorial notary to get himself into trouble. In the early fourteenth century Barthélemy Adalbert spent over twenty-two years in service to the inquisitors of Carcassonne. What brought about his downfall was the investigation of Michel Maurin of Rouvenac. Maurin managed to bribe Barthélemy, who had been detailed to receive testimony against him, to alter the information collected. Barthélemy's actions ultimately came to the attention of the inquisitors. A jurisdictional dispute between the inquisitor of Carcassonne and the bishop delayed the final disposition of his case for over two years, during which time Barthélemy languished in prison. When the inquisitor Pierre Brun finally sentenced him in November 1328, he took into account Barthélemy's long record of service and gave him a relatively light sentence, consisting only of a money fine, fasts, and some penitential pilgrimages.[27]

Since inquisitorial agents had frequent contacts with heretics and since some agents were recruited from the ranks of former heretical sympathizers, one would expect a few to prove vulnerable to the ideological temptations of heresy. Yet apparently no servants of the Languedocian inquisitors were seduced in this way. The only example of an inquisitorial agent who adopted the very heresy he had set out to persecute involves a man who was not native to Languedoc. Jean Philibert, a priest, was living in the Gascon town of Castelnau-Barbarens when he came to the attention of Bernard Gui. Jean had come originally from Burgundy, where he had been in the employ of the inquisitors. Sometime in the late 1200s he was sent to Gascony, which contained a fairly large Waldensian community, to seek out a fugitive Waldensian named Ruste Jaubert. The Gascon Waldensians made a great impression on Philibert. After completing his mission and returning to Burgundy, he came back to Gascony, settling in the diocese of Auch. There he was persuaded by some Burgundian immigrants to become a Waldensian. At some point he once again returned to Burgundy, for, according to his testimony, he was interrogated around 1298 by the inquisitor of Burgundy, Guido de Remis. When first questioned by this inquisitor, he refused to swear an oath to tell the truth, a strong indication of Waldensian beliefs. Ultimately he did confess, but he concealed many things concerning his associates. Having abjured heresy, he returned to Gascony, where he was arrested by Gui. Ultimately he was handed over to the secular authorities on 30 September 1319 to be burned as a relapsed heretic.[28]

---

[26] Figures derived from Cabié, "Compte des inquisiteurs."
[27] Doat, 27: fols. 112v–18r.
[28] *LS*, pp. 252–55.

## STRUCTURAL CONSTRAINTS IN THE LANGUEDOCIAN SOCIAL AND POLITICAL ARENA

Without the active assistance of other power holders, the Languedocian inquisition was not capable of carrying out its repressive tasks. Despite the fulminations of popes and the decrees of kings, this assistance was not always easy to secure. Languedoc was a confused and complex political arena, in which powers of command and coercion were split among a host of institutions—royal and seignorial governments, town and village consulates, and so on—each with its own, jealously guarded bag of rights and privileges. The inquisitors were constantly required to negotiate ever-shifting arrangements with this multitude of political actors.

### The Role of the Parish Clergy

Key to the success of the inquisitors was their ability to enlist the support of the parish clergy. At first glance it may seem surprising to label this group as part of the Languedocian "power elite." Most parish priests, after all, were recruited from fairly humble social backgrounds. The profits they derived from their benefices gave them only a modest economic position in society and they had few of the powers of coercion available to even the most humble of secular lords. Yet it would be a mistake to minimize their political importance. Their land holdings, although tiny compared to the great endowments of monasteries and bishoprics, were often substantial when set beside those of their parishioners. Their smattering of learning, insignificant as it must have seemed when set against that of members of the mendicant orders or of the upper levels of the clergy, was still sufficient to give them a real cultural hegemony in the village. Moreover, as we have seen above, many parish priests occupied the strategic role of middleman, mediating contacts between the small world of the village and the big world beyond it. The strategic role of the parish priest in combating heresy was recognized even before the establishment of the inquisition in Languedoc. In 1229 the Council of Toulouse ordered the bishops of Languedoc, as well as exempt abbeys, to nominate in each parish under their jurisdiction a priest and two or three laymen of good reputation. These men were to examine all buildings, caves, and other places where heretics and their sympathizers might hide. If they discovered any, they were to report them to the appropriate authorities.[29]

With the organization of the Dominican inquisition, the secular "synodal witnesses" declined in importance, but parish priests continued to play a vital role in the detection and repression of heresy. They assisted the inquisitors in many ways, citing witnesses to appear to give testimony and supervising penitents.[30] More important, they were potentially some of the best channels through

---

[29] Mansi, 23: col. 194.
[30] For examples, see *Registre*, 1: 154, 275, 2: 432.

which information could be funneled to the inquisitors. The first stop on the itinerary of many an informant was the parish priest. For example, in the spring of 1322 Bernard Gombert of Ax-les-Thermes engaged in a conversation with a number of people in the village plaza of Ascou about the intemperate nature of the weather. When Bernard made the pious observation that they should patiently endure whatever God sent them, Raimond Sicre replied, "Bernard, it is very necessary for us that the wheat is well disposed and grows, because when there isn't any bread in the stomach, there is no soul there either."[31] After he and the others reprimanded Raimond for his evil words, which savored of heresy, Bernard set out for Ax. Although Raimond followed him and begged him not to get him in any trouble on account of what he had said, Bernard went to the rector of Ax and told him what had happened so that the priest could write about it to Jacques Fournier.[32]

The confessional also provided many priests with information about heresy. In the thirteenth century the church mounted a major effort to get ordinary believers to confess and receive communion at least once a year. In Languedoc, however, because of the problem of heresy, people were required to confess three times a year: at Easter, Pentecost, and Christmas.[33] When hearing confessions, parish priests were required to inquire diligently about heresy. If they learned anything, they were to put it in writing and send it on, together with the penitent, to their bishop.[34] Many, in fact, seem to have done so, like the chaplain who sent Arnaude Mainie of Montréal, who had confessed to dealings with the Béguins, to the inquisitor of Carcassonne.[35]

Immersed in local life, parish priests were also in a position to pick up incriminating rumors and gossip. This is nicely illustrated by the testimony that Guillaume Auriol, the rector of Pradières, gave to Jacques Fournier on 9 November 1324. On the preceding Monday, between vespers and compline, he had been on the road from Foix to Pradières. Among his traveling companions had been Fortanier de Pompiac, servant to a canon of the cathedral of Pamiers, and a man whose name he did not know. This unknown man drew the priest aside to ask his advice. In the preceding July he had visited the valley

---

[31] Ibid., 2: 357.

[32] Ibid., 2: 357–58. For a similar example, see 1: 191–92.

[33] Decree of Council of Toulouse, 1229; Mansi, 23: col. 197.

[34] This was ordered by the archbishop of Tarragona in late 1241 or early 1242 (Doat, 36: fol. 236v). This decree has survived only in a seventeenth-century copy of a document originally preserved in the archives of the inquisition of Carcassonne (fols. 226v–41v). The priest could send his penitent to the bishop only if the penitent was willing to be identified. If the penitent was unwilling to be identified, the priest should, without divulging the penitent's name, seek the advice of those learned in the law about what he should do (Douais, "Saint Raymond de Peñafort," pp. 321–22). For some remarks on the canonical problems raised by the duty of parish priests to report on heresy while not violating the seal of the confession, see Gy, "La Précepte de la confession annuelle."

[35] Doat, 28: fol. 197r. For another example, see 27: fol. 199r.

of Bargilière during the harvest. While staying in the home of Pierre Bernard of Alavac, he had shared a bed with a certain young man. As they chatted one night, this young man had said that the host that priests consecrated during mass was no more than a piece of radish or turnip. Auriol's interlocutor said that he had rebuked the youth for these incautious words. The priest told his companion that he had done ill by not reporting the conversation to the bishop. He also asked for the young man's name. This his companion did not know, but he believed that he was from near La Bastide-de-Sérou and that he was one of Pierre Bernard of Alavac's servants. Guillaume called over three other people in his party and made his companion repeat the story. Guillaume then said that they ought to take the man to the bishop, since he had concealed this heretical conversation. Fortanier de Pompiac offered the opinion that this would not be necessary, as long as they learned their traveling companion's name. The unknown man, however, refused to identify himself. Fortanier thereupon drew his dagger, seized him by the hood of his tunic, and demanded that he identify himself. Thus threatened, he revealed that he was Bernard Maestre of L'Herm. Guillaume and his companions let Maestre go, but the priest brought this conversation to Fournier's attention. The bishop summoned Maestre and on the basis of his information began a heresy investigation against the talkative young man, one Pierre Acès of Esplas-de-Sérou.[36]

Many an inhabitant of Languedoc learned to his chagrin that loose or intemperate words uttered in the presence of a cleric could have unfortunate consequences. For example, in 1276 Roderigo Ferrand, a native of Portugal who was serving as a priest at Lagarde, reported to the inquisitor Pons de Parnac some suspicious words he had heard from Pons des Monts. When Roderigo had been sprinkling the cemetery at Lagarde with holy water a little before Christmas, Pons had volunteered that holy water was no good to anyone, living or dead. Indeed, nothing, neither prayers nor masses, was of any use to the dead. The only thing that profited a man was what he made "with his own hand" (*quod facit propria manu*) while alive. A few months later, angered because the priests of Lagarde planned to bury his niece without any candles, he announced that henceforth he would always be against the church "for the rest of his life" (*toto tempore vitae suae*).[37] Similarly, in June 1245 Pierre Raimond de Crozet of Le Mas-Saintes-Puelles reached back in his memory to recount to the inquisitors an incident twenty-six years earlier, when he had been an acolyte. He and some other people had been playing dice in the home of Pierre Gauta. One Bernard de Quiders climbed up onto a chest. From this perch he urinated on Pierre Raimond's head, "to the dishonor and disparagement of the entire Catholic Church."[38] Even relatively innocent behavior, such as the words that Isambard

---

[36] *Registre*, 3: 455–56.
[37] Doat, 25: fols. 227r–28v. The fate of Pons des Monts is unknown.
[38] MS 609, fol. 3v: "in obprobrium et vituperium totius ecclesie catholice." Bernard in his own

de Saint-Antonin in the Rouergue muttered to his companions in church some-time in 1274 or 1275 about a friar's very long-winded sermon, could be enough to get one haled before the inquisitors.[39]

In addition to reporting rumors and suspicious behavior, parish priests often took a more activist role in the suppression of heresy. In the early days of the inquisition before 1250, when many Cathar *perfecti* were willing to convert to Catholicism, priests often acted as intermediaries between them and the inquisitors. For example, Arnaud Jean of Préserville had been a Good Man for about four years, two of which he had spent in the Cathar stronghold of Montségur. Sometime in 1244 he decided to abandon the sect. He made his way to Préserville, to the home of his uncle, Arnaud Beneeh, and begged him to arrange his surrender. His uncle went to the priest of Odars and said, "My lord priest, if my nephew, Arnaud Jean the heretic, wants to convert, can he find mercy with the clerics?" The priest replied with an emphatic yes. When Arnaud presented himself, the priest sent him with explanatory letters to the inquisitor Ferrier and his colleague.[40]

Some parish priests, especially in the mid-thirteenth century, took on them-selves the task of apprehending heretics and their sympathizers. In the early 1240s the priest of Sorèze, Guillaume de Belleserre, was so active in pursuing heretics that his servant Bernard Barra could describe him as *prosecutor haereti-corum*. One night in the early 1240s Guillaume learned that Arnaud Hugues, a Cathar deacon, and his companion had come to the house of Pierre Raimond de Dreuilhe to give him the *consolamentum*. Taking a number of men with him, the priest set a watch at the door of the sick man's house. On this occasion, how-ever, the heretics escaped. They left the house by a hole in the wall, passed into another building, slid down a rope, and made off.[41] Other priests had better luck. For example, early in May 1245, Arnaud de Cletenx of Les Cassès encoun-tered two *perfectae*, Marquesia and Raimonde, while he was traveling toward the village of Vaux. Since Arnaud was known to sympathize with heretics, the women agreed to go with him to Les Cassès. They remained in his house for twelve days, spinning and doing other work. Arnaud went to the priest at Saint-Paulet and informed him that heretics were staying with him. The priest, a crafty individual, recommended taking no immediate action since more heretics might make their way to Arnaud's house. Marquesia had two sons who were

---

testimony stated that he had done what he had done out of anger over the fact that the players had been swearing (fol. 18v).

[39] Doat, 25: fols. 207r–v.

[40] MS 609, fol. 206v: "Domine Capellane, et si Arnaldus Johannis nepos meus hereticus vellet converti, posset invenire misericordiam cum clericis?" For other examples, see 209v–10r, and Doat, 26: fol. 23r.

[41] Doat, 25: fols. 292v–93r.

*perfecti* and Arnaud expected them to arrive at any time. The priest waited four days. At the end of that time, he arrested Marquesia and Raimonde.[42]

Finally, a zealous priest could do much to keep his parishioners isolated from contaminating contact with suspicious individuals. Parish priests were urged to keep a watch over the deathbeds of those whose faith was suspect to ensure that they did not receive the *consolamentum*.[43] Some priests tried to cut off all contact between their parishioners and those suspected of heresy, like the priest of Lassur who in the early fourteenth century ordered that no one in the village should receive in his or her home anyone who had been cited to appear before Jacques Fournier to answer concerning heresy.[44]

The parish priest thus had a key role to play in the repression of heresy. But unfortunately for the inquisitors, many priests were not prepared to play their assigned part. There were many reasons why some parish priests were unwilling or unable to help the inquisitors. A few seem to have been supporters of the heretics. If the records can be believed, sympathy for the Cathars was fairly widespread among all ranks of the clergy in the Albigeois and the Carcassès in the 1280s. Among clergymen implicated in heresy were a bishop of Carcassonne, canons of Sainte-Cécile and Saint-Salvi in the city of Albi, the prior of Saint-Affrique, the abbot of Caunes, the archdeacon of Carcassonne, the official of the diocese of Carcassonne, and numerous minor clerics and parish priests.[45] The best-known case of a priest who supported heresy is, of course, that of the rector of Montaillou, Pierre Clergue. Together with his brother, at times *bayle* of the village, Pierre deflected attention from Cathar activity in his parish for many years.

To be sure, most parish priests were not heretical sympathizers, yet fear deterred some from cooperating with the inquisitors. Pierre Bela, the rector of Pech, knew that in the first decade of the fourteenth century Cathars were being sheltered in the home of Ermengarde Albiès of Lordat, yet he did nothing. When the heretics were finally arrested, he admitted to one of his parishioners that fear had kept him from denouncing them.[46] In some cases, more important than fear may have a priest's simple desire to get along with his parishioners, people with whom he had to live on a day-to-day basis and many of whom were his relatives. Some priests were willing to put up with a good deal of anticlericalism

[42] MS 609, fols. 222r, 224v. He should have been more patient; on the night of the very day he arrested the heretics, Marquesia's sons arrived at Arnaud's house. For more examples of parish priests arresting heretics, see 44r, 142r, 144r, 187v, 223r; Doat, 23: 289v; 26: fol. 14v.

[43] Mansi, 23: col. 197. For an example of a priest carrying out these instructions, see Doat, 26: fols. 43v–44v.

[44] *Registre*, 2: 351.

[45] The bishop was Guillaume Arnaud Morlane: Doat, 26: fols. 153v–54v; canons: MS 12856, fols. 43r, 45r, 47r; the prior: MS 12856, fol. 43v; the abbot: Doat, 26: fols. 137v–38r; the archdeacon and the official of Carcassonne: Doat, 26: fols. 250r–53v, 261v–65v, 267r–71v; for examples of numerous minor clergy, see MS 12856, fols. 9r–v, and Doat, 26: fols. 163r, 165r, 168v–69v, 174v–75v, 179v, 180v, 182r, 183r, 187v, 189v.

[46] *Registre*, 1: 484.

and heterodox sentiments for this reason. One such priest was Raimond Frézat, rector of Quié, who displayed unusual tolerance for the fulminations of one of his parishioners, Pierre den Hugol. When Raimond de Laburat of Quié was condemned to the *mur* on 19 June 1323[47] for, among other things, making some critical remarks about the alacrity with which the clergy excommunicated the people of the Sabarthès, Pierre den Hugol was outraged. In the presence of Frézat and a number of other people, Pierre said that "the lord bishop and the inquisitors had found on the soles of their feet that law by which they had condemned Raimond de Laburat to the *mur*, on account of what he had said and believed concerning the sentence of excommunication. And, as he said, 'It's easy for them for such a tiny thing to condemn men, who cost so much to raise up.' "[48] Although the rector rebuked him for these words, Pierre managed to win his way back into Frézat's good graces by giving him a dinner. But Pierre made a habit of venting unorthodox opinions in the priest's presence, and they quarreled yet again. The occasion of this later falling out was the reburial of one Bernard Gosiald, who had been posthumously reconciled to the church. The day after the burial a number of people, including Frézat and Pierre den Hugol, ate together in the dead man's house. There the two started arguing. Finally, the exasperated priest said to Pierre, "If I don't reveal to the lord bishop those things I've heard you say, I will get into a lot of trouble; I will go to the lord bishop and reveal to him what you have said." However, this disagreement was patched up by a mutual friend and Frézat did not denounce Pierre.[49]

In addition to fear and complacency, there were also some structural factors at work that reduced the willingness or ability of parish clergy to cooperate with the inquisitors. The Languedocian parish clergy, like that of much of the rest of western Europe, was relatively poorly supervised and disciplined. The church did not have formal institutions in which to train candidates for parochial positions and to socialize them into the norms of the international church. Most priests owed their positions more to the patronage of some local potentate, secular or ecclesiastical, than to the local bishop, their ostensible superior.[50] Training was a haphazard, hit-and-miss affair. Most parish priests were trained through a form of apprenticeship; they learned their craft by assisting the local clergy. When priests were nominated for a particular living, they were supposed to be examined by the bishop to see if they were suitable, but standards were low. Once appointed, priests had a species of property right in their livings. It was highly unusual for priests to be removed from office except for the most scandalous misbehavior. By the end of the thirteenth century, clerical pluralism and the attendant absenteeism were also beginning to become problems. As pluralists accumulated livings, more and

[47] *LS*, p. 393.
[48] *Registre*, 3: 435.
[49] Ibid., 3: 435.
[50] Fournié and Gazzaniga, "La Paroisse," p. 402.

more parishes were served by poorly paid, and possibly poorly motivated, stipendiary priests. Finally, the frequent disputes between bishops and others, especially local monasteries, over the patronage of parish churches undoubtedly did little to help maintain high standards of behavior.[51]

There is nothing unique to Languedoc about these factors. What may be more distinctively Languedocian are the endless disputes over parochial revenues. In much of the south of France, the clergy confronted something of a financial crisis. The end of large donations by wealthy laymen, as well as the often feeble revenues of local bishops and chapters, forced ecclesiastics to cast about for new sources of income. They took a sharper interest in the fees that could be charged for the administration of the sacraments and the saying of prayers for the dead. Perhaps most vexing and divisive was the tithe question.[52]

All across Languedoc in the thirteenth and fourteenth centuries the church was engaged in a determined struggle to increase its tithe income.[53] The tithe issue could, paradoxically, either rally the parish clergy behind the church's leaders or alienate them from those same leaders. In the diocese of Pamiers, tithe disputes perhaps solidified support for the local bishop. That Jacques Fournier's inquisitorial register contains several examples of parish clergy acting as informants may be an outgrowth of the acrimonious dispute over tithes that agitated much of the diocese in the early years of the fourteenth century. The campaign to recover tithes could, however, lead bishops into conflict with their parish clergy. Some bishops endeavored to pry tithe revenue out of the hands not only of the laity, but also of the clergy. The best documented case of such a prelate is Bernard de Castanet of Albi. According to his critics, it was Castanet's practice, whenever a church that received all of the tithe revenue attached to it fell vacant, to appropriate two-thirds of the tithes for himself. The result had been, so it was claimed, the intrusion into church livings of men who were *viles* and *ydiote*. Castanet also seized whatever goods the rectors of parish churches had in their possession when they died.[54]

The higher clergy's efforts to impose a new and more exacting code of sexual behavior on the laity also brought it into conflict with parish priests. Again the diocese of Albi under Bernard de Castanet provides some good examples. Castanet decreed that only certain forms of sexual intercourse were licit, excommunicating those who transgressed these norms.[55] Those who confessed to infringements of these rules could not be absolved by their confessors but had to

---

[51] On these disputes, see Avril, "Les Dépendances des abbayes," pp. 312–15.

[52] See Chiffoleau, "Vie et mort de l'hérésie," pp. 89–94, and "Sur l'économie paroissiale," pp. 96–103.

[53] On this, see Biget, "La Restitution des dîmes" and "Le financement des cathédrales." For disputes over tithes in Provence, see Chiffoleau, "Sur l'économie paroissiale," pp. 98–101.

[54] Collectorie 404, fols. 7r, 20r, 77r, 86v–87r, 167v–68r, 59r, 91v–92r.

[55] Ibid., fol. 7r. See also Biget, "La Législation synodale," p. 201.

present themselves to the bishop. Out of shame, many refused to do this, which greatly disturbed some confessors.[56] The bishop also decreed that all clerics who engaged in sexual intercourse were excommunicated; if within eight days they did not reveal their sin to the bishop, they were liable to suspension, even if they had previously confessed and been absolved.[57] Not only did this strike priests as a violation of the seal of confession, it tended to bring disgrace to the entire clergy, for if any priest went to see the bishop, suspicion immediately arose that he was guilty of fornication.[58]

I have dwelt at length on the parish clergy because their role in effectively prosecuting heresy was so important and because historians have rarely commented on the factors that worked against their filling that role. When we look at other societal factors that hindered the inquisitors, we will be on ground trodden more often; therefore my treatment will be briefer.

### The Role of Royal and Seignorial Agents

As noted above, the inquisitors were largely reliant on royal or seignorial officials for the actual business of hunting down and arresting fugitive heretics.[59] Even though the inquisitors had the right to excommunicate anyone who refused to assist them, they often found representatives of the secular authorities less than enthusiastic partners.

Some royal or seignorial agents were outright sympathizers with heresy, like the *bayle* of Montaillou, Bernard Clergue. Clergue was an agent of the count of Foix, but even royal servants were susceptible to the lures of Catharism. Between 1275 and 1306 the inquisitors assembled information that implicated thirty royal servants or members of their families.[60] These included *viguiers* of Carcassonne and Albi, a constable of Carcassonne, judges of the Minervois, the Rodez, and Albi, and castellans of Montréal, Cabaret, Quertinheux, and Surdépine.[61]

If most royal and seignorial servants were deaf to the ideological appeal of heresy, many were attentive to the clinking of hard cash. For example, sometime around 1233 the *bayles* of Fanjeaux, Ainard and Guillaume Hugues, arrested four Cathars, including the famous Bernard Marty, at the home of Bernard Forner. Forner's wife, Causida, went to Bernard de Cailhavel, the source of our information about this incident, and asked him to accompany her to Peytavin Armieu's workshop. There she told Peytavin that they could buy Marty for 300 sous of

---

[56] Collectorie 404, fols. 93r, 161r.

[57] Ibid., fol. 7r.

[58] Ibid., fol. 93r.

[59] For some examples, see *Registre*, 1: 217, 467; 2: 128, 204, 273; Doat, 24: fols. 115v–16r; MS 609, fols. 44r, 246r; MS 4270, fols. 231r–32v, 238r–v.

[60] See the table in Friedlander, "Les Agents du roi," pp. 208–11.

[61] Viguiers: Davis, *The Inquisition at Albi*, pp. 144, 258; a constable, judges, and castellans of Montréal: Friedlander, "The Seneschalsy of Carcassonne," pp. 378–80; and castellans of Cabaret: Doat, 26: fol. 179v; of Quertinheux: fols. 182v–83r; and of Surdépine: fols. 182v–83r.

Toulouse. Marty's followers thereupon embarked on a frenzy of money raising and the next day secured his release.[62] Almost a century later Pierre den Hugol of Quié saved his house from being destroyed as a punishment for a *consolamentum* having been administered there by giving 15 l.t. to Guillaume Cortète of Fanjeaux, the count of Foix's procurator.[63]

Some opposition by royal agents may not have been due solely to heretical sympathies or to corruption. During the major anti-inquisitorial agitation that gripped Albi and Carcassonne in the late thirteenth and early fourteenth centuries, many royal agents were apparently disturbed by the inquisitors' behavior. As a result, some set about hindering the inquisitors and helping their enemies. Until Geoffroy d'Ablis made the fortunate discovery that Guillaume de Pezens was descended from heretics and thus ineligible for public office, this man exploited his post as royal *viguier* of Albi to further the work of the anti-inquisitorial league. Among other things, he used his authority to force reluctant inhabitants of Albi to help subsidize the league's work.[64] His lieutenant, Pierre Nicholay, also took steps to block the publication of the inquisitor of Carcassonne's excommunication of the royal *enquêteur*, Jean de Picquigny, for his removal of prisoners from the Carcassonne *mur*.[65]

## The Role of the King

A more significant problem for the inquisitors than obstructionism and foot-dragging by royal officials was the wavering support of the French monarchy in the late thirteenth and early fourteenth centuries.[66] Philip IV, confronted with widespread anti-inquisitorial agitation in Languedoc and involved in disputes with the papacy, flirted for several years with the inquisitors' opponents. In April 1291 he wrote to his seneschal of Carcassonne, noting that the inquisitors had been accused of extracting false confessions from the innocent by means of torture. He therefore instructed the seneschal to refrain from arresting anyone on the order of the inquisitors, unless the person in question was a self-confessed heretic or was held to be a heretic by *fama publica*, which had to be supported by the opinion of individuals whom the seneschal thought worthy of credence.[67] In September Philip took steps to protect Jews from the inquisitors, who had jurisdiction over converted Jews who returned to their former religion. He informed the seneschal of Carcassonne that no Jew was to be arrested on the demand of a friar of any order, no matter what his authority, unless the approval of the king's

---

[62] MS 609, fol. 152v.

[63] *Registre*, 3: 381.

[64] MS 4270, fol. 266r.

[65] Hauréau, *Bernard Délicieux*, pp. 176–87.

[66] The best discussion of royal policy toward the inquisition in this period remains that of Lea, in *Inquisition of the Middle Ages*, 2: 58–99.

[67] *HL*, 10: *Preuves*, cols. 273–74. The gist of this order was repeated in another letter of 14 June 1291 (col. 274).

seneschal or *bayle* was obtained.[68] Similar constraints continued through the middle of the 1290s. In January 1296 King Philip repeated his earlier order that no one suspected of heresy should be arrested without prior approval of the royal court. He did, however, make a significant modification to his previous orders: if it was feared that a suspect might flee, he or she could be arrested immediately and held until the royal curia had been consulted.[69] In the opinion of H. C. Lea, Philip's decrees rendered the inquisition virtually powerless.[70]

In 1296 and 1297 the king became involved in a dispute with Pope Boniface VIII over the issue of clerical taxation. In this atmosphere Philip was not prepared to be very cooperative in dealing with the inquisitors. But when the king and the pope patched up their quarrel, Philip returned to the traditional royal policy of active support for the inquisitors. A letter dispatched in September 1298 to all of the king's vassals and administrators in effect canceled the restrictions previously imposed on the inquisitors.[71]

Yet, a few years later, Philip proved once again accommodating to the inquisitors' opponents. The heresy trials in 1300 of several leading citizens of Albi set off a major protest. In 1301 the king arrested Bernard de Saisset, the bishop of Pamiers, on suspicion of planning a revolt. This act involved him in another quarrel with Boniface VIII. In this disturbed atmosphere Philip was once again prepared to restrain the inquisitors. He seized the temporalities of the see of Albi and secured the removal of Foulques de Saint-Georges, the inquisitor of Toulouse. He also required that the inquisitors now act in concert with the local bishops. The *mur* at Toulouse was to be administered by a man selected by both the bishop and the inquisitor. If the inquisitor wanted to arrest anyone, he had first to get the assent of the bishop. If he and the bishop could not agree, the matter was to be submitted to an assembly composed of officials of the cathedral as well as members of the Franciscan and Dominican orders. Actual arrests were to be carried out only by the king's seneschal.[72]

In the summer of 1303 the royal *enquêteur*, Jean de Picquigny, removed from the *mur* in Carcassonne those inhabitants of Albi who had been imprisoned there and lodged them in the royal fortress in the *cité* of Carcassonne. At Christmas the king himself came to Toulouse. After a stormy session in which he entertained complaints about the inquisitors, he issued a new decree. He ordered his agents, in company with the inquisitors, to visit those imprisoned for heresy and to see to it that their prisons were secure but not so harsh as to be punitive. Trials that had not yet been completed were to be dealt with expeditiously, under the joint supervision of the bishops and the inquisitors.[73] This action, which did

---

[68] Lea, *Inquisition of the Middle Ages*, 2: 63–64.
[69] *HL*, 10: *Preuves*, cols. 274–75.
[70] Lea, *Inquisition of the Middle Ages*, 2: 65.
[71] *HL*, 10: *Preuves*, cols. 276–78.
[72] Lea, *Inquisition of the Middle Ages*, 2: 79–81; *HL*, 10: *Preuves*, cols. 379–84.
[73] *HL*, 10: *Preuves*, cols. 428–31; MS 4270, fol. 139v.

not satisfy the critics of the inquisitors, was as much as Philip was willing to do. The death of his old nemesis, Boniface VIII, made the king less inclined to serve as a moderating influence on the inquisitors. Moreover, the new pope, Benedict XI, was a Dominican, and Philip's desire to negotiate with Benedict made him reluctant to take action against the Dominican inquisitors. Finally, when he began his attack on the Templars in 1307, he needed the aid of the inquisitors and hence was loath to restrict their powers.[74]

### The Role of the Papacy

The papacy, which had created and fostered the inquisition, was itself at times willing to trim its powers, influenced by political concerns and the desire to see that justice was done. At times those suspected of heresy felt that they stood a better chance of receiving clement treatment from the current pope than from the inquisitors. Accordingly, in the late thirteenth and early fourteenth centuries there was a small but constant stream of Cathar believers flowing toward the papal curia. For example, the arrest at Limoux in September 1305 of the Good Men Jacques Autier and Prades Tavernier created near panic among their followers. Seven people from the village of Arques, together with an inhabitant of Cubières and a cleric from Rieux-en-Val, set off for the papal court, which was then at Lyon.[75] Their confessions were heard by Bérenger Frézouls, bishop of Béziers and papal penitentiary, who was acting with Geoffroy d'Ablis, the inquisitor of Carcassonne, and Foulques, prior of the Dominican convent of Le Puy. Frézouls imposed penances that were exceedingly light by the standards of the inquisitors. Thus Guillaume Escaunier was required merely to fast on bread and water every Friday for three years and, on the occasion of these fasts, to give alms; on the feasts of the Virgin Mary, he was to put a candle on her altar, wherever he happened to be. Escaunier and his companions also recovered the property that had been sequestrated by the lord of Arques.[76]

Of the people sentenced by Bernard Gui between 1308 and 1323, a total of seven had sought out the ear of the papal penitentiary. Recourse to the papal court did not save everyone from the consequences of his or her actions: Gui burned as relapsed heretics two of those who had previously visited the curia.[77] Nevertheless, for some a direct approach to the papacy seems to have lightened their punishment.

At times the popes intervened directly in the affairs of the inquisitors. Several popes instructed Languedocian inquisitors not to molest the consuls and people

[74] Lea, *Inquisition of the Middle Ages*, 2: 91.

[75] There is a good discussion of this incident in Griffe, *Le Languedoc cathare et l'inquisition*, pp. 291–94.

[76] *Registre*, 2: 8, 18; 3: 145–46.

[77] *LS*, pp. 90, 110–11, 126, 161, 169. Those burned were Pierre Guillaume of Prunet on 5 April 1310 (pp. 90–91), and Pierre Andreas of Castelnaudary of La Rabinia on 23 April 1312 (pp. 169–70).

of Montpellier.[78] Various popes also took it upon themselves to moderate or set aside penalties imposed by the inquisitors. In 1248 Innocent IV sent Algisius de Rosciate, his penitentiary, to Languedoc, empowering him to commute the sentences of those signed with crosses or condemned to prison; such persons could fulfill their penances by participating in the next crusade to the Holy Land.[79] On 24 December 1248 Innocent wrote to his penitentiary concerning seven people who had been imprisoned. Noting that some were in their sixties and had endured the severity of the *mur* for more than four years, he ordered Algisius to release them, imposing what seemed to him to be sufficient and salutary penances.[80] Similarly, in the early fourteenth century Clement V interfered frequently with the work of the inquisitors. When Geoffroy d'Ablis excommunicated Jean de Picquigny for removing prisoners from the Carcassonne *mur*, Picquigny appealed to the pope. Although the *vidame* died, his son continued to press his case. Clement entrusted the matter to a number of cardinals for examination. On 23 July 1308 they found that the excommunication was illegal and unjust and declared it null and void.[81] Clement also ordered the release from prison of Guillaume Garric of Carcassonne, who, in addition to being implicated in the plot of the mid-1280s to steal the inquisitors' records, had been a leader of the anti-inquisitorial movement.[82]

The popes at times proved receptive to complaints about the inquisitors. It was not uncommon for them to order investigations into the proceedings of inquisitors and their agents. Some of the more notable examples of such interventions have been discussed above and I shall here mention only a few others. In 1249 Innocent IV ordered the bishop of Albi and the abbot of Candeil to look into the proceedings of Brother Ferrier against Jean Fenasse and his wife, Arsende. According to the complaint of their sons, both clerics, their parents had died good Catholics. Nevertheless, five years later, Ferrier and his fellow inquisitor had condemned them as heretics.[83]

Even the imperious Boniface VIII was not deaf to the entreaties of those who felt ill used by the inquisitors. Around 1297 a delegation of Carcassonnais, which included Aymeri Castel, against whose father the inquisitors had begun an investigation, petitioned Boniface to take action against the inquisitors. Their requests were seconded by a number of Franciscans, a Cistercian, the duke of Burgundy, and King Philip IV's advisor, Pierre Flote. The pope resolved to have the bishop of Vicenza make inquiries, but the investigation never took place. As part of the deal to get the inquiry approved, the Carcassonnais had promised to give 10,000 florins to Pierre Isarn, a papal referendary. However, Aymeri and his fellows

[78] *Bullaire*, pp. 44 (1318), 349–50 (1363).
[79] *HL*, 6: 800, 8: *Preuves*, col. 1240.
[80] Doat, 31: fols. 152r–53r; printed in *Documents*, 2: pp. 45–47 n. 1.
[81] Doat, 34: fols. 114v–22r.
[82] *HL*, 10: *Preuves*, cols. 526–27. On Garric's career, see Douais, "Guillaume Garric."
[83] Doat, 31: fols. 169r–70v.

backed out of this arrangement, thinking they could get better terms through the good offices of Flote and the duke of Burgundy. This proved a serious miscalculation. When Boniface learned of what the Carcassonnais had done, he was enraged and said, "We certainly know in whom they trust, but by God all the kings [in the world] shall not save those people of Carcassonne from being burned, and especially the father of that Aymeri Castel."[84]

In the pontificate of Clement V, the people of Albi had better luck. Their complaints, and some judicious bribes, persuaded the pope in 1306 to send two cardinals to Languedoc to investigate the inquisitors. In April they arrived in Carcassonne.[85] There they heard the complaints of the people of Albi and Carcassonne, as well as statements from the inquisitor of Carcassonne and a representative of the bishop of Albi. The cardinals then adjourned further hearings to Bordeaux in January. If these hearings actually took place, no evidence of them has survived.

While in Carcassonne, the cardinals visited the *mur*. There they found forty prisoners, who complained bitterly of their treatment. Swayed by what they had learned, the cardinals removed from office all the jailers, except the principal one. To him they added another "principal guardian," to be appointed by the bishop of Carcassonne. Each guardian was to have a set of keys to all the cells. Neither was to speak secretly with any prisoner outside the presence of his fellow guardian. The prisoners were to receive, without any diminution, the provisions given to them by the king or by their friends and relatives. Those afflicted by old age or illness were to be moved from the lower dungeons to the upper levels of the prison as soon as these could be made fit for habitation. The cardinals also ordered that the prisoners should, as long as the current investigation lasted, be let out of their cells and allowed to walk about in the prison's passageways.[86]

Cardinal Pierre Taillefer de la Chapelle also visited the bishop of Albi's prison. There he found prisoners who had been held up to five years without their trials being concluded. He ordered that those who were bound in chains were to be freed from their fetters and that more light was to be let into the cells. He also directed that three or four new rooms, "better and lighter" than those in which the prisoners were currently housed, were to be constructed within a month. Finally, he added to the two principal guardians of the prison a third, Isarn de Sales, a Cistercian monk of Candeil, and issued regulations on the conduct of the guards similar to those already laid down for the *mur* at Carcassonne.[87]

---

[84] MS 4270, fol. 120r: "bene scimus in quibus sperant, et, per Deum, omnes reges non liberabunt illos Carcassonenses quin comburantur, et specialiter pater illius Aymerici Castelli." See also Lea, *Inquisition of the Middle Ages*, 2: 69.

[85] The records of this investigation are in *Documents*, 2: 302–49. See also Lea, *Inquisition of the Middle Ages*, 2: 92–94.

[86] *Documents*, 2: 322–29.

[87] Ibid., 2: 331–33.

In the late thirteenth and early fourteenth centuries no pope went as far as to suspend the inquisition in Languedoc altogether, as Gregory IX, for diplomatic reasons connected with his Italian wars, had done between 1238 and 1241.[88] None troubled the inquisitors as much as had Innocent IV, whose interference in matters of the assigning or commuting of penances so irritated the Dominican inquisitors that they withdrew from office for a period during the 1240s and 1250s.[89] Nevertheless, Clement V, moved by the anti-inquisitorial agitation of the first decade of the fourteenth century, took steps to restrain the inquisitors' freedom. At the Council of Vienne in 1312, he issued the bull *Multorum querela*.[90] This gave bishops equal authority with the inquisitors to pursue heretics. Bishops and inquisitors could both, acting independently of one another, investigate, cite, and arrest those suspected of heresy. For certain matters, however, they were required to cooperate with one another. If a person was to be placed in harsh conditions of confinement, submitted to torture, or given a final sentence, the inquisitor and that person's bishop had to act in concert. The pope also decreed that each *mur* was to have two principal guardians, one appointed by the inquisitor, the other by the bishop. These guardians were to follow the same prescriptions as the investigating cardinals had enjoined on the guardians of the *mur* of Carcassonne in 1306.[91]

These rules were bitterly protested by the inquisitors of Toulouse and Carcassonne, who in the pontificate of John XXII asked that Clement's decree be quashed and that they be allowed to act independently of the bishops.[92] Among other things, they claimed that the requirement to secure the assent of a suspect's bishop before torturing him was a grave hindrance. The jurisdictions of Toulouse and Carcassonne covered several dioceses and securing the required permission led to inconvenient delays. This was especially vexing when the inquisitors had arrested some guides or messengers of the Cathar Good Men, who knew where the *perfecti* could be found. If these captives could be promptly tortured to make them divulge the whereabouts of the Good Christians, the inquisitors had a good chance of arresting them. However, the delay involved in contacting the relevant bishop before the prisoners could be put to the question made it possible for the *perfecti* to escape.[93] Despite the carefully reasoned complaints of the inquisitors, John proved deaf to their supplication.

The inquisitors were hampered on the one hand by factors intrinsic to their own organization—the institutional weaknesses of virtually all medieval administrative

---

[88] Dossat, *Crises*, pp. 137–45.

[89] Ibid., pp. 168–88.

[90] This decree, along with other canon law enactments adopted by the council, was not put into effect until 1317, in the pontificate of John XXII (Lea, *Inquisition of the Middle Ages*, 2: 96).

[91] *Corpus iuris canonici*, 2: cols. 1181–82 (Clem. 5.3.1).

[92] Doat, 30: fols. 90r–132v. See also *HL*, 9: 334–37.

[93] Doat, 30: fols. 100r–101v.

organs, perhaps exacerbated by their lack of an independent source of revenue—and, on the other hand, by factors rooted in the structures of the Languedocian political arena. Neither the parish clergy nor the local power holders, including the king, provided reliable assistance. Even the papacy, the very institution that had given the inquisitors their mission, occasionally found it expedient to interfere with inquisitorial investigations.

Most medieval rulers and administrators had to cope with environments similar to that in which the inquisitors found themselves. In the political arenas of medieval Europe, authority was fragmented and divided among a host of competing interests. Medieval administrators did not have the luxury of operating as the agents of a unified organization that enjoyed a legally recognized monopoly of coercive authority. In the fractured and decentered polities of medieval Europe, all political actors were required constantly to negotiate and renegotiate both their roles and the extent of their authority. In doing so, they had to deal with other power holders who were still, to use Weber's term, "patrimonial" rulers, whose personalistic style of government, swayed more by personal animosity and favoritism than by institutional imperatives, often produced shifting and uncertain policies. In such a context, it is a tribute to the inquisitors that they enjoyed as much success as they did.

# CONCLUSION

# THE INQUISITORS AND THE EXERCISE OF POLITICAL POWER IN MEDIEVAL EUROPE

I N THIS BOOK I have attempted to describe power as it was exercised and conditioned in one medieval society. We have seen how the inquisitors of Languedoc went about the business of identifying, prosecuting, and punishing heretics and their sympathizers. We have looked at how some people sought to protect themselves from the inquisitors and how others endeavored to exploit the inquisitors and their institution. Finally, we have tried to grasp how the structures of local society both facilitated and impeded the inquisitors in their work. At the end of this study, we are left with an impression that may seem rather ambiguous, if not outright contradictory. On the one hand, the work of the inquisitors testifies to just how draconian and compelling the exercise of power could be in a medieval society; on the other hand, it reveals the existence of rather severe limits to even the most determined efforts to exert discipline and control.

## THE POSSIBILITIES AND LIMITATIONS OF MEDIEVAL POWER

One cannot read the Languedocian inquisitors' records without coming to feel a grudging admiration for the ingenuity and determination that many of them displayed in their campaign against heresy. Over the years they developed an impressive array of mechanisms for the discovery of "the truth." Their refinement of methods of interrogation and coercion, their familiarity with the nature of the people and of the deviancy with which they dealt, and their skillful and active use of record keeping made it possible for them to discover a reality that their victims would often have preferred to keep obscure. The success enjoyed by the inquisitors in ferreting out the last Cathar heretics in Languedoc is eloquent testimony to just how effective these medieval techniques could be when wielded with enthusiasm and determination.

The inquisitors were not, however, the mere slaves of reality. Their investigative techniques allowed them to create their own, tailor-made truth. Through their interrogation procedures the inquisitors could make concrete the ideas, fears, and fantasies that resided only in their own minds. In a sense they could

213

make these phantasms objectively real.[1] For example, one of the individuals whom Jacques Fournier interrogated was the commander of the leper house in Pamiers, a man named Guillaume Agasse.[2] Agasse's confession is part of one of the darkest episodes in early-fourteenth-century history: a major persecution of lepers based on the wholly fantastic notion that they intended to poison wells and streams all over France.[3] Agasse's arrest and prosecution grew out of this campaign. Tortured by agents of Bishop Fournier, he produced an amazing tale of how he and delegates from forty other leper houses in the Midi had held a council at Toulouse in May 1320. There they had agreed to poison all the healthy people in their corner of France so that they would either die or become lepers. For his part in this utterly fantastic and nonexistent conspiracy, Agasse was sentenced to imprisonment on 5 July 1322. As far as we know, he died in prison.

The most famous example of the way in which inquisitorial techniques could be used to bend truth to fit the needs of authority was the trial and destruction of the order of the Knights Templar. In his campaign against the Templars, King Philip IV of France made good use of inquisitorial techniques and personnel. When the French Templars were arrested en masse in 1307, they were first interrogated by royal agents, who made liberal use of torture. When the brothers had had a chance to learn their lines, they were turned over to the ecclesiastical inquisitors. These were under the direct supervision of the general inquisitor of France, who happened to be the king's Dominican confessor, Guillaume de Paris. Not surprisingly the Templars confessed to a whole array of monstrous untruths: denial of the church and its sacraments, homosexual practices, demon worship, and so forth. Ultimately some Templars, thinking they could get the ear of papal commissioners delegated to investigate the affair, tried to resist. But when they recanted their confessions, they were simply treated as relapsed heretics and burned. The other Templars decided that it would be best to stick to their stories. As a result, the entire order was suppressed.[4]

More is involved here than the undoubted capacity of medieval people to lie and deceive. The inquisitors had perfected techniques by which the very fabric of reality itself could be altered. By the mid-thirteenth century the creation of various fantasies and their projection onto certain out-groups, such as the widespread belief that Jews indulged in ritual murder, had become an integral feature of western European culture.[5] The inquisitors had devised methods of using

---

[1] On the ability of inquisitors to manufacture heresy, see Grundmann, "Ketzerverhöre des Spätmittelalters."

[2] Agasse's deposition is in *Registre*, 2: 135–47.

[3] On this episode, see Chrétien, *Le Prétendu complot*; Vidal, "La Poursuite des lépreux"; Barber, "Lepers, Jews, and Moslems"; and Bériac, *Des lépreux aux cagots*, pp. 120–38.

[4] Good discussions of this affair can be found in Barber, *The Trial of the Templars*, and Partner, *The Murdered Magicians*, pp. 59–85.

[5] On Jews and ritual murder, see Langmuir, "Thomas of Monmouth" and "The Knight's Tale," and Moore, *Formation of a Persecuting Society*, especially pp. 116–23.

power and coercion to give such fantasies a legally validated and socially accepted reality. Now not only could the despised and rejected members of society be made objects for the projection of the fears and fantasies of Western culture, but they, or virtually anyone else, could be made to admit that those fantasies were true and to suffer the terrible consequences of being guilty of behavior that existed only in the imaginings of their persecutors. The inquisitors could, if they wished, script a role for almost anyone who appeared before them and make that person play that preassigned and largely prewritten part. As the Franciscan Bernard Délicieux told Philip IV, had St. Peter and St. Paul appeared before the inquisitors, they would have been found to be heretics.[6] This capacity to bend the very fabric of reality and to force acceptance of that new shape was a radically new development in the political history of medieval Europe.[7] With the inquisitors of medieval Languedoc, we are squarely on the road that will lead to some of the more reprehensible episodes of European history, including the persecution of Jews and Muslims in Spain and the great witch craze of the sixteenth and seventeenth centuries.[8]

Yet one should not exaggerate the inquisitors' effectiveness. Their techniques of investigation and coercion, no matter how vigorously wielded, were deployed in an overall political framework that was still loose and relatively disorganized. To achieve their goals, the inquisitors had to rely on the assistance of other governing organizations. And government in thirteenth- and early-fourteenth-century Languedoc was still decentralized, characterized by what some Marxist historians term the parcelization of sovereignty.[9] Powers of coercion were widely dispersed among the hands of a hereditary ruling elite, who regarded their authority as part of their family patrimonies. Many towns, and even many villages, had their own share of political power. Moreover, rights to the exercise of political authority were often assigned by prescriptive title rather than by ability, merit, or even interest. In such an environment it was difficult for the inquisitors effectively to penetrate and reshape the recalcitrant political

---

[6] MS 4270, fol. 139r: "He [Bernard] said that he had then said that 'if the blessed Peter and Paul were alive today and it was thrown up against them that they had adored heretics, and if it were proceeded against them concerning this adoration as has been done by some inquisitors at some times against many others, they would not have a way of defending themselves'" (*Dixit etiam tunc se dixisse quod, "Si hodie viverent beati Petrus et Paulus et contra eos impingeretur quod hereticos adorassent, si procederetur contra eos super huiusmodi adoratione sicut per aliquos inquisitores istarum partium aliquando contra multos fuit processum, nec pateret eis via deffensionis"*).

[7] To use Richard Cobb's formulation, the inquisitors were a police who ruled, rather than merely informed (*The Police and the People*, p. 18).

[8] The literature on the Spanish Inquisition is vast, but see Lea, *Inquisition of Spain*; Kamen, *Inquisition and Society in Spain*; and Dedieu, *L'Administration de la foi*. For an argument that stresses how learned judges used inquisitorial techniques to transform popular magical practices into an antihuman conspiracy of witches in league with the devil, see Cohn, *Europe's Inner Demons*.

[9] Anderson, *Passages from Antiquity to Feudalism*, p. 148.

and social structures with which they were confronted. In this they seem typical of most medieval rulers. For the most part medieval government was a matter of doing (more or less) justice and extracting tribute. Both processes tended to be episodic and ultimately dependent on force. Hence, government tended to float on the surface of medieval society.[10] This is not to say that medieval governments were incapable of impressive efforts. When confronted by military challenges, late medieval states could mobilize resources on a huge scale. But these resources were devoted to purposes of destruction. Few medieval states ever mobilized resources on such a grand scale for constructive ends.

The process of governing has two faces: the self-organization of the rulers and the organization of the ruled. The High Middle Ages saw important advances in the first aspect of governance, the self-organization of the rulers. The second aspect of government, the organization of the ruled by the rulers, was a much more difficult and protracted task, which was just barely getting under way in the thirteenth and fourteenth centuries. Indeed, one of the things that makes the inquisitors so very interesting is their position at the forefront of this process.

Despite the admiration one may feel for the assiduous way in which the Languedocian inquisitors went about their task of regulating religious belief and practice, one can never forget that their institution was above all dedicated to repression and that its agenda was essentially negative. Inquisitorial methods were designed to root out dangerous ideological tendencies; they were intended to eradicate opposition, not to activate and mobilize support.[11] The inquisitors' techniques were designed to break existing social relations among men and women; they did not form new ties or reorganize old ones so that they could be put to use to serve the interests of the rulers. Moreover, these techniques were designed to work on individuals, not on social collectivities. The inquisitors incapacitated individuals by cutting them out of the social networks in which they were embedded. By processing people through their penitential system, they could alter their conduct. But their techniques of rule were not as effective in demobilizing or restructuring the organizations to which those individuals belonged. This is illustrated by the great difficulties that the inquisitors had with the townspeople of Languedoc. Though the inquisitors could counter the acts of individual urban residents, they did not necessarily make the entire urban community compliant. Indeed, as we have seen with the cities of Albi and Carcassonne, towns, even with many of their leaders under suspicion of heresy, could organize effective resistance.

---

[10] For an effort to grapple with those conditions that did make it possible for a medieval government to reshape a social formation's structures, see Given, *State and Society*.

[11] On this score, the medieval inquisitors are an interesting contrast to the inquisitors of early modern Spain, who, with their hordes of familiars scattered across the Iberian kingdoms, penetrated local society much more effectively.

In effect, the inquisitors ruled through the systematic creation of social marginality. Many of their techniques relied on a strategy of isolation. This isolation could take several forms, ranging from committing a suspect to prison for extended interrogation to inserting a confessed and penitent heretic or heretical sympathizer into a disadvantaged sociojuridical status. Such creation or maintenance of sociocultural marginality seems to have been an essential aspect of the strategy of power generally in the Middle Ages. As we have already noted, one of the distinguishing features of the medieval political system was the wide dispersion of powers of command and coercion. This presented at least two problems for rulers. First, their desires and goals were often largely irrelevant to the concerns of their subjects, who managed most of their own affairs through traditional, local mechanisms. Second, it was difficult to create a "state elite" with the requisite degree of autonomy from the structures of civil society to carry out a self-consciously articulated state policy. Most rulers had to piggyback their governments on local organizations, leaving the execution of what governmental policy there was to local agents—many of whom were, in effect, self-selected. The result was that it was all too easy for a ruler's policy, and even his government, to be coopted by local politicians.[12]

One solution to these problems was to resort to a group of outsiders, people with a minimum of connection to the structures of local society. The most extreme examples of this can be found in the eastern Mediterranean, among the Ottoman Turks and the Mamluks of Egypt. Ottoman imperial organization was fundamentally dependent on the ability to sever ties between the state elite and civil society. The pillars of Ottoman authority, its Janissary infantry and its upper-level bureaucrats, were slaves, recruited from among the Christian population of the Balkans.[13] Likewise, the Mamluks in Egypt depended on a slave army, recruited in the hinterlands of the north coast of the Black Sea and the Caucasus and imported to Egypt by Genoese merchants.[14]

In western Europe we find a similar recourse to outsiders. The Emperor Frederick II, for example, used Muslim troops recruited in southern Italy for his bodyguard.[15] In fourteenth-century Navarre the kings regularly employed Islamic Mudejars in their government and armies, where they were often responsible for the new, and crucial, technologies associated with gunpowder.[16] In Scotland the local kings built up their authority in the twelfth century in large part by successfully importing a foreign, Anglo-Norman speaking nobility from the kingdom of England. When Wales and large parts of Ireland came

---

[12] On this, see Given, *State and Society*, pp. 204–6.

[13] Hodgson, *The Venture of Islam*, 3: 101–4, and Anderson, *Lineages of the Absolutist State*, pp. 365–68.

[14] Ehrenkreutz, "Implications of the Slave Trade," pp. 341–43.

[15] Abulafia, *Frederick II*, pp. 147–48.

[16] Harvey, *Islamic Spain*, pp. 144–45.

under English domination in the late Middle Ages, one of the mechanisms that the English conquerors used to cement their rule was the importation of ethnically English peasants and burgesses, who devoted much effort to emphasizing their cultural differences from the native Welsh and Irish.[17]

Creating marginal groups could serve other purposes than providing a loyal state elite. Marginalized individuals, such as those who inhabited the criminal underworld of late medieval Paris described by Bronislaw Geremek, were a fruitful source of manpower for the armies of late medieval Europe. They also constituted a reserve from which the hired thugs who made up many an aristocratic retinue could be recruited. This criminal *lumpenproletariat* could be used both to incapacitate the lower orders and to bind them more firmly to their masters. On the one hand, the less wealthy were constantly faced by the threat of being forced into the ranks of the *lumpenproletariat* itself. On the other, the fear of this criminal underclass made many members of the subordinate classes willing to submit to control from above.[18]

Finally, as R. I. Moore has argued, the successful stigmatization of individuals as social outcastes was an integral aspect of the struggle for power and influence among those who sought to lodge themselves in the structures of the new governing organizations that took shape from the twelfth century on. In the new courts of Europe, accusations of sodomy and witchcraft were freely traded among contestants for power. Clerics on the make also endeavored to exclude Jews, whose cultural attainments in the twelfth century were equal if not superior to those of Christians.[19]

The invention and elaboration of marginality thus seem to have been among the distinctive hallmarks of the exercise of power in the Middle Ages. As the inquisitors demonstrated, a skillful use of social isolation, along with systematic stigmatization and marginalization, could accomplish a great deal. But the heavy reliance on such techniques of rule also indicates just how frail was the grasp of power on the social formations of medieval Europe.

## THE PROBLEM OF DISCIPLINE

When social scientists interested in the long-term flow of Western history look back at the Middle Ages and the early modern period, they are often struck by the importance of coercion and repression. For many Marxists, of course, the notion of extraeconomic, politically conditioned surplus extraction is key to their concept of feudalism.[20] And, since the mid-nineteenth century, sociologists have

---

[17] On Wales, see Given, *State and Society*, p. 216. On Ireland, see Frame, *Colonial Ireland*, pp. 131–34.

[18] An idea I derive from Garland, *Punishment and Modern Society*, p. 150. Geremek describes fears of the criminal class in fifteenth-century France in *Margins of Society*, pp. 270–75, 290–98.

[19] Moore, *Formation of a Persecuting Society*, especially pp. 146–50.

[20] See Anderson, *Passages from Antiquity to Feudalism*, pp. 147–48.

seen the phenomenon of "discipline" as a central problem of their field of inquiry. Many accounts of the development of European society argue that sometime in the early modern period, Europeans moved away from "traditional" forms of social organization into modernity, and the rise of discipline was an important aspect of this transition to modernity.

As Robert van Krieken has put it, "being modern means being disciplined, by the state, by each other and by ourselves; . . . the soul, both one's own and that of others, became organized into the self, an object of reflection and analysis, and, above all, transformable in the service of ideals such as productivity, virtue and strength."[21] For such thinkers as Max Weber, Norbert Elias, and Michel Foucault, what is distinctive about this discipline is that it is an inner, self-discipline.[22] The disciplinary practices of the Middle Ages and the early modern period had been, so they believed, basically negative in nature. They simply drew boundaries and inflicted horrible, exemplary punishments on those who transgressed them. In contrast, in the modern period there came into existence an elaborate series of disciplinary systems—schools, workhouses, hospitals, factories, armies, and churches—that penetrated the soul and made it self-disciplining. In Foucault's formulation, repression was replaced by a "society of normalisation." The punishment of those who violate the prince's rules gave way to the inspecting gaze of truth-producing, scientific discourses, "a gaze which each individual under its weight will end by interiorising to the point that he is his own overseer."[23] The disciplinary regimes characteristic of modern society seek to correct rather than punish, to induce conformity rather than impose retribution.[24]

Our examination of the work of the inquisitors should have made it clear that repression in the Middle Ages was not simply a matter of the drawing of boundaries and the infliction of punishment on those who went beyond them. To be sure, as I have argued above, the inquisitors pursued an agenda that was primarily negative, repressive, and demobilizing. Nevertheless, they did aspire to more than the simple production of negative effects, conceiving of their work as therapeutic, as the reconciliation of sinners to the church. And the way in which they manipulated those they processed certainly transcends any simple model of negative, boundary-keeping repression. Moreover, the great *sermones generales* were staged as impressive spectacles designed to teach the masses about the correct nature of orthodox belief and the dire fate that awaited those who opposed the church. To the followers of Foucault, Elias, and

[21] Krieken, "The Organisation of the Soul," p. 353.
[22] See, for example, Weber, *The Protestant Ethic*; Elias, *The Civilizing Process*; and Foucault, *Discipline and Punish*.
[23] Foucault, *Power/Knowledge*, pp. 106–8, 118–19, 131–33. The quotations are from pp. 107 and 155.
[24] See Garland, *Punishment and Modern Society*, p. 145.

Weber, we can reply that medieval Europe, as well as modern Europe, knew its own disciplinary offensives.

The struggle to penetrate the souls of ordinary men and women and reshape them according to elite conceptions of proper behavior and right order had already begun in the Middle Ages. But in a sense the Webers, the Eliases, and the Foucaults are right. The disciplining offensive of the Middle Ages was not as all-embracing as it would become in later centuries. The full weight of the coercive apparatus of the inquisition was brought to bear on only a relatively small number of individuals. And the process to which these unfortunates were subjected was not exactly a "normalizing" one. When they emerged from it, they had not been reshaped and reintegrated into the "normal" community. Instead they had, along with lepers and Jews, been inserted into a clearly delineated out-group.

With the foundation of the mendicant preaching orders and the institution of a requirement for the laity to confess their sins and receive communion regularly, the church authorities had already begun a more far-reaching campaign of normalization; but these offensives would require centuries before they fully bore fruit. And it would be a long time before the appearance of the characteristic features of the modern world—unified, powerful, and intrusive states and a worldwide, all-encompassing market economy—would force Europeans to reshape their characters into bundles of readily marketable traits. Nevertheless, medieval people did not live, as some people would like one to believe, in a wild, unrestrained psychosocial environment, unconstrained by anything but an occasional display of frightful physical punishment. The full panoply of repressive, corrective, and normalizing institutions, which modern Europe would characterisically combine with an interiorized worldly asceticism, was still a long way off, but we can discern some of the lineaments of what was to come in the work of the medieval inquisitors.

# BIBLIOGRAPHY

## PRIMARY SOURCES

### Manuscripts

Archives Municipales, Albi:

| | |
|---|---|
| Series FF | Miscellaneous legal documents |

British Library, London:

| | |
|---|---|
| Add. MS 4697 | Bernard Gui's *Liber sententiarum* |

Bibliothèque Nationale, Paris:

| | |
|---|---|
| Collection Doat, vols. 21–37 | Seventeenth-century copies of miscellaneous documents relating to the Languedocian inquisition |
| MS Lat. 4270 | Seventeenth-century copy of the 1319 trial of Bernard Délicieux |
| MS Lat. 12856 | Sixteenth-century copy of inquisitorial proceedings in Albi, 1286–87 |

Bibliothèque de la Ville, Toulouse:

| | |
|---|---|
| MS 609 | Proceedings of Bernard de Caux and Jean de Saint-Pierre, inquisitors of Toulouse, 1240s–50s |

Archivio Segreto Vaticano, Vatican City:

| | |
|---|---|
| Collectorie 404 | Investigation of the conduct of Bernard de Castanet, bishop of Albi, 1307 |

Bibliotheca Apostolica Vaticana, Vatican City:

| | |
|---|---|
| MS Vat. Latin 4030 | Inquisitorial register of Jacques Fournier, bishop of Pamiers |

### Printed Sources

Blaquière, Henri, and Yves Dossat. "Les Cathares au jour le jour: Confessions inédites de cathares quercynois." In *Cathares en Languedoc*, pp. 259–98.

Cabié, E. "Compte des inquisiteurs des diocèses de Toulouse, d'Albi et de Cahors, 1255–1256." *Revue Historique, Scientifique et Littéraire du Département du Tarn* 22 (1905): 110–33, 215–29.

221

Cayla, Paul. "Fragment d'un registre d'inquisition." *Mémoires de la Société des Arts et des Sciences de Carcassonne*, 3d ser., 6 (1941–43): 282–89.

Clouzot, Etienne, ed. *Pouillés des provinces de Bésançon, de Tarentaise et de Vienne*. Recueil des Historiens de la France, Pouillés, 7. Paris, 1940.

Compayré, Clément. *Etudes historiques et documents inédits sur l'Albigeois, le Castrais et l'ancien diocèse de Lavaur*. Albi, 1841.

*Comptes royaux (1285–1314)*, edited by Robert Fawtier and François Maillard. Recueil des Historiens de la France, Documents Financiers, 3. 3 vols. Paris, 1953–54.

*Comptes royaux (1314–1328)*, edited by François Maillard. Recueil des Historiens de la France, Documents Financiers, 4. 2 vols. Paris, 1956.

*Corpus iuris canonici*, edited by E. Friedberg. 2 vols. Leipzig, 1879–82.

Davis, Georgene W., ed. *The Inquisition at Albi, 1299–1300: Text of Register and Analysis*. New York, 1948.

Devic, Claude, and Joseph Vaissète. *Histoire générale de Languedoc*, edited by Auguste Molinier. 16 vols. Toulouse, 1872–1904.

Döllinger, Johann Joseph Ignaz von, ed. *Beiträge zur Sektengeschichte des Mittelalters*. 2 vols. Munich, 1890.

Dondaine, Antoine, ed. *Un Traité néo-manichéen du XIIIᵉ siècle: Le Liber de duobus principiis, suivi d'un fragment de rituel cathare*. Rome, 1939.

Dossat, Yves, ed. *Saisimentum comitatus tholosani*. Paris, 1966.

Douais, Célestin, ed. *Documents pour servir à l'histoire de l'inquisition dans le Languedoc*. Société de l'Histoire de France, 299–300. 2 vols. Paris, 1900.

——, ed. "Les Hérétiques du Midi au treizième siècle: Cinq pièces inédites." *Annales du Midi* 3 (1891): 367–81.

——, ed. "L'Inquisition en Roussillon: Cinq pièces inédites." *Annales du Midi* 4 (1892): 533–40.

——, ed. *La Procédure inquisitoriale en Languedoc au quatorzième siècle d'après un procès inédit de l'année 1337*. Toulouse, 1900.

——, ed. "Saint Raymond de Peñafort et les hérétiques: Directoire à l'usage des inquisiteurs aragonais, 1242." *Moyen Age* 12 (1899): 305–25.

Duplès-Agier, Henri, ed. *Registre criminel du Châtelet de Paris du 6 septembre 1389 au 18 mai 1392*. 2 vols. Paris, 1861–64.

Duvernoy, Jean, ed. "Cathares et faidits en Albigeois vers 1265–1275 (Ms Mb161 de la Bibliothèque Municipale de Carcassonne extrait du Fonds Doat t. XXV de la Bibliothèque Nationale de Paris)." *Heresis* 3 (1984): 5–34.

——, ed. "Confirmation d'aveux devant les inquisiteurs Ferrier et Pons Gary (juillet-août 1243): Fragment de registre - Manuscrit 3 J 596 des Archives Départementales de l'Aude." *Heresis* 1 (1983): 9–23.

——, ed. *Le Registre d'inquisition de Jacques Fournier (1318–1325)*. 3 vols. Toulouse, 1965.

——, trans. *Le Registre d'inquisition de Jacques Fournier (évêque de Pamiers), 1318–1325*. 3 vols. Paris, 1978.

Etienne de Bourbon. *Anecdotes historiques, légendes, et apologues*, edited by A. Lecoy de la Marche. Paris, 1877.

Eymerich, Nicholas. *Directorium inquisitorum F. Nicholai Eymerici Ordinis Praedicatorum, cum commentariis Francisci Pegñae sacrae theologiae ac iuris utriusque doctoris*. Venice, 1595.

Finke, Heinrich, ed. *Acta aragonensia: Quellen zur deutschen, italienischen, französischen, spanischen, zur Kirchen- und Kulturgeschichte aus der diplomatischen Korrespondenz Jaymes II (1291–1327).* 3 vols. Berlin, 1908–22.

Font-Réaulx, Jacques de, ed. *Pouillés de la province de Bourges.* Vol. 1. Recueil des Historiens de la France, Pouillés, 9. Paris, 1961.

Germain, A. C. "Inventaire inédit concernant les archives de l'inquisition de Carcassonne." *Mémoires de la Société Archéologique de Montpellier* 4 (1855): 287–308.

Grayzel, Solomon. "The Confession of a Medieval Jewish Convert." *Historica Judaica* 17 (1955): 89–120.

Gui, Bernard. *De fundatione et prioribus conventuum provinciarum Tolosanae et Provinciae Ordinis Praedicatorum,* edited by P. A. Amargier. Monumenta Ordinis Fratrum Praedicatorum Historica, 24. Rome, 1961.

———. *Manuel de l'inquisiteur,* edited and translated by G. Mollat. 2 vols. Paris, 1926–27.

———. *Practica inquisitionis heretice pravitatis,* edited by Célestin Douais. Paris, 1886.

Kantorowicz, Hermann U. *Albertus Gandinus und das Strafrecht der Scholastik.* 2 vols. Berlin, 1907–26.

Limborch, Philipp van. *Historia inquisitions, cui subjungitur Liber sententiarum inquisitionis Tholosanae ab anno Christi MCCCVII ad annum MCCCXXIII.* Amsterdam, 1692.

Mahul, M., ed. *Cartulaire et archives des communs de l'ancien diocèse et de l'arrondissement administratif de Carcassonne.* 6 vols. Paris, 1857–82.

Mansi, J. D., ed. *Sacrorum conciliorum nova et amplissima collectio.* 39 vols. Paris, 1901–27.

Martène, E., and U. Durand, eds. *Thesaurus novus anecdotorum.* 5 vols. Paris, 1717.

May, William Harold, ed. "The Confession of Prous Boneta, Heretic and Heresiarch." In Mundy, Emery, and Nelson, *Essays in Medieval Life and Thought,* pp. 3–30.

Moneta of Cremona. *Adversus catharos et valdenses libri quinque,* edited by Thomas Augustinus Ricchinius. Rome, 1743.

Oliger, Livarius, ed. "Summula inquisitionis auctore Fr. Angelo de Assisio O.M. (1361)." *Antonianum* 5 (1930): 475–86.

Pales-Gobilliard, Annette, ed. *L'Inquisiteur Geoffroy d'Ablis et les cathares du comté de Foix (1308–1309).* Paris, 1984.

Pelhisson, Guillaume. "The Chronicle of William Pelhisson," translated by Walter L. Wakefield. In Wakefield, *Heresy, Crusade, and Inquisition,* pp. 207–36.

———. *Chronique (1229–1244), suivie du récit des troubles d'Albi (1234),* edited and translated by Jean Duvernoy. Paris, 1994.

Peters, Edward, ed. *Heresy and Authority in Medieval Europe: Documents in Translation.* Philadelphia, 1980.

Powell, James M., ed. and trans. *The Liber Augustalis, or Constitutions of Melfi Promulgated by the Emperor Frederick II of Sicily in 1231.* Syracuse, N.Y., 1971.

Preger, Wilhelm, ed. "Der Tractat des David von Augsburg über die Waldesier." *Abhandlungen der Historischen Classe der Königlich Bayerischen Akademie der Wissenschaften* 14 (1876): 182–235.

Sanjek, François. "Raynerius Sacconi O.P. *Summa de Catharis.*" *Archivum Fratrum Praedicatorum* 44 (1974): 31–60.

Selge, Kurt-Victor, ed. *Texte zur Inquisition.* Texte zur Kirchen- und Theologiegeschichte, 4. Gütersloh, 1967.

Stones, E. L. G., and Grant G. Simpson, eds. *Edward I and the Throne of Scotland, 1290–1296: An Edition of the Record Sources for the Great Cause.* 2 vols. Oxford, 1978.

Tardif, Ad. "Document pour l'histoire du *Processus per inquisitionem* et de l'*Inquisitio heretice pravitatis.*" *Nouvelle Revue Historique de Droit Français et Etranger* 7 (1883): 669–78.

Vidal, Jean-Marie, ed. *Bullaire de l'inquisition française au XIV$^e$ siècle et jusqu'à la fin du Grand Schisme.* Paris, 1913.

Wakefield, Walter L., and Austin P. Evans, eds. *Heresies of the High Middle Ages: Selected Sources Translated and Annotated.* New York, 1969.

## SECONDARY WORKS

Abels, Richard, and Ellen Harrison. "The Participation of Women in Languedocian Catharism." *Mediaeval Studies* 41 (1979): 215–51.

Abulafia, David. *Frederick II: A Medieval Emperor.* London, 1988.

Adams, Richard N. "Brokers and Career Mobility Systems in the Structure of Complex Societies." *Southwestern Journal of Anthropology* 26 (1970): 315–27.

Albe, E. "L'Hérésie albigeoise et l'inquisition en Quercy." *Revue de l'Histoire de l'Eglise de France* 1 (1910): 271–93, 412–28, 460–72.

Amargier, Paul. "Eléments pour un portrait de Bernard Gui." In *Bernard Gui et son monde*, pp. 19–37.

Anderson, Perry. *Lineages of the Absolutist State.* London, 1979.

———. *Passages from Antiquity to Feudalism.* London, 1974.

Asad, Talal. "Medieval Heresy: An Anthropological View." *Social History* 11 (1986): 354–62.

Assis, Yom Tov. "The Papal Inquisition and Aragonese Jewry in the Early Fourteenth Century." *Mediaeval Studies* 49 (1987): 391–410.

*Assistance et charité.* Cahiers de Fanjeaux, 13. Toulouse, 1978.

Audisio, Gabriel. *Les "Vaudois": Naissance, vie et mort d'une dissidence.* Turin, 1989.

———. *Les Vaudois du Luberon: Une Minorité en Provence (1460–1560).* Marseilles, 1984.

Avril, Joseph. "Les Dépendances des abbayes (prieurés, églises, chapelles): Diversité des situations et évolutions." In *Les Moines noirs*, pp. 309–42.

Bailey, F. G. *Stratagems and Spoils: A Social Anthropology of Politics.* New York, 1969.

Barber, Malcolm. "Lepers, Jews, and Moslems: The Plot to Overthrow Christendom in 1321." *History* 66 (1981): 1–17.

———. *The Trial of the Templars.* Cambridge, 1978.

Baron, Salo Wittmayer. *A Social and Religious History of the Jews.* Vol 11. 2d ed. New York, 1967.

Bartlett, Robert. *Trial by Fire and Water: The Medieval Judicial Ordeal.* Oxford, 1986.

Bartoli, Marco. "Jean XXII et les Joachimites du Midi." In *La Papauté d'Avignon et le Languedoc*, pp. 237–56.

Battifol, Louis. "Le Châtelet de Paris vers 1400." *Revue Historique* 61 (1894): 225–64; 62 (1895): 225–35; 63 (1896): 42–55, 266–83.

Beals, Alan R., and Bernard J. Siegel. *Divisiveness and Social Conflict: An Anthropological Approach.* Stanford, 1966.

Becamel, Marcel. "Le Catharisme dans le diocèse d'Albi." In *Cathares en Languedoc*, pp. 237–52.

Bellomo, Manlio. *The Common Legal Past of Europe, 1000–1800*, translated by Lydia G. Cochrane. Washington, D.C., 1995.

Belperron, Pierre. *La Croisade contre les albigeois et l'union du Languedoc à la France (1209–1249)*. 2d ed. Paris, 1967.

Benad, Matthias. *Domus und Religion in Montaillou: Katholische Kirche und Katharismus im Überlebenskampf der Familie des Pfarrers Petrus Clerici am Anfang des 14. Jahrhunderts*. Tübingen, 1990.

Bériac, Françoise. *Histoire des lépreux au Moyen Age: Une Société d'exclus*. Paris, 1988.

———. *Des Lépreux aux cagots: Recherches sur les sociétés marginales en Aquitaine médiévale*. Bordeaux, 1990.

———. "La Persécution des lépreux dans la France méridionale en 1321." *Moyen Age* 93 (1987): 203–21.

Bériou, Nicole. "Autour de Latran IV (1215): La Naissance de la confession moderne et sa diffusion." In *Pratiques de la confession*, pp. 73–93.

Berlioz, Jacques. "'Quand dire c'est faire dire': Exempla et confession chez Etienne de Bourbon (m. v. 1261)." In *Faire croire*, pp. 299–335.

Berlioz, Jacques, with Colette Ribaucourt. "Images de la confession au début du XIVᵉ siècle: L'Exemple de l'*Alphabetum narrationum* d'Arnold de Liège." In *Pratiques de la confession*, pp. 95–115.

*Bernard Gui et son monde*. Cahiers de Fanjeaux, 16. Toulouse, 1981.

Berne-Lagarde, Pierre de. *Bibliographie du Catharisme languedocien*. Toulouse, 1957.

Biget, Jean-Louis. "Autour de Bernard Délicieux: Franciscanisme et société en Languedoc entre 1295 et 1330." *Revue d'Histoire de l'Eglise de France* 70 (1984): 75–93.

———. "Les Cathares devant les inquisiteurs en Languedoc." *Revue du Tarn* 146 (1992): 227–41.

———. "L'Extinction du Catharisme urbain: Les Points chauds de la répression." In *Effacement du Catharisme?*, pp. 305–40.

———. "La Législation synodale: Le Cas d'Albi aux XIIIᵉ et XIVᵉ siècles." In *L'Eglise et le droit dans le Midi (XIIIᵉ–XIVᵉ s.)*, pp. 181–213.

———. "Un Procès d'inquisition à Albi en 1300." In *Le Crédo, la morale et l'inquisition*, pp. 273–341.

———. "Recherches sur le financement des cathédrales du Midi au XIIIᵉ siècle." In *La Naissance et l'essor du gothique méridional au XIIIᵉ siècle*, pp. 127–64.

———. "La Restitution des dîmes par les laïcs dans le diocèse d'Albi à la fin du XIIIᵉ siècle: Contribution à l'étude des revenus de l'évêché et du chapitre de la cathédrale." In *Les Evêques, les clercs et le roi (1250–1300)*, pp. 211–83.

Blanshei, Sarah Rubin. "Criminal Justice in Medieval Perugia and Bologna." *Law and History Review* 1 (1983): 251–75.

———. "Criminal Law and Politics in Medieval Bologna." *Criminal Justice History* 2 (1981): 1–30.

Bonnassie, Pierre. *La Catalogne du milieu du Xᵉ à la fin du XIᵉ siècle: Croissance et mutations d'une société*. 2 vols. Toulouse, 1975–76.

Borromeo, Agostino. "A Proposito de *Directorium inquisitorum* di Nicolás Eymerich e delle sue edizioni cinquecentesche." *Critica Storica* 20 (1983): 499–547.

Borst, Arno. *Die Katharer*. Schriften der Monumenta Germaniae Historica (Deutsches Institut für Erforschung des Mittelalters), 12. Stuttgart, 1953.

———. "La Transmission de l'hérésie au Moyen Age." In *Hérésies et sociétés dans l'Europe pré-industrielle, 11e–18e siècles*, pp. 273–77. Paris, 1968.

Bourin, Monique. "Fortunes foncières, pouvoir local et 'distinction sociale' en Languedoc (XIIIème–XIVème siècles): L'Exemple d'un village dans la basse vallée de l'Hérault." In *La Terre et les pouvoirs en Languedoc et en Roussillon du Moyen Age à nos jours*, pp. 89–101. Actes du LXIIIe Congrès de la Fédération Historique du Languedoc Méditerranéen et du Roussillon (Montpellier, 24 et 25 mai 1991). Montpellier, 1992.

Bourin-Derruau, Monique. *Villages médiévaux en Bas-Languedoc: Genèse d'une sociabilité, Xe–XIVe siècle*. 2 vols. Paris, 1987.

Brémond, Claude, and Jacques Le Goff, with Jean-Claude Schmitt. *L'Exemplum*. Typologie des Sources du Moyen Age Occidental, 40. Turnhout, 1982.

Brown, Peter. "Society and the Supernatural: A Medieval Change." In *Society and the Holy in Late Antiquity*, pp. 302–32. Berkeley, 1982.

Burr, David. *Olivi and Franciscan Poverty: The Origins of the Usus Pauper Controversy*. Philadelphia, 1989.

———. *The Persecution of Peter Olivi*. Transactions of the American Philosophical Society, n.s., 66, pt. 5. Philadelphia, 1976.

Cameron, Euan. *The Reformation of the Heretics: The Waldenses of the Alps, 1480–1580*. Oxford, 1984.

Carbasse, Jean-Marie. "Bernard Gui, évêque de Lodève (1324–1331)." In *Bernard Gui et son monde*, pp. 333–56.

———. "'Currant nudi': La répression de l'adultère dans le Midi médiéval." In *Droit, histoire et sexualité*, edited by Jacques Poumarède and Jean-Pierre Royer, pp. 83–102. Lille, 1987.

Carnoy, Martin. *The State and Political Theory*. Princeton, N.J., 1984.

Carruthers, Mary J. *The Book of Memory: A Study of Memory in Medieval Culture*. Cambridge, 1990.

Castan, Nicole. "La Préhistoire de la prison." In *Histoire des galères, bagnes et prisons, XIIIe–XXe siècles: Introduction à l'histoire pénale de la France*, edited by Jacques-Guy Petit et al., pp. 19–44. Toulouse, 1991.

*Cathares en Languedoc*. Cahiers de Fanjeaux, 3. Toulouse, 1968.

Cazelles, Raymond. *La Société politique et la crise de la royauté sous Philippe de Valois*. Paris, 1958.

Cazenave, Annie. "Aveu et contrition: Manuels de confesseurs et interrogatoires d'inquisition en Languedoc et en Catalogne (XIIIe–XIVe siècles)." In *La Piété populaire au Moyen Age*, pp. 333–52. Paris, 1977.

———. "Les Cathares en Catalogne et Sabarthès d'après les registres d'inquisition: La Hiérarchie cathare en Sabarthès après Montségur." *Bulletin Philologique et Historique (jusqu'à 1610) du Comité des Travaux Historiques et Scientifiques*, 1969, 1: 387–436.

———. "Déviations scripturaires et mouvements sociaux: Le Languedoc médiéval." In *Crises et réformes dans l'église de la réforme grégorienne à la préréforme*, pp. 117–34.

———. "L'Entraide cathare et la chasse à l'hérétique en Languedoc au XIIIe siècle." In *Pays de Langue d'Oc, Histoire et Dialectologie*, pp. 97–125. Paris, 1978.

Chenu, M.-D. *Nature, Man, and Society in the Twelfth Century: Essays on New Theological Perspectives in the Latin West*, edited and translated by Jerome Taylor and Lester K. Little. Chicago, 1968.

Cheyette, Frederic L. "Inquest, Canonical and French." In *Dictionary of the Middle Ages*, 6: 478–80. New York, 1985.

Chiffoleau, Jacques. *Les Justices du Pape: Délinquance et criminalité dans la région d'Avignon au quatorzième siècle.* Paris, 1984.

———. "Sur l'économie paroissiale en Provence et Comtat Venaissin du XIIIe au XVe siècle." In *La Paroisse en Languedoc*, pp. 85–110.

———. "Vie et mort de l'hérésie en Provence et dans la vallée du Rhône du début du XIIIe au début du XIVe s." In *Effacement du Catharisme?*, pp. 73–99.

Chiffoleau, Jacques, Lauro Martines, and Agostino Paravicini, eds. *Riti e rituali nelle società medievali.* Spoleto, 1994.

Chrétien, H. *Le Prétendu complot des Juifs et lépreux en 1321.* Châteauroux, 1887.

*Les Cisterciens de Languedoc (XIIIe–XIVe s.).* Cahiers de Fanjeaux, 21. Toulouse, 1986.

Clanchy, M. T. *From Memory to Written Record: England, 1066–1307.* 2d ed. Oxford, 1993.

Cobb, Richard. *The Police and the People: French Popular Protest, 1789–1820.* Oxford, 1970.

Cohen, Esther. *The Crossroads of Justice: Law and Culture in Late Medieval France.* Leiden, 1993.

——— "'To Die a Criminal for the Public Good': The Execution Ritual in Late Medieval Paris." In *Law, Custom, and the Social Fabric in Medieval Europe*, edited by Bernard S. Bachrach and David Nicholas, pp. 285–304. Kalamazoo, Mich., 1990.

Cohn, Norman. *Europe's Inner Demons: An Inquiry Inspired by the Great Witch-Hunt.* London, 1975.

Coulet, Noël. "Un Moine languedocien accusé de béguinisme." In *Les Moines noirs*, pp. 365–89.

Coulton, G. G. *The Inquisition.* London, 1929.

———. *Inquisition and Liberty.* Boston, 1959.

*Le Crédo, la morale et l'inquisition.* Cahiers de Fanjeaux, 6. Toulouse, 1971.

*Crises et réformes dans l'église de la réforme grégorienne à la préréforme.* Actes du 115e Congrès National des Sociétés Savantes, Avignon 1990, Section d'Histoire Médiévale et de Philologie. Paris, 1991.

Dahl, Robert A. "The Concept of Power." *Behavioral Science* 2 (1957): 201–15.

Darwin, Francis. "The Holy Inquisition: Suppression of Witnesses' Names." *Church Quarterly Review* 125 (1940): 226–46; 126 (1941): 19–43.

Dedieu, Jean-Pierre. *L'Administration de la foi: L'Inquisition de Tolède, XVIe–XVIIIe siècle.* Madrid, 1989.

Delaborde, H.-François. "Les Classements du Trésor des Chartes antérieurs à la mort de Saint Louis." *Bibliothèque de l'Ecole des Chartes* 62 (1901): 165–80.

Delpoux, Charles. "Alphonse de Poitiers et l'inquisition." *Cahiers d'Etudes Cathares*, 2d ser., no. 69 (1976): 47–55; no. 70 (1976): 27–44.

———. "Les Cathares et l'inquisition dans la région de Béziers." *Cahiers d'Etudes Cathares*, no. 14 (1953): 91–100.

———. "Le Catharisme en Albigeois: La Croisade et l'inquisition aux XIIIe et XIVe siècles." *Cahiers d'Etudes Cathares*, no. 18 (1954): 81–91; no. 19 (1954): 145–56.

———. "Le Catharisme en Armagnac." *Cahiers d'Etudes Cathares*, 2d ser., no. 48 (1970–71): 28–34.

———. "Guillaume Pagès, diacre cathare du Cabardès." *Cahiers d'Etudes Cathares*, 2d ser., no. 82 (1979): 22–36.

———. "L'Inquisition à Narbonne." *Cahiers d'Etudes Cathares*, 2d ser., no. 84 (1979): 29–37.

Delumeau, Jean. *L'Aveu et le pardon: Les Difficultés de la confession, XIIIᵉ–XVIIIᵉ siècle.* Paris, 1990.

———. *Sin and Fear: The Emergence of a Western Guilt Culture, 13th–18th Centuries,* translated by Eric Nicholson. New York, 1990.

Diehl, Peter D. "Overcoming Reluctance to Prosecute Heresy in Thirteenth-Century Italy." In Waugh and Diehl, *Christendom and Its Discontents,* pp. 47–66.

Dmitrewski, Michel de. "Fr. Bernard Délicieux, O.F.M., sa lutte contre l'inquisition de Carcassonne et d'Albi, son procès, 1297–1319." *Archivum Franciscanum Historicum* 17 (1924): 183–218, 313–37, 457–88; 18 (1925): 3–32.

———. "Notes sur le Catharisme et l'inquisition dans le Midi de la France." *Annales du Midi* 35 (1923): 294–311; 37–38 (1925–26): 190–213.

Dognon, Paul. *Les Institutions politiques et administratives du pays de Languedoc du XIIIᵉ siècle aux Guerres de Religion.* Toulouse, 1895.

Dondaine, Antoine. "Le Manuel de l'inquisiteur (1230–1330)." *Archivum Fratrum Praedicatorum* 17 (1947): 85–194.

———. "Le Registre d'inquisition de Jacques Fournier: A propos d'une édition récente." *Revue de l'Histoire des Religions* 178 (1970): 49–56.

Dossat, Yves. "Le 'Bûcher de Montségur' et les bûchers de l'inquisition." In *Le Crédo, la morale et l'inquisition,* pp. 361–78.

———. "Les Cathares d'après les documents de l'inquisition." In *Cathares en Languedoc,* pp. 71–104.

———. "Les Confréries du Corpus Christi dans le monde rural pendant la première moitié du XIVᵉ siècle." In *La Religion populaire en Languedoc,* pp. 357–85.

———. *Les Crises de l'inquisition toulousaine au XIIIᵉ siècle (1233–1273).* Bordeaux, 1959.

———. "Du début de l'année en Languedoc au Moyen Age." *Annales du Midi* 51–55 (1942–43): 520–29.

———. "Innocent IV, les habitants de Limoux et l'inquisition." *Annales du Midi* 61 (1948): 80–84.

———. "L'Inquisiteur Bernard de Caux et l'Agenais." *Annales du Midi* 63 (1951): 75–79.

———. "Le Massacre d'Avignonet." In *Le Crédo, la morale et l'inquisition,* pp. 343–50.

———. "Les Origines de la querelle entre prêcheurs et mineurs provençaux: Bernard Délicieux." In *Franciscans d'Oc,* pp. 315–54.

———. "Le Plus ancien manuel de l'inquisition méridional: Le *Processus inquisitionis* (1248–49)." *Bulletin Philologique et Historique (jusqu'à 1715),* 1948–50, pp. 33–37.

———. "Les Priorats de Bernard Gui." In *Bernard Gui et son monde,* pp. 85–106.

———. "La Répression de l'hérésie par les évêques." In *Le Crédo, la morale et l'inquisition,* pp. 217–51.

———. "Les Vaudois méridionaux d'après les documents de l'inquisition." In *Vaudois languedociens et Pauvres Catholiques,* pp. 207–26.

Douais, Célestin. *Essai sur l'organisation des études dans l'ordre des Frères Prêcheurs au treizième et au quatorzième siècle (1216–1342): Première province de Provence - province de Toulouse.* Paris, 1884.

———. "Guillaume Garric, de Carcassonne, et le tribunal de l'inquisition (1285–1329)." *Annales du Midi* 10 (1898): 5–45.

———. *L'Inquisition: Ses Origines—sa procédure.* Paris, 1906.

——. "Les Manuscrits du château de Merville." *Annales du Midi* 2 (1890): 36–64, 170–208, 305–64.

——. "Les Sources de l'histoire de l'inquisition dans le Midi de la France aux XIIIᵉ et XIVᵉ siècles." *Revue des Questions Historiques* 30 (1881): 383–459.

Dufau de Maluquer, A. de. "Le Pays de Foix sous Gaston Phoebus: Rôle des feux du comté de Foix en 1390." *Bulletin de la Société des Sciences, Lettres et Arts de Pau*, 2d ser., 28 (1898–99): 1–280.

Durkheim, Emile. *Moral Education: A Study in the Theory and Application of the Sociology of Education*, translated by Everett K. Wilson and Herman Schnurer. New York, 1961.

Duvernoy, Jean. "Bertrand Marty." *Cahiers d'Etudes Cathares*, 2d ser., no. 39 (1968): 19–35.

——. "Le Catharisme en Languedoc au début du XIVᵉ siècle." In *Effacement du Catharisme?*, pp. 27–56.

——. "L'Edition par Philippe de Limborch des sentences de l'inquisition de Toulouse." *Heresis* 12 (1989): 5–12.

——. "Une hérésie en Bas-Languedoc: L'Affaire des Béguins (1299–1329)." *Etudes sur l'Hérault*, 2d ser., 4 (1988): 85–90.

——. "La Noblesse du comté de Foix au début du XIVᵉ siècle." In *Pays de l'Ariège*, pp. 123–40. Paris, 1969.

——. "Pierre Autier." *Cahiers d'Etudes Cathares*, 2d ser., no. 47 (1970): 9–49.

Edgerton, Samuel Y., Jr. *Pictures and Punishment: Art and Criminal Prosecution during the Florentine Renaissance*. Ithaca, N.Y., 1985.

*Effacement du Catharisme? (XIIIᵉ–XIVᵉ s.)*. Cahiers de Fanjeaux, 20. Toulouse, 1985.

*L'Eglise et le droit dans le Midi (XIIIᵉ–XIVᵉ s.)*. Cahiers de Fanjeaux, 29. Toulouse, 1994.

Ehrenkreutz, Andrew. "Strategic Implications of the Slave Trade between Genoa and Mamluk Egypt in the Second Half of the Thirteenth Century." In *The Islamic Middle East, 700–1900: Studies in Economic and Social History*, edited by A. L. Udovitch, pp. 335–45. Princeton, N.J., 1981.

Elias, Norbert. *The Civilizing Process: The History of Manners*, translated by Edmund Jephcott. New York, 1978.

Emery, Richard Wilder. *Heresy and Inquisition in Narbonne*. New York, 1941.

Esmein, A. *A History of Continental Criminal Procedure with Special Reference to France*, translated by John Simpson. Boston, 1913.

*Les Evêques, les clercs et le roi (1250–1300)*. Cahiers de Fanjeaux, 7. Toulouse, 1972.

*Faire croire: Modalités de la diffusion et de la réception des messages religieux du XIIᵉ au XVᵉ siècle*. Rome, 1981.

Faury, Jean. "Les Collèges à Toulouse au XIIIᵉ siècle." In *Les Universités du Languedoc au XIIIᵉ siècle*, pp. 274–93.

*La Femme dans la vie religieuse du Languedoc (XIIIᵉ–XIVᵉ s.)*. Cahiers de Fanjeaux, 23. Toulouse, 1988.

Foreville, R. "Les Status synodaux et le renoveau pastoral du XIIIᵉ siècle dans le Midi de la France." In *Le Crédo, la morale et l'inquisition*, pp. 119–50.

Foucault, Michel. *Discipline and Punish*, translated by Alan Sheridan. New York, 1977.

——. *Power/Knowledge: Selected Interviews and Other Writings, 1972–1977*, edited by Colin Gordon, translated by Colin Gordon et al. Brighton, 1980.

Fournié, Michelle, and Jean-Louis Gazzaniga. "La Paroisse dans le Midi de la France à la fin du Moyen Age: Eléments pour une enquête." *Annales du Midi* 98 (1986): 387–411.

Fowler-Magerl, Linda. *"Ordines iudiciarii" and "Libelli de ordine iudiciorum."* Typologie des Sources du Moyen Age Occidental, 63. Turnhout, 1994.

Fox, Robin. *Kinship and Marriage.* Harmondsworth, 1967.

Fraher, Richard M. "Conviction According to Conscience: The Medieval Jurists' Debate concerning Judicial Discretion and the Law of Proof." *Law and History Review* 7 (1989): 23–88.

———. "Preventing Crime in the High Middle Ages: The Medieval Lawyers' Search for Deterrence." In Sweeney and Chodorow, *Popes, Teachers, and Canon Law in the Middle Ages*, pp. 220–33.

———. "The Theoretical Justification for the New Criminal Law of the High Middle Ages: '*Rei publicae interest, ne crimina remaneant impunita.*'" *University of Illinois Law Review*, 1984, no. 3: 577–95.

Frame, Robin. *Colonial Ireland.* Dublin, 1981.

*Franciscans d'Oc, les Spirituels, ca. 1280–1324.* Cahiers de Fanjeaux, 10. Toulouse, 1975.

Frank, Rosalyn M., Monique Laxalt, and Nancy Vosburg. "Inheritance, Marriage, and Dowry Rights in the Navarrese and French Basque Law Codes." *Proceedings of the Fourth Annual Meeting of the Western Society for French History* 4 (1976): 22–31.

Frank, Rosalyn M., and Shelley Lowenberg. "The Role of the Basque Woman as *Etxeko-Andrea*, the Mistress of the House." *Proceedings of the Fourth Annual Meeting of the Western Society for French History* 4 (1976): 14–21.

Frederichs, Jules. *Robert le Bougre: Premier inquisiteur général en France (première moitié du XIIIᵉ siècle).* Ghent, 1892.

Freedman, Paul. *The Origins of Peasant Servitude in Medieval Catalonia.* Cambridge, 1991.

Friedlander, Alan Ralph. "The Administration of the Seneschalsy of Carcassonne: Personnel and Structure of Royal Provincial Government in France, 1226–1320." Ph.D. diss., University of California at Berkeley, 1982.

———. "Les Agents du roi face aux crises de l'hérésie en Languedoc, vers 1250–vers 1350." In *Effacement du Catharisme?*, pp. 199–220.

———. "Jean XXII et les Spirituels: Le Cas de Bernard Délicieux." In *La Papauté d'Avignon et le Languedoc*, pp. 221–36.

———. "Les Sergents royaux du Languedoc sous Philippe le Bel." *Annales du Midi* 96 (1984): 235–51.

Garland, David. *Punishment and Modern Society: A Study in Social Theory.* Oxford, 1990.

Garrigue, Gilbert. "Marques distinctives des hérétiques du Midi de la France au XIIIᵉ et XIVᵉ siècles." *Cahiers d'Etudes Cathares*, 2d ser., no. 62 (1974): 53–58.

Gauvard, Claude. "Pendre et dépendre à la fin du Moyen Age: Les Exigences d'un rituel judiciaire." In Chiffoleau, Martines, and Paravicini, *Riti e rituali nelle società medievali*, pp. 191–211.

Gavrilovitch, Michel. *Etude sur le Traité de Paris de 1259, entre Louis IX, roi de France et Henry III, roi d'Angleterre.* Paris, 1899.

Gazzaniga, Jean-Louis. "La Création de la province ecclésiastique de Toulouse par Jean XXII." In *La Papauté d'Avignon et le Languedoc*, pp. 143–55.

Geertz, Clifford. "The Javanese Kijaji: The Changing Role of a Cultural Broker." *Comparative Studies in Society and History* 2 (1960): 228–49.

Geremek, Bronislaw. *The Margins of Society in Late Medieval Paris*, translated by Jean Birrel. Cambridge, 1987.

Giordanengo, Guido. "La Féodalité." In *La France médiévale*, edited by Jean Favier, pp. 183–99. Paris, 1983.

Given, James. "Factional Politics in a Medieval Society: A Case Study from Fourteenth-Century Foix." *Journal of Medieval History* 14 (1988): 233–50.

——. "The Inquisitors of Languedoc and the Medieval Technology of Power." *American Historical Review* 94 (1989): 336–59.

——. "A Medieval Inquisitor at Work: Bernard Gui, 3 March 1308 to 19 June 1323." In *Portraits of Medieval Living: Essays in Memory of David Herlihy*, edited by Samuel K. Cohn, Jr., and Steven A. Epstein, pp. 207–32. Ann Arbor, Mich., 1996.

——. "Social Stress, Social Strain, and the Inquisitors of Medieval Languedoc." In Waugh and Diehl, *Christendom and Its Discontents*, pp. 67–85.

——. *Society and Homicide in Thirteenth-Century England*. Stanford, 1977.

——. *State and Society in Medieval Europe: Gwynedd and Languedoc under Outside Rule*. Ithaca, N.Y., 1990.

Gonnet, Giovanni. "Bibliographical Appendix: Recent European Historiography on the Medieval Inquisition." In *The Inquisition in Early Modern Europe: Studies on Sources and Methods*, edited by Gustav Henningsen and John Tedeschi, pp. 199–233. Dekalb, Ill., 1986.

Gonnet, Giovanni, and Amedeo Molnár. *Les Vaudois au Moyen Age*. Turin, 1974.

Goody, Jack. *The Development of the Family and Marriage in Europe*. Cambridge, 1983.

Goyheneche, Eugene. "Medieval French Basque Economic and Political Structures." *Proceedings of the Annual Meeting of the Western Society for French History* 4 (1976): 1–13.

Gramsci, Antonio. *Selections from the Prison Notebooks of Antonio Gramsci*, edited and translated by Quintin Hoare and Geoffrey Nowell Smith. New York, 1971.

Green, Thomas Andrew. *Verdict According to Conscience: Perspectives on the English Criminal Trial Jury, 1200–1800*. Chicago, 1985.

Griffe, Elie. *Les Débuts de l'aventure cathare en Languedoc, 1140–90*. Paris, 1969.

——. *Le Languedoc cathare au temps de la croisade (1209–29)*. Paris, 1973.

——. *Le Languedoc cathare de 1190 à 1210*. Paris, 1971.

——. *Le Languedoc cathare et l'inquisition (1229–1329)*. Paris, 1980.

Grundmann, Herbert. "Ketzerverhöre des Spätmittelalters als quellenkritisches Problem." *Deutsches Archiv für Erforschung des Mittelalters* 21 (1965): 519–75.

——. *Religiöse Bewegungen im Mittelalter: Untersuchungen über die geschichtlichen Zusamenhänge zwischen der Ketzerei, den Bettelorden und der religiösen Frauenbewegung im 12. und 13. Jahrhundert und über die geschichtlichen Grundlagen der deutschen Mystik*. 2d ed. Hildesheim, 1961.

Guenée, Bernard. *Between Church and State: The Lives of Four French Prelates in the Late Middles Ages*, translated by Arthur Goldhammer. Chicago, 1991.

Guiraud, Jean. *Histoire de l'inquisition au Moyen Age*. 2 vols. Paris, 1935–38.

——. *L'Inquisition médiévale*. Paris, 1978.

Gy, Pierre-Marie. "La Précepte de la confession annuelle (Latran IV, c. 21) et la détection des hérétiques: S. Bonaventure et S. Thomas contre S. Raymond de Peñafort. *Revue des Sciences Philosophiques et Théologiques* 58 (1974): 444–50.

Hamilton, Bernard. *The Medieval Inquisition*. London, 1981.

Hanawalt, Barbara A. *Crime and Conflict in English Communities, 1300–1348*. Cambridge, Mass., 1979.

Harding, Christopher, Bill Hines, Richard Ireland, and Philip Rawlings. *Imprisonment in England and Wales: A Concise History*. London, 1985.

Harvey, L. P. *Islamic Spain, 1250 to 1500.* Chicago, 1990.

Haskins, Charles Homer. "Robert le Bougre and the Beginnings of the Inquisition in Northern France." In *Studies in Mediaeval Culture,* pp. 193–244. New York, 1958.

Hauréau, B. *Bernard Délicieux et l'inquisition albigeoise (1300–1320).* Paris, 1877.

Heers, Jacques. *Parties and Political Life in the Medieval West,* translated by David Nicholas. Amsterdam, 1977.

Henriet, Patrick. "Du nouveau sur l'inquisition languedocienne." In *Effacement du Catharisme?,* pp. 159–73.

Herlihy, David, and Christiane Klapisch-Zuber. *Tuscans and Their Families: A Study of the Florentine Catasto of 1427.* New Haven, 1985.

Higounet, Charles. "Granges et bastides de l'abbaye de Bonnefont." In *Paysages et villages neufs du Moyen Age,* pp. 275–83. Bordeaux, 1975.

———. "Le Groupe aristocratique en Aquitaine et en Gascogne (fin X$^e$–début XII$^e$ siècle)." *Annales du Midi* 80 (1968): 563–71.

Hilton, R. H. *A Medieval Society: The West Midlands at the End of the Thirteenth Century.* London, 1966.

Hindess, Barry, and Paul Q. Hirst. *Pre-Capitalist Modes of Production.* London, 1975.

*Historiographie du Catharisme.* Cahiers de Fanjeaux, 14. Toulouse, 1979.

Hobsbawm, E. J. *Primitive Rebels: Studies in Archaic Forms of Social Movement in the 19th and 20th Centuries.* Manchester, 1959.

Hodgson, Marshall G. S. *The Venture of Islam: Conscience and History in a World Civilization.* 3 vols. Chicago, 1974.

Hyams, Paul R. "Trial by Ordeal: The Key to Proof in the Early Common Law." In *On the Laws and Customs of England: Essays in Honor of Samuel E. Thorne,* edited by Morris S. Arnold et al., pp. 90–126. Chapel Hill, N.C., 1981.

*Juifs et judaïsme de Languedoc, XIII$^e$ siècle–début XIV$^e$ siècle.* Cahiers de Fanjeaux, 12. Toulouse, 1977.

Justice, Steven. *Writing and Rebellion: England in 1381.* Berkeley, 1994.

Kamen, Henry A. F. *Inquisition and Society in Spain in the Sixteenth and Seventeenth Centuries.* London, 1985.

Kelly, Henry Ansgar. "Inquisition and the Prosecution of Heresy: Misconceptions and Abuses." *Church History* 58 (1989): 439–51.

———. "The Right to Remain Silent: Before and after Joan of Arc." *Speculum* 68 (1993): 992–1026.

Kieckhefer, Richard. *European Witch Trials: Their Foundations in Popular and Learned Culture, 1300–1500.* Berkeley, 1976.

———. "The Office of Inquisition and Medieval Heresy: The Transition from Personal to Institutional Jurisdiction." *Journal of Ecclesiastical History* 46 (1995): 36–61.

———. *Repression of Heresy in Medieval Germany.* Philadelphia, 1979.

Kolmer, Lothar. *Ad capiendas vulpes: Die Ketzerbekämpfung in Südfrankreich in der ersten Hälfte des 13. Jahrhunderts und die Ausbildung des Inquisitionsverfahrens.* Bonn, 1982.

Krasner, Stephen D. "Approaches to the State: Alternative Conceptions and Historical Dynamics." *Comparative Politics* 16 (1984): 223–46.

Krieken, Robert van. "The Organisation of the Soul: Elias and Foucault on Discipline and the Self." *Archives Européennes de Sociologie* 31 (1990): 353–71.

Lafont, Robert, et al. *Les Cathares en Occitanie.* Paris, 1982.

Lambert, Malcolm. *Franciscan Poverty: The Doctrine of the Absolute Poverty of Christ and the Apostles in the Franciscan Order, 1210–1323*. London, 1961.
———. *Medieval Heresy: Popular Movements from the Gregorian Reform to the Reformation*. 2d ed. Oxford, 1992.
Langbein, John H. *Torture and the Law of Proof: Europe and England in the Ancien Régime*. Chicago, 1976.
Langlois, Ch.-V. *L'Inquisition, d'après des travaux récents*. Paris, 1902.
Langmuir, Gavin I. "Anti-Judaism as the Necessary Preparation for Antisemitism." In Langmuir, *Toward a Definition of Antisemitism*, pp. 57–62.
———. "The Knight's Tale of Young Hugh of Lincoln." In Langmuir, *Toward a Definition of Antisemitism*, pp. 237–62.
———. "Thomas of Monmouth: Detector of Ritual Murder." In Langmuir, *Toward a Definition of Antisemitism*, pp. 209–36.
———. *Toward a Definition of Antisemitism*. Berkeley, 1990.
———. "The Transformation of Anti-Judaism." In Langmuir, *Toward a Definition of Antisemitism*, pp. 63–99.
Lea, Henry Charles. *A History of the Inquisition of Spain*. 4 vols. London, 1906–1907.
———. *A History of the Inquisition of the Middle Ages*. 3 vols. New York, 1955.
Lebois, Michèle. "Le Complot des Carcassonnais contre l'inquisition (1283–1285)." In *Carcassonne et sa région*, pp. 159–63. Carcassonne, 1970.
Lerner, Robert E. *The Heresy of the Free Spirit in the Later Middle Ages*. Berkeley, 1972.
Le Roy Ladurie, Emmanuel. *Montaillou: Village occitan de 1294 à 1324*. Paris, 1975.
Little, Lester K. *Religious Poverty and the Profit Economy in Medieval Europe*. Ithaca, N.Y., 1978.
———. "Les Techniques de la confession et la confession comme technique." In *Faire croire*, pp. 87–99.
Llobet, Gabriel de. *Foix médiéval: Recherches d'histoire urbaine*. Foix, n.d.
———. "Variété des croyances populaires au comté de Foix au début du XIVᵉ siècle d'après les enquêtes de Jacques Fournier." In *La Religion populaire en Languedoc*, pp. 109–26.
Lodge, Eleanor C. *Gascony under English Rule*. London, 1921.
Lot, Ferdinard, and Robert Fawtier. *Histoire des institutions françaises au Moyen Age*. 3 vols. Paris, 1957–62.
Lukes, Steven, ed. *Power*. Oxford, 1986.
Maddern, Philippa C. *Violence and Social Order: East Anglia, 1422–1442*. Oxford, 1992.
Magnou-Nortier, Elisabeth. *La Société laïque et l'église dans la province de Narbonne: (Zone cispyrénéenne) de la fin du VIIIᵉ à la fin du XIᵉ siècle*. Toulouse, 1974.
Maisonneuve, Henri. "Le Droit romain et la doctrine inquisitoriale." In *Etudes d'histoire du droit canonique dédiées à Gabriel Le Bras*, 2: 931–42. 2 vols. Paris, 1965.
———. *Etudes sur les origines de l'inquisition*. 2d ed. Paris, 1960.
———. *L'Inquisition*. Paris, 1989.
Manselli, Raoul. "Bernard Gui face aux Spirituels et aux Apostoliques." In *Bernard Gui et son monde*, pp. 265–78.
———. "Eglises et théologies cathares." In *Cathares en Languedoc*, pp. 129–76.
———. "Les Opuscules spirituels de Pierre Jean-Olivi et la piété des béguins de Langue d'Oc." In *La Religion populaire en Languedoc*, pp. 187–201.

——. "Per la Storia della fede albigese nel secolo XIV: Quattro documenti dell'inquisizione di Carcassona." In *Studi sul medioevo cristiano offerti a Raffaello Morghen*, 1: 499–518. 2 vols. Rome, 1974.

——. *Spirituali e Beghini in Provenza*. Rome, 1959.

——. *Spirituels et Béguins du Midi*, translated by Jean Duvernoy. Toulouse, 1989.

Martin, Ernest. *Histoire de la ville de Lodève, depuis ses origines jusqu'à la Révolution*. 2 vols. Montpellier, 1900.

Martin, Hervé. "Confession et contrôle sociale à la fin du Moyen Age." In *Pratiques de la confession*, pp. 117–36.

Marx, Jean. *L'Inquisition en Dauphiné: Etude sur le développement et la répression de l'hérésie et de la sorcellerie du XIV^e siècle au début du règne de François I^er*. Paris, 1914.

Marx, Karl. *The Eighteenth Brumaire of Louis Bonaparte*. In *The Marx-Engels Reader*, edited by Robert C. Tucker, pp. 594–617. 2d ed. New York, 1978.

McDonnell, E. W. *The Beguines and Beghards in Medieval Culture, with Special Emphasis on the Belgian Scene*. New Brunswick, N.J., 1954.

Mellinkoff, Ruth. *Outcasts: Signs of Otherness in Northern European Art of the Late Middle Ages*. 2 vols. Berkeley, 1993.

Ménard, Léon. *Histoire civile, ecclésiastique, et littéraire de la ville de Nîmes*. 7 vols. Nîmes, 1873–75.

*Les Mendiants en pays d'Oc au XIII^e siècle*. Cahiers de Fanjeaux, 8. Toulouse, 1973.

Merklen, Pierre. "Les Brulés de Beoulaygues: Un Episode agenais du drame cathare (1249)." *Cahiers d'Etudes Cathares*, 2d ser., no. 45 (1970): 20–35.

Merlo, Grado Giovanni. "Coercition et orthodoxie: Modalités de communication et d'imposition d'un message religieux hégémonique." In *Faire croire*, pp. 101–18.

Michaud-Quantin, Pierre. *Sommes de casuistique et manuels de confession au Moyen Age*. Louvain, 1962

——. "Textes pénitentiels languedociens au XIII^e siècle." In *Le Crédo, la morale et l'inquisition*, pp. 151–72.

Michel, Robert. *L'Administration royale dans la sénéchaussée de Beaucaire au temps de Saint Louis*. Paris, 1910.

*Les Moines noirs (XIII^e–XIV^e s.)*. Cahiers de Fanjeaux, 19. Toulouse, 1984.

Molinier, Auguste. "Etude sur l'administration de Louis IX et Alfonse de Poitiers (1226–71)." In *HL*, 7: 462–570.

——. "Etude sur l'administration féodale dans le Languedoc (900–1250)." In *HL*, 7: 132–213.

——. "Etude sur les démêlés entre l'évêque d'Albi et la cour de France au treizième siècle." In *HL*, 7: 284–95.

Molinier, Charles. *L'Inquisition dans le Midi de la France au XIII^e et au XIV^e siècle: Etude sur les sources de son histoire*. Paris, 1880.

——. "Rapport à M. le Ministre de l'Instruction Publique sur une mission exécutée en Italie de février à avril 1885." *Archives des Missions Scientifiques et Littéraires, Choix de Rapports et Instructions*, 3d ser., 14 (1888): 133–336.

——. "Un texte de Muratori concernant les sectes cathares: Sa Provenance réelle et sa valeur." *Annales du Midi* 22 (1910): 180–220.

*Le Monde des chanoines (XI^e–XIV^e s.)*. Cahiers de Fanjeaux, 24. Toulouse, 1989.

Moore, R. I. *The Formation of a Persecuting Society: Power and Deviance in Western Europe, 950–1250*. Oxford, 1987.

———. "Heresy, Repression, and Social Change in the Age of Gregorian Reform." In Waugh and Diehl, *Christendom and Its Discontents*, pp. 19–46.

———. *The Origins of European Dissent*. London, 1977.

Moorman, John. *A History of the Franciscan Order: From Its Origins to the Year 1517*. Oxford, 1968.

Muchembled, Robert. *Le Temps des supplices: De l'Obéissance sous les rois absolus, XVe–XVIIIe siècle*. Paris, 1992.

Mundy, John Hine. *Liberty and Political Power in Toulouse, 1050–1230*. New York, 1954.

———. *Men and Women at Toulouse in the Age of the Cathars*. Toronto, 1990.

———. *The Repression of Catharism at Toulouse: The Royal Diploma of 1279*. Toronto, 1985.

Mundy, John Hine, Richard W. Emery, and Benjamin N. Nelson, eds. *Essays in Medieval Life and Thought, Presented in Honor of Austin Patterson Evans*. New York, 1955.

*La Naissance et l'essor du gothique méridional au XIIIe siècle*. Cahiers de Fanjeaux, 9. Toulouse, 1974.

Nelson, Janet L. "Society, Theodicy and the Origins of Heresy: Towards a Reassessment of the Medieval Evidence." In *Schism, Heresy and Religious Protest*, edited by Derek Baker, pp. 65–77. Cambridge, 1972.

Nicholas, Ralph W. "Factions: A Comparative Analysis." In *Political Systems and the Distribution of Power*, edited by Michael Banton, pp. 21–61. London, 1965.

Nickson, M. A. E. "Locke and the Inquisition of Toulouse." *British Museum Quarterly* 36 (1971–72): 83–92.

Omont, Henri. "La Collection Doat à la Bibliothèque Nationale: Documents sur les recherches de Doat dans les archives du sud-ouest de la France de 1663 à 1670." *Bibliothèque de l'Ecole des Chartes* 77 (1916): 286–336.

———. "Mémorial de l'inquisiteur d'Aragon à la fin du XIVe siècle." *Bibliothèque de l'Ecole des Chartes* 66 (1905): 261–68.

Ourliac, Paul. "Le Pays de la Selve à la fin du XIIe siècle." *Annales du Midi* 80 (1968): 581–92.

*Paix de Dieu et guerre sainte en Languedoc au XIIIe siècle*. Cahiers de Fanjeaux, 4. Toulouse, 1969.

Pales-Gobilliard, Annette. "Bernard Gui inquisiteur et auteur de la *Practica*." In *Bernard Gui et son monde*, pp. 253–64.

———. "Le Catharisme dans le comté de Foix des origines au début du XIVe siècle." *Revue de l'Histoire des Religions* 189 (1976): 181–200.

———. "L'Inquisition et les juifs: Le Cas de Jacques Fournier." In *Juifs et judaïsme de Languedoc*, pp. 97–114.

———. "Pénalités inquisitoriales au XIVe siècle." In *Crises et réformes dans l'église de la réforme grégorienne à la préréforme*, pp. 143–54.

*La Papauté d'Avignon et le Languedoc (1316–1342)*. Cahiers de Fanjeaux, 26. Toulouse, 1991.

Parkes, M. B. "The Influence of the Concepts of *Ordinatio* and *Compilatio* on the Development of the Book." In *Medieval Learning and Literature: Essays Presented to Richard William Hunt*, edited by J. J. G. Alexander and M. T. Gibson, pp. 114–41. Oxford, 1976.

*La Paroisse en Languedoc (XIIIe–XIVe s.)*. Cahiers de Fanjeaux, 25. Toulouse, 1990.

Partak, Joëlle. "Structures foncières et prélèvement seigneurial dans un terroir du Lauragais: Caignac dans la seconde moitié du XIII$^e$ siècle." *Annales du Midi* 97 (1985): 5–24.

Partner, Peter. *The Murdered Magicians: The Templars and Their Myth.* New York, 1982.

Paul, Jacques. "Jacques Fournier inquisiteur." In *La Papauté d'Avignon et le Languedoc*, pp. 39–67.

———. "La Mentalité de l'inquisiteur chez Bernard Gui." In *Bernard Gui et son monde*, pp. 279–316.

———. "La Procédure inquisitoriale à Carcassonne au milieu du XIII$^e$ siècle." In *L'Eglise et le droit dans le Midi (XIII$^e$–XIV$^e$ s.)*, pp. 361–96.

*Pays de l'Ariège.* Fédération des Sociétés Académiques et Savantes Languedoc-Pyrénées-Gascogne. Actes du XVI$^e$ Congrès d'Etudes, Foix, 28–30 mai 1960. Paris, 1969.

Pazzaglini, Peter Raymond. *The Criminal Ban of the Sienese Commune, 1225–1310.* Milan, 1979.

Péano, Pierre. "Les Béguins du Languedoc ou la crise du T.O.F. dans la France méridionale (XIII$^e$–XIV$^e$ siècles)." In *I Frati Penitenti de San Francesco nella società del due e trecento*, edited by Mariano d'Alatri, pp. 139–59. Rome, 1977.

*Le Pèlerinage.* Cahiers de Fanjeaux, 15. Toulouse, 1980.

Pélissier, E. "La Lutte des classes à Foix au XIV$^e$ siècle." *Bulletin Périodique de la Société Ariégeoise des Sciences, Lettres et Arts et de la Société des Etudes du Cousserans* 14 (1914–16): 96–103.

Pennington, Kenneth. *The Prince and the Law, 1200–1600: Sovereignty and Rights in the Western Legal Tradition.* Berkeley, 1993.

———. "*Pro Peccatis Patrum Puniri*: A Moral and Legal Problem of the Inquisition." *Church History* 47 (1978): 137–54.

Peters, Edward. *Inquisition.* New York, 1988.

———. *The Magician, the Witch, and the Law.* Philadelphia, 1978.

———. "Prison before the Prison: The Ancient and Medieval Worlds." In *The Oxford History of the Prison*, edited by Norval Morris and David J. Rothman, pp. 3–47. New York, 1995.

———. *Torture.* New York, 1985.

Petrucci, Armando. "Lire au Moyen Age." *Mélanges de l'Ecole Française de Rome, Moyen Age–Temps Modernes* 96 (1984): 603–16.

Platon, G. "Du Droit de la famille dans ses rapports avec le régime des biens en droit andorran." *Bulletin du Comité des Travaux Historiques et Scientifiques, Section des Sciences Economiques et Sociales*, 1902, pp. 144–214.

Pocock, David. "The Bases of Faction in Gujerat." *British Journal of Sociology* 8 (1957): 295–306.

Pontal, Odette. "De la Défense à la pastorale de la foi: Les Episcopats de Foulque, Raymond du Fauga et Bertrand de l'Isle Jourdain à Toulouse." In *Effacement du Catharisme?*, pp. 175–97.

Porteau-Bitker, Annik. "L'Emprisonnement dans le droit laïque du Moyen Age." *Revue Historique de Droit Français et Etranger*, 4th ser., 46 (1968): 211–45, 389–428.

Poulantzas, Nicos. *Political Power and Social Classes*, translated by Timothy O'Hagan. London, 1973.

Poumarède, J. "Les Coutumes successorales dans les Pyrénées au Moyen Age." *Revue du Pau et du Béarn* 2 (1974): 23–34.

Poux, Joseph. *La Cité de Carcassonne, histoire et description.* 2 vols. Toulouse, 1922–31.

*Pratiques de la confession: Des Pères du désert à Vatican II.* Paris, 1983.

Presle-Evesque, Alix de la. "Une Famille d'Albi face à l'inquisition aux XIIIe–XIVe siècles." In *Crises et réformes dans l'église de la réforme grégorienne à la préréforme*, pp. 135–42.

Pugh, Ralph B. *Imprisonment in Medieval England*. Cambridge, 1968.

Ramière de Fortanier, Charles. *Chartes de franchises de Lauragais*. Toul, 1939.

*Raymond Lulle et le Pays d'Oc*. Cahiers de Fanjeaux, 22. Toulouse, 1987.

*La Religion populaire en Languedoc, du XIIIe siècle à la moitié du XIVe siècle*. Cahiers de Fanjeaux, 11. Toulouse, 1976.

Robert, Ulysse. *Les Signes d'infamie au Moyen Age: Juifs, Sarrasins, hérétiques, lépreux, cagots et filles publiques*. Paris, 1891.

Roquebert, Michel. "Le Catharisme comme tradition dans la 'Familia' languedocienne." In *Effacement du Catharisme?*, pp. 221–42.

Rouse, Richard H., and Mary A. Rouse. "*Statim invenire*: Schools, Preachers, and New Attitudes to the Page." In *Renaissance and Renewal in the Twelfth Century*, edited by Robert L. Benson and Giles Constable, with Carol D. Lanham, pp. 201–25. Cambridge, Mass., 1982.

Rudé, George. *The Crowd in History: A Study of Popular Disturbances in France and England, 1730–1848*. New York, 1968.

Ruggiero, Guido. "Constructing Civic Morality, Deconstructing the Body: Civic Rituals of Punishment in Renaissance Venice." In Chiffoleau, Martines, and Paravicini, *Riti e rituali nelle società medievali*, pp. 175–90.

Russell, Jeffrey Burton. "Interpretations of the Origins of Medieval Heresy." *Mediaeval Studies* 25 (1963): 26–53.

Saint-Blanquat, Odon de. "Comment se sont crées les bastides du Sud-Ouest de France." *Annales: Economies, Sociétés, Civilisations* 4 (1949): 278–89.

*Saint Dominique en Languedoc*. Cahiers de Fanjeaux, 1. Toulouse, 1966.

Schmidt, C. *Histoire et doctrine de la secte des Cathares ou Albigeois*. 2 vols. Paris, 1849.

Schnapper, Bernard. "Les Peines arbitraires du XIIIe au XVIIIe siècle (doctrines savantes et usages français)." *Tijdschrift voor Rechtsgeschiedenis* 41 (1973): 237–77; 42 (1974): 81–112.

Schüßler, Martin. "Statistische Untersuchung des Verbrechens in Nürnberg im Zeitraum von 1285 bis 1400." *Zeitschrift der Savigny-Stiftung für Rechtsgeschichte, Germanistische Abteilung* 108 (1991): 117–93.

Scott, James C. *Domination and the Arts of Resistance: Hidden Transcripts*. New Haven, 1990.

——. *Weapons of the Weak: Everyday Forms of Peasant Resistance*. New Haven, 1985.

Segl, Peter, ed. *Die Anfänge der Inquisition im Mittelalter: Mit einem Ausblick auf das 20. Jahrhundert und einem Beitrag über religiöse Intoleranz im nichtchristlichen Bereich*. Cologne, 1993.

Seillan, G. "Un Inquisiteur dacquois en Languedoc cathare, Guillaume Bernard, O.P. (1257–1263)." *Bulletin de la Société de Borda* 114 (1989): 523–34.

Selge, Kurt-Victor. *Die ersten Waldenser*. 2 vols. Arbeiten zur Kirchengeschichte, 37. Berlin, 1967.

Semkov, Georgi. "Le Contexte socio-économique du Catharisme au Mas-Saintes-Puelles dans la première moitié du 13e siècle." *Heresis* 2 (1984): 35–53.

Shannon, Albert Clement. *The Popes and Heresy in the Thirteenth Century*. Villanova, 1949.

———. "The Secrecy of Witnesses in Inquisitorial Tribunals and in Contemporary Secular Criminal Trials." In Mundy, Emery, and Nelson, *Essays in Medieval Life and Thought*, pp. 59–69.

Sheehan, W. J. "Finding Solace in Eighteenth-Century Newgate." In *Crime in England, 1550–1800*, edited by J. S. Cockburn, pp. 229–45. Princeton, N.J., 1977.

Shorter, Edward, and Charles Tilly. *Strikes in France, 1830–1968*. London, 1974.

Silverman, Sydel F. "Patronage and Community-National Relationships in Central Italy." *Ethnology* 4 (1965): 172–89.

Sivéry, Gérard. *Saint Louis et son siècle*. Paris, 1983.

Skocpol, Theda. "Bringing the State Back In: Strategies of Analysis in Current Research." In *Bringing the State Back In*, edited by Peter B. Evans, Dietrich Rueschemeyer, and Theda Skocpol, pp. 3–37. Cambridge, 1985.

———. *States and Social Revolutions: A Comparative Analysis of France, Russia, and China*. Cambridge, 1979.

Spierenburg, Pieter. *The Spectacle of Suffering: Executions and the Evolution of Repression: From a Preindustrial Metropolis to the European Experience*. Cambridge, 1984.

Stella, Alessandro. *La Révolte des Ciompi: Les Hommes, les lieux, le travail*. Paris, 1993.

Stock, Brian. *The Implications of Literacy: Written Language and Models of Interpretation in the Eleventh and Twelfth Centuries*. Princeton, N.J., 1983.

Strayer, Joseph R. *Les Gens du justice du Languedoc sous Philippe le Bel*. Toulouse, 1970.

———. *Medieval Statecraft and the Perspectives of History*. Princeton, N.J., 1971.

———. *The Reign of Philip the Fair*. Princeton, N.J., 1980.

———. "Viscounts and Viguiers under Philip the Fair." In Strayer, *Medieval Statecraft and the Perspectives of History*, pp. 213–31

Sweeney, J. R., and S. Chodorow, eds. *Popes, Teachers, and Canon Law in the Middle Ages*. Ithaca, N.Y., 1989.

Tanon, L. *Histoire des tribunaux de l'inquisition en France*. Paris, 1893.

Tentler, Thomas N. *Sin and Confession on the Eve of the Reformation*. Princeton, N.J., 1977.

———. "The *Summa* for Confessors as an Instrument of Social Control." In *The Pursuit of Holiness in Late Medieval and Renaissance Religion*, edited by Charles Trinkaus and Heiko Oberman, pp. 103–26. Leiden, 1974.

Thouzellier, C. "L'Inquisiteur et saint Dominique." *Annales du Midi* 80 (1968): 121–30.

———. "Réponse au R.P. Vicaire." *Annales du Midi* 80 (1968): 137–38.

Tilly, Charles. *The Contentious French*. Cambridge, Mass., 1986.

———. *From Mobilization to Revolution*. New York, 1978.

Timbal, Pierre. *Un Conflit d'annexion au Moyen Age: L'Application de la coutume de Paris au pays d'Albigeois*. Toulouse, 1950.

Toulouse, Bibliothèque Municipale. *Catharisme et cathares: Bibliographie établie à partir des ouvrages imprimés de la Bibliothèque Municipale de Toulouse*. Toulouse, 1983.

Trabut-Cussac, J.-P. *L'Administration anglaise en Gascogne sous Henry III et Edouard I de 1254 à 1307*. Geneva, 1972.

Trusen, Winfried. "Der Inquisitionsprozeß: Seiner historischen Grundlagen und frühen Formen." *Zeitschrift der Savigny-Stiftung für Rechtsgeschichte, Kanonistische Abteilung* 74 (1988): 168–230.

———. "Von den Anfängen des Inquisitionsprozeßes zum Verfahren bei der *Inquisitio Haereticae Pravitatis*." In Segl, *Die Anfänge der Inquisition*, pp. 39–76.

Turley, Thomas. "John XXII and the Franciscans: A Reappraisal." In Sweeney and Chodorow, *Popes, Teachers, and Canon Law in the Middle Ages*, pp. 74–88.

Ullmann, Walter. "The Defence of the Accused in the Medieval Inquisition." *Irish Ecclesiastical Record* 73 (1950): 481–89.

*Les Universités du Languedoc au XIIIᵉ siècle.* Cahiers de Fanjeaux, 5. Toulouse, 1970.

Vacandard, E. *L'Inquisition: Etude historique et critique sur le pouvoir coercitif de l'église.* Paris, 1912.

*Vaudois languedociens et Pauvres Catholiques.* Cahiers de Fanjeaux, 2. Toulouse, 1967.

Vekené, Emil van der. *Bibliotheca bibliographica historiae Sanctae Inquisitionis.* 2 vols. Vaduz, 1982–1983.

Ventura i Subirats, Jordi. "Catharisme et Valdéisme en pays catalan." *Cahiers d'Etudes Cathares,* 2d ser., no. 63 (1974): 30–39.

———. "Les Derniers contacts entre le Catharisme et la Catalogne." *Cahiers d'Etudes Cathares,* 2d ser., no. 26 (1965): 8–19; no. 28 (1965–1966): 26–37; no. 29 (1966): 3–12.

Vicaire, Marie-Humbert. "L'Action de l'enseignement et de la prédication des Mendiants vis-à-vis des cathares." In *Effacement du Catharisme?*, pp. 277–304.

———. "Les Cathares albigeois vus par les polémistes." In *Cathares en Languedoc,* pp. 105–28.

———. "Note sur la mentalité de saint Dominique." *Annales du Midi* 80 (1968): 131–36.

———. "Saint Dominique et les inquisiteurs." *Annales du Midi* 79 (1967): 173–94.

Vicaire, Marie-Humbert, and Henri Gilles. "Rôle de l'université de Toulouse dans l'effacement du Catharisme." In *Effacement du Catharisme?*, pp. 257–76.

Vidal, Jean-Marie. "Les Derniers ministres de l'albigéisme en Languedoc: Leurs Doctrines." *Revue des Questions Historiques* 79 (1906): 57–107.

———. "Doctrine et morale des derniers ministres albigeois." *Revue des Questions Historiques* 85 (1909): 357–409; 86 (1909): 5–48.

———. *Un Inquisiteur jugé par ses "victimes": Jean Galand et les Carcassonnais (1285–1286).* Paris, 1903.

———. "Menet de Robécourt, commissaire de l'inquisition de Carcassonne." *Moyen Age* 16 (1903): 425–49.

———. "Les Origines de la province ecclésiastique de Toulouse (1295–1318)." *Annales du Midi* 15 (1903): 289–328, 469–92; 16 (1904): 5–30.

———. "La Poursuite des lépreux en 1321 d'après des documents nouveaux." *Annales de Saint-Louis-des-Français* 4 (1900): 419–78.

———. *Le Tribunal d'inquisition de Pamiers.* Toulouse, 1906.

———. "Le Tribunal d'inquisition de Pamiers: Notice sur le registre de l'évêque Jacques Fournier." *Annales de Saint-Louis-des-Français* 8 (1903–1904): 377–435; 9 (1904–1905): 5–87; 10 (1905–1906): 5–52.

Wakefield, Walter L. "The Family of Niort in the Albigensian Crusade and before the Inquisition." *Names* 18 (1970): 97–117, 286–303.

———. *Heresy, Crusade, and Inquisition in Southern France, 1100–1250.* Berkeley, 1974.

———. "Heretics and Inquisitors: The Case of Auriac and Cambiac." *Journal of Medieval History* 12 (1986): 225–37.

———. "Heretics and Inquisitors: The Case of Le Mas-Saintes-Puelles." *Catholic Historical Review* 69 (1983): 209–26.

Walker, Sue Sheridan. "Punishing Convicted Ravishers: Statutory Strictures and Actual Practice in Thirteenth- and Fourteenth-Century England." *Journal of Medieval History* 13 (1987): 237–50.

Walsh, William Thomas. *Characters of the Inquisition.* New York, 1940.

Waugh, Scott L., and Peter D. Diehl, eds. *Christendom and Its Discontents: Exclusion, Persecution, and Rebellion, 1000–1500*. Cambridge, 1996.

Weber, Max. *Economy and Society: An Outline of Interpretive Sociology*, edited by Guenther Roth and Claus Wittich, translated by Ephraim Fischoff et al. 2 vols. Berkeley, 1978.

——. *The Protestant Ethic and the Spirit of Capitalism*, translated by Talcott Parsons. New York, 1976.

Wolf, Eric R. "Aspects of Group Relations in a Complex Society." *American Anthropologist* 58 (1956): 1065–78.

Wolff, Philippe. "Les Luttes sociales dans les villes du Midi français du XIIIᵉ au XVᵉ siècle." In Wolff, *Regards sur le Midi médiéval*, pp. 77–89.

——. "Réflexions sur l'histoire médiévale de Montauban." In Wolff, *Regards sur le Midi médiéval*, pp. 333–45.

——. *Regards sur le Midi médiéval*. Toulouse, 1978.

——. "Rôle de l'essor économique dans le ralliement social et religieux." In *Effacement du Catharisme?*, pp. 243–55.

——, ed. *Histoire de Toulouse*. 2d ed. Toulouse, 1974.

——, ed. *Histoire du Languedoc*. Toulouse, 1967.

Wolfgang, Marvin E. *Patterns in Criminal Homicide*. Philadelphia, 1958.

Yates, Frances A. *The Art of Memory*. Chicago, 1966.

Yerushalmi, Yosef H. "The Inquisition and the Jews of France in the Time of Bernard Gui." *Rutgers Hebraic Studies* 1 (1965): 1–60.

Zorzi, Andrea. "Rituali e cerimoniali penali nelle città italiane (secc. XIII–XVI)." In Chiffoleau, Martines, and Paravicini, *Riti e rituali nelle società medievali*, pp. 141–57.

# INDEX

Abbeville, Nicholas d', inquisitor of
    Carcassonne, 41, 44, 131–33, 137,
    140, 171, 188
Ablis, Geoffroy d', inquisitor of
    Carcassonne, 42, 109–10, 122, 133,
    136, 156, 159–60, 188, 192, 206,
    208–9
Acès, Pierre, of Esplas-de-Sérou, 107, 107
    n. 44, 108, 200
Acolyte, 200
*Ad abolendam*, 13
Add. MS 4697 of the British Library,
    29–33
Adhémar, Alazaïs, 41 n. 51
Adhémar, Pierre, of Prades d'Alion, 53,
    100, 153–55
Adoration. *See Melioramentum*
Agasse, Guillaume, commander of leper
    house of Pamiers, 118 n. 9, 214
Agenais, 17
Aiguebelle, 106
Aigues-Juntes, 124
Ainard, *bayle* of Fanjeaux, 205
Alamans, Bertrand d', de Saint-Germier,
    of Caraman, 126–27
Alanh, Germain d', episcopal inquisitor of
    diocese of Narbonne, 89
Albi, 53, 65, 133–37, 139, 146, 170,
    189, 210
    bishop of, 89, 170, 209
    council at, 27
    diocese of, 137, 204, 207
    heresy trials at, 14, 35, 41, 132, 146,
        170–73
    judge of, 205
    opposition to inquisitors in, 131–39, 187
    riots in, 116–17, 128–29

Albiès, Ermengarde, of Lordat, 202
Albigensian crusades, 12, 16, 88, 170
Alboara, Guillaume, Cathar Good Man, 97
Alegre, Martin, of Clermont-l'Hérault, 77
Alexander III, pope, 11
Aliguer, Bernard, of Mirepoix-sur-Tarn,
    30, 101 nn. 22, 23
Alion, Guillaume d', of Pamiers, 157–58
Alix, Cathar Good Woman and grand-
    mother of Guillaume de Pezens, 42
Alms giving, as punishment, 208
Alzon, 36
Amiel, Guillemette, 112 n. 4
Amiel, Hugues, inquisitor, 82, 97
Amiel, Pierre, 122
Amilhac, Barthélemy, stipendiary priest of
    Mézerville, 82–83, 100, 102–3, 121
Amorosa, Jacquette, of Lodève, 96
Andorran, Galharde, 41 n. 51
Andorran, Guillaume, 41 n. 51
Andreas, Pierre, of Castelnaudary, of La
    Rabinia, 208 n. 77
Anhaus, Guillaume d', 41 n. 51
Anti-inquisitorial league, of Albi,
    Carcassonne, and Cordes, 134, 187
Aragon
    inquisitor of, 193
    kingdom of, 38, 90, 103–4, 107–8, 195
    kings of, 16
Archives, 26, 33–34
    of inquisitors, 26–27
    retrieval of information from,
        35–39, 41–42
    as source of information, 34–39
    as source of power, 39–42
    of inquisitors of Carcassonne, 27–28,
        48–49, 118–19, 130, 209

Undergraduate Lending Library

James Buchanan Given is Professor of History
at the University of California at Irvine.